Literature, in Theory: Tropes, Subjectivities,
Responses & Responsibilities

Also available from Continuum:

Derrida: A Guide for the Perplexed, Julian Wolfreys

Literature, in Theory: Tropes, Subjectivities, Responses & Responsibilities

Julian Wolfreys

continuum

Continuum London
The Tower Building
11 York Road
London SE1 7NX

Continuum New York
80 Maiden Lane, Suite 704
New York
NY 10038

www.continuumbooks.com

British Library Cataloguing-in-Publication Data
A catalogue record for this book is available from the British Library.

ISBN: 978-1-4411-6152-9 (hardcover)
         978-1-4411-2324-4 (paperback)

Library of Congress Cataloguing-in-Publication Data
A catalog record for this book is available from the Library of Congress.

Typeset by Pindar NZ, Auckland, New Zealand
Printed and bound in Great Britain by CPI Antony Rowe, Chippenham, Wiltshire

Contents

and is propounded or accepted as accounting for the known facts; a statement of what are held to be the general laws, principles, or causes of something known or observed'. Such a statement may not be systematic, or, more precisely, the system may not be regular, coherent or consistent within itself. But then, the universe of the literary, every singular manifestation, accords to its own laws. This is, at least, literature, in theory.

Dickens's writing of the city moves therefore through manifestations of the urban for a subject constituted by and placed within those manifestations, which present themselves sequentially and serially. An object, or fragment of an object, is presented, only to be supplemented by another, as each 'builds' in the imagination through a concatenation not objectively explicit. This is given us to read at the opening of an article titled 'Wapping Workhouse', published in *All the Year Round* early in 1860. In directing himself towards the 'East-end of London', and on leaving Covent Garden, the narrator, having 'got past the India House', is caused to reflect in desultory fashion on 'Tippoo-Sahib and Charles Lamb'. These phantasms are supplanted in turn by the little wooden mid-shipman, Aldgate Pump, the Saracen's Head, his already 'swarthy countenance' disfigured by an 'ignominious rash of posting bills' (Dickens 1997a, 366). These phenomena are juxtaposed with an 'ancient neighbour', another Inn, the name of which is not to be remembered distinctly as a result of its having long disappeared, and its becoming conflated with another coaching inn, The Bull, which was to be torn down six years after this article was published.

While items, names, images and objects accumulate, already in meaningful ways, the journey moves forward but the narrating subject displaces himself from the present both spatially and temporally. Names and figures – India House, Tippoo-Sahib, the Saracen's Head – hint at an 'orientation' which is also a disorientation, the journey to the East of London invoking another, Orientalist East, and with that, other temporal and historical frames. Topographical motion brings about a slippage in the mind, into Gothic codes of 'the barbaric or Oriental' (Miles 1993, 44), as if the physical act of perambulation, in its causing the chance encounter with various signs of alterity, releases an unconscious desire, as language itself succumbs to an inadvertent revelation of the perception or anticipation of excess. A doubling temporality is opened from within the present for the subject, who later confesses himself, in another Orientalist turn, in a 'Turkish frame of mind' (Dickens 1997a, 367), for he walks on quite blind to place and historical moment, lost in the pasts of coaching inns and a phantasmic, quite possibly Gothicized, East, before emerging in both 'the age of railways' and Whitechapel Church (Dickens 1997a, 366). The signs of the city lose the subject in a phenomenological miasma between Leadenhall Market and what was likely to be the church of St Mary Matfelon (destroyed in the Second World War), a distance of just under a mile. In the presentation of objects, a street scene, the details of atmosphere, the listing of proper names by encounter and association, or, as elsewhere, details of a building or room, the object or group of objects being represented, manifesting themselves through the communication of traces in an often febrile adumbration, disappear behind the phantasm woven out of the collective web of signs. Concomitantly, the urban subject finds himself lost, once more. As the narrator had found himself in a disorientating experience in Seven Dials almost three decades before, so here it is confessed that 'I gave myself up as having lost my way, and abandoning myself to the narrow streets in a Turkish frame of mind' (Dickens 1997a, 367). As if to enforce the Gothic transformation of place and subject, the narrator then recounts how a young man is encountered, whose 'puffed sallow face, and . . . figure all dirty and shiny and slimy . . . may have been . . . the drowned man' of local advertizing hoardings (Dickens 1997a, 367). This 'figure' defined three times as an 'apparition' and having a ghastly grin and a watery gurgle for a laugh (Dickens 1997a, 367) erases the narrator's own sense of individualism, causing the latter to feel himself to be anonymous, a 'General Cove, or member of the miscellaneous public' (Dickens 1997a, 368).

The subject is given up, and gives himself up to the city. Being addressed by it, he becomes a psychic palimpsest of its structures, flows and manifestations. Objects and places are revealed as being veiled by the traces of themselves, traces which bespeak the tenor, the tone if you will, of other identities, meanings and times, and which in turn direct the subject away from the present materiality, through the lightning flash impressions that they leave perceptually. Moreover, the object in Dickens, that material form belonging to the technique of urban representation, is 'never grasped as distinct from what reveals it. In short', observes Renaud Barbaras (on whose phenomenology of perception I am drawing), 'the manifestation presents the object [whichever experience of London, whichever location, event or scene to which Dickens addresses himself, and by which he is addressed] as what itself remains unpresentable' (Barbaras 2006, 14) – hence the Fabricated Gothic East with its wild boar, dismembered Muslims and aqueous ghouls. (I cannot help wondering, in passing, if Dickens's narrator had not encountered a variation of Phlebas the Phoenician, while, in turn, the Saracen, no longer any body, may have resigned his nomadic role to the narrating subject in a moment of gothic-comic transference and displacement.)

The concern I am stressing here though is that Dickensian urban mapping and representation proceeds by telegraphic shorthand and phatic adumbration, in order simultaneously to outline the experience of perception and to present that which is unavailable to full presentation. That very act of sketching nevertheless presents the object 'rigorously as what requires formulation', which is to say the subject's apperception of the truth of the urban, as the object transforms itself into perceived subject and as the subject who perceives must necessarily receive, decipher and so perceive both 'the manifestation and what appears, [as these are] affected by a double constitutive ambiguity' (Barbaras 2006, 14). Perception, always the perception of some subject, thus reveals itself as the 'identity' of that other subject, the city for the human subject who, in producing this identity, obliterates the objective reality. And 'as for the object', Barbaras continues, 'it is [therefore] simultaneously present in the sense that it is attained in person and indefinitely absent in the sense that no series of adumbrations can exhaust the tenor of being'. The Dickensian manifestations of London generated in fragmentary surges – themselves communicated through the fragment, the ruin, the otherwise unorderable collocation of traces, elements and aspects both structural and phantasmic – project, rather than represent, 'the identity of a coming to presence and a retreat into the unpresentable' (Barbaras 2006, 14). The subject sees the city. The subject *is* the city. Conscious experience becomes the place where, and the screen on which, the apparent unity of the urban is found and projected contingently, before giving way to the haunting implication, always at work, of 'an eidetic abyss between experience and reality' (Barbaras 2006, 14). Half glimpsed as it were, the city in full retreats, its various manifestations never becoming a totality but perceived as an ungraspable totality, which can only be apprehended in the present if it is linked with an historical or fictive past – hence, that drive we identify through the adjective *Dickensian*, that restless rapid pulse at the heart of urban representation in the text of Dickens. And if 'the Gothic novel remains unhistorical precisely because it lacks this link' between the 'historical reality' of the past and 'the present' (Iser 1974, 84), then Dickens situates the interconnection explicitly between historical reality and subjective historicity, through the tropes of Gothic discourse.

This somewhat modified Husserlian reading remains to be explained further. What I am suggesting though about Dickens's response to London and thus, by extension, about the ways in which representation in writing is translated by the subject's experience of the metropolis, is that the phenomenon that is London from the early nineteenth century onwards causes or gives to be known a radically different mode of apprehension and representation, in which it is no longer possible to represent the material world 'as if there were only a single manner of existing and therefore a single adequate modality of access to existing' (Barbaras 2006, 16). London brings about the revelation of the ruin of representation – its reduction to 'nothing other than the vital movement of the coexistence and the interweaving of original formations and sedimentations of meaning' (Husserl 1989, 174) – in terms of the limits of a purely presentist mimetic adequation, and so forces on the subject a new identity, with an historically and materially grounded urban specificity, from which must be generated an inventive 'idiocultural' writing. Such inscription, while grounded in empirical or historical fact, whether solicited 'in the present through experience or . . . as a fact in the past, necessarily has its *inner structure of meaning*' and thus is founded on an 'immense structural a priori', the disclosure of which gives to the act of writing its 'historical becoming' (Husserl 1989, 174). Such a writing is 'inventive' in the sense that the writing subject is forced by the object to find the trace of alterity within what is already there, rather than create some wholly new mode, in order to communicate perception and experience from its partial and subjective location as this takes place. And it is 'idiocultural', to borrow and adapt this term of Derek Attridge's, inasmuch as Dickensian urban invention, through its adumbrated and telegraphic phatic fluxes, attests in a performative manner, thereby doing in words the very thing it describes, to the 'individual's grasp on the world [of the modern city, as this] is mediated by a changing array of [historically given] interlocking, overlapping and often contradictory cultural systems' that mark the urban scene as a 'complex', and which therefore is 'necessarily unstable and subject to constant change' (Attridge 2004, 21).

IV

Dickens affirms in his writing of the city, in his invention of a singularly urban and metropolitan mode of presentation *through* perception that 'the complexity of a cultural field or an idioculture [given singular expression as 'London in the nineteenth century'] is something we can barely fathom; it is certainly not something

to which we can achieve direct access' (Attridge 2004, 22), as anyone familiar with
the city of Dickens's novels, early or late, will know. The description of Snow Hill
and Newgate in *Nicholas Nickleby* draws on the already established journalistic
register and gives sharp expression to the unstable complexity and its power to
confound the subject:

> ... at the very core of London, at the heart of its business and animation, in the
> midst of a whirl of noise and motion: stemming as it were the giant currents of
> life that flow ceaselessly on from different quarters ... stands Newgate; and in
> that crowded street on which it frowns so darkly ... scores of human beings,
> amidst a roar of sounds to which even the tumult of a great city is as nothing,
> four, six, or eight strong men at a time, have been hurried violently and swiftly
> from the world, when the scene has been rendered frightful with excess of human
> life ... (Dickens 1986a, 89)

Unfolded as an excessive countersignature to anything the name 'Snow Hill'
might signify to someone not from London (as Dickens prefaces this remark),
the city is unveiled in all its terrifying force as obviously a living and yet inhuman
phenomenon, challenging both comprehension and the limits of representation, as
these are historically determined at a given moment. London is to be felt as much
as seen, and in this Dickens appears, in his fashioning of the city and its effects on
its subjects, to be anticipating Conrad's injunction in the preface to *The Nigger of
the Narcissus*. The narrative subject as individual form has disappeared, the subjects
being both the city and those who inhabit the machine, the principal purposes of
which are to replicate itself and execute the criminal. What is precisely disquieting
here, and that which, I believe, gives access to that singular idiocultural mode of
historical becoming being referred to as the urban Gothic, is that equivalent excess
of violent motion: a body without a head, the capital city, swarms, roars and thrives;
and yet, in this tumult of unthinking surfeit of dark energy, it targets destructively
at a moment that appears engendered out of the fright and frightfulness of the
'excess of human life'. And once more, we witness the Dickensian performative; the
sentence is entangled in itself, clause after clause, driving itself and being driven,
as the written form offers a perception of the city through the analogy of its own
excessive deformity in 'a complex relationship both to historical verisimilitude and
to ... processes of authentication' (Robertson 1994, 93) through that performative
becoming-monstrous. It is as if Dickens's writing, in order to prove its truth beyond
mere empirical veracity, must become that which it describes.

Thus, it is that Dickens's writing of London 'comes into being as a challenge to
cultural norms [of representation] and retain[s] that challenge ... because it is never
fully accommodated' (Attridge 2004, 46). Yet, although it cannot be fully accommodated, there is, nevertheless, that strange, disquieting feeling of the 'experience
of intimacy ... a sense that the work speaks to my inmost, most secret being', its
haunting and uncanny singularity striking me 'afresh' (Attridge 2004, 78). At the
same time, the demand made on me is clearly akin to the demand made on Dickens
by the city. The demand that London imposes on Dickens is also a demand that

'this specific collocation of words, allusions, and cultural references makes on me, in the event of my reading, *here and now*' (Attridge 2004, 67; emphasis added). I read the Dickensian subject encountering the city: I *am* that subject – or at the very least, phantasmically, it is *as if* I were that subject. This experience and perception are thus the manifestation of a singularity, and the 'experience of singularity involves an apprehension of *otherness*, registered in the event of apprehension' (Attridge 2004, 67). So it is that we find ourselves back, once again, with that abyss between experience and perception. In this, we therefore are simultaneously at a remove and yet impossibly close to Dickens's own encounter with the abyss, that very opening which writing could never suture, and which intuition may serve in part to explain the motivation behind the Dickensian invention of a specifically modern, idiocultural urban gothic. Or, let us just suggest, for Dickens, the urban *was* Gothic and what was Gothic was precisely the apprehension of a terror in the face of an abyss which could never be bridged or closed, and which, in turn, drove Dickens on to write repeatedly of the city as a topography and architecture that could never be mapped or given totalized, finite representation. Reading Dickens on the city, the experience becomes one involving something akin to Dickens's encounters with London: an inventive and singular – singular every time I pick up another text – appreciation and *analogical apperception*; as Attridge has it, this is a 'living through, of the invention that makes the work not just different but the creative re-imagination of cultural materials' and material culture (Attridge 2004, 67).

If I experience that sense of a 'living through' – in the sense of duration and its endurance – as a vicarious, phantasmic event, it is in Dickens's creative re-imagining of various dimensions of the Gothic in culturally and historically specific terms iterable in the urban contexts. Additionally, my phenomenal, haunting experience is marked by both the replication and iteration of Dickensian subjectivity's fall into the world and anonymity. The anonymous narrator-effect delivers us to, and marks the limits of, a threshold between subject and world and the Gothic translated is all the more immanently troubling, if less solidly represented, because identity is lost in the urban. The anonymous comes to pass, glimpsed in this act and articulation of the city in its bearing witness to place and what takes place; for: 'the anonymous is a constitutive feature of the social' (Natanson 1979, 534). As the anonymous subject disappears into the urban (think if you will of Master Humphrey's 'disappearance'), so I too experience this estranged, ironic displacement. Therefore, the anxiety in the face of London's haunting traces is more nearly felt, more intimately available, if not to perception, then to apperception (a distinction I shall make clear shortly). For now, it is enough to remark that in indirect apprehension the city is experienced or suffered as a possibly occult threatening, inhuman, yet vital force, which can swallow us, suffocate us, lose us forever, and prevent our escape. The flows of London consolidate around the nameless subject all too easily, becoming reified as both material locations *and* Gothic structures of the imagination.

V

By the phrase 'Gothic structures' I want to suggest the forms of particular locations in Dickens's essays as simultaneously always real *and* imaginary, and I have in mind not only those aspects of setting and place that resonate with the more obvious settings of the Gothic narrative. As I have already intimated, I am also reading the various 'worlds' of Dickens's London as mappings of material structures, the streets, buildings and so on, which, in their complexity, fragmentation, their 'barbarous' or 'rude' qualities, are suggestive often anachronistically of a dark otherness and also a tendency towards excess of detail and irrationality in design. There is always the sense, for example, in reading Dickens, of passages that lead nowhere, and to nothing, whether those passages are narrative cul-de-sacs or dark streets (reflect once more on 'Seven Dials' or 'Wapping Workhouse'). The street may be found on the map, but its phenomenological phantasm, palimpsest and countersignature are not. If Dickens produces the city as always in some sense the obliquely significant labyrinth, this may well have to do with the abyssal immanence felt by the urban subject in the early nineteenth century. Nicholas Freeman remarks of tropic irregularity and Gothic excess in Dickens's text, 'the labyrinth encapsulates the bewildering confusion of proliferating and dangerously similar streets, engendering frightening claustrophobia or even deadening ennui . . . the city is a realm of tangled passages and monstrous artifice' (2007, 162). This is absolutely, undeniably so; but what Freeman also gestures towards here is that performative palimpsest of Dickensian writing, equally informed by 'tangled passages' of representation and 'monstrous artifice' in the conjunction of design and phenomenological effect; at the always moving centre of which is the urban subject. The subject is always there and always about to be swallowed.

Hence a passage such as the following, in which all estranges even as every detail feels uncannily familiar, and familiarly uncanny. The passage comes from 'Spitalfields', an article from 1851. After 'we cross a many cornered square and enter a sort of gateway', in which geometry and the threshold collude in our initiation, we encounter this 'Gothic structure' in the paragraph that follows:

> Along a narrow passage, up a dark stair, through a crazy door, into a room not very light, not very large, not in the least splendid; with queer corners, and quaint carvings, and massive chimney-pieces; with tall cupboards with prim doors, and squat counters with deep dumpy drawers; with packages, out of whose ends flash all the colours of the rainbow – where all is as quiet as a playhouse at daybreak, or a church at midnight – where, in truth, there is nobody to make a noise, except one well-dressed man, one attendant porter (neither of whom seem to be doing anything in particular), and one remarkably fine male cat, admiring, before the fire, the ends of his silky paws – where the door, as we enter, shuts with a deep, dull, muffled sound, that is more startling than a noise – where there is less bustle than at a Quakers' meeting, and less business going on than in a Government office – the well-dressed man threads the mazes of the piles, and desks, and cupboards and counters, with a slow step, to greet us, and to assure us, in reply

to our apology, that we have *not* made any mistake whatever, and that we are in the silk warehouse which we seek . . . (1997, 295).

This is not the end of the sentence, and its monstrous growth is so serpentine and excessive that the collective subject is all but lost, appearing barely after what seem to be innumerable clauses. All the more remarkable in this ravelling up of subjectivity is the fact that the sentence or 'narrow passage' does not only distend itself disorientatingly, its multiple clausal facets lose the reader in the many layered density of the structure. Intensity, density and duration combine to overwhelm, to lose, and to render space no longer clearly imaginable. How much time do we need to register all that is here, and all that combines to delay passage and yet impinge on perception with a sense of discontinuous but endless duration? So much does the Dickensian city rely on the iterability of such effects and forms that the endless-ness is itself suggestive that not only is London an unfathomable and illimitable labyrinth but that, formally, reiteration of device and aspect produces that type of 'ritualization of mystery' typical of Gothic fiction identified by Fiona Robertson (1994, 72). Arguably also, Dickens's London resembles Frank Kermode's com-mentary on Gothic in *The Genesis of Secrecy*, with that narrative's production of 'something irreducible, therefore perpetually to be interpreted; not secrets to be found out one by one, but Secrecy' (Kermode 1979, 143). There is nothing 'behind' Dickens's iterable perceptions of the city, merely the one 'secret' that here, as everywhere, is London, irreducible to definition and, so, control. And it is this very irreducibility that drives Dickens on, to describe, inscribe, and reinscribe, the ineffable and ineluctable performative of a tropic and topic manifestation of the same-everywhere and everywhere as other. Dickens thus anticipates a later writing of the city, even if he does not obviously present such a London himself. In the combination of manifest labyrinth, replicated at and resounding between, the levels of form, content, and interpretation, the Dickensian narrator opens the city into what Nicholas Freeman, again, calls, apropos late-nineteenth-century urban discourse, 'the wider vocabulary of visionary experience' and the 'unsolved puzzle' (Freeman 2007, 163). But while for later writers, concealed within such experience was the promise of occult or mystical revelation, for the reader of Dickens there can be no such 'outside' the city and concomitantly, no solution, no relief, and no possibility of freeing oneself from the simultaneously *material* and *phantasmic* vision in which one is trapped.

In that understanding of the 'something irreducible . . . perpetually to be interpreted', we read the Dickensian anticipation of what Edmund Husserl was to call, in *Cartesian Meditations*, the experience of 'appresentation' or 'analogical apperception' (1995, 108ff.). London Gothic in its Dickensian mode is not logical, it is analogical; one grasps it, if at all, indirectly through the limitless comparison between its singular sites, events and experiences, and the literary manifestation and invention of its phenomena. I grasp at the next image, and the next, even as sentences such as the one above to which I feel myself bound, in which I find myself enmeshed, and to which my subjectivity is sentenced, move, replicate, double and displace every element of themselves beside, within, and from themselves.

And Dickens does not so much present, represent, perceive or invite the reader to perceive the city directly (this being impossible), as the city figures itself as an other through the apperceptive realization of its immensity, its sublime terror and endless awful wonder. One's consciousness cannot grasp the whole, and so moves feverishly and with an anxiety of inadequacy, from sign to sign, the totality immanent and always at a remove, however proximate or intimate, from the street, the room, the shop window, and so on.

Dickensian narration therefore gives us to apprehend how 'experience', in Husserl's words, 'is original consciousness' (1995, 108), this consciousness being always consciousness of an other. In its encounter with alterity, consciousness has itself reflected back to itself as a '"there too"', as Husserl puts it (1995, 109). Dickensian consciousness is a focused reflection on the materiality of place and the (a)material traces that register on subjectivity. To return to 'Spitalfields', in a gesture of parabasis, the reader is interrogated over his or her knowledge or experience of Spitalfields (Dickens 1997a, 294). Supposing the reader only to have a vague impression of a place never visited, the narrator proceeds to ask if the reader will accompany him there. Perceiving myself to be thus mediated by my experience of the other, I come to a mediated awareness of place, a being '"there too"', but my consciousness of myself is simultaneously opened to me as never being capable of achieving a pre-originary sense of 'an "itself there"' (Husserl 1995, 109). In being made to perceive myself not as pure presence but as being made '"*co-present*"' (Husserl 1995, 109), I am presented to myself as an other: thus, I am conscious of myself through, in Husserl's word, an *appresentation*. Doubled and divided, I am haunted as much as I haunt myself.

In pieces such as 'Spitalfields', the Dickensian narrator maintains this mode of appresentation and doubling after his initial rhetorical gambit by shifting to speaking of what 'we' observe: 'Turning ... out of ... Bishopsgate, we suddenly lose the noise that has been resounding in our ears' (Dickens 1997a, 294). Location and loss, placement and displacement mark the transition of the self and the experience of this district of London. The city as both material entity and experience and perception of a material entity thus breaks up irrevocably the Romantic compact between solitary consciousness and Nature, which simultaneously makes me at one with Nature whilst giving to my consciousness the illusion that I am in control, I master Nature in perceiving it for myself, and myself alone. Nature vouchsafes me the perception of an '"immanent transcendency"' (Husserl 1995, 110). But everywhere in the urban location I encounter others, like myself and yet not myself, urban subjects. I am thus reduced in relation to that something irreducible (to recall Kermode's phrase) to the situation of being an other, *comme les autres* as it were, and yet other than each and every other. The city thus produces in my appresentative consciousness, inscribing in me indirectly, the analogical apperception of myself as one more urban subject, a fragment of an impossible, infinite and monstrous form. I enter into, and am found to myself, given subjectivity through my '"*analogizing" apprehension*' (Husserl 1995, 111) of my subjectivization.

This, argues Husserl, is not a 'thinking act' though. For

Every apperception in which we apprehend at a glance, and noticingly grasp, objects given beforehand – for example, the already-given everyday world – . . . points to . . . an *analogizing transfer* . . . [and] to the extent that there is givenness beforehand [given that we know the material world in which we find ourselves is always already there in its brute, mute materiality, a materiality the immensity of the city enforces with a particular violence in the first decades of the nineteenth century], there is such a transfer . . .

Such analogizing transfer arrives between the discontinuous motion of object after object, clause after clause, experience after experience, and subject substituted for subject. Such transfer, such translation takes place in me through the iterable material condition translated as the equally iterable fragmentation and singular-seriality of the urban. Thus, the Dickensian revelation is that the subject 'merely becomes conscious' of that which is always already at work, the narrative and constitutive 'creation' being 'only the explication of an already constituted concept' that is encountered (Derrida 1989a, 40). This is witnessed also in the article and analogical transference of Spitalfields into the textual matrix of traces that bear its name as itself and not itself, and which, in turn, though irreducible to any given meaning, are simply the fragments that Dickens shores against the ruin of representation. In this, Dickens is responding rather than creating; he happens to be on hand in order to receive and so set free 'a possibility' in representation 'which is nothing less than historical, in order to hand it to us' (Derrida 1989a, 39). If, as Husserl reminds us, and as Dickens gives us to know here, the '*radical differentiation of apperceptions*' as so many 'different levels' of the same experience (Husserl 1995, 111) comes down to the disappearance of any separable subjectivity into that anonymous doubled self haunted by the urban, by its irreducibility, then this phenomenal experience is already mapped in the broken heap of images.

Dickens, in sum, receives and grasps objects, traces, signs, and so on. In repeating them, in transferring them from their material historicity to the materiality of the letter, he constructs the labyrinth of an urban subjectivity through the transformation of objects into tropes. These, in turn, lead both nowhere and back to where one begins, where the subject finds him- or herself constituted. The London in Dickens's text is therefore invented through the mediation of the Gothic device of employing 'narrative and architectural [as well as topographical] passages which seem to lead nowhere [but which] in fact lead', if not to a secret past as Fiona Robertson observes of the typical Gothic narrative (1994, 74), then to the uncanny revelation of one's own fundamental displacement within the world, *by the historical and material facticity of that world*. As in Gothic narrative, Dickens's London essays and articles 'disrupt the reader's conventional expectations about the working of cause and effect' (Robertson 1994, 76). What Dickens also achieves is a displacement of Gothic effect from the subject in the narrative to the reading subject, as has been witnessed. Whereas, in Gothic narrative, the protagonist's consciousness is represented as apprehensive and anxious, and whereas this is in part the effect that Dickens reworks on his characters in his novels (think Pip at the beginning of *Great Expectations* prior to his encounter with Magwitch), in the journalism, the reading subject is produced as anxious and apprehensive through the presentation of the particular areas of the city as labyrinthine, dark and confusing, without the balm or false hope of a resolution.

VI

Dickens's writing of London mediated through the Gothic serves then, and in conclusion, two purposes at least. On the one hand, in its invention of an idio-cultural discourse appropriate to time and place, it mediates the historically determined experience of the modern urban subject at the beginning of the nineteenth century. On the other hand, its revision of the Gothic in response to the urban condition as experience and perception of serial fragmentation generates a performative fragmentation in prose, which has the possibility to assume 'limitless shapes of being [and] in the special way of responding and vibrating to the encounter of one's glance ... [which in turn] evokes all sorts of variations' (Merleau-Ponty 1973, 62–3), causing to appear to the reader's perception the indirect manifestation of London's otherwise inaccessible reality.

In this, Dickensian perception inaugurates an order of 'coherent deformation imposed on the visible' (Merleau-Ponty 1973, 91), precisely so that the truth of place is available if not to representation then, at least, and in no small measure, to processes of perception that exceed the merely present and empirical. London, we conclude, needs a language equal to itself. Fashioning this from what is found in the past memory of literary formation, Dickens enacts a mode of indirect and analogi-cal appresentation and apperception in which communication, however ruinous, causes London to appear not as such, to repeat myself, but as it is, in its irreducible secrecy, a place in which signs are made and given continually, but like the unfortunate freemason who speaks at the close of 'Wapping Workhouse', "I am in this unfortunate position ... [for there is never received] the countersign!"' (Dickens 1997a, 375) There is only, instead, the haunting revelation and knowledge of what Merleau-Ponty calls 'the meaninglessness of association through contiguity' (Merleau-Ponty 1995, 15). What is all the more terrible here for the subject is that the immediate and local impression given the Dickensian subject can only arouse other images because it is 'already *understood* in the light of the past experience' of 'the psychic fact' (Merleau-Ponty 1995, 17, 115) that I am only ever trapped within, and speak out of, this confounding place, time and again.

2

Houses, Homes, Rooms and Tombs: The Unhomely Spaces and Monstrous Economies of *Dombey and Son*

I

In the previous chapter, we wandered the streets with Charles Dickens, reflecting on the estrangement of subjectivity in the face of London and the impossibility of finding a narrative language adequate to any direct representation of the city. At the same time, I also considered to what extent London had come to constitute a modern subjectivity, marked by the signs of its own, and also the city's, historicity, and to begin an 'inaugural mutation' (Derrida 1989a, 39). Dickens's language is a mutation but also originary in its invention of the urban. It breaks with conventions of representation of the city, while at the same time 'developing something ... potentially inscribed' in the language of urban representation (Derrida 1989a, 10). The invention of such a language is necessary to the transmission of a 'material ontology', as a 'unity of traces' that is at once originary *and* bound to a tradition (Derrida 1989a, 31, 29). Writing the city thus admits to, and causes to come into being a history, or, more precisely, a historicity that affirms 'the historical dimension of a priori possibilities' (Derrida 1989a, 39) in both the 'sensible figuration' and the 'psychological lived experience' of the urban subject (Derrida 1989a, 41). Dickensian subjectivity as consciousness is also 'the consciousness of historicity ... where sense is indissociable from being' (Derrida 1989a, 46). In this formulation, it is capable of transmitting its experience to future readers, making available a true reading of historicity apropos consciousness, without falling into 'the philosophical nonsense of a purely empirical history' (Derrida 1989a, 51). Staying with Dickens for this chapter, we will leave the streets to enter a house, which is distinctly unhomely, and, in its own fashion, as monstrous an architecture as the streets were perceived as being. In entering the house, we will also reflect on the relationship between 'house' and 'home', what it means to 'dwell', and how the homely, the familiar, the habitual in the idea of home come to be informed by an uncanny estrangement.

II

Before the house – or, rather, the houses of Dombey and son, and daughter – a journey abroad, away from home, away from the familiar and all regular habit. Charles

Dickens began *Dombey and Son* while on holiday with his family in Lausanne, Switzerland. He announced this in a letter, dated 28 June 1846, to John Forster, the author's lifelong friend and first biographer. He had had the idea for the novel as early as January of the same year, but no work had begun in earnest until halfway through the year. As Peter Ackroyd observes of Dickens's time in Switzerland, no writing could begin until 'the "big box" which contained all the appurtenances of his desk arrived . . . not just his writing materials . . . but also the bronze images of two toads duelling, of a dog-fancier . . . a paper-knife, a gilt leaf with a rabbit upon it'. Ackroyd goes on to explain that 'so great was [Dickens's] love of habit and order that he could not write without their silent presence in front of him' (Ackroyd 1990, 503). Another way to look at this is to suggest that Dickens's fetishes served to induce the habitual, to reconstitute in part the necessary dwelling place, where the family, the familiar, habit and habitat form a matrix, from within which the self finds itself. If, as Gaston Bachelard assumes, a 'house constitutes a body of images that give . . . proofs or illusions of stability', then through such objects 'we are constantly re-imagining' the reality of home; 'to distinguish all these images would be to describe the soul of the house' (Bachelard 1994, 17).

If Dickens *needed* the image of the part of home that was most authentically the expression of his selfhood, constituted through a constellation of material objects, he also required a physical distance to write what is at once his most fantastic melodrama of the modern home. In part, Dickens's purpose for the novel was to examine the world of home and capitalism from the perspective of a child, the strangely prescient, somewhat uncanny Paul Dombey, who, Dickens wrote in his working notes, was 'born to die'. Here, we have, albeit indirectly, the first acknowledgement that this is to be a haunted and haunting, domestic melodrama, and one in which the home plays a particular role. Indeed, Dickens's vision of 'home' is dark and complex in *Dombey and Son*. It is not a safe haven, a family hearth, a familiar locus. The home in *Dombey* is distinctly unhomely. A corollary of this, As John Butt and Kathleen Tillotson argued back in 1957, is that 'the pervasive suggestion [of Dickens's seventh novel] remains that a family cannot be run on business lines' (1957, 87). Though capitalism sustains the home, its violence rends the very idea. Thus, *Dombey and Son* bears witness to, and takes responsibility to convey, the unseen effects of economic systems on the home, as they haunt it, transforming it on occasions into a tomb, a sepulchre where sense and being, once again, attest to the consciousness of historicity.

Two motifs that are now familiar to critics of Dickens, and much discussed, recur throughout the novel, outside the house and the home: the sea and the railways. Though not of home, these symbols and forces of nature and society make their forces felt throughout the Victorian interiors of *Dombey*, in their shared, inhuman indifference, and the link they assume between alterity and violence, otherness and death, by which mortality is revealed to humans. In this action, the natural and mechanical forces in question trouble because the intimate spaces of safety that the home promises are thus rendered subject to a violation. 'Images of immensity' (Bachelard 1994, 184), the sea and the railways give to the reader the perception of selfhood at threat, and thus intimate the fragility of one's dwelling on the earth, through the 'effects of harsh dialectics' (Bachelard 1994, 184). In Chapter Sixteen, sea whispers to Paul Dombey in his sickroom of death, the 'old fashion', as Dickens calls it, with the 'golden ripple' (Dickens 1985, 297) rolling across the wall, while, in general, the building of the railways demolishes homes and shakes the foundations of those that remain standing. Trains bespeak, and reveal to view the ruination of the home, we read of 'jagged walls and falling houses'; we read also of 'battered roofs and broken windows, wretched rooms'. The railway suggests the 'want and fever [that] hide themselves in many wretched shapes' inside the same houses, while the exteriors, with their 'crowded gables, and distorted chimneys, and deformity of brick and mortar' mirror as they enclose 'deformity of mind and body' (Dickens 1985, 355). For Paul's father, the train particularly announces and serves as a mnemotechnic of death, in passages from Chapter Twenty that are frequently quoted, passages where Dickens has to shift from past to present tense, in order to maintain the inexorable speed and monstrous force that unveils itself to Dombey Senior in the process of his journey.

Allied to these oppositions of nature and civilization, there is also the contest between female and male, for Dickens, universal as opposed to historical principles. In a novel 'acutely attuned to contemporary issues', there remains a sense, as one Dickens critic, Alexander Welsh, argues, that in the failure of the male line in the novel, which foreshadows the collapse of the capitalist venture embodied by Dombey Senior, 'only [an] unchanging female principle makes death and history acceptable' (Welsh 1987, 101). If Paul is uncanny though, the first of several 'unearthly' characters in Dickens's fiction, then Florence, his sister, is, equally, not drawn according to realist conventions; instead, she belongs to both the eighteenth-century sentimental tradition and the conventions of fairy tale, in order that Dickens can 'explore taboos and fantasies' (Schlicke 1999, 186). Nowhere, Dickens shows us, are taboos and fantasies unearthed more intimately and painfully than in the home, the place from which the novel begins, and which image it seeks to redeem in the face of Victorian modernity and the historical consciousness of an inescapable destiny, of technological and economic destruction, with which *Dombey* toys. Thus, *Dombey and Son* realizes, in the words of Gaston Bachelard, that, apropos any discussion of the home, the house, its rooms and related spaces, 'it is not a question of describing houses, or enumerating their . . . features'. The house is not just a backdrop or stage-set, on which characters act out their lives and relationships. Instead, through consideration of the ways in which Dickens figures interior and domestic spaces, we come to perceive how the world is 'our first universe' and how 'we inhabit our vital space', how we 'take root' or are uprooted (Bachelard 1994, 4). Dickens is the novelist of home *par excellence*, as well as being the writer who, more than any other, perceives how precarious a thing is home. At the same time, though, it is this very same vulnerability that gives to the poetics of the home in Dickens a place for the possibility of making appear to his characters their own homelessness, and so the concomitant possibility of learning what it means to dwell in relation to, and in care of, one another.

III

This last remark is traced by Martin Heidegger's reflection on the nature of 'dwelling' as a constituent aspect of one's being, as opposed to mere building or existing, and is germane to this discussion of *Dombey and Son*. (See also, Chapter Eleven, pp. 200–15.) I will therefore suspend the close consideration of Dickens's text in order to clarify this relation, if possible. My purpose in so doing is to illuminate for the reader how Dickens's novel leads to a revelation of dwelling rooted in, and disclosed through, the novel's fairy-tale and feminine principles, which the novel seeks to set against the masculine world of enterprise, capitalism and business houses (aspects of which I will go on to explore, further on in the present chapter). The novel is thus constructed along a trajectory that aims to recover through disclosure an apprehension of dwelling.

For Heidegger, dwelling does not define one's existence in a given place. It is irreducible to any notion of building, construction or activities producing material habitats. Drawing on the etymology of 'dwelling' (*bauen*) in German, and showing its relation to the conjugated forms of the verb of being (*Ich bin, du bist*), and the imperative form, *bis*, meaning 'be' (2001a, 144–5), Heidegger presents the notion of dwelling as part of being's ontology in its historicity, as that which serves to define what it means to exist as a mortal, or what Heidegger would describe as being-towards-death, on, and in knowing relation to, the earth. This 'dwelling' is an active and conscious consideration and reflection on what it means to be, being mindful of one's temporal and material condition, and to exist in such a manner that demonstrates care for being. Building, construction, architecture and building 'as cultivating', as Heidegger puts it, and so on (2001a, 145): all are (capable of being apprehended as) merely expressions of one's being and one's dwelling, for 'building as dwelling, that is, as being on the earth . . . remains for man's everyday experience that which is from the outset "habitual" – we inhabit it' (2001a, 145). Because 'building' is habitual, that to which we are accustomed, which we do with that forgetfulness that defines habit and custom, so we 'inhabit' unthinkingly a manner of existence that, in its forgetfulness, occludes the true condition of being as dwelling, which is, 'to be on the earth as a mortal' and so forget also that dwelling (and here Heidegger returns to the etymological and semantic resonances of *bauen*) 'means at the same time to cherish and protect, to preserve and care for' (2001a, 145; One might also reflect on the idiomatic use of 'dwell' to get closer to the Heideggerian sense; when you say you will 'dwell on' a subject for a certain amount of time, or when you ask someone to dwell on the consequences of what they have done, then you are invoking a self-conscious process of thought concerning the relation between existence and thinking).

One other aspect of 'dwelling' in Heidegger requires consideration, however briefly, this being what the philosopher calls 'the fourfold'. Dwelling, as mortals, places us in the 'fourfold' (2001a, 148). To be mortal means to die, 'to be capable of death *as* death', and this capability is given only to humans (2001a, 148). Obviously, it might be said, animals die also. Strictly speaking though, they do not, they cease to exist. For Heidegger, only humans have the capability of thinking death, of conceptualizing the notion of death and constructing around this various practices, customs, rituals and so forth. Equally, and as a result, only the human animal can 'think' death. Against this, human dwelling is a way of preserving, of bearing in mind, of 'saving' the earth (Heidegger 2001a, 148). 'Saving' here is not used in the sense of protecting, but, as Heidegger reminds us, of excepting, of keeping safe by excepting. So the earth is preserved, excepted from the thinking of mortality, in order that there is dwelling-to-come, for others. If earth and being in its mortality are two dimensions of the fourfold, the other two in Heidegger's geometry of dwelling are the sky and what he calls the divinities. The sky is perceived as that which, not of the materiality of the earth, has collectively its own passages and temporality (2001a, 48). The 'divinities' is a collective conceptualization, regardless of a specific religion, given to humans to think as that which is hoped for beyond all rational hope or empirical experience, that which is other and to come. Thus dwelling is constituted through the human reflection on and reception of – a 'staying with' rather than simply existing (Heidegger 2001a, 149) – the three dimensions of the fourfold not categorized as being.

Before turning back to close readings of particular passages from *Dombey and Son*, it should be helpful to consider Dickens's novel in a somewhat general fashion, in possible relation to the Heideggerian consideration of dwelling. Inasmuch as death makes itself manifest in stark, violent and markedly different ways through the agency of nature and human construction (the sea, the railways), it is clear that mortality as that which is nearest to one's being is borne home to Dombey Senior, and in a false anticipation to Florence also, in the inaccurate report of Walter's death. That the novel begins with death in childbirth indicates the striking intimacy and proximity of life and death within, and as, determinants of what it means to dwell, but, moreover, what is closest to home, what strikes home, one might say, with the most powerful immediacy, and thus comes to haunt the very idea of the home, from the start *and as an inaugural mutation of homeliness*. While death for Paul is 'natural', part of nature, in the images of death that the train journey encompasses and projects repeatedly for Paul's father, death is a destructive force, imagistically projected from the material experience and phenomena of the Victorian age in particular expressions of its industrial-capitalist manifestations. Death is one more product, an outcome if you will of steam, mechanization, industrialization, urbanization, mercantile mass-production and systems of exchange, the destruction of the land.

As we have already seen, houses in *Dombey* are ruined materially, but nineteenth-century mercantilism, and the economic system that supports it, destroys homes in other ways also. However, for Paul, death arrives 'naturally' (he is, after all, 'born to die'; but, then, so are we all), the waves and the sea engulfing the room figuratively. In a gesture of *poiesis*, of making things appear through poetic creation, Dickens discloses Paul's being gathered into the natural world, Heidegger's earth and sky, as that which calls us to dwell, to 'think of what is called man's existence by way of the nature of dwelling' (Heidegger 2001a, 213). Poetic creation unveils the truth of dwelling through language, as that which, most nearly, through its tropological work calls the reader to his or her responsibility towards being. Language measures being in its dwelling, as Heidegger argues (2001a, 219–20) and Dickens completes the reminder of one's being in the fourfold, if I can put it like this, gesturing towards the divinities and thus expressing that weak hope through a gesture of theological apostrophe, by which Chapter Sixteen comes to a conclusion (1985, 297–8). In comparison, death, as that which haunts Mr Dombey's train journey, arrives as a reminder of all that he has forgotten. Such forgetfulness is not personal to Dombey, however. It is, *Dombey and Son* seeks to remind us, that which is the condition and the price – the very historicity itself – of the period, the 'age of steam', the 'age of industry', and so on. Dombey only learns to remember, and so to dwell authentically, in the conclusion of the novel, when the waves speak finally to him, and to Florence, in rhythmic imitations of the heart, 'murmuring . . . of love, eternal and illimitable, extending still, beyond the sea, beyond the sky, to the invisible country far away' (Dickens 1985, 975). In a final moment of parabasis, Dickens refuses closure to *Dombey and Son*, instead opening it to 'us' (1985, 975) through the hope of the arrival of all those voices of the other, and leaving us to dwell as the narrative flows into the illimitable ocean, in a call that seeks a response, an affirmation, and so a responsibility to being, in the face of the material conditions of the subject's historicity in the mid-nineteenth century.

IV

This is to place the novel in a large historical and philosophical frame, and if the question is raised as to why a Heideggerian reading might not be malapropos, I shall answer this further in the chapter, in addressing the question of melodrama in relation to different registers of historical reading, and the textual manifestation of historicity. It now remains, though, to address the specificity of singular homes. In the first chapter of *The Poetics of Space*, Bachelard sets out the grounds for a phenomenology of the home and house. As he argues, the house, 'quite obviously, is a privileged entity' for such a study, because it appears to us as a complex unity, comprising both 'dispersed images and a body of images' simultaneously (Bachelard 1994, 3). Much of Victorian fiction deals with such 'privileged entities'. While a number of the novels of the eighteenth century take place in part or to a large extent on the road, with the road offering a parallel to the narrative trajectory, the representation of the house in fiction of the nineteenth century is often integral to apprehending the novel's purpose. From Northanger Abbey, in Jane Austen's novel of the same name, to *Wuthering Heights*, the house and the home are forcefully significant, to the extent that they might be considered characters in their own right. Later in the century, there is the house of Henry Jekyll in *The Strange Case of Dr Jekyll and Mr Hyde* with its front and back doors, the abbeys and castles of *Dracula*, or the houses of John Galsworthy's *The Forsyte Saga* that enclose scenes of infidelity, guilt and rape. How a house looks, what it contains, how its rooms are appointed – all such concerns demand the reader's attention, whether in the *fin de siècle* Gothic of Richard Marsh's *The Beetle* or George and Weedon Grossmith's social comedy, *The Diary of a Nobody*. (For discussion of these and other novels of the suburbs, see Chapter Six.) Each invites us to comprehend how domestic spaces, architectural form and the elements that make up their rooms – furnishing, colour, material objects – serve to inform the reader about character, class, ideology, and a particular family's past or its secrets. Such spaces also serve as complex coded representations of the contemporary cultural moment, and thus give us access not only to history, in the sense of 'how people lived', but also to the historicity of a particular novel, how the novel has embedded the traces of its moment in its writing.

For all that criticism of the Victorian novel will explicate matters of social and economic force, political struggle, and large historical fluxes (see Chapter Four, on the contested grounds of epistemological and political identity mediated through nineteenth-century texts), the Victorian novel is as much, if not more, concerned with the private and familial, and the relations or power struggles that are mapped through the domestic *economy* of this symbolic site. (In using the term *economy*, I am thinking less of matters of money or finance, than I am of the etymology of the word, coming from the Greek meaning 'control of the house'.) Consequently, it is important that we consider the role of rooms in Victorian novels, as these operate beyond immediate staging places for narrative events, and become in themselves, non-linear narratives of identity and history. *Dombey and Son* is particularly important in this regard, because it plays on the very idea of the 'house', of what constitutes a house, who controls and who inherits it. As in all Dickens novels, there is more than one house, each house being either a place of secrets and the past, or the place of redemption and so a future, which may be desired but which cannot be programmed, which cannot be made subject to any economy.

Houses are prisons in Dickens, but they are also places of sanctuary. As the very first chapter of *Dombey* shows us, a particular room can be a locus of both life and death. A room can be a tomb, even though one is still alive, and there is always the violent possibility that one can be expelled from the home, made an outcast, homeless, in one of the most stereotypical of Victorian narrative effects. More than this, *Dombey*, from its very title, plays on the doubleness and duplicity of the house. What appears normal or perfectly ordered from the outside is far from familiar, once we find ourselves inside that structure. Regarding *Dombey's* doubleness, there is Dombey's house of business but also his home. *Dombey and Son* names both a family relationship and a professional organization. The title thus doubles up, economically, on what is being identified, even as that very same title offers a confusion of locations, business and home. Indeed, to give the novel its full title – *Dealings with the Firm of Dombey and Son, Wholesale, Retail and for Exportation* – it is unequivocal that the novel intends to 'deal' with the very idea of business, and to address the mercantile structure and operation. Dombey's business house, the structural relation that names it, informs the first sentence, indeed the first paragraph, of the novel:

> Dombey sat in the corner of the darkened room in the great armchair by the bed-side, and Son lay tucked up warm in a little basket bedstead, carefully disposed on a low settee immediately in front of the fire and close to it, as if his constitution

were analogous to that of a muffin, and it was essential to toast him brown while
he was very new. (Dickens 1985, 49)

Son, capitalized, is anonymous except for his relation to the father. Moreover,
in this opening scene there is something that is both vaguely comical and, at the
same time, uneasily, disquietingly menacing. Dombey, we learn is 'eight-and-forty'.
For the Victorian reader, this would have registered immediately, for the year of
publication in book form was 1848, the year of publication also of *Vanity Fair*,
Wuthering Heights, *Jane Eyre*, and *The Tenant of Wildfell Hall*, all novels, in one
way or another, about finding a proper home, or the impossibility of such a quest
(on *The Tenant of Wildfell Hall*, see the following chapter). Dombey Senior is thus
as old as the century, the most typically Victorian of men. Son is 'about eight-and-
forty minutes' of age, Dickens taking care to drive the historical analogy home, to
mark beings with the historical and temporal coincidence, for even the most obtuse
of readers, reiterating this later in giving the number of railings, counted by Miss
Tox, around the Princess's Arms (Dickens 1985, 49, 143).

It is as if Dickens intends Dombey, the father, to signify the spirit of the age,
to be its material embodiment or reified personification and all that this implies. Certainly, Dombey is a singular exemplar of everything that draws out of
Dickens such ambivalence towards his epoch, in this and in other fictions such
as *A Christmas Carol* or *Little Dorrit*. A powerful patriarchal figure, a successful
modern man of business, Dombey Senior is also the most callous and indifferent
of parents, concerned only with genetic reproduction as the necessary coadjutant
of economic success, in a fabulous representation of capitalist survival of the fittest.
This is given clearly, when Dombey remarks to his silent wife that 'The House will
once again, Mrs Dombey . . . be not only in name but in fact Dombey and Son'
(Dickens 1985, 49). The home is subordinate to the House *de facto* and *de jure*, the
one merely a domestic factory for producing the product that will continue the
other, the cost of business being the death of Mrs Dombey. While Mrs Dombey
'had always sat at the head of [her husband's] table, and done the honours of his
house' (Dickens 1985, 51), her purpose has been merely subsidiary to principal
interests.

As Dombey puts it, in announcing Son's name as Paul, the coining of a new
male Dombey in the image of a previous male member of the family is paramount.
Paul, after all, is the name that has passed from male Dombey to male Dombey, the
'Junior' being a mere inconvenience, only of 'a private and personal complexion'
(Dickens 1985, 50). More significantly, the 'signature' of the House 'remains the
same' (Dickens 1985, 50). The inscription of the proper name maintains a symbolic
refiguring of the imagined space of the business house, acting as its guarantor, and
in this there is announced a question of maintaining the capital investment. In contrast, having already remarked of six-year-old Florence Dombey that she belongs
to the category of 'no issue . . . worth mentioning', Dickens observes, somewhat
archly, that '[i]n the capital of the House's name and dignity, such a child [as
Florence] was merely a base coin that couldn't be invested – a bad Boy – nothing
more' (Dickens 1985, 51).

I shall return to the interior spaces of *Dombey and Son* shortly. What we can see from the very first page of Dickens's novel, though, is that, in its mediation of its historicity, *Dombey* announces the 1840s, in the words of Raymond Williams, 'as the decisive period in which the consciousness of a new phase of civilization was being formed and expressed' (Williams 1985, 11). In this sketch of family relations and their economic interdependency, we come to realize already that this consciousness, in *Dombey and Son* especially and in other novels of the period, is produced as a violent birth out of the dialectic struggle between domestic and public, home and house, and often female and male. In relation to the inner space, though, in response to what appears in that space and the various combinations that the elements of the domestic interior impose on our consciousness, we see from Dickens immediately how 'imagination', as Bachelard argues, 'augments the values of reality' (Dickens 1985, 3). Thus, Dickens takes us into the home at a point of personal and historical crisis in the opening pages, and inflects that crisis through the melodrama of family, which suffers its own crisis as a result of the larger issue of identity in the mid-nineteenth century.

Returning to rooms and Bachelard: if imagination augments the values of reality, when I look at a room with which I am familiar, items, objects, the otherwise heterogeneous phenomena that make up such a space, assume meaning through their constellations and interplay. Photographs, souvenirs or mementoes are simultaneously exteriorized traces of memory, and displayed, cryptic displacements of my identity, an identity that, in any given room, is available as both public *and* secret. A room is, thus, in principle, an act of memory work, a mnemotechnic, and, additionally, simultaneously, an archive. Projected beyond myself, it returns to me, projections of myself, so that, in effect, I return to myself as both myself and an other; or a room, or some other place with which I associate my identity, can remind me, in the words of Stephen Dedalus, that 'I am another now and yet the same' (Joyce 2008, 11). The Dickensian room anticipates the modernist and phenomenological temporal awareness of one's being, but emphasizes also the historicity of that being through the singular phenomena that stand in for, and act as so many prostheses of, the self on a material, and, therefore, historical plane. A room, particularly a domestic interior, but, by extension, other rooms with which I associate myself, in which I am in familiar surroundings, as the saying goes; all are prosthetic extensions of my selfhood or dispersed fragments of an I, which consciousness reassembles every time I enter that space. At once material, they are also phantasmic spaces that remind me of who I am. It is therefore not too great a shift to suggest that a city can be home; or parts of it at least. Streets take on an aspect of habit, or otherwise express the spirit of the *habitus*.

Bachelard cautions, 'it is not enough to consider the house as an "object" on which we make our judgments and daydreams react' (Bachelard 1994, 3). *How* we see the spaces we inhabit must also be considered, and Dickens, with his toasting babies and darkened rooms, helps us focus in particularly acute ways. More generally, the novel is perhaps *the* fictional space where the phenomenology of house and home is brought to our attention most intimately and repeatedly. As we have already seen, novels invite us to enter the homes of strangers. They take us into their drawing rooms, their boudoirs, kitchens and bedrooms. They show us around, make us familiar with their furniture and other possessions. Occasionally, they describe the decoration of a room. Frequently, they allow us a voyeuristic insight into how people live, eat, talk, make love, give birth, and many other things also. The strangest thing of all, though, in the narrative act of causing others' rooms – and so their lives – to appear, is that the writer or narrator 'furnishes' us with the material details of these rooms in such a manner that we too become inhabitants. The paintings, carpets, beds, wash stands and chairs are already there; and yet, uncannily, they are not merely objects composing the larger 'object' of the room, inside the still larger 'object', the house. As well as being material fixtures and fittings, the phenomena of a given fictional room are presented and inscribed in fiction in such a way as to assume particular meanings, which, strictly speaking, should only be familiar or proper (that is to say also, *of* the family, the property *of*) the house owner or occupier. In seeing someone else's property in so familiar a fashion, there is something not a little improper.

V

We now turn to Chapter 3 of *Dombey and Son*, 'In which Mr Dombey, as a Man and a Father, is seen at the Head of the Home-Department' (74). Dickens's ironic title speaks directly to us of the extent to which the idea of home has been elided, occluded even, by the 'House' of business by the 1840s. Home is merely an extension of capitalist enterprise, a department of the business operation, run on modern lines. Now, it has become something of a commonplace in criticism to remark of a narratorial voice that its omniscience – when, indeed, *if* it is omniscient – gives the reader access to the characters' thoughts, desires and wishes, and this is true. The narratorial rhetoric makes mediated observations, to which, properly speaking, no one should have access to other than a given character. Yet, it is also true that the rhetorical projection and replay we call 'narrator' – a kind of fictive recording medium, which in being so named, gives ghostly manifestation or appearance, hardly 'presence', to an otherwise disembodied voice – causes to 'appear' the emotional or psychic resonance, if I can put it like this, of inanimate objects in their particular conjunctions and as these are associated with a given family. Not every novel engages in the revelation of the familial spirit through its furniture and domestic interiors, or associated external spaces in equal degree, of course. But amongst those novelists for whom the room is an archive and expression of memory, Dickens is peculiarly attuned to the 'voices' of such spaces, and what they might have to whisper, of family secrets, family histories, and, of course, family romances, as we witness in the third chapter of *Dombey*.

The chapter begins with a reflection on Mrs Dombey's funeral in particular, and funerals in general, from the point of view of the 'neighbourhood', 'which is generally disposed to be captious on such a point, and is prone to take offence at any omissions or shortcomings in the ceremonies' (Dickens 1985, 74). Thus, omniscience, so-called, is displaced from within itself by a more limited and partial perception. Disinterestedness gives way to partiality. As readers we are having our perspective positioned, as we are made aware of perspective. If 'no structure [in this case a structure of perception] can exist apart from a certain purposefulness in its own formation' (Karatani 1995, 26), the purpose of the Dickensian structure of perception and narration is to introduce the social and cultural dimensions of narrative, to assume responsibility for bearing witness, in order that the trace of historicity in relation to a given event may survive, and 'natural' relations demystified. Narration takes responsibility for limited expressions of social history, thereby dismissing the illusion of omniscience and transcendence, as these are implied in the idea that narrative can take a view 'of the whole process of social history' (Karatani 1995, 83). Here the private world of grief and mourning becomes subject to scrutiny as public ritual and a communal perspective on such events. The 'small world' (Dickens 1985, 74) of the house is thus always implicitly open in its comings and goings in its immediate vicinity, and is defined in this manner, even as it mirrors, in however distorted a fashion, the 'great one out of doors' (Dickens 1985, 74). The identity of the house disposed of in this fashion, Mr Dombey's servants 'subsided', as Dickens has it, 'into their several places in the domestic system', wherein death appears as a 'dream', in order that the machinery of the domestic system can resume its normal operation (Dickens 1985, 74). If the familiarity and comfort of a home or room comes from the 'synthesis of immemorial and recollected' in order to create within the walls of that home a 'community of memory and image', as Bachelard asserts (1994, 5), then the house of Dombey is striking for its being so very forgetful, as if its communal memory were wiped, so that business as usual can continue.

Only after the system resumes its proper order does the Dickensian narrator describe the house and its interior spaces. The house, we read, 'was a large one, on the shady side of a tall, dark, dreadfully genteel street in the region between Portland Place and Bryanstone Square' (Dickens 1985, 74). The topographical specificity of the location stands in contrast to the anonymity of the home itself. We are told of the exterior form in its totality that:

> It was a corner house, with great wide areas containing cellars frowned upon by barred windows, and leered at by crooked-eyed doors leading to dustbins. It was a house of dismal state, with a circular back to it, containing a whole suite of drawing-rooms looking upon a gravelled yard, where two gaunt trees, with blackened trunks and branches, rattled rather than rustled, their leaves were so smoke-dried. (Dickens 1985, 74–5)

In short, this is a parody of a house; bereft of life, yet uncannily animate, with its crooked-eyed doors and barred windows that frown and leer, Dombey's home has something monstrous about it, to the extent that the trees are blasted and the sun rarely shines there.

Such a dismal and unprepossessing condition is doubled and echoed internally, for, we are informed, 'it was as blank a house inside as outside' (Dickens 1985, 75). This has little to do with the fact that a death has recently occurred or a funeral more recently taken place. All 'consciousness' of home, if it can be expressed thus, is 'dispersed' or 'cast out'. The very blankness suggests that all is surface, that this is an anti-home, the very antithesis of what a home should be. It is also as if the house itself is death, or, at the very least, aridity and sterility, the 'great world' of business and capitalism contaminating the domestic small world. Dombey's house becomes an unhomely simulacrum of the home proper, defining itself by what it is not, haunting us through all that we know to be absent. It is nothing less than a tomb for the Victorian family, and the very idea of the family home. Dickens produces an uncanny house that is all the more discomforting for being so materially *of its epoch*, so much a distilled condensation of the historical moment.

Dickens takes us deeper into this strange place. Dombey orders the furniture to be covered. 'Accordingly', we are told, 'mysterious shapes were made of tables and chairs, heaped together in the middle of rooms, and covered over with great winding sheets' (Dickens 1985, 75). Furniture becomes its own corpse, remaining in its proper location but becoming improperly other than itself. The passage continues:

> Bell-handles, window-blinds, and looking-glasses, being papered up in journals, daily and weekly, obtruded fragmentary accounts of deaths and dreadful murders. Every chandelier or lustre, muffled in Holland, looked like a monstrous tear depending from the ceiling's eye. Odours, as from vaults and damp places, came out of the chimneys. The dead and buried lady was awful in a picture frame of ghastly bandages. Every gust of wind that rose, brought eddying round the corner from the neighbouring mews, some fragments of the straw that had been strewn before the house when she was ill, mildewed remains of which were still cleaving to the neighbourhood: and these, being always drawn by some invisible attraction to the threshold of the dirty house to let immediately opposite, addressed a dismal eloquence to Mr Dombey's windows. (Dickens 1985, 75)

Everything is covered, hidden; nevertheless everything 'speaks', though not as itself but in the fragmentary voices of the dead and the murdered, transcribed for, and reported in, the daily and weekly newspapers. That sense of the external house being an animate but inhuman monstrous form considered earlier, returns here through the 'monstrous' tears, as the house turns its gaze inwards. Mrs Dombey's portrait, not only a reminder of the dead mistress of the house, becomes an awful effigy of herself, as if resurrected from the grave, and framed by 'ghastly bandages'. There is, in this passage, what architectural theorist Anthony Vidler calls an 'abyssal drive towards' death (Vidler 1992, 38), and, in addition, the return, the revenance of death's ghostly traces, as the essence of home is dismembered. We can only imagine the home from what is not there. Drawing on all his resources from Gothic fiction, Dickens imagines the unimaginable, the modern home, an 'especially favoured site for uncanny disturbances: its apparent domesticity, its residue of family history [as figured in the accusatory painting of Mrs Dombey] and nostalgia, its role as the last and most intimate shelter of private comfort sharpened by contrast' with the remainders and reminders of death (Vidler 1992, 17). The entire productive activity of Dickensian representation tends towards this making unhomely the home as a complex entity produced through both historical, material and psychic phenomena.

Dickens is projecting an image of the house through a matrix of effects, which has the opposite effect of Gaston Bachelard's analytical principles. While Bachelard suggests that we approach 'the house images with care not to break up the solidarity of memory and imagination', so that 'we may hope to make others feel all the psychological elasticity of an image that moves us at unimaginable depths' (1994, 6), Dickens seeks to make us see and feel through negating all that holds memory and imagination together in the idea of home. Perhaps the most disquieting aspect of the death of the home that Dickens enacts here is that part of the house is kept open, including those 'apartments which Mr Dombey reserved for his own inhabiting' (Dickens 1985, 75). In contrast to the dead rooms of the house, Dombey's rooms are sensuously drawn, comprised of various smells, 'hot-pressed paper, vellum, morocco, and Russia leather . . . the smells of divers pairs of boots' (Dickens 1985, 75). Arguably, such smells encode the passage with a particularly masculine memory that excludes by implication. Such is the gap between the dead spaces and Dombey's apartments that he is glimpsed 'sitting in the dark distance . . . among the dark heavy furniture . . . as if he were a lone prisoner in a cell, or a strange apparition that was not to be accosted or understood', unless he 'came to be . . . invested in his own person . . . with all the mystery and gloom of his house' (Dickens 1985, 76). A spectre is haunting the house of Dombey; the spectre of capitalist masculinity. Victorian man, the man of the age, has become his own, most uncanny, Gothic, double – and Dickens presents us with a disquieting perspective on this, in his portrait of the capitalist as a middle-aged man. For Dombey's 'inhabiting' is nothing other than the reification of habits, generated through a taxonomy of commodity forms in a constellated presentation of the room as what Marx calls in *Capital* a 'social hieroglyphic' (Marx 1976, 167). Dombey does not understand what it means to dwell, and is surrounded, composed we might say, by the ghosts, the scents of commodities, which announce the secret of Dombey's estranged, unhomely being.

VI

Dickens has effected a remarkable trajectory in Chapter Three. Beginning with the representation of the house's exterior, suggesting in the process that the house has something uncannily alive about it, he has moved through the house, tracing in the parallel erasure of the memories of home and Mrs Dombey the death of the homely, to arrive at a distanced, partially obscured vision of Dombey, seen as if 'through a glass, darkly' (as 1 Corinthians 13.12 has it). The reader travels from external façade to the dark heart of the unhomely home, a distorted parallelism being implied between the inhuman house and the inhuman Dombey. The metaphors of prison and haunting offer a striking contrast, in that one condition could not be more materially the opposite of the other, while both are evocative of an older, Gothic sensibility. It is as if, Dickens proposes, through his perception of the modern home, that in murdering the home and, with that, family, the capitalist murders himself. There is, for Dickens, a psychic crime that is no less dreadful than the real equivalent, as those uncannily readable scraps of newspapers serve to remind us. What Bachelard calls 'topoanalysis' (1994, 8), that is, the analysis of place and what is inscribed onto place through human relationships and events so as to make it meaningful, opens for us a means of reading rooms in fiction that addresses the effects of material history from the inside. In doing this, it posits the room, the domestic or interior space, as hypothetical or theoretical place for writing to experiment with the poetics, as well as the politics of historical inscription. If the room figures 'compressed time', as Bachelard avers (1994, 8), that time is not only the personal time of an individual in a fictional work, such as a novel. It is also the time of the epoch that serves to generate such a representation, through the 'countless intermediaries between reality and [the] symbols' (Bachelard 1994, 11). The author finds appropriate traces of his age. In the details of a given room, writing gives the tone, through the poetics of interior representation, to what Bachelard calls 'the mode of our inner space' (1994, 12). That is, as with the movement from outside to inside, from architecture to psyche in Chapter Three, so the poetics of space trace the relationship between how the world exists and how this determines the inner life of a character such as Mr Dombey. Dickens makes possible a phenomenology of the haunted house, which situates the ghosts firmly as projections of the self. Dickens thus opens the form of the home to a closer scrutiny; he 'opens the space of an inextricably convoluted tangle of traits' (Weber 1996, 27), which it then becomes the purpose of the novel to pursue, and, if possible, redeem, thereby positing the possibility of a home to come in the place of the crypt that has taken the place of the house at the beginning of *Dombey and Son*.

VII

A small, but significant, moment in *Dombey and Son* arrives with Florence's dream, and this dream has to do with the home. Freud had yet to be born when Dickens published *Dombey*, and the psychoanalyst's major study, *The Interpretation of Dreams*, was not to be completed until 1899, so while there was some interest in dreams, dream-states and their narratives in mid-nineteenth century psychology, there was hardly a fully-formed systematic model of interpretation or explanation available. In the world of fiction, the dream occupied a similarly marginal place. As Kerry McSweeney observes, 'not all nineteenth-century novelists were interested in dreams' (McSweeney 2005, 163). George Eliot, for example, saw no purpose for them in fiction except as obvious devices to propel the story in a distinctly unrealistic manner. In an article on dreams in the novel, McSweeney recognizes that the dream has something foreign about it, its agency belonging to Dostoevsky and Tolstoy more than the so-called 'Classic Realist Text' of middle-class English fiction. The two obvious exceptions to this exclusion of the dream in nineteenth-century fiction are *Wuthering Heights*, published in the same year as *Dombey and*

Son, and Lewis Carroll's *Alice's Adventures in Wonderland*, wherein the majority of the narrative coincides with Alice's sleep. So, when Dickens includes a dream in the novel, which, arguably, offers his first major social commentary, it is worth our while to turn our attention to it.

In 1851, Dickens had observed in a letter the following concerning dreams: 'taking into consideration our vast differences in point of mental and physical constitution', there is a 'remarkable sameness' in dreams. He continues, 'We all fall off that Tower ... we all take unheard-of trouble to go to the Theatre and never get in ... or to read letters, placards, or books, that no study will render legible ... we all go to public places in our night dresses, and are horribly disconcerted, lest the company should observe it (Dickens 1988, 278–9). The various 'scenarios' Dickens describes here all have a common subject: anxiety (McSweeney 2005, 165), and this is used on occasion by the novelist in his work. The other kind of dream Dickens recognizes and 'makes good use of', as McSweeney demonstrates, is 'what is called hypnagogic dreaming. This occurs "in a physiological 'twilight' setting" ... [integrating] the psychic event and the dreamer's physical surroundings' (McSweeney 2005, 166). One could argue that Scrooge's 'experience' of the three spirits of Christmas is an acutely observed condensation of both dream forms, the anxious and the hypnagogic, the latter defined by Dickens in *Oliver Twist*, when he remarks that 'a kind of sleep ... steals on us sometimes, which, while it holds the body prisoner, does not free the mind from a sense of things about it' (Dickens 1986b, 309). To take a last comment by Dickens on dreams from his letters, the author also notes that the relation between dreaming and waking states is hardly maintained through content: 'I should say the chances were a thousand to one against anybody's dreaming of the subject closely occupying the waking mind – except ... in a sort of allegorical manner' (Dickens 1988, 276–7). What takes place in the daytime may surface in our dreams, but if it does so it arrives heavily veiled, deeply encrypted.

What might be the relation between dreams and the idea of the home then? Certainly, Gaston Bachelard draws out a connection between daydreams, memory, familiarity and domestic spaces in *The Poetics of Space*. More significantly, however, there is, in Chapter Nine, the discussion of the dialectics of outside and inside (Bachelard 1994, 211–21). If Dickens uses the interior of the home and house and the dismantled identity of the family as the social phenomena that should oppose or act as concepts in distinction to the outside world of finance, mercantilism and big business, he also exploits the opposing actions of 'inside' and 'outside' through the opposition or juxtaposition of what is identified, in the author's letters, as mental and physical constitution. Dickens relies on a series of parallel oppositions, analogous with one another. As there is the exterior world beyond the house, and the interior world of the home, so there is the exterior world of action and event, and the interior world of thought, reverie and dream. Importantly, Dickens erases the distinctions at crucial narrative junctures and in significant ways in the act of narrating. What might appear 'realist' about Dickens's fiction, conventionally understood, undergoes at strategic moments a transformation, becoming distinctly anti-realist and even surreal, phantasmagorical, uncanny, as if the narrator were himself in a hypnagogic state. (Recall the various discussions of disorientated and

fanciful narrators, finding themselves lost in London, from the previous chapter.)
This takes place in *Dombey and Son* in the scenes of Paul's death and in Dombey
Senior's railway journey, already mentioned. I will return to the first of these examples shortly, but first, there remains to be considered what must surely be one of the
strangest sequences of events, and, more significantly, representation of events, in
any novel of the nineteenth century.

Shortly before Florence's dream, which arrives on the night of Dombey's marriage to Edith, the reader witnesses the bridegroom-to-be in his dining room, in
Chapter Thirty, a chapter that has begun: '. . . the enchanted house was no more,
and the working world had broken into it' (Dickens 1985, 500). Although it
arrives halfway through the novel and refers to the Feenix household, you might be
forgiven for thinking we had yet to leave the first chapter and the original Dombey
house, so fitting an aphorism for the entire novel does this sentence seem. That
aside, though, Dombey is witnessed in a reflective state, not quite a waking dream
but close enough to one, as, thinking of Edith, he 'picture[s] to himself, this proud
and stately woman doing the honours of his house . . . The dignity of Dombey
and Son would be heightened and maintained, indeed, in such hands' (Dickens
1985, 509). The phrase echoes Dombey's earlier thoughts on the role of the first
Mrs Dombey. In this reiteration, where a 'false' Mrs Dombey is about to be located
in the house and place of the 'true' Mrs Dombey in a gesture of uncanny doubling,
we are given a glimpse of the extent to which Dombey's imaginary 'world' is
trapped by its own mechanisms and desires. Once again, through Dombey's reverie
– a delusion as much as an illusion – we read how the woman, subservient to the
needs of the house, bears the weight of representation for the business also, as the
home is elided, once more, by the House of Business.

In this mood, Dombey remains sitting 'alone at the dining-table', musing 'upon
his past and future fortunes' (Dickens 1985, 509). His pensive apprehension is
echoed in the exterior of the room, as if its furnishings, its 'scant and gloomy state'
were, somehow, the displaced expression of his own psyche, in a fine example of
pathetic fallacy:

> . . . the room, in colour a dark brown, with black hatchments of pictures blotch-
> ing the walls, and twenty-four black chairs, with almost as many nails in them as
> so many coffins, waiting like mutes, upon the threshold of the Turkey carpet; and
> two exhausted negroes holding up two withered branches of candelabra on the
> sideboard, and a musty smell prevailing as if the ashes of ten thousand dinners
> were entombed in the sarcophagus below it . . . the room had gradually put itself
> into deeper and still deeper mourning for him, until it was become so funereal
> as to want nothing but a body in it to be quite complete.
>
> No bad representation of the body, for the nonce, in his unbending form, if
> not in his attitude, Mr Dombey looked down into the cold depths of the dead
> sea of mahogany on which the fruit dishes and decanters lay at anchor: as if the
> subjects of his thoughts were rising towards the surface one by one, and plunging
> down again. (1985, 509–10)

We have slipped from Dombey's 'dream' to the dream- or nightmare-like condition of the unhomely room, tomblike in its hallucinatory and phantasmagoric appearance. The room is an oceanic abyss, all the more uncanny because its fathomless depths are described through the solidity of mahogany, chairs bearing a resemblance to coffin nails, a sideboard reminiscent of a sarcophagus. In the midst of this, Dombey rises and sinks repeatedly in his thoughts, as if, psychically at least, he were in the process of drowning. There is a clear marking here of outside and inside, but the former – in the hallucinatory manifestation of the room – and the inside – Dombey's thoughts – flow into and out of one another. There is thus figured here what Bachelard calls an 'implicit geometry' to thought and representation, a geometry of imaginary space, through which spatial mapping in the doubling analogy of thought and room, narrative realism founders in 'the immense domain of imagination' (Bachelard 1994, 212). Dream 'logic' dictates the association of unlike forms, dream rhetoric allowing for the movement between those distinct, dissimilar figures. In this, Dickens finds a mode of expression that loosens words from their mimetic associations. He 'loosens their intimate ties', to borrow a phrase of Bachelard's (1994, 213). But in doing this, in freeing the syntax of representation from its role in merely directing us to the presumption of reality, Dickens takes us into the depths of the psyche, in order to illustrate how what Dombey, singular representative of capitalism, has caused to happen – the murder of the home and the family – returns now to engulf him.

Which leads, from this moment of unreal suspension, through the acceleration of the week – Dickens writes and repeats that the days 'fled fast', 'fled faster', 'fled faster' (Dickens 1985, 511) – to Edith Granger's 'unquiet spirit' restlessly moving, 'to and fro, and to and fro, and to and fro again, five hundred times' in the 'dead of night' (Dickens 1985, 515). A virtual double of herself, haunted by her own past and avoiding catching a glimpse of herself in the mirror, Edith is transfigured by Dickens into the image of the most uncanny of spectres: it is as if she is her own phantom, as if she is there for herself only as a tormenting ghost, a ghost moreover arriving to haunt the house of Dombey and Son. She cannot stand to see herself because she knows that sight would reveal her interior truth, and Dickens can only figure this self-horror in representing Edith through the language of the ghost story and the haunted house. In effect though, what we have witnessed here, together with the earlier scene of Dombey's own self-haunting thoughts, is that there is no such thing as a house that is not haunted, after a fashion. Dickens is not asking us to believe in literal ghosts. He knows, however, that conditions approaching dream-states are the modern manifestation of being haunted, that the apparition comes not from outside but from the very interiority of our being.

In this, Dickens anticipates not only Freudian psychoanalysis but also later novelists, contemporaries of Freud such as Henry James and Thomas Hardy. Dickens anticipates the apprehensions of modern perception by doubling inside and outside as distorted translations of one another. In *Dombey and Son*, we come to read, citing Bachelard once more, how 'inside and outside, as experienced by the imagination [and given external form in narrative ostensibly directed towards representations of the material world], can no longer be taken in their simple reciprocity'.

Through Dickensian narrative, we 'come to realize that the dialectics of inside and outside multiply with countless diversified nuances' (Bachelard 1994, 216). To give this a less abstract, more material definition: if the house becomes the space where the mercantile world imposes itself internally, it is also the locus where psyche and being exteriorize themselves.

Rooms and homes are thus privileged sites that do double service rhetorically and imaginatively, poetically and ideologically. While, on the one hand, they refigure the monstrous machinery and economy of the greater world beyond their walls, on the other hand, they become the crypts, the sarcophagi, in which are secreted the phantoms and phantasms, the ghosts, if not the skeletons in the closets of family identities. To paraphrase an observation of Bachelard's on the loss of one's sense of being, both Dombey and Edith have, each in their own way, lost their meaning (and from this, one might suggest, they have forgotten the truth of dwelling, the authentic condition of one's being). They have become ghosts, or 'shades' of themselves, in being no longer attached in a proper manner to family or home. They find themselves only in a 'horrible inside-outside' existence (Bachelard 1994, 217). Dickens disrupts their identities from inside, through the unfolding of Dombey and Edith's thoughts and feelings. In the rooms they haunt, their identities are dispersed, only to be condensed subsequently in the intimate, claustrophobic spaces of the very same rooms, their minds in turn, 'banished from the realm of possibility' (Bachelard 1994, 218); which is to say banished from the world and any meaningful future. 'Intimate space' thus 'loses its clarity' (Bachelard 1994, 218) and the home is anticipated as a nightmare.

VIII

On the other hand, nightmares and dreams offer radical views of the home; they recall us to the thought of dwelling. '[H]aving rambled through the handsome house, from room to room' and finding it 'strange and new' (Dickens 1985, 532), Florence puts on her mourning clothes once more following the wedding. Shortly thereafter, in Chapter Thirty-five, a chapter much concerned with the appearance of houses, in which Mr Dombey and his bride return home, Florence's dream is told in detail:

> In her sleep ... Florence could not lose an undefined impression of what had so recently passed. [Note here how the waking experience remains, but does so indirectly, leaving its trace only as an 'undefined impression', and therefore doubly indistinct.] It formed the subject of her dreams, and haunted her; now in one shape, now in another; but always oppressively; and with a sense of fear. She dreamed of seeking her father in wildernesses, of following his track up fearful heights, and down into deep mines and caverns; of being charged with something that would release him form extraordinary suffering – she knew not what, or why – yet never being able to attain the goal and set him free. Then she saw him dead, upon that very bed, and in that very room, and knew that he had

never loved her to the last, and fell upon his cold breast, passionately weeping. Then a prospect opened, and a river flowed, and a plaintive voice she knew, cried, 'It is running on, Floy! It has never stopped! You are moving with it!' And she saw him at a distance stretching out his arms towards her, while a figure such as Walter's used to be, stood near him, awfully serene and still. In every vision, Edith came and went, sometimes to her joy, sometimes to her sorrow, until they were alone upon the brink of a dark grave, and Edith pointing down, she looked and saw – what! – another Edith lying at the bottom. (Dickens 1985, 591)

Despite the fact that the chapter begins in present tense with a somewhat strained, and undeniably ironic, encomium on the homeliness of the newly resurgent Dombey home, Florence's is a dream, which, in its terrifying substitutions, Paul for Walter, Edith for her other secret self, presents an image of only homelessness, the impossibility of dwelling on the one hand, and unhomeliness, the uncanny eruption of the unfamiliar from within the familiar on the other, through the absence of the father, and death. Dombey is only found, once he is dead. In possibly the most disquieting moment of the dream, his body is finally found, on Florence's bed, substituted, in Florence's imagination for Walter, who has been sent to sea by Mr Dombey and who, as Florence imagines, has drowned, in an uncanny visionary echo of Dombey's own metaphorical drowning, discussed earlier. The substitution of Walter and Mr Dombey is one that disturbs the very idea of the home, whilst maintaining the house as a seemingly endless series of spatial repetitions, each suggestive of death. As Bachelard points out about nightmares, there is no shelter, and 'space is nothing but a "horrible outside-inside"' (Dickens 1985, 218). The logic of the dream makes it plain that either one is absent, banished, abject in the wilderness, or one is enclosed in rooms, which are also tombs, the marriage bed or lovers' bed (as it will become for Walter and Florence) simultaneously the most intimate space of absolute exteriority, expulsion from being, death. That Edith comes to Florence as a result of the latter's nightmare, holding out her arms as the vision of Paul had done in her dream, only serves to illuminate how the interiority of the dream is reiterated in the exteriority of the waking moment.

Florence's dream is not an allegory, clearly. It projects itself, in what Kerry McSweeney describes as a 'melodramatic prolepsis of what is to come in the con-cluding sections of *Dombey and Son*' (2005, 168). Or, to see this differently, the melodrama of the nightmare is an exaggerated articulation of the novel's awareness of the extent to which the home is a disturbed and disturbing place. In producing his narratives of the modern unhomely, Dickens is not only framing a modern discourse, shaped through a distinctly modern sensibility. He has recourse, as is well known, and as I discuss in the first chapter, to older, pre-Victorian narrative forms and modes of representation, not least Gothic.

Signs of Gothic are always in Dickens's writing, and *Dombey and Son* offers a surprising updating of the genre. As Paul dies, the passage of life-to-death is recorded with a distinctly Gothic inflection: 'as the reflection [of the sun] died away, and a gloom went creeping up the wall, he watched it deepen, deepen, deepen, into night' (Dickens 1985, 292). Paul is dying; the reader is aware of this, but Dickens intensifies the apprehension of the impending death through the temporal shift registered here and, with that, the arguably Gothic motion of the creeping gloom, with that repetitious, 'deepen, deepen, deepen'. Perhaps also Gothic here, though less visible than felt, one might say, is the sense that, in that repetition, the sentence assumes what speech act theory would describe as a performative effect: repetition 'deepens' the reading subject's awareness and reception of the encroaching, consuming darkness, which is simultaneously real and perceptual, phenomenologically apprehended. Later comes a repetition, this time in Paul's perceptions, as the day, again, moves on towards night: 'he ... would ... be troubled with a restless and uneasy sense again – the child could hardly tell whether this were in his sleeping or his waking moments' (Dickens 1985, 293). Here we read the hallucinatory shift in subjective ground, a destabilization of perception that in the Gothic-proper is attributed to external forces, at least initially. Here, however, the condition is a matter of Paul's subjective perception; it is phenomenological, psychosomatic – and Dickens conveys this performatively, as I have averred, through the formal passage of writing moving in the direction of death, opening up the boundary or limit of being to its other.

Paul's corporeal-psychological condition changes to the extent that the world of his room is the scene of constant shifting hallucination, so that 'the people round him changed unaccountably' (Dickens 1985, 294). Finally, there appears to Paul an unnamed figure 'with its head upon its hand' (Dickens 1985, 294), who returns, and again, but never speaks. Dickens constructs the passage in such a manner that Paul's uncertainty about the character – is it his father? – becomes the reader's uncertainty also. What we read, therefore, is that representation itself is haunted by the disturbance to Paul's perception. As it is Paul's interior perception, so this is externalized in the third-person narration, the ambiguity coming to trouble the reader through the imaginative space of the narrator. This transgression is double. The most familiar location, home, is written as inescapably haunted once more, ruptured by phantasmic intrusion, as the spectralization of the Gothic is in full force here. For, unlike earlier Gothic novels, the effect is neither local, nor is it maintained within the narrative frame. The haunting, we might say, *is* the narrative; the narrative voice is the voice of an apparition, unseen but always there. In this, through Paul's dying and his coming death, Dickens traces the threads between different modes of apprehension and representation, the Gothic and the phenomenological (as I have already intimated in the discussion of *Dombey* in relation to the Heideggerian reflection on being and dwelling), and so discloses the weave of a disquietingly modern subjectivity.

IX

Such strange, restless and disturbing inventions in Dickens might best be termed a *figurative economy*, which is informed by 'impulse, excess, and misdirection' (Bowen 2000, 79). Dickens's fictional, figurative economy is one in which the 'interest in radical social change' shared with its 'Romantic precursors' (Bowen

2000, 77). In assuming such an economy, Dickens invites his readers to *feel* as well as to *see*. He therefore structures the possibility of perception and vision through sentiment, excess and melodrama. Like Wordsworth, Dickens understands contemporary social conditions as examples of 'evacuated ontology', to use Alan Liu's phrase. Or to say this more simply, we know the meaning of something in *Dombey and Son* through what is missing, what is lacking. *Dombey and Son* is informed and structured by 'absences that [are] the very possibility of the "here and now"' (Liu 1989, 39). There are no *homes* in the here and now of 1848. Furthermore, Dickens conveys absence and negation through melodrama, excess and sentiment rather than a more restricted and mimetically faithful realism: 'sentiment is Dickens's *forte* . . . melodrama provides Dickens with a mode that is "historical" in its insistence on a past that is lost but not forgotten' (Crosby 1991, 70). In the example of *Dombey*, the past that is lost but not forgotten – at least not forgotten by Florence and the narrator – is *home*, the place of the imaginary and memory. Dickens wagers everything on the past not being forgotten through the structuring forces of sentiment and melodrama and what those forces carry with them from one moment to another.

Sentiment and melodrama are then significant, alternative, historical modes of representation. Dickens's historicizing 'system', his 'fictional economy', is one determined by 'loss and gain, of absence and presence'. In hinting at an imaginary world close enough to be remembered by its readers, a world vanishing from sight as 'the ever receding ground of the present' (Crosby 1991, 96), *Dombey and Son* projects the very possibility of nineteenth-century middle-class cultural identity given specific form of the evacuated and haunted family as a condition of loss, absence and undecidability. The novel thus constitutes the lack or absence around a meditation, an act of dwelling, on the inauthenticity of its contemporary subject, and the forgetfulness on the subject's part of its own historicity. It does so in two principal ways: first, through its close attention to matters of the rhetoric of domestic spaces; and second, through its relentless confusion of forms, images and purposes of the domestic. Like Walter Scott before him, Dickens responds to a 'demand for an approach to the past that would interest a middle-class public by treating aspects of experience with which they could empathize . . . in a manner that would engage their imaginations and their sympathies, thus allowing them, as it were, to experience the past anew' (Rigney 2001, 71).

In the case of Dickens, empathy is made possible through the idea of a pre-Victorian family, which, like a dream, is never there, only intimated through all that the family of Dombey is not. However, Dickens is never without the possibility of redemption. For if the ghosts of family and home are those traces of a past that haunt the present of *Dombey and Son* and 1848 in the Dickensian imagination, then they are also the spectres of a future conditional tense. By the force of sentiment, achieved through the perspectives and the death of children, Dickens's novel thus situates the memory of a cultural childhood lost in the historical maturation of successful middle-class Victorian identity, as that which is the burden of Florence's character might cause to return. Criticism of Dickens has failed in part to recognize the significance of Romantic thought to the novelist, even as it has not addressed adequately the possibility that alternative epistemological models are at work within Dickensian representations of mid-nineteenth century culture. As a result, 'the significance of some kind of "feeling" … as a mode of historical manifestation is an underexplored or undeveloped *insight*' (Rancière 2004, 4; emphasis added). Dickens knows that, more than merely mawkish feeling, sentiment can be a powerful, conservative tool. Sentiment is not simply an emotional distortion, even though too much of it can cause this. It should be remembered that sentiment can cloud our vision. It can make us, or more importantly, the novelist, misty-eyed, as in the ending of *The Old Curiosity Shop*.

Not taken too far though, sentiment, the *OED* tells us, is awareness gained from vague sensation, a mental feeling. It is the feeling or meaning intended by a particular passage in literature, or it is a wish or view expressed as an epigraph. When not taken to extremes, sentiment gives another name to the structural play of perception and conscious experience. Put another way, sentiment figures simultaneously the inescapability of perspectival perception and the risk of a certain misapprehension arises from the very same situated consciousness. Sentiment thus doubles itself in a contradictory, not to say paradoxical, fashion. Inseparable from itself into two distinct conceptual formations, the notion of sentiment oscillates undecidably. How do we decide whether sentiment offers the proper perspective or an overly coloured view? If, as Raymond Williams argues, 'there is no natural seeing and therefore … [no] direct and unmediated contact with reality' (Williams 1981, 167), how, in conclusion, can, or does, Dickens avoid a dishonest over-emotionalism? There is no absolute answer to this. As Dickens realizes, one always has to risk everything in sentiment, recognizing that while for some 'home' is the most sentimental of figures, for others it remains a promise, to come. That the question remains undecidable, in response to *Dombey and Son*, is perhaps itself an answer of sorts. For, in 1848, when *Dombey* had completed its serial publication and had appeared in volume form, the world of men like Dombey was still very much an historical force, presenting one possible image of the future, a vision that exploited, even as it marginalized, notions of the family and home. Thus, if there is some conclusion, without prediction, it is that, knowing there to be no unequivocal response, Dickens sought through what Gaston Bachelard terms 'exaggeration of images' (1994, 221) to disturb his readers just enough, in order that they might, in turn, have the possibility of becoming aware of their own *inner disturbances* (Bachelard 1994, 220), in their homes and in themselves. Dickens's writing of the home risks 'put[ting] language in danger' (Bachelard 1994, 220) through the melodramatic extremity of the estranged domestic image, in order that the reader might begin to grasp the historical crisis of the idea of the family at its very centre, the notion of home.

3

In Visibility, or the Appearance of 'True Histories': Truth, Confession and Revelation in Anne Brontë

I

Revealing the truth of narrative through narrative means puts fiction to work in the service of both past and future. The act of disclosing or discovering the truth as that which motivates an account but remains hidden within the tale as the promise for bearing patiently with the act of reading is a gesture always attuned to an other – I promise, dear reader, if you will be faithful to me, to tell, or show, you the truth – and involves a retrospective ravelling of times passed, and time past. Thus, the narrative must, in moving forward, return to the past it narrates, as that past is, itself, moving forward in its folding back over the ground whereby it comes to speak. Forward temporal motion is thus always already inscribed in the recursive process, the purpose being, ostensibly, to join the 'I' which narrates with the 'I' being narrated, and so reunite the 'I' I once was, and which I was on successive occasions, in the I speaking in a present always slipping away from me. The self recounts itself as an other self, bearing witness to its selves, in order that it can reach a moment where narration comes to a close in a silent future, which is implied by the end of each and every narrative.

The process of telling the story informed by the 'historical' truth of a subject is thus only apprehended through that narrative gesture of reduction to the various instances and events of the self, which are assumed to be coherent, and thus the truth of the subject who speaks, or who writes. (For other aspects of this hypothesis of recursive narration apropos subjectivity, see Chapter Eleven on the circularity of being.) Such coherence, or, equally, the perception of accord between the narrating subject who speaks and the narrated subject of whom the narrator speaks on the part of the reader, relies on an 'inner possibility' (Heidegger 1998, 143) of intra-subjective consonances, irreducible to mere historical fact. The distinct 'selves' must 'sound together', implying a proximity that closes up temporally discrete moments, but narration must effect this in such a manner that consonance is the inner possibility between the I who recounts the autobiographical fiction, and the I who reads. The truth of the subject must therefore be one revealed in acts of reading and writing, along with their experience, which 'assures us an experience of an experience of a concealed essential ground of the human . . . and in such a manner that the experience transposes us in advance into the originarily essential domain of truth' (Heidegger 1998, 143–4). 'Truth', thus understood, is not factual accuracy, so much as it is 'unconcealment' (Heidegger 1998, 144). Such unconcealment, along with other aletheic modes, constitutes the truth of the subject's acts of attestation, experience and historicity in the novels of Anne Brontë. Indeed, unconcealment, disclosure, indirect revelation, and other contingent modalities, Brontë gives us to understand, are all that are possible for narrative, in the absence or impossibility of another's being witness to a now invisible past. Before turning to matters of vision and invisibility in relation to the particular aletheic modalities of *The Tenant of Wildfell Hall*, I wish to sketch a brief reading of *Agnes Grey*, regarding the 'true histories' that it intimates through a meagre illumination (1988, 61).

II

The youngest of the three Brontë sisters, Anne Brontë (1820–1849) wrote *Agnes Grey* (1847) at the same time as Emily produced *Wuthering Heights* and Charlotte composed *The Professor*. The first of just two novels Anne was to write before her untimely death at the age of twenty-nine, *Agnes Grey* relates its eponymous hero-ine's experience as a governess with two families, the Bloomfields and the Murrays. Though the date of *Agnes Grey*'s action is not specified, this is an 'historical' novel inasmuch as its events occur quite some time before Agnes Grey recounts her life as a governess, as we learn towards the end of the novel when Agnes refers to her three children (Brontë 1988, 251). Like *The Tenant of Wildfell Hall*, *Agnes Grey* plays on the interdependence of narrative structure, along with the duration and order of narration, and the passage of historical time as the inevitable motion towards revelation.

In comparison with either Anne Brontë's sisters' novels or, indeed, her sub-sequent novel, *Agnes Grey* is initially remarkable for its lack of melodrama or sensational event. There are no mad women in attics, no wild snowstorms or house fires, no ghosts whose wrists are dragged across shards of broken windowpanes. Instead, wilfully reckless children and thoughtless young women have fits of temper (Brontë 1988, 100); they pull the wings off birds and 'persecute the lower creation' (Brontë 1988, 103); they encourage their dogs to hunt and kill hares, worrying at them until their bodies are 'lacerated' (Brontë 1988, 208). Such small moments, though horrible, are relatively few and far between in the novel. These are banal instances of cruelty and the manifestation of everyday, thoughtless evil in comparison with the more Gothic aspects of *Wuthering Heights* or *Jane Eyre*. Yet such occasions, along with her other duties as governess, lead Agnes to reflect upon feelings of degradation and shame: 'I sometimes felt myself degraded by the life I led, and ashamed of submitting to so many indignities' (Brontë 1988, 128–9).

This statement is strikingly personal, confessional even. If *Dombey and Son* is marked by moral, ethical and other manifestations of metaphorical blindness, *Agnes Grey* revels in bearing witness: to Agnes's shortcomings and to the ignorance and cruelty of others. The words *confess* and *confession* appear several times through-out the novel, usually uttered by Agnes. Much of the narrative engages in processes of reflective self-revelation, if not self-reading. For example:

... *in truth*, I considered myself pretty nearly as good as the best of them, and wished them to know that I did so, and not to imagine that I looked upon myself as a mere domestic, who knew her own place too well to walk beside such fine ladies and gentlemen as they were – though her young ladies might choose to have her with them, and even condescend to converse with her when no better company were at hand.

Thus – *I am almost ashamed to confess it* – but indeed I gave myself no little trouble in my endeavours (if I did keep up with them) to appear perfectly unconscious or regardless of their presence ... (Brontë 1988, 162; emphases added)

Or, again, here:

I have omitted to give a detail of his words, from a notion that they would not interest the reader as they did me, and not because I have forgotten them. No; I remember them well; for I thought them over and over again in the course of that day and many succeeding ones, I know not how often; and recalled every intonation of his deep, clear voice, every flash of his quick, brown eye, and every gleam of his pleasant, but too transient smile. *Such a confession will look very absurd, I fear: but no matter: I have written it: and they that read it will not know the writer.* (Brontë 1988, 175)

The 'truth' of confession has to do, obviously, with a sense of shame, absurdity, fear or anxiety. Equally, it is conveyed through the private and anonymous act of writing. Yet, there is an ironic undercutting, a countersignature in the gesture, by which truth is revealed, despite the fact that the 'confessions' are maintained within the narrator's conscience, or else, transmitted to readers who are supposed not to know the writer. For, is it not the case that the truth of the writer, Agnes Grey, is presented through both the confession and the accompanying emotional reflection attendant on the confession? Even a chapter titled 'Confessions' (Brontë 1988, 192–202) opens with a confession of vanity, Agnes paying attention to her dress, and spending 'as much as two minutes in contemplation of my own image in the glass' (Brontë 1988, 192). While, on occasions, 'confession' takes place as a deliberate, conscious strategy on the part of the narrator, at other times Agnes gives away aspects of her self, her psyche and private thoughts and emotions in narrative response to incidents such as those described above. Thus, much, if not all, of *Agnes Grey* is a confessional novel, for it confesses the self as observer, as someone whose writing enacts the 'inner' truth of what has been seen in the absence of the experience. *Agnes Grey* is an observer's novel, therefore, its narrative issuing from a liminal and ostensibly passive place, that of the governess. Agnes enfolds herself in her own 'obscurity' and confesses from the beginning that, with regard to the merits or usefulness of her autobiography, she is 'hardly competent to judge' (Brontë 1988, 62). In this, representation is made problematic, recollection subject to a suspension regarding its accuracy, while confession of the self is understood as necessary to the revelation of truths unavailable to any form of sight, save insight.

Despite this, however, the narrative codes of confession are inseparable from the material culture in which they are produced. The positions that Agnes espouses and mediates are all marked by their historicity. As Sally Shuttleworth has it in her study *Charlotte Brontë and Victorian Psychology*, the various discursive traces of *Agnes Grey*, in their mediation and interanimation, point to the ideological ways in which such 'languages' come to be 'recast within the dominant social paradigms of an era' (Shuttleworth 1994, 68). If this is the case, the possibility is also that confession problematizes the 'dominant social paradigms' from within which it seeks to tell the truth of what can no longer be experienced. Furthermore, the discursive intertextuality that generates *Agnes Grey* also in certain ways serves as a commentary on the material transformation of narrative. It does so particularly in its representation of the behaviours and cultural codes of the provincial gentry, in their relation to one another, their servants and the rural poor with whom they come into brief contact. For, it may be argued, *Agnes Grey* portrays the upper-middle classes in the singular examples of the Bloomfields and Murrays as cultural and fictive anachronisms. Fiction thus reveals the truth of historical transformation, albeit indirectly. Agnes' acts of confession, reflection, self-reading and interpretation effectively centre and historicize the otherwise liminal location that she occupies, whilst simultaneously decentring the significance of the families for whom she works. Obviously enough, Agnes' agency is not powerful enough to effect such a displacement in any real way. Importantly, however, *Agnes Grey* does produce the narrative of the family as worn out, decadent in some respects, and belonging to older fictional paradigms. This is entirely in keeping with the historical displacement of the narrative itself, which is written some years after the events it details.

Perhaps *Agnes Grey* may be understood, at least in part, as a moral *bildungs-roman* that proposes a vision of cultural transformation through the subject's articulation of a theologically determined assumption of personal duty and respon-sibility. *Agnes Grey* is effectively a testamentary text. It attests to the sustenance of faith in the figure of the isolated subject, Agnes herself, in a visibly cruel world, the material, visible culture of which is bereft of spiritual, that is to say, invisible values and truths. The novel effects this 'confession' through Agnes's own strug-gling discourse that articulates and 'refuses to arrest a dynamic spiritual process that is ongoing in history in what must paradoxically must be understood as a most material way' (Zemka 1997, 103). This dynamic movement is what takes place in Agnes's self-revelation, the subject she produces through memory and writing, and it is a movement that does not come to a halt in any single manifestation, identity or representation. As for Thomas Carlyle in *Heroes and Hero-Worship*, there is for Anne Brontë no 'iconic or narratological representation' (Zemka 1997, 103) of Christ or God. There is only the most indirect apprehension of God through the perception that 'God is Love', such a truth revealed indirectly through the experi-ence of the other. As Elizabeth Deeds Ermath argues, for Anne Brontë, 'what we call "social issues" are at bottom moral and religious ones' (Ermath 1997, 16).

In common with other writers of the period, Anne Brontë tends towards the possibility of a 'universalist' or 'restorationist' eschatology, expressing through Agnes Grey 'the opinion that all will be ultimately saved' (Farrar cit. Wheeler

1994, 75). The condition of this of course is that one learns one's duty on earth. This is articulated both indirectly and directly on a number of occasions. The promise of redemptive reward is implicit towards the end of *Agnes Grey* when the narrator visits her erstwhile charge Rosalie Murray, now Lady Ashby: 'I exhorted her to seek consolation in doing her duty to God and man, to put her trust in Heaven . . .' She goes on to remark directly to Rosalie: 'The end of Religion is not to teach us how to die, but how to live' (Brontë 1988, 238). Clearly, Agnes's role in this novel, both for her charges and for the reader, is simultaneously kerygmatic and didactic – she seeks to preach and to teach, and thus is figured within the discursive frameworks of the text as a doctrinal medium, seeking to exhort others, Rosalie or her readers, to assume responsibility for themselves. That her agency is mobilized both intra- and extradiegetically is signalled in a number of places in the text.

If Agnes is an observer of others, she is also a critical observer of herself, as has been remarked. She reads herself in relation to others. As this implies, the universalist theological sentiment that remains imminent in the commentary on, and directed towards, Rosalie is also given voice more directly when addressing – confessing – Agnes's own hopes and beliefs to the reader. The eschatological hope is presented at the end of the novel when, some years after the principal events of the narrative, and Agnes's marriage to Mr Weston, she reflects one final time on her married life, to which we have not been witness, whilst also expressing the hope for an afterlife:

> We have had trials, and we know we must have them again; but we bear them
> well together, and endeavour to fortify ourselves and each other against the final
> separation – that greatest of all afflictions to the survivor but if we keep in mind
> the glorious heaven beyond, where both may meet again, and sin and sorrow are
> unknown, surely that too may be borne . . . (Brontë, 250–1)

Such hope articulates and anticipates that which obviously can never be known as such, which can never arrive to be experienced first-hand. It is thus a discourse of indirection, announcing that which otherwise is 'too fine and subtle to be grasped by words, and, therefore, indescribable – but deeply felt at heart', as Agnes puts it elsewhere (Brontë 1988, 248). This apprehension of that which is to come announces also the coming to a close of the novel, as if narrative and life were, if not parallel, then analogous expressions of faith, arriving through self-interrogation and analysis. As the remark to Rosalie, already quoted, has it: 'The end of Religion is not to teach us how to die, but how to live'. The end of the novel – *end* in the sense of both purpose *and* conclusion – would appear to be the same, given the trajectory that Agnes's moral, psychological and theological investigations have taken in the course of her story as a governess. If she has taught no one in the novel, she has at least taught herself, or come to terms with the idea of 'how to live' within the discursive structures by which she is framed, and in which she presents herself. It is thus that she closes the novel with the following sentence, which is also the final paragraph of *Agnes Grey*: 'And now I think I have said sufficient' (Brontë 1988, 251). That reflective pause – *I Think* – indicates just a little hesitation, the undecidability perhaps, that was remarked on the first page, when Agnes reflected that she was hardly competent to judge.

So the novel returns – albeit with a difference – to where it began; and with the admission – the confession – as well in its self-reflective address that also moves beyond itself in the hope, if not risk, not only of a heaven but also of the transmission of a truthful communication to its readers, that there is a limit to words, to what can be said, taught, represented, and that we must pass over in silence that whereof we cannot speak, to paraphrase Wittgenstein. This apparently somewhat circular gesture intimates that the narrative presents its universalist belief as an example of *Apocatastasis*: the doctrine that ultimately all free moral creatures – angels, men and devils – will share in the grace of salvation. Salvation remains to come, but its possibility is there to be heard indirectly, the narrative of Agnes Grey being a 'true history', a history that recounts the past in such a manner as to be true to the hope in that which is to come. Thus while the emphasis throughout the novel is always on what Ermath describes as 'human relatedness', however 'realistic' the novel's scenes of interaction or revelations of psychology appear from certain critical perspectives, 'they belong to a narrative that relies on already understood plots [and narrative codes] that have to do with salvation' (Ermath 1997, 16), and thus bear witness to a modality that exceeds representation of the material or temporal world. In this is the expression of a hope in the truth of what lies in the unseen, in, once again, the experience of the other.

III

Sight, vision, reading, interpretation, representation: these are, if not the only themes or interests of *The Tenant of Wildfell Hall*, then amongst its most persistently noticeable, if you read and look carefully. Why they should be there is another matter, not quite so easy to discern or decipher. Looking is not the same as reading. One may look and understand nothing, or misread the situation or text entirely. Frequently, and conversely, we speak of seeing metaphorically, as in the phrase 'I see what you mean', where the tropes of sight and vision have to do with perception and comprehension. In *The Tenant of Wildfell Hall*, there are more than a hundred acknowledgements that someone 'saw': saw something or someone; or understood or believed they had comprehended something. Much greater frequency and mention is given to the act of looking, with nearly four hundred references to 'look', 'looking' and 'looked'. There are over two hundred references to eyes, seventeen uses of 'gaze', fifty of 'glance', and eighty-nine of 'appear' or 'appearance'. There are, additionally, around eighty references to books, not to mention other forms of text, such as letters, journals and so on, which are material objects placed directly before the readers in the book and those outside it – that is to say, us – which, implicitly, if not explicitly, require that seeing and comprehension or perception, vision and consciousness be connected. The references to texts are not simply local either; for, importantly, this is a densely structured novel in which one text after another frames the other texts prior to it.

There will be more to say about framing and embedding, about the materiality of the letter also. Returning to sight and vision for now, though, it has to be
admitted that not all such references are of importance in and of themselves, when
considered singly. This is the reason, in all probability, why someone, considering
himself or herself a good reader, may not notice them. In looking for something
else – story, narrative movement, events of significance to the narrative as a whole,
the obvious signs of a surface history –, or, at least, the *something else* by which
one may connect statement to the actual, the hypothetical reader fails to see, or,
better yet, is blind to sight, seeing, looking, glancing and appearance. Yet, in a
novel where seeing and perception, and equally, initially, misunderstanding, are
intimately related; and, furthermore, in a text where seeing and comprehension or
apprehension (in which latter two the act of reading is necessarily involved), have
such significance for the eventual outcome of the novel; then, it becomes undeniable that, taken together, all such references to the look, the gaze and to sight form
or are rhetorical moments of punctuation in a matrix, from out of which right
perception, and so meaning, is generated.

In a world where external signs are the only indicators of possible secrets, and
where emotion is the visible expression of invisible mental conditions, everything
relies on seeing as an act of reading and interpretation. For example, on encountering Eliza Millward, Gilbert Markham observes that they had not met 'since the
evening of the tea-party', and on the subsequent meeting, 'there was no visible
emotion either of pleasure or pain' (Brontë 1993, 105). There appear to be no
signs to read, nothing visible to the eye, except for 'a depth of malice in her too
expressive eye, that plainly told me I was not forgiven' (Brontë 1993, 105). The
eye speaks, even if the face remains both blank and mute, in a coded language of
vision, a discourse that Anne Brontë remarks as being all the more complex when
it becomes reciprocal, as in the moment shortly after the one just observed, when
Markham, following the reception of a 'sidelong glance – intended to be playfully
mischievous – [but being] really, brimful and running over with malice' leads to an
act of 'sternly repelling her odious glances with my eyes' (Brontë 1993, 105). Such
reciprocity is, in principle, endless. For Markham's act of representing this war of
the eyes hands over its fortunes to other eyes, the eyes of his first reader, Halford,
and subsequently to other readers, those of us who read the book. Markham is thus
subject to his own writing rather than being its master.

In this manner, Gilbert Markham 'marks' himself in writing, as a figure produced
through writing, and thus structurally absent, except as the phantom effect of his
own writing, giving (to) the reader 'the experience of a world without substance'
(Kamuf 2005, 144). This has consequences for thinking about vision and sight in
the novel. In the absence of a living being, the act of seeing, and with that the acts
of perception and interpretation, are made all the more fraught; as when all the
reader has to go on is a text, or series of texts, dated at least twenty years before, and
some further back than that. The written text is all we see, experience unavailable
except as experience of the other. If truth relies on the 'inner possibility' of a certain
consonance, it must also be available as an experience of a certain heteronomy.
The written text – whether we call it fiction or literature – is the material form

that reminds us that history and the past are always already absent. Additionally, the written text is only ever a tissue of other texts woven together to produce an image, whether those texts be those referred to, reproduced, composed from the dialogues between characters, or, not infrequently in *The Tenant of Wildfell Hall*, the various biblical allusions and quotations that 'produce' particular characters, their 'subjective' being. Markham, for example 'constitutes' himself in the first chapter by remarking that he was 'burying [his] talent in the earth, and hiding [his] light] under a bushel' (Brontë 1993, 9), both observations taken from the Gospel of Matthew.

The novel is thus an act of writing structured as a memoir of absence, which it must supplant or supplement in some manner. While this is a general observation, true of all writing, Anne Brontë makes this quality of writing and textuality urgently important in the survival and salvation of Helen Graham. Brontë demands therefore that we take seriously the work of fiction in the revelation of a truth beyond the merely factually or historically true or false, inasmuch as her fiction 'takes seriously the demands made by an exteriority [the past, the narrated event] that can no longer be . . . *seen* at all' (Kamuf 2005, 146; emphasis in original). Despite this invisibility, what is illuminated is the responsibility to take writing seriously in the absence of proofs, and, concomitantly, that fiction takes place as 'a telling and not a showing, a writing and not a pointing to objects as they already are in the world' (Kamuf 2005, 146).

Only if we comprehend this fully, and assume responsibility in our act of reading is there the chance of a 'salvation' and 'survival'. In this 'salvation' and 'survival', Gilbert Markham is not the principal authority or 'sovereign' master of reading and writing. He is blind to his own function, and necessarily so: for, in always looking at others, he does not understand how he, himself, is 'seen', as it were, by the reader outside his text. While Gilbert 'gains' Helen Graham, having deciphered her secret, a secret as much of writing as of the self, so his secret is made clear: he is also a subject of his own writing, subject to its own tropic play, and handed over to the authority of another reader, other readers: locally, J. Halford, but more generally all of us. In that passage of journals and letters to another reader, so we see how, in the words of Jacques Rancière, 'any human being' is 'seized by writing', given meaning and incarnated only through 'the reality of writing' in the form of 'a bodyless word that attests' to the impossibility of any final meaning or presence (Rancière 2004a, 93). The implication is not that Brontë's novel has no meaning; rather, meaning resides in the decoding of historical significance as an ethical responsibility that does not rest within the representation of Victorian culture in general, or in the institutional abuse of women that *The Tenant of Wildfell Hall* particularly addresses. The ethical responsibility resides in making visible the invisible, albeit indirectly. The revelation of such invisible and secret practices rests in seeing properly, that is to say, a reception and perception on the part of the reader; and, unlike *Agnes Grey*, in which hope resides in a Messianic desire for what remains to come, *The Tenant of Wildfell Hall* urges a responsibility to the unveiling of truth in the reading of given historical moments. As readers, Brontë requires that we engage in an act of seeing that is also an act of transformative reading. We have to become conscious of cultural and historical invisibility, in order that representation does not simply repeat the past, but opens to a future where representation serves as a corrective through the transmission of an ethical and cultural truth.

IV

Published in the same year as *Dombey and Son*, *The Tenant of Wildfell Hall* seeks, in the words of the author from the preface of the second edition, to 'tell the truth, for', as she asserts, 'truth always conveys its own moral to those who are able to receive it' (Brontë 1993, 3). Truth, here, is not empirical fact. Grounded on the empirical fact of Helen Graham's abuse by Huntingdon, the 'truth' of *The Tenant of Wildfell Hall* resides in a greater historical secrecy and invisibility. It is something else, which cannot plainly be seen, witnessed or encountered. We can tell this from Brontë's comment. Something not materially there, yet communicated to those capable of receiving it, and so belonging to perception and consciousness, if one happens to be the appropriate recipient of such a truth, it passes from narration in the material form of the novel to the reader. 'Truth', thus understood, is received and perceived, or, more specifically, truth is a matter of *apperception*. One does not receive it directly, but only indirectly – hence *apperception* rather than perception – through the medium of fiction, a medium that conveys or communicates truth through its own form. Such a form is neither truthful nor untruthful. Fiction, and by extension literature, produces a kind of third term, neither truth nor lie. Having the quality of an analogy, fiction's 'truth', this 'moral' message that the author sends us is dependent on our ability to see, and so to interpret through the fictional characters and events, as these, in turn, are represented by the narrative in the fictional representation of a material reality unavailable except in the act of telling. So, sight, vision, reading, interpretation, and representation: all mediums, perhaps *media*, of Anne Brontë's phantom truth machine. And *The Tenant of Wildfell Hall* is a machine of sorts, for its purpose is to make the truth appear, but also to *make* the truth, to invent a complex ethical statement that, in being caused to be produced in the material form of the novel, demands we question the conventions and blind spots of a communal morality. Form is thus as significant as content.

How does Brontë construct her machine? What are the devices by which the technology of the novel, or, more properly, *tele-technology*, puts its narrative components to work? How is that which is otherwise invisible, this strange 'truth', made manifest in a markedly material world? I referred to 'tele-technology' just now, and the phrase, though familiar to some, requires some unpacking before we proceed, especially as this has to do with the matter of sight, and of the invisible, and therefore to the work of the novel itself in its ability to represent the world and the past. 'Technology' is derived from the Greek, *tekhne*, meaning to make, to cause to appear, and pertains to art and craft before its more modern usage in relation to machines or engineering. *Tele-*, as in *telephone*, *television*, and so forth, and again Greek, is etymologically related to *telos*, meaning *place*, and signifies that which is far off, afar. So, *tele-technology* is that which makes anything not present appear, but which comes from some other place, far away, in time or in space. The novel is just this particular mode of the tele-technological, which causes through its making our ability to see what is otherwise invisible, unseen or unseeable. Any novel effects this, and can do so only through an act where, in seeing words, we are caused to see images that are neither real nor unreal, but projections or representations of the real world.

Like other novelists, Anne Brontë's purpose is to represent the materiality of the world. To do so, though, she must 'translate' this materiality into another materiality: that of the letter, of writing and text. None of these is insignificant. The novel begins with a letter from Gilbert Markham to J. Halford, Esq., a letter the principal function of which is to determine Markham's consciousness as well as his existence for the reader. In what initially appears in 1848 to echo a past and, by then, anachronistic form of the novel, the epistolary fiction, Brontë sends out Markham's letter, a letter which, of course, must have been written *after* his own journal and, additionally, after Helen Graham's journal. My point here is that the post is sent via Brontë and thus immediately draws attention to the temporal and historical manipulation that writing enables. Truth is thus contingent on, and in correspondence with, an act of unconcealing, of opening the experience of the other's being, and so bringing it into being, albeit in the phantom form that literature enables. This is a small but important issue, because it has to do, from the beginning, with reception and perception; the question concerns to what extent we see, and so pay attention, to form.

As Markham acknowledges, this is only the latest in a series of exchanges, which have been touched by a refusal on Markham's part to convey a story (Brontë 1993, 7). The particular letter admitting to this refusal or avoidance is there, even though the others to which it refers are not. It follows the title page and the preface but appears before the first chapter. It is thus, clearly, not a preface, but, more properly perceived, a pretext, a text that arrives before the text-proper, without having a proper place, directed moreover specifically towards a named reader, as a material form, which we chance to read. The letter, or a copy of it, is thus reproduced, materially, on and as the page, one voice transmitted to, communicating with another. Without 'showing' us either Markham or Halford, it makes them appear through their communications and specifically as the subjects of writing. The letter is, as already acknowledged, an answer, a response, to a demand for a story, and its condition as writing is deliberately announced, being the medium by which is introduced a journal, found 'among the letters and papers I spoke of'. This 'faded old journal' is both the prosthesis of memory and it material supplement to 'memory alone' (Brontë 1993, 8). The letter, an act of writing and thus a material artefact, introduces another written text. It is produced, furthermore, on a given occasion, in a specific place, a library, the pen having been taken up as we are told (1993, 7–8). 'Old letters and papers' cause Markham to muse on 'past times' (1993, 8), which activity has placed him in 'a very proper *frame* of mind' (1993, 8; emphasis added).

The metaphor of the frame is no more incidental than the various references to libraries, books, papers etc. While the metaphor is, in a sense, *only metaphorical*, being indicative in a somewhat poetic mode of the manner in which Markham is produced as a subject of reading, placed or located by the interaction of reading and thought, it is also a trope that governs the structure of *The Tenant of Wildfell Hall*, with its successive frames of texts within texts, of which the 'faded old journal' is just one. And *frame* is, also, a reminder that there is nothing there as such. The discovery of this journal is thus a pretext for the narrative, as well as being the bearer of the narrative. Implicitly, this journal must be edited by Markham, revised and rewritten. It is given coherent form in a narrative directed towards Halford, which we just happen to read, which we chance to receive, as if we were spying on a secret being shared, and in which, with Halford, we 'must go back with [Gilbert Markham] to the autumn of 1827' (1993, 9).

Thus, from before the very start, Brontë makes us aware that there is no access to reality that is not mediated; there is no immediate reality. There is always interpretation or translation between transmission and reception and perception, or the consciousness of the reader. For as much as we read what is called a first-person narration, we always have, between us and the world, another's perception, another's consciousness, and so another's interpretations, those of Gilbert Markham. To make matters more complicated, that perception or consciousness, those 'translations' of a material reality and past no longer directly available, are already doubled, in being those of Markham as he writes, and edits his journal, and also those of his interpretations in the late 1820s. What Markham makes us realize is that there is always a filter between the self and the world. Brontë exploits this to a great extent, in a novel where vision, sight, eyes and looking are tropes, the frequency of which throughout *Wildfell Hall* should give us pause to stop and reflect on their purpose, especially as these are not infrequently connected to matters of representation, whether in Brontë's references to novels or books in general, or to Helen Graham's paintings and sketches. From the outset though, we are, or should be, aware, that we do not have direct access to that reality, to the material world of the narrative for two reasons. On the one hand, there is always writing between us and the world we are attempting to see. This is the case whether we consider our role as readers, or whether we attempt to 'see' Gilbert Markham, as he perceives himself. (And this is true for any character, of course, though with Markham, there is a self-reflexive reference to the act of writing insistently, in his reminders that there is always text to be navigated.) On the other hand, in having taken place a generation or so before, *Wildfell Hall* is a novel that seeks to remind us how all narrative is implicitly historical. Writing generates a past that cannot be present as such, and thus must construct from the traces of memory and the text, an indirect material approximation of the past. Markham's letter provides an inauguration but also a frame, within which the substrate of the journal returns, on which the traces of the past are assembled.

V

One of the chief difficulties in *The Tenant of Wildfell Hall* concerns comprehension through vision. If we do not have any trouble 'seeing' the narrative in its general trajectory or sense, then we perceive that Markham, as the narrator, is both frustrated and frustrating in his inability to present a clear vision. Indeed, his comprehension reaches its limits and he requires the arrival of another text in order to help clarify, if not vision, then at least perception, this other act of writing being represented through Chapters Sixteen to Forty-five, the extended internally framed narrative of Helen Graham's journal. What we understand from Markham's experience in Chapter Twelve of an empirical impasse or aporia – he cannot get past what he believes himself to have seen, in witnessing Helen with another – is that empirical evidence counts for very little, and with that comprehension and perception are hindered, rather than aided, by sight.

Comprehension for Markham results in what Paul de Man describes as a 'paradigmatic totalization of the apprehended trajectory' (de Man 1996, 77) – that is to say, in Markham's case, witnessing Helen Graham with another man leads the narrator to draw a false conclusion as the totality of possibilities from the 'evidence' of his own eyes, based erroneously on a single, and singular, event. Taking the empirical evidence as truth, evidence which is only evidence regarding the fact that you cannot judge from what you see any more than you cannot judge a book by its cover, Gilbert constructs a paradigm, a typical pattern, and creates a totality from this concerning Helen's 'truth': the truth of the secret of Helen Graham. And he does so by projecting from this instance of misperception and misreading an 'apprehended trajectory': he projects a line from this encounter and the false witness of his own eyes, to an implied, projected conclusion: that Helen is false, that she has a secret lover, and that she will never be his.

The false revelation is prefaced by a number of references to sight and vision, as Chapter Twelve, 'A Tête-à-tête and a Discovery', reaches its climax. Leaving Wildfell Hall, following a disappointing conversation with Helen Graham, Gilbert Markham takes 'one look back' before closing the door, only see 'her leaning forward on the table, with her hands pressed against her eyes, sobbing convulsively' (Brontë 1993, 98). As he walks away, commenting that his own internal monologue 'would almost fill a volume in itself' (Brontë 1993, 98), and thereby hinting at the endless relay of text upon text, Markham 'turned to look at the old hall', turning back 'to get a better view of it'. Getting 'sight' of the hall, Markham pauses 'a moment to look', and the pause in turn becomes 'contemplation'. It is as if Wildfell Hall becomes an external material reality that in some manner will, in being comprehended, reveal its inner secret, the 'truth' of Helen Graham (Brontë 1993, 98). Markham continues, by remarking that he 'could see the red fire-light dimly gleaming from her parlour window . . . my eyes [being] fixed upon the lattice' (Brontë 1993, 99). Sight and the material barrier of the Hall itself combine to produce first thwarted perception and comprehension in Markham, as his thoughts repeatedly reach a limit, until the same activities of looking and reflection pull him physically to vault 'over the barrier, unable to resist the temptation of taking one glance through the window' (Brontë 1993, 99). It is at this point that he hears Helen ask someone to come outside, and so witnesses the following scene:

> I stood ... in the shadow of the tall holly-bush, which, standing between the window and the porch, at present screened me from observation, but did not prevent me from *seeing* two figures come forth into the moonlight: Mrs. Graham followed by another – not Rachel, but a young man, slender and rather tall. O heavens, how my temples throbbed! *Intense anxiety darkened my sight*; but I thought – yes, and the voice confirmed it – it was Mr. Lawrence!
>
> [...]
>
> ... they had sauntered slowly past me, down the walk, and I heard no more of their discourse; but *I saw him put his arm around her waist*, while she lovingly rested her hand on his shoulder; – and then, *a tremulous darkness obscured my sight*, my heart sickened and my head burned like fire. (Brontë 1993, 99–100; emphases added)

Notice how sight interprets with great speed. Witness to the situation, Gilbert misreads what he sees, and representation does nothing to counter that, because, of course, this is first-person narration, and the older Gilbert, the one writing to his friend, Halford, does nothing to correct the initial impression first received. It is as though Markham wishes to darken – to use his own image – the vision of the reader, whether Halford or us, to keep us in the dark as to what we see and how we read it; and through that, Brontë teaches us how to distrust sight, especially in that doubling of the trope of the darkening of vision, of vision in the night becoming darkened, and so leading to a concomitant and inner emotional 'darkening' of the subject.

As a result, this scene embodies the problem of sight and vision in the novel, and provides one of several lessons from which Brontë desires the good reader will learn. For comprehension, understood as interpretation based on reading and representation, 'grows', as de Man argues, 'increasingly difficult as the space covered by apprehension grows larger' (de Man 1996, 77). Beginning with a letter, and moving from there to a narrative concerning a stranger who takes up the tenancy of Wildfell Hall, Brontë's second novel utilizes the faulty reasoning and perception of a narrator who is caught within a web of sight lines and modes of perception, in order to illuminate, and make more visible for the reader, the increasing difficulty of apprehension, and the concomitant displacement or deferral of a truth irreducible to empirical evidence or direct vision. Thus, it is that the novel operates around an absent centre, which the presence of Helen Graham does nothing to close. What Markham cannot realize – but what the reader can, if s/he reads carefully, and looks with equal care – is that 'comprehension discovers its own limitation, beyond which it cannot reach' (de Man 1996, 77).

VI

Chapters Sixteen to Forty-five reproduce the pages from Helen Graham's book that are torn out and given to Gilbert Markham. Dated initially 1821, the chapters and pages move forward to the point at which Helen takes up residence at Wildfell Hall, in 1827. Another text, set within a text, removes us to a further moment in the past, whilst also communicating that past to the reader through Markham. However, what is important here is that Gilbert Markham removes himself from the scene for the duration of Helen's first-person narrative. We are thus left to do all the work ourselves, to experience Helen's emotions, her perceptions and her responses to her situation with her. There is no distance between Helen and us, but despite this, truth is still mediated through a narrative relay. This text arrives, importantly, as a corrective to what Markham had mistakenly believed he saw and heard earlier, and rather than correct him directly, Helen Graham requires that he read the text, and so work out the truth for himself, through the act of perception and interpretation. Truth is thus, once more, a matter of reading, of consciousness as an adjunct to vision, and perception the medium that connects the materiality of the letter to the subject's understanding. Truth is revealed indirectly. It is irreducible to direct factual representation but is instead that which is subject to being projected from out of narration. There is a relay of readers, then, an 'open chain', so that whoever has last read the novel has also to turn his or her eyes to the deciphering of evidence in the form of a writing. Truth is the condition of reading not what one sees or witnesses empirically. The chain of readers begins with Helen as her own reader, someone who belatedly realizes how poorly vision has revealed the truth of Huntingdon to her. She is her own reader as well, because in being the writer of her journal, a journal lasting six years, she reads herself as her own construction, her own character. After Helen, the next reader is, of course, Markham, who then inserts the text in his own rewriting, so that his text is the frame to Helen's. Halford is the third reader, and then we follow in a long line of readers from 1848 onwards.

The novel thus constructs itself through successive framing devices – historical and perceptual or phenomenal – onto which each reader in turn links him- or herself. Like Markham's text, though positioned differently, Helen Graham's journal has to do with sight and vision, but more particularly with empirical, if metaphorical, 'blindness'. Empirical sight blinds Helen to the perception and interpretation of Huntingdon. Importantly though, every reading is a *first* reading, even though the text has been previously read. It arrives as a return posting from the past, and demands, in return, that we return our judgement, and so return truth to the traces of the past, as we read. This, in effect, is what the novel enables. At its centre, in the case of *The Tenant of Wildfell Hall*, a large centre of twenty-three chapters and more than two hundred and fifty pages, is a narrative, which – at first a secret – gradually unveils its enigma. *Tenant* is structured around the absence of the truth, around a gap, which writing must fill as best it can. That gap or absence, in which Helen's consciousness becomes aware of its own fault or myopia concerning Huntingdon is necessary as the condition for redemption and reconciliation, in a gesture of a weak transcendence, which is the only hope the novel can hold out as bourgeois epic and secular substitution for Biblical promise. *The Tenant of Wildfell Hall* assumes that dimension of modern epic described by Rancière, which is as the 'epic of totality that is lost but still striven for', which totality is the closing up desired by the individual of the distance and him [or her] and his [or her] God' (Rancière 2004a, 72).

Transcendence into what, though, it must be asked. If we are links in the open chain that Brontë's related tropes of vision and text demand be constructed as the necessary historical and ethical responsibility of a 'true' reading, then we also are in some sense entrapped within the 'complicated framing device', as Tess O'Toole calls it (1999, 715). As she also remarks:

> ... in proceeding through the multilayered narrative and remaining for a surprisingly protracted time in Helen's painful account of her nightmarish marriage, the reader experiences a sensation that might be labelled narrative claustrophobia. The text thus produces an effect on the reader that mimics the entrapment Helen experiences in her marriage. (O'Toole 1999, 715)

As persuasive a local reading as this is, it fails to take account of the fact that, as suggested by, on the one hand, the evidence of constant textual referral and framing, and, on the other, the concomitant troubling of empirical evidence based on the faultiness and partiality of perception grounded in sight and vision, in the singular example of *The Tenant of Wildfell Hall*, 'the immanence of meaning in life has become a problem' (Rancière cit. Hegel 2004a, 72). Rancière is citing Hegel here, but the problem of modernity that Hegel identifies is at the heart of Brontë's novel also. There can only ever be a 'weak' transcendence in that closure promised in the love of Helen and Gilbert for one another. This is merely strategic transcendence, by which the novel closes the book on endless writing and rewriting, framing and reframing, in its narrative substitution for transcendence proper, which is the absence on which is founded the '"modern" epic of the novel' in Rancière's words (2004a, 72). The modern novel is thus always founded on a deferred fulfilment – unless one looks in another direction.

VII

If *The Tenant of Wildfell Hall* presents vision as everywhere but limited, communication in the form of written texts as always indirect, and truth as something to be deciphered, not immediately available, then this, as I have been suggesting, is as much a question of form as it is of content. *How* the narrative of hidden abuse comes down to us is as significant as the fact that it is gradually revealed through various third parties. True knowledge – knowledge of Helen's identity and her past, but also Gilbert's nature as it reveals itself to him through communication with Helen – has to pass through what Pascal calls 'un pensée de derrière', that is to say, the thought that 'sees behind the apparent evidence of things' (de Man 1996, 66).

Like Gilbert, we have to learn to see behind the apparent evidence, behind what is presented to our eyes, and thus *The Tenant of Wildfell Hall* makes a distinction, albeit implicitly, between a mere surface empirical evidence conjured by gossip and opinion – a stranger comes to town, the stranger must have a past, otherwise she would not wish to remain a stranger, an enigma – and the interpretative discernment of a knowledge that illuminates the dark corners of the past. This is the 'true' as opposed to the 'false' transcendental promise of the novel, the true 'transcendental' principle, if you will, of *The Tenant of Wildfell Hall*, which is achieved only when the narrative retreats from the space of representation – representation of Helen from others' perspectives, including Gilbert Markham's – to become first-hand knowledge, through which the true history of Helen Graham can be written. Such a retreat into the past enables the arrival of a vision to come in the future.

There are, then, other places where one might locate the possibility of transcendence, and so see through to the possibility of truth. This is intimated towards the end of the novel, in its conclusion, in a scene that offers a telling summary of what the novel seeks to show us, as opposed to what its story merely *tells* us. The 'weak' transcendence of love and marriage is a gesture by which Brontë 'wrong-foots' the bad reader, the conventional reader. For the good reader, there is always the possibility of a revelation. The conclusion begins with Markham in a gloomy 'reverie', lost and blinded by a kind of waking dream, his sight turned inward. Soon, this inner vision is overtaken by a plethora of visual and visible signifiers, or direct reference to their absence. Markham is disturbed, brought back to the real world by the arrival of a carriage, from which emerges Arthur's voice. Although Markham does 'not raise' his 'eyes', he supposes that 'mamma looked', as a result of hearing a 'joyous though suppressed excitement in the utterance of those few words' (Brontë 1993, 459). Revelation, literally a removal of a veil, a disclosure of truth, thus arrives through the reception of the voice. Not looking, not seeing, Markham is forced to listen in order to hear a truth in the tone of voice before any sight can mislead or confirm. Hearing in this example is akin to a careful reading, a blind reading that 'shows' with apodictic certainty, or what Samuel Taylor Coleridge called 'truths of apodictic force' (Brontë 1993, 358), more than mere representation can.

Having 'heard' the truth of Helen Graham, conveyed in the voice, Markham looks up, 'and met the eye', not of Helen, but of 'a pale, grave elderly lady surveying me from the open window' (Brontë 1993, 459). From this, a 'hand was put *silently* put forth' from the carriage window; 'I knew that hand, though a black glove concealed its delicate whiteness and half its fair *proportions*' (Brontë 1993, 459; emphases added). Notice how there is either sound or vision, but not both at the same time. The voice is heard, the hand follows 'silently'. And more than this, it is an indirect revelation, because the hand is both the hand and yet not itself, being a gloved hand, and a glove moreover that conceals in its blackness the whiteness of the hand as well as the hand, whilst also concealing its 'proportions'. It is as if the scene is constituted through a geometry of delays, deferrals and relational differences. To push this strong reading here, it is as if the passage were about learning to read: first hearing in default of seeing, seeing and inferring through a structural replacement of direct evidence, seeing only a representation – the glove – of the hand, which itself is made to represent the whole of Helen: so the glove, as metonymy masking the hand, synecdoche for Mrs Graham. The opening gambit of the conclusion of *The Tenant of Wildfell Hall* is to replay in miniature, through a kind of micronarrative, the stages by which one has to learn to decipher signs so as to reassemble the material elements into a meaningful whole.

Kissing the hand impetuously, Gilbert releases it, only to hear once again 'the low voice of its owner' (Brontë 1993, 459). In itself a strange phrase, we receive this as if the voice, hand, and the person to whom they both are a part, are somehow separated, however partially, from one another. Responding to the voice, the owner of which Markham feels 'was attentively surveying my counte- nance from behind the thick black veil with which the shadowing panels entirely concealed her own [face] from me', Gilbert lies, stammering that he came to 'see the place' (Brontë 1993, 459). Still unable to see Helen Graham, Markham sees instead the trace of her image indirectly manifested in Arthur, now, at seven, a 'tall, slim young gentleman with his mother's image visibly stamped upon his fair intelligent features, in spite of the blue eyes' (Brontë 1993, 460). After pausing on the steps to look around him, Gilbert notices, as they continue inside, that 'Helen eyed me as I entered with a kind of gentle, serious scrutiny' (Brontë 1993, 460), following which Rachel greets him with 'an almost friendly smile of recognition', a sign, he takes it, in an observation that connects metaphorical and axiomatic vision with imperfect empirical interpretation, that 'she had *seen* the error of her former estimation' (Brontë 1993, 461; emphasis added). There is something of an irony in Markham's perception, directed as it is to the interpretation of another's hitherto faulty vision, a condition he is all too guilty of elsewhere in the novel.

Finally, there is an apocalyptic dis-covery, literally an uncovering or disclosure, which is also revelation:

> When Helen was divested of her lugubrious bonnet and veil, her heavy winter cloak etc., she looked so like herself that I knew not how to bear it. I was par- ticularly glad to see her beautiful black hair unstinted still and unconcealed in its glossy luxuriance. (Brontë 1993, 461)

Helen remains silent, as first Arthur, then Mrs Maxwell talk *at* Gilbert in a manner that serves as an 'antidote', as he puts it 'to those emotions of tumultuous excite- ment'. At the same time, however

> I was sensible that Helen was standing within a few feet of me beside the fire. I dared not look at her, but I felt her eye was upon me, and from one hasty, furtive glance, I thought her cheek was slightly flushed, and that her fingers, as she played with her watch chain, were agitated with that restless trembling motion which betokens high excitement. (Brontë 1993, 461)

What might it mean to look 'so like' oneself? What, in such a true resemblance, in which one is doubled as one's true self and being visible as the appearance of oneself is there – this is the logic of Gilbert's statement, that visibility signifies and doubles the truth of a person – that it is unbearable to witness: 'I knew not how to bear it . . . I dared not look at her'. The veil and outer clothing removed, Brontë's narrative imagines the sight of Helen for Gilbert in the form of some, possibly avenging, angel, whose 'higher and better self', Helen reflects, 'is indeed unmarried' (Brontë 1993, 243).

Helen's doubleness, her life-preserving duplicity – she appears as a mystery and is not what she appears – aside, if this appears too strong a reading, it should not be forgotten that Anne Brontë's vision is one of 'suffering and dark enlightenment' as embodied in Helen, allied to Brontë's own uncompromising 'Protestant vision', as Stevie Davies, editor of the Penguin edition, puts it in a convincing reading of the theological dimensions of *The Tenant of Wildfell Hall* (Davies 1996 xx, xxi), wherein she also speaks of Brontë's 'radical Protestantism' (xx). To quote Davies again, this is a novel in which 'the cosmic and the domestic occupy the same page' (vii), through a narrative wherein 'moral disease has become a norm' (vii). Contamination comes chiefly from men, 'hell-bent souls recklessly playing away the hope of heaven, within a patriarchal system that licenses the soulless pleasures of "gentlemen"' (vii). Like *Dombey and Son*, then, *The Tenant of Wildfell Hall* presents us with a vision of the Victorian world where gross materialism and masculinity, power and patriarchy go hand in hand. If Helen is, for most of the novel, a woman without a home, an 'unaccommodated woman' as Stevie Davies describes her, in a 'landscape of biblical texts as well as moorlands and pasture' (xi), her lone stand is the material expression on Brontë's part of a proto-feminism, a feminism that is lived before the word can determine it historically, but which is nonetheless real for that. But this proto-feminism is intimately part and parcel with Brontë's religious faith, hence the frequency with which fragments of biblical texts appear throughout the novel – almost as often as eyes, in fact. The Bible is thus a privileged textual material that sutures the absences, the gaps and omissions, the silences that make up the narrative.

A Victorian reader may well have recognized such textual threads, with an immediacy that many of us, today, do not. To put this differently, we cannot see what we do not know to be there, on the surface, and so are blind to the material weave of discourses from out of which the novel figures material experience and stresses a different vision of the world within the experience of that same world. Recognizing this, however belatedly, gives us insight, and so invites us 'to witness', in the words of Jacques Rancière, the specific relationship between writing and fiction that is here revealed. Anne's unveiling at the close of the novel is a manner of secular incarnation, and, at the same time, a measure of 'the distance of every truth of the book from the truth of the Incarnate Word' (Rancière 2004a, 90). Helen's 'revelation' of herself, her 'resurrection' from the funereal black, and those coffin-like panels that momentarily obscure sight of her body, make known Brontë's local truth as analogy for a theological truth in which she had faith, even if we do not. To borrow from Rancière's discussion of Don Quixote, Helen Graham stands in for an unavailable and invisible truth in the mid-Victorian period, the truth of Scripture, by being the visible substitute, the 'specific fiction of a quasi-body'

(Rancière 2004a, 90), as part of the transcendent fantasy, the proto-feminist fable that imbues *The Tenant of Wildfell Hall* with such power.

The quasi-body is of course the written text. That is Brontë's one hope of expressing faith in the possibility of the impossible; hence, the layering of text within text. And text – the appearance of the journals, letters and books – reminds the reader that all local meaning, all local truths are only substitutes, fictions, whereby 'the "fictionality" of meaning . . . forms the limit of every exegesis of the condition of the truth of the life story' (Rancière 2004a, 84). One fiction stands in for another, one frame surrounds the next, and it is in this spirit that we have to take this narrative of the suffering female body. Brontë's novel struggles therefore, and in conclusion, between all merely empirical vision and what Paul de Man describes, in his account of the Kantian perception of the sublime, as a *'material vision'* (de Man 1996, 82). As de Man remarks of Kant's perception of the ocean, the land, the heavens, there is 'no mind' involved in the *materiality* of the vision of Helen. There is 'no mind' for two reasons: first, less significantly, Gilbert cannot bear to look directly at her, as if the overwhelming vision of her unveiled is some sublime experience; second, there is no mode of judgement, and hence no mode of representation that can give merely local meaning beyond the statement that there she stands. Something else, something unspeakable is seen in this moment, but what is seen – as vision's truth – is, to quote de Man again, 'how things are to the eye . . . and not to the mind' (de Man 1996, 82). That which is seen is not to be seen. That which overwhelms Gilbert's vision cannot be translated, conveyed, articulated, communicated. There and yet not there, Helen stands before us on the page, 'devoid of any semantic depth' (de Man 1996, 83), briefly, it may be inferred, as 'a purely sublime and aesthetic vision' to which we have no direct access (de Man 1996, 83). In the blink of an eye, she is there as herself and also her 'higher and better self' (to recall Helen's own words), and then she is gone, rendered only in corporeal fragments as a flushed cheek and fingers playing with a watch-chain, captured in a hasty, furtive glance. 'Truth' withdraws, or, putting this another way, we witness, *through the failure and limit of Gilbert's vision*, what Philippe Lacoue-Labarthe describes as the '"withdrawal" of the divine', wherein retreat or withdrawal is not denial or withholding, but that which saves or 'preserves . . . and separates the human from the divine, what retraces the limit of finitude' (Lacoue-Labarthe 1999, 77), which, ultimately, it is the purpose of narrative to enact. The *material* vision, of the other Helen, the higher Helen, within the woman who will become Helen Markham, is thus the incarnate expression of what de Man describes as a 'quasi-theological necessity that follows necessarily from our fallen condition' (de Man 1996, 84).

Either you see this or you do not, and no amount of narrative description or representation can make you see it. As with the meaning of parables, you remain either side of the apprehension/incomprehension divide: if you receive the vision, no amount of explanation or description is necessary; if you do not, nothing will ever explain it in a way that will give you access to the immediacy of that vision. Thus the sight of Helen operates in an 'essentially negative way' (de Man 1996, 85). It remains only for Gilbert Markham to conquer his surprise, his fear bordering on terror, in order that the implicit, yet somehow direct threat that Helen figures, can be overcome, in the imagination at least. For as Paul de Man argues: 'Taming this delectable, because imaginary terror . . . and preferring to it the tranquil satisfaction of superiority, is to submit the imagination to the power of reason . . . [for] the imagination's security depends on the actual, empirical physical attraction' (de Man 1996, 85–6). In this 'complicated and somewhat devious scenario', Gilbert's imagination closes its eyes to the blinding vision, and in so doing 'reconciles pleasure with pain', returning in the process to the 'stable order of reason' (de Man 1996, 86), and to the conventional banality of marriage as that which places the seal on narrative, closing the book, and hiding its characters from our sight. We cannot remain with or in sight of truth. The finitude of the novel bespeaks the finitude of being itself. But such a revelation 'also supposes that the divine be subject to the very history its epiphany – or retreat – sets into motion' (Lacoue-Labarthe 1999, 77). Perhaps this is the secret truth of Anne Brontë: that, in this withdrawal of the divine, apophatically presented, there remains the possibility of the divine 'still to come' (Lacoue-Labarthe 1999, 77). Withdrawal is not closure, Brontë might be read as suggesting, it is merely an opening, the openness 'of the truth of Being [that] remains intentionally undeveloped' (Heidegger 1998, 154).

4

Contested Grounds: Historical, Epistemological and Political Identities in Nineteenth-Century Literature

I

'[T]he historicity of past texts and the historicity of present interpretation must of necessity differ' (Liu 1989, 217). Thus, Alan Liu in his *Wordsworth: The Sense of History*. He continues: 'but in their difference they will agree – thus making critical interpretation and understanding possible'. As a result, ideological and epistemological difficulties or those disagreements, intellectual and otherwise, which persist in the study of literature, in university departments for example, or what Liu called in 1989 '[o]ur chosen controversies ... reproduce with a critical difference the controversy in' literary texts that map controversies of their day (1989, 217). The assumptions here are many, not least that the day of a particular text is separate and separable from the 'day' of the critical act. (Which day might that be? Perhaps 1989 – the day of publication of Liu's book; or its starting point, signalled as eight years prior [1989, 500]; or 2009, that in which – and in a different academic culture from that in which Liu produced his major study of William Wordsworth – I am, 'at this very moment', so to speak, writing?)

That aside, the agreement in difference alerts us to something that is symptomatic in interpretation: the need – perhaps the desire – to put into one's own words what has already been said, so as to cause to appear and so become transmissible that to which the text being read has already attested. More than a 'need' or 'desire', both of which situate too readily the locus of event in the reading subject, there is also the demand from the other that I respond to, and take responsibility for, the other's words, and, in reiterating them, bear witness to the other, opening transmission onto others and an unprogrammable future reception. I would amend this by suggesting that whatever we take as 'past texts' be understood not as literature as opposed to criticism or theory, as appears implicit in Liu's dialectical distinction between 'past texts' and 'present interpretation', but that we also begin to appreciate the extent to which 'past texts' are also interpretations, whether novels or poetry. Accepting this symptomaticity, one might venture that the act of interpretation takes place precisely from a necessary blindness to one's own historicity. I write and leave to chance or fate the destination and reception of these words because, while I know myself to be a being whose being is material and

therefore informed by the signs of a particular historicity, I cannot say for sure what
constitutes the singularity of such historicity.

Writing is a making sense of the self (the self becoming in the making of the
self as other) without the self having full access to that sense. Writing signals a
historicity yet to be perceived and, 'most crucially, it opens up the interval between
then and *now*, and, in doing so, creates the essential space of . . . the epochal divide
between the other and the same that is the aporetic ground . . . of historical understanding' (Liu 1989, 457). In this, despite my intention, what I mean to say – and
this is true, equally, for each and every writer, every other writer and every reader,
each and every reader as an other – is traced in a writing which 'is thus radically
sceptical in its ontology but positive in its displaced locus of epistemology. It would
know the shape and dimensions of the divide itself together with the imprint of
such impending division, or becoming, *within* the other – a palpable absence . . .'
(Liu 1989, 457). With this in mind, I want to seek to read several such moments
of becoming in 'Victorian' or, more properly, nineteenth-century literature, so as
to mark the extent to which literature forms itself, in every singular instance, as one
of so many absent, or possibly phantom manifestations of 'theoretical' reflection.
Putting this differently, literature accounts for the historicity of identities and
subjectivities by proposing narrative structures and trajectories that institute and
imply epistemologies of becoming, without seeking to map a mistaken ontological
formation.

II

The novels conventionally defined as 'social-problem novels' are *Hard Times*
(Dickens), *Mary Barton* and *North and South* (Elizabeth Gaskell), *Alton Locke*
(Charles Kingsley, whose *Yeast* might also be added to this list), *Sybil* (Benjamin
Disraeli), and Eliot's *Felix Holt* (Guy 1996, 3; see also Ingham [1996a], who discusses Gaskell, Dickens and Eliot, and Childers [1995], who discusses Kingsley and
Gaskell). What distinguishes such novels for the historicist critic is their interest in
representations of class- and labour-relations, even though, as Josephine Guy points
out, the novels were not thought of as a 'group by their nineteenth-century readers
or critics' (Guy 1996, 3). The labels 'social-problem' or 'industrial novel' have been
affixed in the second half of the twentieth century as a typical phenomenon of the
role of institutionalized literary criticism (as Guy's study makes plain; 3–63). The
institutional definition or identification of such a sub-genre goes hand in hand with
the interest in the related questions of literature and culture, literature and history,
and what is all too broadly defined as literature's context.

However, what might be read also is criticism's own act of mapping its 'chosen controversies', to recall Alan Liu's phrase, onto a disparate range of fictional
productions. From the 1980s onwards, through the 1990s, the cultural and ideological discourse wars are staged in the reading of the industrial or social-problem
novel, whereby 'history' returns to the stage of academic criticism. In part, this
was doubtless a reaction to, as well as part of the so-called 'theory wars', so many

semi-bloodless but nonetheless occasionally hysterical coups taking place in English and Comparative Literature departments on both sides of the Atlantic. (Liu's study of Wordsworth is, itself, a product of such struggles, and seeks, throughout its length to justify the ways of the historicist to allegedly formalist critical modalities, whether the older New Criticism, or the misread 'deconstruction' of so-called post-structuralism.) Historicization was a necessary process, it was argued, against all the dehistoricizing, formalist, playful retreat from politics on the part of so-called theory (for which, one might conveniently read the proper names Derrida, Lacan, Kristeva, Cixous, Irigrary). In the US, historicists of the emergent variety had their own French theorist, Michel Foucault, and through Foucault, to the reading of other French historicist critical texts. In the UK, critics turned to versions of Marxism, as a practical and pragmatic political discourse. While it is my intention in this chapter to examine the traces of historicity, epistemology, and the political, as these, in turn, serve to mediate subjectivities in nineteenth-century novels and poems, it is necessary primarily to reflect briefly on this turn to Marxism, contra 'theory', as a way of understanding the readings that have been presented that assert a reading of history. This is not to offer counter-readings of particularly politically inflected historicist analyses of the 'social-problem novel' – indeed, the chapter opens from such an inaugural point to read other texts of the nineteenth century about which such criticism has largely remained silent, considering both novels not obviously belonging to the institutionally invented genre of the 'social-problem', and also poems, which trouble political, historical and epistemological identity; instead, the purpose is to suggest that what has been taken to be a Marxist criticism has been marked by a cultural identity that has not been fully or adequately reflected on in the development of politicized or historicist critical modalities.

In turning to something called Marxism, what particular historicist critics in British universities *returned* to, in fact, without necessarily having systematically or actively read in the tradition of Anglo-Saxon modernity, was a model of thought and interpretation of the world dictated by a culture of empirical distrust of ideas, stretching back through the formation of orthodox and middle-class English cultural identity to the seventeenth century, and given a dialectical and apparently radical spin. Put another way, Marx's legacy could not have been so intellectually successful anywhere other than England, especially given the systematic, transcendent spin put on it by Friedrich Engels. As a result of Engels' Hegelian 'tidying-up' of Marx, many so-called Marxists accepted, and still accept, what Kojin Karatani describes as a 'an unexamined version of the Smithian notion of the "division of labour"' (Karatani 1995, 84), alongside a certain discernibly Ricardian influence. There is little wonder in this, as Engels himself did not examine the notion to any great extent. To offer a rough and admittedly reductive equation, 'Marxism', on this account, equals, therefore, an uneasy, and ill-thought alliance between the ideas of Adam Smith and G. W. F. Hegel (economics + metaphysics) informed by a native tradition of empiricism and materialism (Hobbes, Locke, Hume), and always already traced by a 'systematic scepticism about the nature of history and of "change"' (Ackroyd 1976, 13–14). In other words, and to put it, perhaps, too briefly, particular aspects of Marxist criticism in the twentieth century replicated *in other words* a wholly nineteenth-century, not to say 'Victorian', manifestation of economic and political discourse already overdetermined by particular conventions and modes in the tradition in English thought.

The sign that this tradition has remained unthought and in-place manifests itself (even today), ironically, not in the materialist critique of (so-called) 'high theory' of an alleged retreat from the political or the historical into endless formalist play, but more markedly in the native distrust of linguistic 'conceits', of 'jargon' and 'obfuscation' (or, 'eloquence' and 'complexity', if you happen to stand the other side of the divide). This is no mere, modern, institutional argument, a result of the theory wars. It belongs, whether one reads Thomas Sprat, John Dunton or John Locke, to the emergence of Anglo-Saxon modernity. It instigates a tradition of polemic 'directed against ... apparently opaque style which can spin disputation and subtlety out of thin air, out of nothing' (Ackroyd 1976, 14). The 'new language' of English empiricism and rationalism, that is to say the language of bourgeois orthodoxy, by which humanist and Marxist critics alike remain enthralled in the English university, is motivated by 'Reason', it claims mastery over, and so pretends to transform, the 'natural world', by speaking and writing in a manner that is 'continuous, plain, familiar, simple, solid, sensible' (Ackroyd 1976, 14–15). Hence the critical turn, in the names of politics and history, to the invention of a genre, the 'social-problem novel', and to the reading of literature not tropically, but in terms of text and context. Thus, the turn to a bastardized Marx.

While Marx had sought to emphasize history as 'natural history', and to read the historicity of social formation as inevitable and organic processes of, manufacturing, differentiation, division and intercourse ('accidental and transverse connection' [Karatani 1995, 86]) reliant on the contingency of *Naturwüchsigkeit*, 'the anarchic [and natural] drive of a society' (Karatani 1995, 85), Engels sought to define and so control such processes in terms of a deliberate and transcendent consciousness. Marx's aim had been to read the deconstruction of Hegelian dialectics, through an inversion of 'those aspects of Hegel's thought that asserted a view of history as "making" and *Geist* as a maker of that world history' (Karatani 1995, 86). Reintroducing the Hegelian notion of a conscious human will into the thinking of human productivity – and thereby laying the groundwork for a Leninist-Marxist perception of social control through the transformation of human productivity in terms of the transformation of society into a 'gigantic factory' (Karatani 1995, 85) – Engels also reintroduced temporal precedence and succession, as ordered and rational manifestations of human will and 'consciousness of purpose' (Karatani 1995, 88), rather than seeing such conceits as 'themselves products of the division of labour, products of a consciousness (philosopher) that, by the grace of the division of labour, was enabled to think itself autonomous' (Karatani 1995, 89).

Class struggle understood 'as the motor of history' is thus 'a fiction, even though the class struggle itself is undeniable' (Karatani 1995, 89). But, more importantly, it is a fiction co-opted by writers of the nineteenth century, given order in narrative and poetics of the age as a means of rationalizing and ordering – thereby making sense of – the otherwise inchoate and organic transformation of society over a couple of generations. Writers identified today as 'Victorian' produce fictions of historical struggle as a way of formulating epistemological comprehension, and so producing narrative as the expression of both historicized identity and historicized consciousness. What is occluded in this process of seeking to come to terms and comprehend the new world of 'Victorian' consciousness is the rapid transformation of English society and culture from its largely agrarian identity to an identity that is industrial and urban. Marxist and related criticisms of the 1990s in (re)turning to historicist and rationalist modalities reiterate the occlusion of earlier English cultures and identities. (See Chapter Six on English diaspora.)

Coming back to the study of the 'social-problem' or 'industrial novel', as Josephine Guy makes clear, the rise in interest in the 'industrial novel' is, itself, a historical phenomenon which first occurs in critical discourse a couple of generations before the Marxist turn in 1980s and 1990s criticism, as the debate around the importance of the historicized study of literature and literary production is taken up, insisted on, for example, by Oxford critic F. W. Bateson on the one hand, and dismissed, on the other, by Cambridge critic F. R. Leavis. (There is, in this, a politics of interpretation and a political history of literary criticism, which it would be well to read with regard to the question of canonization.) However, as Guy goes on to show, the modern critical perception has, until recently, been at odds with the contemporary reception of the novels in question, not least for the variance between the mid-nineteenth and late-twentieth century comprehension of problems as, on the one hand, individual and, on the other, social (1996, 9–10). This disjunction calls to account the very role of historical knowledge for Guy in the interpretation of literary texts, so that, whether from what she describes as Marxist, contextualist or New Historicist perspectives, there is a shared 'attempt to explain social-problem novels in terms of the historical circumstances which produce them' (1996, 5). Ironically, the three analytical modes share for Guy a lack of awareness of the 'political and social topicality' of the texts in question (1996, 8). This occurs, at least in part because, in the words of Patricia Ingham (citing Mary Poovey), '[l]iterary critics . . . seem readily to overlook the possibility that the representation of social class and that of industrial society were similarly "in the making" and "open . . . to dispute"' (Ingham 1996a, 2). Moreover, critical tendencies assuming similarity rather than difference have, to some degree, tended to overlook the complex mediations of competing and frequently contradictory discourses which come together in nineteenth-century texts, as Elizabeth Deeds Ermath has been at pains to stress (1997, 84–93). In relation to the politics of gender in the Victorian novel, so-called, Poovey shows how any narrative account of gender is 'both contested and always under construction; because it was always in the making, it was always open to revision, dispute and the emergence of oppositional formulations' (Poovey 1988, 3). What may appear today, about supposedly Victorian representations of politics, class and gender, as coherent and organically of a piece, was, in the nineteenth century, 'actually fissured by competing emphases and interests' (Poovey 1988, 3).

Change is a keyword in the nineteenth century, and was, furthermore, according to Joseph Childers, 'lived at "such a depth" and so saturated society that it attained

hegemonic status' for the Victorians (Childers 1995, 23). One aspect of change
was the 'new language of class', first critically identified by Asa Briggs (1967), but
subsequently given further development as a subject of critical inquiry in relation
to the political novel by Patricia Ingham (6). The language of class – itself a signifier of modernity which separates the Victorians discursively and politically from
their ancestors – dependent on a perception of the relation between economic and
social status, transforms what might be identified provisionally as Victorian self-
awareness, as it replaces the more static, hierarchically fixed and organic language
of rank and station (Ingham 1996, 4–5). That the emphasis is on language, that
is to say on signifying systems, rather than on some simply assumed reality and
its unproblematic representation, is telling. Both Ingham and Childers, in their
studies of political discourse in the Victorian text, bring out with great subtlety
the complex interanimation through the medium of language between the areas of
politics and literature, in order to demonstrate the constant process of change taking place both socially and linguistically during the 1830s, 40s and 50s, a period in
which political, economic and social crisis was matched and mediated by 'linguistic
crisis or conflict of discourses' (Ingham 1996a, 3). There is thus not available to us
a 'univocal totality without contradictions', as Childers suggests (23), whether one
analyses political discourse as a language of progress emanating from Parliament
or other political sources, or via its manifestations in literary texts. Moreover,
'politics and the novel are two major systems that often overlap each sharing
certain aspects of its language and interpretations with the other' (Childers 1995,
35). It is such interweaving for which we should read, and which, in turn can give
us to comprehend the novel in the nineteenth century as political in the broadest
sense imaginable, thereby allowing our critical acts to move beyond the restrictive
categorization of the 'social-problem', 'industrial', or 'condition of England' novel.

III

Coningsby, like George Eliot's *Felix Holt: the Radical*, is set in the period of the
1832 Reform Act (a narrative strategy used again by Eliot in *Middlemarch* [1871–
1872]), by which the franchise was extended in Great Britain. In doing so, Disraeli
(and, arguably, Eliot) relies for the cogency of his various narrative and ideological
perspectives on a reading of founding political moment for both the modern era to
which he belongs, and for the construction of a narrative which imply politics as
that which offers to the Victorian reader what Eliot is to refer to in *Daniel Deronda*
as 'the make-believe of a beginning' (Eliot 1986, 35). As Joseph Childers puts it,
Coningsby, 'besides being arguably the first English political novel, combines and
examines two major interpretive systems of nineteenth-century Britain: the novel
and parliamentary politics':

> In doing so, it maintains not only that political representations of the world may
> be 'factitious' but that the truth claims of fiction often may carry more weight
> than their political counterparts. This is particularly momentous for the status

of the novel in Victorian England. For, in spite of Disraeli's often paradoxical explications of social and political change, *Coningsby*'s assertion that novels can offer workable . . . explanations of the rapidly changing world helps establish the genre as an instrument of social criticism and an interpretive discourse that actively informs Victorian culture. (Childers 1995, 12)

I quote Childers at some length, for the argument he puts forward, drawing on the exemplary status of the text of Disraeli, is precisely the argument presented in this chapter, which is that in order that one not occlude historical difference, there remains the necessity of reading the political differently: not simply as a critical-theoretical gesture, but also as a (political) response and understanding of the work as a novel of the nineteenth century. The status of the novel as cultural object and discursive event is, itself, political, and that status changes as the discourses comprising literary and fictional prose actively take on the facticity, as Childers puts it, of political discourse and event. To write from the make-believe of a beginning which is the First Reform Act is not only to 'ground' the play of fiction on a historical fact; it is also to acknowledge the sense in which the world and its representations are actively textual.

The First Reform Act is not, of course, the only political event of the first third of the nineteenth century, even though its significance was undeniable inasmuch as it doubled the number of those who could vote, from approximately 500,000 to one million. In the years following the Act of 1832, up to the coronation of Queen Victoria, other equally significant Acts of Parliament were passed, along with other events, which today can be read as both determining what we understand as the narrative of the Victorian period, while providing for the Victorians themselves a variety of narrative details which are themselves political, and by which the Victorians can define a self-aware narrative of modernity separating them from their Hanoverian predecessors.

Amongst the political changes that took place was the 1834 Poor Law Amendment Act. This decreed that no able-bodied person was eligible for poor relief unless he or she entered the workhouse. The fear of the workhouse was so public and so long-lasting that if one takes the works of Dickens, one will find ambivalent reference to its horrors and abuses from *Oliver Twist* (1838), through Scrooge's Malthusian allusion in *A Christmas Carol* (1843), again in *Bleak House* (1853) and *Little Dorrit* (1857) in the figure of Nandy, the workhouse occupant, and, finally his last completed novel, *Our Mutual Friend* (1865), with the character of Betty Higden, who would rather kill herself and baby Johnny than be taken to the workhouse (Dickens 1997b, 324). If we pause at Dickens before returning to Disraeli, we can suggest that the Dickensian text gives us the possibility of reading the complex and persistent, encrypted manifestation of, and response to, politics, to which, if we are not attendant, then we are liable to make assumptions that certain novels are political while others are not. In the case of Dickens, it is very much a question of reading a different appearance of politics and reading politics differently. This might be enabled in the thinking of how those most threatened by the 1834 Act are given voice in the novel, in order that the ideological positioning

of the Act might most immediately be apprehended, from the position of the pow-
erless. The text of Dickens persistently manifests the trace and discursive effect of
the Poor Law Amendment Act. In fact, we can suggest that the Act, though hardly,
if ever, named as such, nonetheless returns in a reiterative fashion as the spectral
trace of political discourse and institutional practice, haunting the Dickensian text.
At the same time, thinking the question of the political differently, and paying
attention to such 'incidental' traces, allows us to read Dickens's novels as political
novels, as well as epistemological discourses taking responsibility for particular
identities in the face of new networks of state and institutional power, albeit different in degree, rather than kind, from more apparently obviously politically engaged
novels, such as *North and South*. In Dickens, the poor are not a group, but historical
subjects, whose singular experience of the early and mid-Victorian world is made
visible and articulated for bourgeois consciousness. Characters such as Nandy,
Betty Higden, even Oliver: all are written in the process of 'becoming *historical
agents* [, no] longer the simple "bearers" of social relations, whose misfortune is
not being unaware of real conditions but of not being *equal* to what they bear'
(Rancière 2004b, 121).

The year following the Poor Law Amendment Act saw the 1835 Factory Act,
which ensured, in principle at least, inspection of working conditions in factories,
while, in the same year there came about the abolition of slavery in those states
belonging to the British Empire. During this year, closer to home, but with
profound political ramifications, was the Municipal Corporation Act, which
transformed the political management and government of local boroughs and the
towns therein, in ways that have lasted piecemeal to the present day. In 1836, the
working-class movement known as the People's Charter, or Chartism, as it is more
commonly called, came to be established, demanding universal suffrage, while, in
1838, the Anti-Corn Law League was also established (lasting eight years) in order
to combat the political fixing of corn prices in favour of domestic product, which
led directly to artificially high bread prices (Hobsbawm 1996, 41).

These, then, are some of the overtly political domestic events taking place between the moment in which *Coningsby* is set and the year in which it is published.
If we recall the complications of the idea of the political novel put in place above,
the following comment from Thom Braun, the editor of the Penguin edition of
the novel, is instructive: '[h]is novels of the 1840s were political, not just in being
about politics, but in being themselves manipulative, and in attempting to present
disparate, paradoxical and often contradictory views within an artificially created
organic whole' (Disraeli ed. Braun 1989, 8). To an extent I agree with Braun's assessment, but where we part company is over the aesthetic inflection of the editor's
remark, where *political*, in being equated obliquely with conscious effort, becomes
a sign of awkward, dishonest construction. As is implied throughout this chapter
(and recalling the remarks of Guy, Ingham, Ermath and, particularly, Childers's
description of 'Disraeli's often paradoxical explications of social and political
change'), contradiction and paradox in *Coningsby* are *just* the conditions of discursive flow and mediation, particularly as the traces they leave are those determining
the historicity of a moment so obviously in the throes of cultural transition.

Disraeli's novel *is* political, certainly, but not simply in the double sense afforded it by Braun. The political is, moreover, a matter of perception, inasmuch as perception, constituted through epistemological transformation and ideological positioning is marked, even as it traces, the encrypted signs of a subject's historicity. Disraeli gives us to understand this in a conversation between Coningsby and a 'stranger' met by chance in an inn. In a dialogue that self-reflexively marks its own modernity as belonging to the tradition of the novel, by signalling its historical difference from traditions and conventions with reference to 'Cervantes' and the 'age of adventures', Coningsby bemoans the absence of travel in his life, to which the stranger replies, 'You are travelling ... Every moment is travel, if understood' (Disraeli 1989, 141). Through a solicitation of fictional conventions and narratives of the previous century, and, as a result, and epistemologies that undergird such forms, Disraeli invites a reflection on the transformation of both narrative and the English subject, both fictional *and* historical subjectivity. Being is, for the stranger, a *becoming*, motion and travel, philosophical as well as material categories, the self a motivating force, and agent driving 'the motor of history' (Karatani 1995, 89). 'Travel' is the metaphorical vehicle or engine itself in the self-differentiation of the subject, properly historicized and apprehended in this epistemology of the 'new generation's' epistemological reflection, mediated by the self-referential discourse on cultural identity as previously learned from the form of novel (exemplified in the allusion to Cervantes). Hence, equally, the 'Age of Ruins' and the 'age of adventures' are past (Disraeli 1989, 141) but only as a fiction or myth of the subject's constitution; for, as the stranger affirms, 'adventures are for the adventurous' (141), an expression that admits an ideology of personal agency. Athens and the Mediterranean are mere material manifestations of '[p]hantoms and spectres', Manchester is now the goal, and therefore, it is implied, this is culture, history *and* the future; the experience of materiality of the industrial north is what will give to Coningsby his being and his identity (Disraeli 1989, 141).

With Disraeli's *Sybil* (1845) and *Tancred* (1847), *Coningsby* was part of what became referred to as the 'Young England' trilogy. The trilogy mediates the politics of early Victorian England in interesting ways, conceiving 'of history as structured like a spiral, permitting progress or displacement forward provided it is conceptualized in terms that evoke a hallowed past' (Bivona 1990, 3). The collective term for the trilogy is instructive. It points to the youthful modernity which mid-Victorian England was already constructing for itself as the narrative of its own progress and change, as well as signalling an attempted divorce from its regency parents. This is caught in the narrative concerns of *Coningsby* itself, and summarized succinctly in political and ideological terms by Daniel Bivona. Coningsby, 'the aristocratic hero of the novel ...' regains his lost inheritance from his grandfather; this:

> ... and his eventual marriage to Edith Millbank are intended to mark the metaphorical passage of landed wealth from a decadent Regency aristocracy to a youthful, but serious and reform-minded, Victorian one, and, more importantly, a symbolic merger of the manufacturing class with the landed aristocracy: a fantasy empowerment which is presented here as a taming process which softens

and civilizes the unpolished manners of the middle classes as it appropriates their world-historical energies. (Bivona 1990, 5–6)

Thus, the novel is not simply political because it addresses more or less directly political characters and events, or the 'agitation which for a year and a half had shaken England to its very centre' as Disraeli chooses to put it (Disraeli 1989, 36), nor because it works its fictions against a discernibly 'true' historical narrative (however manipulated). It is also political – and this having to do with the politics and epistemology of national identity of a 'new' bourgeois generation and the question of a somewhat self-reflexive narrative mediating the desires of a reading public eager to have presented to it a progressive, yet essentially English vision of itself – in that it tells a 'historicized' tale whereby the new and the old commingle in the name of nation and as an articulation of national discourse. And what perhaps is most telling is that Disraeli's text, and the two subsequent novels of the trilogy, actively mediate the political, social and economic transactions between classes in the instance of national transition, can be read as politically justifying its entire trajectory from that one line, cited above. The rhetoric of agitation and solicitation, touching the very core of Englishness (wherever that core or centre may chance to be located; Disraeli is silent on this point), is so forceful, not to say violent, in condition, that the political necessity, not to say inevitability for political transformation, is all but assured.

IV

History, as Disraeli conceives it at least, is ironic, *Coningsby* capturing 'the quintessence of bourgeois theater' (Rancière 2004b, 133). The 'entertainment' of Thomas Hood's 'The Song of the Shirt', is of a far grimmer variety, belonging alongside Disraeli's spectacle of dehumanized pit workers depicted in *Sybil*, who, coming forth at the 'cessation of *English* toil', number amongst themselves, stripped to the waist and 'clad in male attire', 'the mothers of England!' (Disraeli 1985, 177, 178) Though not often read today, Hood's brief prominence in the early part of the nineteenth century (he died in 1845) coincided with what both contemporaries such as John Stuart Mill (Mill 1964–1991, 410) and, subsequently, critics in the twentieth century have perceived as a crisis in English poetry and what Peter Simonsen has described as 'the decline of the art under commercial pressure' (Simonsen 2006, 41; see also Wolfson 2006, n.p.). That this crisis was experienced, and is attested to, suggests the economic transformation of the ideological superstructure was far-reaching; however, it also points to the fact that so swift, sweeping and far-reaching was the radical alteration of English culture across the generations of the Industrial and French Revolutions, that poetry had, with the generation of the Romantic poets, reached certain limits: in articulation and representation, certainly, but also in perception, so profound was the cultural, material and historical sea-change as its effects were registered on aesthetic subjectivity.

Of Thomas Hood, Susan Wolfson writes: 'the strangest but inescapable feature of Hood's imagination is his seemingly helpless attraction to puns and wordplay, in all kinds of situations, even at the risk of offending – or with the effect of satirizing – decorum. This would be the basic fuel of his fame as the leading English comic poet of the 1830s and 1840s' (Wolfson 2006). Situated by Wolfson as a late Romantic poet whose reputation has suffered in the critical climate of the second half of the twentieth century as a result of being both male and middle class, (2006, n.p.), and yet as someone William Michael Rossetti claimed to be (with not a little hyperbole, perhaps), 'the finest English poet between the generation of Shelley and the generation of Tennyson' (Rossetti 1872, xxxi), Hood has largely been neglected (see Simonsen 2006, 61 n. 4). While attention has been necessary with regard to women poets of the nineteenth century, and particularly the period 1820–1850 as Susan Wolfson argues, subsequent ideological revision and commercial publishing interests in revisionist anthologies has rendered Hood, a 'belated Keatsian' and fierce social satirist, largely inaccessible. This is, perhaps, because his wit, verbal dexterity and punning were forms which, to modern critical sensibilities and institutional orthodoxies, proved incompatible with 'a set of phobias and fears about the vulnerability of the human body to catastrophes of various kinds, and the agonies of poverty and the brutally exploited working class [that] concentrated his energies in his last decade' (Wolfson 2006, http://www.erudit. org/revue/ron/2000/v/n19/005932ar. html). Thus it is, as Peter Simonsen argues vigorously, 'Hood's poetry must be approached in its own terms rather than terms informed by High-Romantic ideals' (Simonsen 2006, 42); which is to say, in his undermining of 'central aspects of High-Romantic conceptions of disinterested, inspired, and spontaneous composition', Hood's 'poetic is predicated on "legibility" rather than sincere self-expression and on achieving an immediate, powerful "effect"' (Simonsen 2006, 47). Fully aware of his market and the power of the many influential and widely read periodicals in which he chiefly published – and not a few of which he also worked on as editor – Hood engaged the market and modern print technology with a directness rarely witnessed in poets. For Hood, we might reflect, if the personal was not the political exactly, then the poetic certainly was.

One of the most anthologized of Victorian poems, and the work for which Hood is principally remembered, 'The Song of the Shirt', published initially anonymously in *Punch*, presents a stark protest against the abuses of labour. William Michael Rossetti, Hood's first editor, remarked that 'it ran like wildfire, and rang like tocsin, through the land' (Rossetti 1872, xxvi). More than this, the poem 'saved both the periodical and Hood's career' (Simonsen 2006, 57). Its force works precisely because of its sentimentalized exploitation of the image by which it seeks to convey the inequities and suffering caused under capitalism. Suffering and sentiment become a powerful dialogical form, exceeding mere representation and engaging in the historicity of contradiction, literally; for the poem not only stages contra-diction in its voices, it is also an act of contra-diction, speaking out against work, and yet staging the work aesthetically in its rhythm and repetition. The poem thus transposes itself from being at one level a constative poetic statement to becoming an analogical performative: making appear the work and the woman working through the 'making' that poetry names, the poem also 'makes' poetry in a modern mode of production – repetitive, exploitative, tedious. The 'technology' of dehumanizing labour is transferred into the technicity of poetic production. Poetry thus debases itself as a sign of the times, countersigning its form with the anonymity of labour, and transforming itself into a recording medium through which the voice of the poor returns, in attempting to offer an analogy for the experience of the other, in this case, the working woman.

That said, this is not a poem that addresses large-scale, organized, industrial work but, instead, the plight of seamstresses. The figure of the seamstress had been 'a feature of a few literary descriptions by John Galt and Dickens in the 1830s' (Simonsen 2006, 57), and indeed Dickens returns to the figure in a haunting Grotesque manner with Jenny Wren, in *Our Mutual Friend* in 1865. However, it was 'not until 1842 [that] writers [began] to pay attention to her as a subject of real suffering' (Simonsen 2006, 57). 'The Song of the Shirt' capitalizes, so to speak, on the gendered subject, extracting and so humanizing the single victimized woman from an otherwise undifferentiated mass of workers in the nineteenth century. To risk a speculation, it may just be that Hood (praised by near contemporary readers as distinct as Engels, Poe and Baudelaire), chose the 'wrong' working-class group to whom the poetic voice was given. This lone working woman, whose gender is thrown into relief by her own clothing, her 'unwomanly rags' (l.3), stitches seemingly unceasingly, from morning to night, and from one year's end to the next. Her condition is foregrounded for the middle-class reader supposedly ignorant of the conditions of the working classes in England by a fragmented, distressed corporeal representation, as well as through some telling analogies that operate effectively in the nineteenth century because of their cultural currency. Concerning the body, the woman is figured '[w]ith fingers weary and worn' and 'eyelids heavy and red' (l.1–2); and again with 'eyes [that] are heavy and dim!' (l.19), from which come tears that hinder work (l.79). Such effects may well 'jar sensibility' (Wolfson 2006), with their intensity of focus and their insistent *petit point* attention to corporeal agony. The reader's eyes are expected to suffer seeing in detail the suffering of another's eyes, as words replace stitches; our hands hold the finely wrought text, as the seamstress's hands hold the textile. Economizing on a monstrous analogy and, once more, capitalizing on gender, Hood fetishes the body in distress through this restricted synecdochic signalling of female frailty and suffering, thereby aestheticizing the politics of representation and seeking to produce a sensuous effect in the reader. As for those analogical elements mentioned, the plight of the English working woman under capitalism is compared with that of Muslim women under Islam, who, though suffering as 'slaves' under the 'Babarous Turk' (ll.13–15), are considered to be comparatively better off than the condition of a woman made abject by 'Christian work' (l.16). The image is then displaced and reiterated, figured through difference and yet made more powerful in the suggestive similarity between foreign and domestic suffering, with reference to the forced labour of criminals (l.52).

Interestingly, the comparative critique, staged through the analogy of the working-class Christian woman's condition and suffering with those of the slave, the Muslim, and the criminal, is almost precisely the same as the comparisons drawn by Disraeli in the representation of the pit workers, in the opening chapter of Part Three of *Sybil*. In the shared representation we read the experience of the other at the heart of aesthetic estrangement as the signs of a differentiated historicity, inasmuch as there is a call to bear witness and so assume ethical responsibility, in order that 'moral law be realized historically', according to Kant (Karatani 2005, 128). Analogy works to cover, though not close up, the gap between a *then* and a *now*, whereby, in Kant's phrase, the writer demands a realization of an ethical imperative, that 'you use humanity, whether in your own person or in the person of any other, always at the same time as an end, *never merely as* a means' (Kant 1970, 44). Both Hood and Disraeli illustrate what happens through assumed historical inevitability 'in the "production and the relation of production" in the commodity economy' (Karatani 2005, 128–9), where humans are only ever means, and not an end, while, through such representation and the analogies they employ, the suffering of humans as *merely* a means historically and materially suggests that being become an end. *How* one reads representation becomes the test of ethical responsibility.

Although such allusions and analogies are powerful, the Gothic dimension of Hood's work ought not to be overlooked. It surfaces briefly in 'The Song of the Shirt', through the seamstress's reflective consideration of a ghostly double

> That Phantom of grisly bone
> I hardly fear its terrible shape
> It seems so like my own –
> It seems so like my own (ll.34–7)

Whilst Gothic effect suits Hood's heightened dramatic form – the spectre of the seamstress doubles the formal doubling – such uncanny ventriloquial power did not sit easily with certain of the poem's critics (see Simonsen 2006, 58). Such 'Gothicization', though, is no more peculiar to Hood than are his comparisons between Christian women, criminals and non-Western women. As already considered in Chapters One and Two, Gothic provides tropic and discursive material and form for Dickens, amongst others, and is perhaps most famously captured in Dickens's own critique of 'uncaring capitalism' in *A Christmas Carol*, published in the same year as Hood's poem. The apparition in 'The Song of the Shirt' foreshadows, of course, the seamstress's death. More than this, though, the haunting of the self by its other figures as an uncanny, irrational excess within the poetic economy. It draws the reader's attention to the poem's central motif of doubling and displacement, and with that the work of iterability and analogy as this is played out in the woman's own repetitious recognition of the familiar resemblance. Arguably, the uncanniness of the moment is captured in the repetition of the line 'it seems so like my own'.

These are not the only reiterated phrases of course. Reiteration is, we might say, the law of economy *and* excess in the poem. As Peter Simonsen observes

> We should not be surprised to find refrain-like and almost incantatory patterns of repetition in poetry that purports to be imitative of a work song, one of whose generic traits is indeed a foregrounding of repetition (hence also its proliferation

76	Literature, in Theory

of alliteration and internal rhyme). Nevertheless, a supplementary explanation of the meaning of these patterns of repetition (which are equally present in Hood's framing stanzas and in the framed work-song) may be sketched: one that sees them as examples of Hood's radical artifice – his extreme foregrounding of the poetic sign ... However, rather than being unintentionally humorous and thus sounding insincere they powerfully enact the mechanical repetition which informs both the nature of the seamstress' labour and that of the professional poet working to meet deadlines. They are not excessive superficial surface effects that disrupt the poem's meaning, but the very opposite.

The chiasmus, 'Seam, and gusset, and band, / Band, and gusset, and seam', for instance, almost physically embodies and figures in an iconic manner the end-lessly circular and repetitive needlework it is about. (Simonsen 2006, 58)

Such circularity and iterable weave does more than physically embody, it transforms the text from within, the linguistic play becoming that which registers its performative dimension. While Simenson is precisely right in his commentary, it does not go far enough to observe that an analogy is drawn between seamstress and poet. Left at this, the remark denies the political urgency of the text, rendering the seamstress as exploited melodramatic figure (however difficult, a poet/editor's hardships are *not* those of a working woman). Rather, in its ventriloquism, Hood's tropes of doubling enact the work. Such doubling marks the poem with a double work of 'sewing up' and continuing the motion, somewhat relentlessly perhaps. Indeed, the poem is framed by such a gesture. Moving in a somewhat circular motion, the text opens and closes with a double image of the woman stitching endlessly and, equally endlessly, singing the 'Song of the Shirt' (ll.1–8, ll.81–9). The poem is thus constructed clearly as a performative loop that enacts the stitching motion, whilst also signifying – *through* the mechanistic motions of the poem – the attempt to 'meet the demands of a thoroughly commercialised system of commodity production' (Simonsen 2006, 59). This larger gesture is reiterated within and across verses through tedious reiterations of phrases such as 'work-work-work' and 'Stitch! stitch! stitch!', and again in the chiasmic reversal of lines 'Seam, and gusset, and band, / Band and gusset, and seam' (ll.19–20). It is through both the image of stitching and the suggestion of the song that the exhausting ineluctability of forced work is inscribed. Such doubling is given an internal echo in the woman's reference to 'Sewing at once, with a double thread, / A Shroud as well as a Shirt' (ll.31–2). Work taken on to maintain mere living existence becomes the inevitable cause of, and connection with, death, itself anticipated in every iterable motion. There is a further doubling and displacement, this time in an ironically contrapuntal effect, and so re-enforced by Hood through the rhyme of 'stitch' and 'pitch'. In this way the text oscillates between its constative, descriptive purpose, and its performative dimension: for not only is the poem 'the song of the shirt', it is also a 'recording', a gesture of attestation to a performance, orally and corporeally, of that song. 'Song' thus refers to the text as literal figure, and to the woman's work and her words, as both metaphor and internalized articulation of the song.

In this manner, Hood plays on the economy of resonance between and across iterable levels, picked out in Hood's needlepoint images that serve to compose his social satire. This precision is captured in several ways by Hood. On the one hand, it is woven *by* and *in* the economics of synecdochic play, from 'rags' to 'shirt' to 'shroud'; life, work, social relation, exploitation and death in the dance of clothing. On the other hand, Hood threads, and so depicts another tapestry of social relation: through the images of a different discursive and ideological relation and order, the anonymous female work who provides the linen for the nation's men is sewn analogically to women of other classes, the sisters and mothers of those who create the work and wear – and wear out, as Hood's pun has it – both the products of labour and the gendered labourers:

> 'Oh, Men, with Sisters dear!
> Oh, men, with Mothers and Wives!
> It is not linen you're wearing out
> But human creatures' lives!' (ll.25–8)

In a disconcerting moment of parabasis, the seamstress makes the direction of her address clear. From being captured and framed by the opening and closing stanzas, her voice turns directly towards the male readers of *Punch*.

The variations between the repetition that makes beginning and end are small but significant. While the first eight lines present the singing, sewing woman, in the final two stanzas, an additional line apostrophizes the song, the woman's work, and the very representation in which the poem has engaged, by turning to its audience in the expression of a desire: 'Would that its tone could reach the Rich!–' (l.88). Ingeniously, in this moment of parabasis, Hood makes the connection between wealth and the exploitation of the poor through labour not directly through the work but through the idea of song itself. The extra line adds a rhyme (pitch/rich), which is 'stitched' (as it were) into the poem's weave through desire that the 'tone' of the song would touch those who have served to directly or indirectly create the conditions of working women in England, and who also are being clothed as a result. In this question of tone the burden of the poem is carried: for it is what is caught in and by the tenor of the text, as a matter of sympathetic vibration in its semantic, ideological, and cultural threads, clews, and weave, that the interconnecting weft of Victorian society comes to be unravelled. As Peter Simsonsen argues, 'The Song of the Shirt' was amongst the most significant ideological texts of its day, for it played 'an important role in ushering in a characteristic interventionist poetry of public, social protest that reflects the Victorian World' (Simonsen 2006, 60). More than this, it inaugurates the possibility of a poetry attendant to the otherwise occluded manufacturing base on which, indirectly, the 'work' of poetry is made possible. Hood's performative 'Grotesque' (Armstrong 1993, 238–9) deforms the polite spaces of poetry, not through excess but through the dehumanization of the mechanical and its almost automated functionary, a voice of working-class protest within a machine not of its own making, which reveals through its 'enslaved consciousness' the material if not the 'historical conditions' of its possibility (Armstrong 1993, 239).

V

It can be argued that part of the historical condition of Thomas Hood's poem is its encrypted alienation or estrangement, which, today and in recent decades, the historicist critic has not always been able to access, much less read. Similarly, as we have seen, Charles Dickens relies on the estranging forces of melodrama, Gothic, the Grotesque, and sentiment in order to enable political and historical critique of material and ideological conditions. *Little Dorrit* constructs a historical narrative of the Victorian Era and Victorian political discourse and institutions by displacing the time of its events to the 1820s, and it is this generational displacement that opens the space of critique through the estranged registration of contemporary crisis. On the surface, *Little Dorrit* appears as less directly political, and yet has more to do with a certain political, or rather, ideological flow, which serves in turn to define the attitudes and perspectives of particular sections of the British public. Moreover, there is readable, in the historical work of the text, a doubling of political commentary, requiring an equally double focus on the part of the reader. Thus the novel is imbued with a certain strategic historicized anachronism, whereby 'time is out of joint', so to speak. On the one hand, one possible reading of the novel's political condition would turn its attention to the political situations of the 1820s, to the transformations and transitions underway, culturally and ideologically, in the Britain of William IV, particularly as these are given a somewhat oblique focus through the estranged cultural figure of Arthur Clennam. Clennam, already in his early forties upon his return to Britain, belongs to another age, and moves, with an 'other' perception or perspective on the Britain that he encounters. He is therefore written by Dickens so as to afford the reader of the 1850s a different vantage point from within English culture from which to view the national, cultural self. On the other hand, Dickens's representation of the Office of Circumlocution (itself a composite) as a figure for the practice, institution, discourse and ideological self-interest of British politics and its close relations with economic matters affecting the lives of all Britons, is readable as a somewhat transgenerational, if not transhistorical, figure.

It may be addressed, therefore, as speaking to the question of, as well as encrypting and analysing in, what Diane Elam describes as an 'alienating' manner (1996, 168), the political configuration in both moments, the 1820s and 1850s. Elam's analysis addresses particularly the question of time – of the several times of the novel (as she puts it, clock, psychic, organic) – which seem anachronistically untimely, and all the more modern for that. Time for Elam is particularly related to matters of debt (168–71), itself a literal and figural, and, indeed, political concern of *Little Dorrit*, wherein one may say that it is debt rather than money which circulates, and which comes back, within time, across time and from time to time (as if there were a manifestation of Nietzschean eternal recurrence haunting the structure of the Dickensian text or, as Elam herself suggests, a somewhat uncanny encounter with Heideggerian concepts of temporality *avant la lettre*; 168ff).

What Elam's reading of time does not specifically address are the related matters of facticity, historicity and the narratives of temporality that these invoke, and to which the question of the novel *qua* political is yoked. From this vantage point, and in order to read politically the very political question of national identity, the reader may come to understand that a persistent characteristic of Englishness in the nineteenth century is a certain mystification and obfuscation with regard to the perpetration and perpetuation of political power. In this political reading of the novel, we may also wish to read the Dickensian construction of the convolutions of political machinery as, itself, a political response, albeit one, which, as a number of critics of the novel have argued, is partially recuperated into the very same political aspects of Englishness which are manifested through the Circumlocution Office. What returns is not only Arthur Clennam; what returns is what is always already in operation, the recurring politics of the political system, a certain historical revenance and recirculation, which both defines and maintains the politics of Englishness and the Englishness of (these) politics.

To take the political reading further, thereby opening the politics of the novel in another fashion: there is also, very much, and very much encrypted in the text, a question of colonial political relations, not least in the references to Arthur Clennam's having worked in his father's business in China for many years and Flora Casby's inane questions concerning received English (narrative) wisdom about mandarins and pigtails. Jeremy Tambling's Foucauldian inflected reading of the text (1995, 98–128) takes full account of the various histories which inform *Little Dorrit*, looking at how both historical past and political present come to inform the novel as an anachronistic and political site. The background of the novel's composition is the Crimean War (99), while the Opium War of 1840–1842 led to another war (1856–1860), in the name of Free Trade (Tambling 1995, 116–17). Yet the Clennam firm's interest in China belongs very firmly to the period between the 1780s and 1820s (the period of Arthur's youth) of the East India Company, colonial trade and imperial expansion (see Tambling 1995, 116). Clennam's return to Britain occurs, arguably, at a point in British history where foreign trade begins to be superseded by domestic economic enterprise.

So, while from one perspective, Clennam may, as Patricia Ingham correctly suggests, draw together the various strands of the narrative by his 'itinerant' activity (Ingham 1996b, 101), temporally, historically, Clennam's mobility, we might say his *motivation* (or at least the motivation behind his agency), is to thread a discontinuous weave between periods and moments of English political and economic endeavour, between the various presents, pasts and futures of the text, so as to open to view the persistence of the national political interest. If, from one perspective, 'change' is a Victorian word, in the text of *Little Dorrit*, maintenance (alongside change) also, equally, has a cogent political valence. As Disraeli had sought to bring together the aristocracy and productive middle-classes, so Dickens, through the figure of Clennam, observes the political and economical transformations *and* inheritances. Clennam tries to adapt, leaving the parental firm because it is no longer of the times, and eventually turns to the economic potential and industry (in more than one sense) of Daniel Doyce. (Although, this also is somewhat anachronistic, Doyce's workshop in Bleeding Heart Yard having more of an artisanal endeavour about it than the mass productivity of the industrial revolution.) Yet this fails also, because Clennam is always figured as hopelessly out of date and out of time.

Thus there is, in *Little Dorrit*'s reading of the condition of England, a sense of political ambivalence: Arthur Clennam, perhaps a typical English businessman, no different except in degree from either the modern entrepreneur Mr. Merdle or the ageing remnant of the late eighteenth century, Mr. Dorrit, fails (despite the projected romantic happiness of the novel's conclusion). For, we read *Little Dorrit* as suggesting that, without radical political transformation, the English imprison themselves, and will continue to do so, metaphorically and philosophically if not literally. They haunt themselves with the spectre of their own failed possibilities, their own identities. Mr. Meagles's brass weighing scales may well be a sign of the times, but of which times we're not exactly sure. 'Do Not Forget', the phrase inherited from Arthur's father (ironically, appropriately) suggests that, whether one is located in the 1780s, the 1820s or the 1850s, in not forgetting, the English can never move on, trapped as they are in a revenant circumlocution of the self-same, an auto-immune myopia.

Given the imminent political and economic rise of the US, particularly, and Germany, shortly thereafter, in the period following the publication of *Little Dorrit*, the novel becomes available as all too prescient in its commentary on a people blind to the ghosts that dwell among them, and which, in recirculating, causes them to reiterate, in their historical condition, the very actions that have always already determined their limits. Yet, the surface of the political aside, it is important that we recognize in a properly politicized reading *apropos* the dialogical temporal frame and the aporia it institutes – a limit registered in and as the historical relation between the 1820s and the 1850s – that *Little Dorrit*'s critique of English economic and political culture is grounded in a reading of that culture as the manifestation of a disabling modernity. As much as *Little Dorrit* is an encrypted narrative addressing the *realpolitik* and the lived individual expressions and consequences of economic and ideological systems, it is also, too, a novel concerned with, or, at least, seeking to express the epistemology of the modern and the crisis at the heart of modernity's representation. In modernity, Maurice Merleau-Ponty suggests, the 'rational universe which is open in principle to human endeavours to know it and act within it, is replaced by a kind of knowledge and art that is characterised by difficulty and reserve, one full of restrictions' (Merleau-Ponty 2008, 77–8). In modernity, Merleau-Ponty continues, we have a representation 'of the world which excludes neither fissures nor lacunae, a form of action which is unsure of itself, or, at any rate, no longer blithely assumes it can obtain universal assent' (Merleau-Ponty 2008, 78). Clearly, Dickens's England of the 1820s is not a rational universe open to human endeavours, whether in principle or in reality. Circumlocution is not merely an office of government, and England is not a police office but a culture of civil servants, procrastinators, and disingenuous dissimulators. Arthur Clennam may offer us the singular personification of someone characterized by difficulty and reserve, but restriction is everywhere, and not just in the material boundaries of the Marshalsea. Fissures, lacunae, gaps, secrets, silences and occlusions structure the fabric of society, a society oblivious to its own tattered and ruined condition – in this, the Clennam house, shored against its own ruin (as it were) is just the most typical English construction. And it is in the fissure opened by the novel between the time of its publication and that of its narrative that we witness the extent to which one generation traces the other.

VI

The matter of epistemological lacunae (touched on repeatedly thus far) that is at the heart of comprehension, interpretation and the perception of historical condition is remarked persistently in narratives of the nineteenth century. Wilkie Collins's *The Moonstone* (1999) addresses such matters in an inventive manner through its multiple narrators and their culturally and epistemologically positioned, partial perceptions, while resisting the efforts to supply pat answers to the problems and questions raised around the status of historically conditioned knowledge. In this, Collins's novel bears a superficial resemblance to another work published in the same year (1868) with multiple narrators or witnesses to events that remain beyond experience, Robert Browning's *The Ring and the Book* (2001).

An apparently, transparently, disingenuous question is asked in *The Ring and The Book*: what is 'the thing signified' (1.32)? One possible, enigmatic response, might be taken from the following: 'The somehow may be thishow' (1.706). There is that which it is difficult, if not impossible, to figure. Yet, despite this, and the aporetic encounter that appears indirectly figured in the 'somehow' may 'somehow' come to be refigured, however apodictically, as the singular manifestation of whatever may make itself known, coming to appear in – or as – the *thishow*; all of which may refer to: the making of a ring; the story of the forging of this object; the spinning of the gold, the pure substance intermixed with alloy to allow for ease of work; the subsequent process by which the alloy is removed, the purity, or, let us say figuratively, the 'truth' of the gold returned by the craft of the artificer, who having shown himself, then vanishes; but in the interim acknowledging that such 'substance of me interfused the gold' (1.682) until 'I disappeared; the book grew all in all' (1.687); in order that the reader might appear to see not only how 'something dead may get to live again' (1.729) but more directly, and without mediation, 'the dead alive once more' (1.799); *as if* there were 'no trope at all' (1.1306); and this in proof that, from out a 'web of words' (1.1277), otherwise a 'cold black score, mere music for the mind' (1.1216), there seems to arrive 'voices we call evidence, / Uproar in the echo'(1.833–34) translated as 'the passage to be conned' (1.1253) in order to produce 'vibrations in the general mind' (1.844) of the 'British public' (1.410, 1379); those who otherwise 'love the level, corn and wine, / Much cattle and the many-folded fleece' (1.1338–39); for readers such as these. the poet risks everything in order that 'What was again may be' (1.1407); so, transformation, interchanging, translation; whereby 'the printed voice ... lives now as then' (1.167); in which, the proof also that 'I fused my live soul and that inert stuff' (1.469), elsewhere apprehended as 'motions of mine / That quickened, made the inertness malleable' (1.701–2), and foregrounded as such; but only so as to produce 'This that I mixed with truth,' (l.701); in this, we are vouchsafed the image that the artificer, the 'I' 'Creates no, but resuscitates, perhaps' (l.719); 'I' enters, as it were, 'spark-like', putting 'old powers to play' (l.755), the self at once both conductor and conduit for 'galvanism' (l.739); and, again, in this, there is 'mistily seen, murmuringly heard' perhaps (l.758), that which remains unnameable, except indirectly, as the 'something else'(l.699), the sign, a 'figure, a symbol, say' (l.31) not merely of mere 'imitative craft' (l.3) but that craft itself, which offers and so translates itself into a 'God-glimpse' (l.596).

Concerning all of which the poet entreats the reader urgently, 'hold that figure fast!' (l.142; is this not a joke?), even as he wonders 'Is fiction which makes fact alive, fact too?' (l.705). The first book of Browning's *The Ring and the Book*, places the reader in front of the figure of an author who, like an over-eager dramatist, steps before his audience before the play has begun, in order to reveal the details of the drama in its entirety. Apparently uncertain as to whether he is offered in the creative act a glimpse of God's creative power, or whether in imitating such divine force, he assumes a god-like condition, Browning risks Faustian (l.759) damnation through a double act of writing and invention in order that the past may be momentarily brought back to life; not as itself but through its traces, through the interfusing of the self with the dead documents, both printed and hand written (l.85), the 'posthumous papers', if you will, of the old yellow book discovered and purchased by Browning in Florence. Putting himself into the work in more ways than one, Browning foregrounds himself in the act of purchase, reading and writing, and so interleaves those found papers with his own writing, itself analogous, he assures us (hold that figure fast), with the work of the goldsmith.

However, in doing so, not only does Browning commune with the past, acting as a spirit guide of sorts for his readers, he also places himself into the work. Becoming one more character, he also enacts his role self-reflexively as one of a series of creators. Moving from the 'imitative craft' of the jeweller to the observation of a statue made by Baccio Bandinella (l.45), and from there to the recollection of da Vinci's *Mona Lisa* (l.72–3), the work of Alexandre Dumas *fils* (l.78), Horace (l.79), possibly Byron and Milton (l.308, 1157, 1201), Luigi Ademollo (l.369), Corelli and Handel (1214), and, in those references to galvanism and resuscitation perhaps even Mary Shelley (if not her monstrous creation), Browning announces himself the latest in a catalogue of artists. Book One is 'interfilleted' (l.138) with a hierarchy – and also a history – of the arts, proceeding from the artisanal and applied arts to those considered aesthetically higher. In this, the argument is made that ultimately a greater purity is capable of being produced, when the artist withdraws himself, the alloy, from the work, much like the goldsmith, to appear indirectly only to act on inanimate writing so as to re-present life, phantoms of lives past, as had Faust, in an imitation of the artificer, the creator God.

There is in this a complex, not to say baroque process at work for Browning in his historical-narrative project. An overlaying, an interweaving, as well as an 'interfilleting', occurs at many different levels, with many different strands and patterns in this first book of a poem, the initials of which are themselves a siglum, being also the poet's initials of course. Not least amongst such interanimations are the translations of the printed and written matter of the yellow book and the various proleptic stagings of their narrative threads, as Book I anticipates in several retellings of the narrative materials of Books II–IX. Such narrative variations are, themselves, retellings of each other, even as Browning informs us, Roman law of the early modern period is written as an anachronistic co-mingling of 'dead' and 'live' language, Latin and Italian, evidence of which – the 'Apostolic Chamber's type' (l.149) – is reported (relayed through Browning's intermediation) indirectly in English. Trope substitutes trope; one form of aesthetic production displaces another, even as it gives way to yet more, each as the appropriate figure, the apposite, figural 'truth'; metaphor drifts, becoming reiterated, supplemented, simulated, in a vertiginous seriality of substitutions at the structural, narrative and thematic levels of the text, whereby different modes and different pasts interpolate one another in Browning's spectropoetic switchboard. And, of course, the differing narratives, anticipated in Book One's staging of the differing précis of the matter of both the trial and the events leading up to it, compete with and displace one another, in a contest of contending claims to truth, 'Adduced in proof . . . on either side' (147).

All of which only begins to unveil the complex conditions to which the poet draws his readers' attention by which poetry is in service to the past, bearing witness, whilst, at the same time, and in the different temporal moments of a reading 'now', irreducible to a present, persists in an ideological intervention through poetry-making regarding the politics and poetics of historicity and witnessing. Undeniably, the question of poetic production is not simply a formal game. It is not just, if at all, a play, which, similarly to and yet differently from *The Moonstone* (published in the same year as Browning began the publication of *The Ring and the Book*), asks to what extent the past is knowable. Like Collins's novel, Browning's poem, or the first book in any case, also asks about the role of the present subject in the invention and interpretation of that past, in however a coded fashion such an interrogation proceeds. Even as Browning toys with the conceit of the role of artist as being analogous with God, that establishment of a spectral heritage of artists across the ages stresses the significance of art in the communication of past in a mode comprehensible to an audience in the present of the work's reception. Every mode of production involves in its invention the introduction of an alterity. In this manner the singularity of event, or experience of that event, may be transmitted in iterable fashion in what Derek Attridge calls the 'transformation of the cultural field' (2004, 25) through the aesthetic projection of the work's idiocultural idiom. A singular articulation in itself, the text or artwork as idiocultural idiom has the possibility to 'make the past live' as the phrase has it, but not as it was – only in translation. However, as Browning appears to realize through his ethical self-interrogation in Book One, the past is neither singular material moment nor available as such. It is there only in phantasmagoric form, mediated as the manifest number of traces, other textual forms, other works of art (poetry, painting, sculpture, architecture, prose, drama), which are the singular idiocultural iteration of other traces of events – and so on, and so forth. The very nature of the old yellow book (as Browning presents it to us) informs us of as much, with its documents conveying a trial and evidence given in that trial, conducted indirectly according to the juridical and legislative pre-texts produced by the heteroglot 'interfilleting' of Latin and Italian, and subsequently inscribed as competing and contradictory tongues.

Thus the poet seeks to bear witness to that which cannot be presented or re-presented, and to assume a responsibility for the dead in risking a response to the various voices, echoes and motions of the pen in different 'tongues'. Opening all the circuits across the centuries, Browning seeks to give a glimpse of a truth concerning the past that exceeds any factual account. As *The Ring and the Book* lets us see, however indirectly, what we call history is irreducible to the fact/fiction binarism. The past is best served, if at all and in the face of all its multiplying, proliferating texts that offer the reader the encounter with the undecidable, through the risk of rendering its traces as poetic truth; or as Browning has it, the production of the 'lingot truth' (1.459), that which is pure within the mix. It is the risk entailed in the assumption of ethical response and responsibility without justification that is captured in the line: 'The somehow may be thishow' (1.706). Browning's caution indicates the impossibility of knowing for sure that his representation of history is either justified or in any manner accurate. His portmanteau word, *thishow* is an effective economical device and worth noting, once more. *This* serves to indicate both a spatial and temporal location, that of the text – this text, this reading, this act of interpretation – and the subsequent supplementary reading that arrives with the reader's reading of Browning. Things are 'this how'. The thing signified is '*this how*'.

Browning's phrase thus appears to decide on the undecidable, and so move beyond his personal experience of the aporia engendered by the encounter with the other, in the effort to read that which the text reveals as unavailable – the truth of historical event. Risking a decision in the face of the crisis of representation, he wagers on figuration in the grounding, the fashioning (to mix my historicist and materialist metaphors), that takes place in this present entity, the poem and the book being held and read, and the present (and the present subject's) moment of interpretation. *This(i/s)how I see it.* The I has it: interpolating oneself into the imagined event, I galvanizes the dead matter, in an *inmixing* of self and other, past and present. Indeed, understanding this, one also understands a process of reversal and inversion in the text. There is no stable binarism of pure/mixed or pure/impure. Indeed, as the poet's example and analogy between ring-making and poetry-making informs us, far from being extrinsic to purity, the 'alloy', a debased but necessary ingredient, is indispensable, crucial to the production of purity, so-called.

For all that Browning remarks of the jeweller's process concerning the sudden acid-erasure of the alloy,[1] which, contaminating the ingot or lingot had made possible the shaping of form, no 'pure' proof or truth would be possible without that contamination. Concomitantly there is no past except as it is 'inmixed' or interfilleted' with the iterable supplement of singular translation, without the arrival of the other's tongue, given and giving tongue in the subject's own mouth, through the present subject's pen. (Which pen, of course, in opening the past in the present in translated fashion, therefore leaves its own singular and idiocultural trace to remain open and iterable in the future.) This 'alchemical', though not necessarily Faustian, process unveils the past within the present as much as the present's apprehension of the past. And as with Mephistopheles's 'staging' of the phantasmagoria of Helen of Troy for Faust, so Browning's *thishow* is also *this show*, this enactment of history's events, in the only manner available. Just as one cannot remain with the undecidable, so one cannot remain with the past, even though the past might just remain with us and in us, though never as itself.

If the processes of inmixing, interpolation, interfilleting and, with these, the effects of the past's interpellation of the present subject admit of inversion also, whereby what was debased becomes elevated, what was marginal becomes central, this is perhaps no accident. Earlier, it was noted how, in Book One, Browning catalogues the arts, his historical trajectory, from the early modern period certainly but also with intimated interpolations from the classics and the Bible, being readable also as an architectonic cataloguing of the types of arts. In this hierarchical order, the goldsmith's or jeweller's craft is perceivable as the lowest and most practical artisanal practice while the work of God (or nature) is the highest. Yet Browning transforms the order, risking implications of a reversal or inversion of location by analogous association in his textual weave. No, more than this he dares to erase the gradations, bringing low and high together in the figure of the poet's attempt to produce the truth of the past. If it concerns him, at one instance that, like Faust he risks damnation in mimicking God, inasmuch as resuscitation imitates the creation of life, then there is another movement at work here. In connecting the divine artificer with the artisan via the medium of poetry (or the medium who is the poet); in implying by the work of analogy that God's productions are like those of the jeweller in their perceived purity, high and low are not only reversed or inverted. They are, in effect, revealed as the same and yet not the same, as singular instances of the other, remaining singular and therefore incommensurable, but apprehended as non-synonymous substitutions in the apprehension of truth. And this takes place not through the offices of the poet, but of poetry. Or, to be more precise, *poetics*, wherein which singular mode of performative articulation 'Art may tell a truth / *Obliquely*' (XII. 859–60; emphasis added), despite *and yet because of* what Browning calls – thereby admitting to impurity as necessary to the medium – 'the mediate word' (XII. 861).

VII

That 'mediate word', the *thishow*, is both translation and position, locus and communication, signature and post. In *Victorian Poetry: Poetry, Poetics and Politics*, Isobel Armstrong offers some brief though significant insights into *The Ring and the Book*. In a chapter that focuses on Browning's work through the 1850s and beyond when the poet and Elizabeth Barrett Browning lived as ex-patriots in Italy until her death in 1861, Armstrong frames her analysis with reference to *The Ring and the Book* at either end of that chapter. In a gesture that is readable as imitative of Browning's own teleological and circular structure, Armstrong identifies the language of Browning's poetry of this time in general as '[i]diosyncratic, bizarre, arcane' (Armstrong 1993, 284). Associating such language with an ostensible retreat from the political, which had marked earlier work, Armstrong points out that the commitment to the political remained, with Browning constantly taking a more radical line, much to the discomfort of conservative critics, such as Walter Bagehot (1826–1877), in England (Armstrong 1993, 284). One particular remark of Bagehot's from an 1869 review of *The Ring and the Book* quoted by Armstrong suggests, in its assessment of the poet, that Bagehot unwittingly plays Gabriel Betteredge to Browning's Franklin Blake: 'The colouring of his mind and the colouring of his work are alike Italian' (Bagehot, cit. Armstrong 1993, 284).

We may read here how the notion of a national identity of the mind is, for some, quite a serious matter and concern; voice is clearly received ideologically, and from within the voice of the poet the ontology of the foreign other is perceived. More than this though, we are offered a glimpse of shared cultural codes that Collins is at pains to parody. In addition to the conservative commentary on the impurities of Browning's cultural and national identity as this is read through *The Ring and the Book*, Bagehot sought to locate Browning's cultural 'tendencies' through the identification of the poet's work as early as 1864 in a review article that compared Tennyson's *Enoch Arden* and Browning's *Dramatis Personae*, according to a modified (some might say distorted) version of Ruskin's definition of Grotesque art. Bagehot does however share, with both Betteredge and Ruskin, a very English distrust of 'notions and abstractions', as well as a tendency 'to philosophise . . . to care for schemes of thought'.[2] As Armstrong explains, in Bagehot's essay on Tennyson and Browning, the categories therein developed are 'Pure' or classical art (Wordsworth), 'Ornate' or Romantic art (Tennyson) and 'Grotesque' or medieval art (Armstrong 1993, 285). The last, medieval art, was highly influential from the mid-Victorian period onwards. Not only did Tennyson and Browning draw on medieval, Arthurian and other pre-modern sources, such were the influences, however seemingly anachronistic this might appear, on avant-garde art movements, such as the Pre-Raphaelites, as has been well documented, and, of course, William Morris's Arts and Crafts movement.

Bagehot's categories need not detain us long, but Armstrong's definitions are invaluable for situating an understanding not only, immediately, of Bagehot's reaction to Browning, but, more importantly, Browning's work in particular historical and ideological contexts. Working according to a somewhat hygienically expressed typology, developed in part from what can only be taken as a misreading of Ruskin's *Modern Painters* (1846) and dictated by a belief that the poet and artist's responsibility is to depict *types* in art as they are found in reality (Bagehot 1999, 1310),[3] Bagehot perceives 'pure' or classical art as 'an antidote to anxieties rather than expressing them'. It expresses a 'pure Type, whole, unified, with . . . verbal economy', and without 'mutilating' its object (Armstrong 1993, 285; Bagehot 1999, 1312). On the other hand, Ornate or Romantic art occludes its anxieties, disguising 'the unpleasing Type by loading it with superfluous and distracting detail [used to produce] . . . a sense of mystery and illusion' (*VP* 285. Finally, the Grotesque, i.e. Browning struggles 'with obstacles'; it is 'encumbered with incongruities'; and it presents the reader with 'distorted and imperfect image[s]' (Bagehot cit. Armstrong 1993, 285; Bagehot 1999, 1316). The Grotesque is thus the aesthetic-ideological antithesis for Bagehot to the 'pure, fixed, universal theological Type'. The problem for Bagehot in regard to Browning is that his poetry is not what Bagehot is pleased to call *literatesque*, a somewhat Grotesque neologism on the critic's part intended to be the literary equivalent of *picturesque*, and defined as that which is 'fit to be put into a book' (Bagehot 1999, 1309). Significantly, in Bagehot's eyes, Browning's poetry is not *literatesque*. It portrays the degraded, the degenerate and the abnormal, as Armstrong makes clear (Armstrong 1993, 285; Bagehot 1999, 1316). Bagehot's model silently – or not so silently – thus aligns the theological with the evolutionary; and these are further employed in the cultural agenda of defining Englishness, when Browning is identified as un-English (and implicitly pre-modern as well as tainted by association with, what for Bagehot would be. undoubtedly Catholic art), foreign both in his thinking and his modes of representation. More than this, Browning is associated, somewhat sneakingly by Bagehot, as '*half* educated', whose poetry is a sign of the times, published in a world where there are greater numbers of readers but few who know how to discern 'quality' (Bagehot 1999, 1318).

I take what appears to be a somewhat lengthy digression away from the immediate task of commenting on *The Ring and the Book* in order to situate through this example of the poet's reception ways in which *The Ring* might be approached in a more affirmative or open manner when considering its 'Grotesque' and 'medieval' force, *pace* Bagehot. Without denying Bagehot's perceptions of this cultural phenomenon, how might the understanding of distortion and incongruity be read for its alterity and singularity? Bagehot's is not the only voice of the period crying in a cultural wilderness, when he dismisses what he calls the '*buried* life [of] the spiritual mediaeval' in Browning's poetry (Bagehot 1999, 1318). Equally, the terms in which Bagehot locates Browning, the historical and cultural locations or sources from which he discerns Browning deriving his work, are not peculiar to Browning alone, as I have already intimated. Idiosyncratic, bizarre, arcane. To Isobel Armstrong's categorization of Browning's poetic language, we might also add, anachronistic. For it is precisely in the strange intensity and violent motions of the language and its interchangeable, morphing analogous tropes that are alluded to in the reading of Book One of *The Ring and the Book* above, that the reader may find all that is strange and estranging for Walter Bagehot. That the critic does not perceive the complexity of pattern, but merely finds such complex 'interfilleting' repulsive and disturbing in its seeming violence of motion, its hybridity, and abstract concentration of detail, the sheer proliferation of which defers direct straightforwardly realist or mimetic modes of representation, hints at that which is both *ultra-modern and untimely in its anachronic mode*.

Browning's mode, it has to be stressed, is anachronic not merely as a result of its subject matter. Not simply historical, *The Ring and the Book* is, like Browning's dramatic monologues, startlingly modern in the temporal and epistemological disjunctions between subject matter on the one hand and psychological and formal apperception and mediation on the other. Like the paintings of the Pre-Raphaelites (though of course singularly different), the excessive attention to detail and the rapidity with which direction is changed, allied with a superabundance of competing and interchangeable motifs, tropes, metonymies, figural devices and effects, forestalls ideal, pure or classical realist representation. As the very translatability between the principal figures of the title, the ring and the book, attest in Browning's phenomenal perception of their becoming suggests, every figure ultimately, though discontinuously, disfigures itself in figuring every other without any proper relation between each. The tropes of the work figured in the first book disorder. Importantly, they disorder representation from within, and perception of representation from without: for in being themselves the figures of the 'thing signified', they signal one another rather than any external world, and so traverse the subject's interpretive horizons without end. It would be more precise to say then that representation disorders itself from within itself, as every moment of disorder, marked by the non-identity of its own violent disorder. Indeed, arguably in such a process of destabilized, mutable dis-figuration there occurs a flattening out of representation; the weave of detail is such, the competition of figures and voices so overwrought, that one is caught up in a web of words, frequently frustrated in the attempt to gain the right distance, as it were, required for achieving any supposedly proper perspective. There is no relief in the world of the text, either in form or narrative; there is no literary *trompe l'oeil* by which the reader may assume mastery over the subject.

Apropos of such motion, analogous with the formal, figural displacements, Armstrong observes of the narrative, *The Ring and the Book*'s tale of violent sexual murder undercuts any authority, as 'no version of the story is ever an exact repetition, whether it is told by the murderer, the victim, factions of the community or the lawyers in the case' (Armstrong 1993, 316). Thus, if 'individual conscience [is situated] against authority, both political and ecclesiastical' (Armstrong 1993, 317), the condition of language is revealed by the poem as central to any such dialectic, for it foregrounds not only the undecidability at the heart of interpretation but also a more urgently political debate concerning the reliability of the witness in bearing witness. As we shall see momentarily, in Book Two, 'Half Rome', witness is pre-empted somewhat by gossip, hearsay, and a somewhat doxastic mode of recounting events leading up to the murder and trial. Such an opening of the text onto the undecidability that troubles representation and the desire to arrive at a *final* and *authoritative* representation and reading of the events of the crime throughout *The Ring and the Book* is one aspect – from a more neutral or even, arguably, radical standpoint than that of Bagehot's – of the Grotesque, in opposition to the Classical.

Seeking to perceive the Grotesque beyond its aesthetic or formal conditions, how might it be comprehended in its historicity, specifically as Browning brings the events of the seventeenth century into collision with a nineteenth-century mode of representation (and, it has to be said, a mode that is never simply of its moment, but overdetermined by the anachronistic traces of other representational modes, of which the 'medieval' is but the most recognizable)? In employing the term and its apparent counterpart, the Classical, in this manner, I am suggesting that one may align the Classical, or otherwise read it, as embodied in the authoritative voice, and with that the individual, 'proper' subject, formed with propriety, and authorized by some mastering discourse to speak on behalf of such authority. The Grotesque, on the other hand, is the figure for excess. It names that ungovernable multiplicity, overflow and impropriety that are implicated also in cultural discourses in notions of the low, the heterodox or heterogeneous, the polyvalent and the apprehension of irreducible alterity.

Authority versus doxa; facts versus hearsay; truth versus interpretation; pure versus alloyed; propriety/impropriety. Such interrelated pairings are at work behind Bagehot's assessment of Browning to be sure. They also inform what Armstrong defines astutely as the '*legal* fiction and the endless work of redefinition it demands' (Armstrong 1993, 317). Having returned to England in 1861 following the death of his wife and the discovery of the yellow book in the previous year, Browning's poem is eventually produced and published seven years later, immediately following the Second Reform Bill (1867). Not only does *The Ring and the Book* continue in extended form the interrogation of 'the nature of . . . fiction and imaginative constructs' (Armstrong 1993, 316) as these are in turn inflected through individual psychological motivations and their ideologically governed expressions that are to be found in the volume that so disturbed Walter Bagehot, *Dramatis Personae*; it also engages, in however markedly and elliptical a manner, with the ideological debate concerning democracy and the constitution of a 'proper' or, let us say, Classical body-politic as one manifestation of national identity. The debate which Browning joins was clearly widespread in the years leading up to *The Ring and the Book*'s publication, two of the most influential and powerful contributions to it being Bagehot's own *The English Constitution* and Matthew Arnold's essays that were to comprise *Culture and Anarchy*, but initially published in *The Cornhill* in 1867–1868 (Armstrong 1993, 317).

Thus it is that this tale of seventh-century murder, which veers between Grotesque farce and revenge tragedy, offers to its reader in the late 1860s 'an exhaustive reading of the implications of *vox populi* and the different forms representation can take' (Armstrong 1993, 317). It does so moreover through 'Linking our England to . . . Italy' (XII. 874). In this last line, there is undeniably a comparison of representations, in which the past and present overfigure one another, by analogy, duplicating and displacing one another. In this, Browning invites us to apprehend that history is not only the past. It is not fixable or representable as such. History is also what takes place *this how*, in the singularity of events specific to and produced out of particular idiocultural matrices. And, as the questioning of the moment being finite as such that opens the last book of *The Ring and the Book* – 'had anything an end' (XII. 1) – history is the spectacle and debate pursued publicly in the *now* of the 1860s – and beyond.

The violence of the murders of Pompilia, her parents Pietro and Violante, and Pompilia's lover Caponsacchi and, more importantly, the spectacle of that violence at the hands of Guido, is strikingly graphic. From the public display of the corpses 'in the church' (II. 18) to the attention to the mutilation of Violante's

face, and the detail of the kind of knife employed ('Triangular i' the blade . . . /
Armed with those little hook-teeth on the edge / To open in the flesh nor shut
again'; II. 147–9), Book Two, 'Half-Rome' would seem, on brief acquaintance, to
share a contemporaneity not with the novels of Trollope and Eliot, but with *The
Godfather*, *Reservoir Dogs*, or the BBC/HBO series *Rome*. We are told for example
that it is a matter of 'honour's sake' (II. 28) that the avenger 'disfigure the subject,
fray the face' (II. 32) in an act of deliberately 'conspicuous punishment' (II. 35).
No less Grotesque is the fascination reported concerning the crowd who wish to
see the mutilated bodies: 'In trying to count stabs, / People supposed Violante
showed the most' (II. 23–24):

> From dawn till now that it is growing dusk
> A multitude has flocked and filled the church
> Coming and going, coming back again
> Till to count crazed one. Rome was at the show
> People climbed up the columns, fought for spike
> O' the chapel-rail to perch themselves upon
> Jumped over and so broke the wooden work
> Painted like porphyry to deceive the eye;
> Serve the priests right! The organ-loft was crammed
> Women were fainting, no few fights ensued
> In short, it was a show repaid your pains;
> (II. 88–98)

It is worth speculating that, in part at least, the scene might have been suggested
to Browning by the July 1866 riots in Hyde Park, known also as Black Monday,
which was initially occasioned by a demonstration begun in the name of universal
male suffrage by the Reform League. Whether or not this is the case though, in
this nearly orgiastic spectacle of display, and in the prurient interest of a crowd too
large to be accommodated by the church, there is a grimly comic sense of theatrical-
ity and melodrama that the narrator of 'Half-Rome' appears to relish, and which
Browning highlights throughout the book.

Leaving aside the theatrical, it is also arguable that in Browning's presentation
of the more graphic aspects of historical representation, there is also to be read
the singular and timely response to a certain Victorian interest in more violent
and bloody representations of the past. Historical novels in particular drew on
Grotesque and Gothic modes of representation. As Franco Moretti asserts, such
fiction was 'the most successful form of the century' (Moretti 1999, 33). If, as
Moretti argues, concerning the specificity of place in historical novels, 'different
forms inhabit different spaces' (Moretti 1999, 34), then, for Victorian writers at
least, the content and mode of representation may serve to inhabit radically different social and cultural spaces simultaneously, thereby estranging both location
and narrative for the purposes of oblique contemporary commentary. For example,
social unrest and trade depression in general and Chartist agitation in particular
give to Dickens's historical novel *Barnaby Rudge*, first published in 1841, an

ideological resonance between that which is taking place historically as the novel is being written and the historical events to which the novel turns, the Gordon Riots and other political events of the 1780s.

As the editor of the Penguin Classics' edition of *Barnaby Rudge*, John Bowen, argues, 'the political activity of the book is deeply enmeshed in Gothic and melo-dramatic material' (Bowen 2003, xxv). So too is *The Ring and the Book*; or, at least in its modes of production, it tends to the exploitation and presentation of such material. It is political not in its being a historical text, but in its apprehension of historicity and witness in the absence of the past as such. To borrow John Bowen's assessment of the mode of historicity of *Barnaby Rudge*, but equally applicable to *The Ring*, 'history is a repetitive and strangely doubled business . . . here things repeat and repeat . . . [and] repetition is of various sorts' (Bowen 2003, xvi). Repetition is not merely historical for Browning. That which is repeatable – or, strictly speaking, iterable – is narrative, with its remarking of difference, and its generation of a 'theoretical' matrix, a structure of voices recorded interacting in order to obscure and reveal perspective, and so from out of this to produce a vision of the past which is also a vision of the historicity of truth and the truth of historicity. In its internal echo-chamber of iterable narrative and repetitive tropic recurrence, *The Ring and the Book* holds commune not only with the temporal moment of its subject matter; it does so in addition with the politics and poetics of fictive historicity in the text of the first half of the nineteenth century.

VIII

Considering the contested grounds of political and historical fictions in the nine-teenth century, the critic has to acknowledge Charles Kingsley, and two novels in particular, *Yeast* and *Alton Locke*, both produced within two years of one another (1848 and 1850 respectively). Although it may be said that Charles Kingsley argu-ably 'embodied the contradictions in the critique of industrial capitalism more fully than any other Victorian writer', (Gallagher 1985, 88) and although his writing is marked by an 'ambivalence about the relationship between character and circum-stances' (89) as does Catherine Gallagher, Kingsley began his career as a novelist in an avowedly polemical manner, with the two novels, *Yeast* (1848) and *Alton Locke* (1850), which, undeniably, address contemporary political concerns and issues. Published in a year of European revolutions, *Yeast* addresses two different, yet prevalent concerns of the mid-Victorian period: the impoverished conditions of the rural working class and their exploitation by the landed gentry, and the abandonment of the Church of England by a number of the younger generation in favour of Catholicism. *Yeast* is one of the few novels of the mid-Victorian moment to take seriously the plight of the rural poor. Its two narratives are not kept separate, but the discourses of Christianity and politics are shown to commingle, in the figure of the responsible individual, in this novel, Lancelot Smith who embodies the mid-Victorian concept of Christian manliness. Through this interanimation, Kingsley structures and reveals the subject's historicity, from which issues the

discourse of both novel and material conditions. (On the subject of Christian manliness and for a reading of Kingsley's *Alton Locke*, see David Alderson 1996, 43–61;
on the subject of muscular Christianity in the nineteenth century in general, see
also Donald E. Hall, ed., 1994, and Norman Vance, 1985.)

A novel in which Kingsley 'illustrates the interconnectedness he finds among
sexual repression, dirt and disease' (Fasick 1994, 95), *Yeast* is unusual among
overtly political novels, in that it deals with the rural, rather than the urban poor,
unlike the novels of Gaskell, Disraeli and Dickens. Causing something of a stir at
the time of its serial publication (it had to be ended abruptly, so many complaints
did *Fraser's Magazine* receive), *Yeast* was derived from three principal sources of
which Kingsley had first-hand knowledge: his own encounters with the conditions
of rural workers, the philanthropic work of his brother-in-law, Sidney Godolphin
Osborne, a Dorset rector who sought to establish better living conditions for farm
hands, and the 1843 *Reports of Special Assistant Poor Law Commissioners on the
Employment of Women and Children in Agriculture*, which provided harsh detail of
the abject state of rural working conditions. However, it is a sign of the contradictory, if not contestatory tussle of political discourse, which marks this, and other
novels, as historically rather than personally determined, that, while Kingsley's
reformist tendencies manifest themselves in full sympathy for workers' conditions,
there is also the sign of political conservatism in the novel's distrust of radical
and systematic Christian doctrine, while, simultaneously, there is a conservative
moral judgement at work in response to the middle-class, land-owning heroine,
Argemone Lavington, whose desire to reject a conventional gender role and sexual
life is read, in the text, as 'unnatural and . . . unhealthy in its consequences' (Fasick
1994, 96).

Like its predecessor, *Alton Locke*, a novel inspired by the Chartist movement,
brings together the reformist concern over working conditions – this time those
of the novel's titular character, an East End London tailor and poet – and the
particular ideological currents of Victorian Christianity in transition. Kingsley,
typical of Victorian novelists of whatever political orientation, focuses on the
individual, as a means of humanizing political struggle, and thereby both mystify-
ing and depoliticizing the rights of the proletariat from certain perspectives. (As
Josephine Guy puts it, 'mid-Victorian writers (of whatever political persuasion)
tended to understand problems in society in individual, rather than social terms'
[1994, 9].) As if to argue against any form of system which does not have as its
centre or origin the idea of the individual, the novel is, as David Alderson puts it,
'a significant text in the representation of the demise of Chartism as being a result
of the movement's own ineptitude' (1996, 44).

To turn to Dickens momentarily, in relation to the Victorian politics of indi-
viduality as opposed to the systematic: consider for example the relatively crude
polarization in Dickens's *Hard Times* between the all-too-human and pathetic
figure of Stephen Blackpool, who is cast against not only the impersonal systems
of the employers but also, disingenuously and ideologically, on Dickens's part, the
equally impersonal, and therefore inhuman union movement. The labour movement is read in the text as monstrous because it has no room to comprehend or

allow for Stephen's personal domestic dilemmas. However, to read the politics of this narrative differently, it is important to understand how the novelist's act of humanization is itself political in that it insists on the primacy of personal, individual emotional experience, over collective political need and class-based rights. Structurally this forms an extended narrative gesture which, undoubtedly, found political resonance in the reading of F. R. Leavis, who, with a disingenuous gesture surpassing Dickens's own, described the novel as a 'moral fable' (Leavis 1948).

Reception aside, however, what can be read is that, while variously outraged at politically charged and engendered conditions, novelists such as Dickens and Kingsley were responding out of personal moral and ethical understandings, rather than consciously political ones; and that this being so, it may be read that both men, despite reformist sympathies and polemical literary activities, evince repeatedly in their writing a distrust of institution, abstract intellectualism and all manifestations of systematicity at the supposed expense of the individual (whether one is speaking of the Tractarian or union movement). The individualism of Victorian political economists, the discursive-ideological focus on the individual, is the inevitable humanist focal point of political democracy in the nineteenth century (Alderson 1996, 45), and, discursively, this interest is translated by the novel (consider how many Victorian novels take individuals' names for their titles), which, in turn, is readable as part of a broad ideological focus, regardless of narrow political or philosophical affiliation. In this we come to read, what Josephine Guy calls the Victorian 'emphasis on the individual as the basic unity of enquiry' (1994, 10).

Comprehending, then, the importance of the representation of the individual at the centre of political turmoil (and all too often the victim of impersonal political forces) is key to any understanding of both the political novel and the politics of the novel in the Victorian era. What is all the more complex, and which therefore requires our more patient focus (for which there is not the space here), is the paradoxical, if not ambivalent, nature of Victorian narrative when comprehended politically. It is not a question of hurrying to judge Dickens, Kingsley, or any other writer for that matter, simply as politically 'right' or 'wrong', but instead, to seek to read the various political traces within texts in all their contradictoriness as signs of the times, so to speak (and from there to begin to come to terms with the ways in which our acts of reading the 'political' novel in the nineteenth century is similarly positioned within the historical limits of our thought).

The Water-Babies takes a somewhat different tack, constructing not a single perspective but what Elizabeth Deeds Ermath describes as a 'perspective system' (1997, 93). Such systems, argues Ermath, are prevalent in the Victorian novel; they are the ways in which a 'historical continuum' (1997, 85) is forged in the form of a narrative out of a range of different discourses, demanding of the reader that she attend 'not to events and characters but to the perception of events and characters – in short to the act of historical attention' (Ermath 1997, 93). Such narrative ordering offers a positive response to political and philosophical dilemmas faced by the Victorians as it mediates its discursive, ideological and philosophical strands in the face of the 'upheaval in the very basis of social order' (1997, 84), which generates such anxiety amongst so many Victorian writers. Kingsley's personal response is to adapt social and political narrative through the mediation of the discursive modes of fantasy and satire in *The Water-Babies*. While it is possible to read this novel as retreat from overtly political narrative, this is still to read within a limited conception of what the political novel might look like. Equally, this fantasy of Tom, the chimney-sweep who dies and becomes a water baby, is readable as a series of oblique commentaries on contemporary political and social matters, not least the exploitation of children as sweeps. When published, 'it was immediately striking as a fresh endeavour by the Reverend Kingsley to express through fiction some of the social and spiritual – and even scientific – dilemmas that were his constant preoccupation' (Kingsley, int. Alderson 1995, xiv). Thus, we would argue, the novel develops a strategy which is itself political in that it seeks to disturb its reception through the estranging mediation of political issues, in order to push the reader into thinking differently about contemporary social matters. And it is a sign of its political effectiveness that, a year later, the 1864 Chimney Sweepers' Act was passed in Parliament, as an attempt to alleviate the plight of exploited children.

IX

At the risk of stating the obvious, narrative or poetic discourse on the political in English society of the nineteenth century will inevitably assume myriad and heterogeneous forms, often becoming readable only partially, and only after the event as fractured, dissonant and contradictory. It is, furthermore, often marked by a limit to which 'thinking the political' can extend within the era in question, and which therefore reveals the manifestation of crisis – in representation, ontology and historical consciousness. There is, then, always a matter of reading the contested grounds of representation and 'theoretical' commentary that narrative and poetry can afford, a contest or conflict that has become doubled, ghosted by, overtly political critical discourses of the twentieth and twenty-first centuries, which reiterate such contested loci in their desire to map onto the literary texts of the nineteenth century particular identities, genres and ontologies. An important step in recognizing the Victorian text *qua* contested ground (the very term 'Victorian' signals both contemporaneously and subsequently in critical reception the very ground to be contested, contest for determination of the ground itself) is to recognize how historicity is a concern, if not an anxiety of the political; it is to see also to what extent the textual matrix we nominate as 'Victorian' (a signifier at once finite and endlessly open) is internally fissured within its articulations, riven by the paradoxes and blind spots that attend any age; this is to see, furthermore, that there emerges 'a new kind of relationship between the novel [and poetry] and the social and political worlds which produced' them (Guy 1996, 3). Such a relationship is itself political in that '[i]n social narratives, novelists [and poets] by the hundreds *experiment* across a whole range of social circumstance with [the] new relationship between individual voice and collective identity. What is at stake here is nothing less than a shift in the way an entire culture constructs identity' (Ermath 1997, 119–20; emphasis added). Such an experiment involves the strategic use of different, though recognisably familiar, historical moments, or the employment of fantasy and satire, and thus literary discourse adapts in a broadly political manner to the transformation of political and social change, thereby implicating itself into the political weave from out of which transitions in literary language take place. What is of especial interest today, I would argue, after the insights made available to critics by what we loosely term 'theory', is that experiment and enquiry, engagement and response are readable. Also available is a perception of the different, differing ways the trace of the political is readable, in those very narrative situations which, on the surface at least, seem, from conventional perspectives, not to treat of politics, narrowly defined: in children's fantasy, in a love story, in social comedy as well as in those most obvious textual sites addressing the question of political activity.

Thus we apprehend, in conclusion, so many fictions of the political: Victorian literature, if that label will hold momentarily, presents its work through unveiling that which, in being occluded as the political, leaves the authenticity of the historical trace to be read. The responsibility of the critic is to recognize the extent to which the Victorian age was self-aware *and* blind, and thus in its literary mediations of its identities was involved actively in the production and dissemination of necessary fictions concerning itself, and the possibilities that representation afforded society for telling itself about itself. Every narrative, monologue or staged presentation of historicized subjectivity is, in some manner, political, though not all are equally so; nor in any measure do the fictions of the political become registered in the same fashion, even though all are, equally, authentic, in one manner or another – that is to say, authenticity, however ideologically positioned, is figured in the work of the trope and the theoretical framework that maintains a network of tropes in the form of novel or poem. Every text will necessarily differ from the next and the political as such cannot, therefore, by definition be defined. Rather, we read perception, perspective and limit; partiality and focus announce the historical conditions by which the political is given aestheticized determination.

In the face of such a recognition, what is needed therefore is for readers of Victorian texts to learn to read the signs of politics as they hide themselves, as they write themselves otherwise, as they display themselves in full view, apparently as though the question were not one of politics at all, but of common sense, historical inevitability, cultural contingency, and so forth. In coming to terms with such diversity, then we might begin to read the trace of the political as the authentic transmission of the subject's historicity: hence, the term *theoretical* and, in no small measure, my use of the term *theory* in the title of the present volume, and throughout, but particularly in the chapters that comprise the latter chapters of *Literature, in Theory*. In its uses amongst critics in recent decades and currently, *theory* is used to refer to that heterogeneous corpus of critical publications and metacritical reflections informed by inter – and multidisciplinary discussions and praxes, opposed to practice. Latterly (that is to say in the last forty years or so), this definition has been increasingly, and distortedly, emphasized – misdirected – as that which is linguistically or philosophically reflexive, playful, formal, as distinct from the allegedly more necessary political or historical work of criticism.

Yet *theory*, at least partly, still retains (and is used throughout this volume implicitly in this way) its earlier and now obscure senses of looking at something, viewing or contemplation, considering and reflecting on a spectacle or sight, a mental view leading to insight. Reminding oneself of this admittedly occluded meaning, it is, I believe, important that we recover such determination, in order that we afford ourselves a different epistemological and historical perception on literature of the nineteenth century. If the 'narrator' or 'voice' of the text bears a relation to the world it presents – such fictional subjectivity is always already, as construct, positioned so as to afford perception rather than unmediated empirical reality – of mind to world, then, necessarily, it must occupy a space between the reader and that which is imagined, offered for speculation, or brought to the mind's eye for reflective contemplation. To the extent that literature of the nineteenth century might be taken as 'realist', or to the extent that it has been read critically to be representing its own historical realities, more or less directly, then, there can be no doubt, it must be perceived as *theoretical*. As such, it is a product of the modernity it figures. Its fictions, narratives and poetics occupy the lacunae or fissures in the otherwise irresolvable problems of the historical moment and any merely empirical apprehension of the events that constitute the historical. In this interpretive and, therefore, *theoretical* role of spectator, the narrator or poetic persona bears witness. In translating event through the politics and poetics of fictive and poetic figuration, literature demands we assume the position of the *theoretical* spectator, and so take responsibility for witnessing the traces of the past.

5

(Sub) Urbi et Orbi: The 'Little Worlds' of London, or, Fear, Whimsy and Singularity

I

If, as I suggested at the end of the previous chapter, literature affords perception rather than unmediated empirical reality then, necessarily, it must occupy a space between the reader and that which is imagined. Such positioning affords distance, and with that, the possibility for the shaping of a world, recognizably one's own and, yet, sufficiently different. To reiterate one of my final statements from the last chapter: 'to the extent that literature of the nineteenth century might be taken as "realist", or to the extent that it has been read critically to be representing its own historical realities, more or less directly, then, there can be no doubt, it must be perceived as *theoretical*. What such theoretical focus makes possible then is that mode of vision that arrives as if it had never been witnessed before. At the same time, however, literature in the nineteenth century was also responding to different phenomena and cultural experiences at an unprecedented rate, so that perception itself was under assault. One particular phenomenon, the 'suburb', presented to the urban writer a congeries of possibilities for narrative and imaginative construction. Yet the problem was one of seemingly endless repetition. So much so, in fact, that the remark was made: 'A modern suburb is a place which is neither one thing nor the other' (Anon., 1876). This remark is taken from *The Times* in 1876. It imposes on the suburb a modernity defined, if not by indefinability, then a certain ambiguity of identity, the result of its hybrid borrowing from more than one source or location. Neither city nor country, the modern suburb of the 1870s is a place allegedly without a sense of itself, without a *genius loci*, except, perhaps, a spirit of anonymity. Appropriate as it is that the derogatory observation was written by our most published, if not most celebrated, author, Anon., how true is the observation? Is the shallow empiricism of such a remark merely one of the signs of an inability to read the ways in which suburbs, seemingly anonymous, keep to themselves secret identities, identities that, for all their plundering of metropolitan or pastoral conceits, produce something that is, singularly, their own inimitable personae?

It might be the case perhaps that in being 'neither one thing nor the other', the suburb's identity is a matter of the immaterial, of perception rather than reality. While a suburb is undeniably what the *OED* defines as the outlying parts, the outskirts or purlieus of a place, it is also defined by the dictionary as a term signifying immaterial things, citations offered by the *OED* referring to the 'suburbs of narrative' or the 'suburbs of sense'. Such figurative use aside though, there is a persistence in the use of the term, mildly suggested by Anon., that the suburbs are places of debased, inferior, or, as the *OED* puts it, *especially* licentious habits of life. While Ben Jonson refers to 'suburbe-humour', in *Every Man in His Humour*, Milton, in *Eikonoklastes*, acknowledges the presence of 'dissolute Sword-men and Suburb roysters' (both cited in the *OED*).

Distinct from such largely pejorative associations, what I wish to suggest is that there are two ways, at least, in which one might read the idea of the suburb. On the one hand, as I shall go on to discuss, the suburb is that which abuts or borders onto the urban-proper, as a satellite of that greater identity. On the other hand, however, the suburb is not simply the adjunct or supplement to the city, it is, as its name appears to encrypt, a little world of its own, a world underneath, and thus escaping, the determination of the city centre. In this, it maps an imaginary territory, which in turn gives place to the projection of the life of other 'little worlds', worlds of whimsy, anxiety, comedy and fear – and this is particularly true of the suburban identities constituted in literary texts from the 1870s to the 1930s, although extending either side of these parameters, of course. For the 'little world' of the suburb concerns very much the projection, and experience of, singular identities, identities caught up in that which resonates in a number of eccentric and ex-centric ways.

In order to illustrate how a location may be configured as a 'little world', consider Russell Square. If Russell Square is about as far away conceivably – geographically, psychically, even psychogeographically – as it is possible to get from the suburb in the conventional sense, yet, historically, there is something of the 'little world' about the area of Bloomsbury. Were you to leave Senate House, for example,[1] exiting onto Russell Square Gardens, crossing the Gardens in a nearly straight line, you would come out into Guilford Street. Walking East-North-East along Guilford Street, passing Coram's fields on the one hand, and Lamb's Conduit Street on the other, you would in a matter of a few minutes be able to turn onto Doughty Street, where there remains one of the early homes of the adult Charles Dickens, now, as many of you know, a museum in his memory, a kind of evacuated stage set, in which, for a modest fee, we are invited to conjure the ghosts, pausing in the stairwell to touch the Little Midshipman, in a brief, whimsical moment. Not far from Dickens's house, coming back in this direction, you will find another blue plaque, this time on what was the home of Dorothy L. Sayers, 24 Great James Street. And, of course, we are in the heart, more or less, of Bloomsbury. A very literary location then, or at the least, an area from out of which come many of our most familiar literary works. More than this though, we might also suggest that location is mapped by the literary, by various palimpsests of the real; or, conversely, the 'real' is merely the material ground for the little worlds of literature and the arts. The streets immediately around us were the haunts – and probably remain so – not only of Dickens and Sayers, but Virginia Woolf, of course, Vanessa Bell also, Charles Darwin, the illustrator Randolph Caldecott, the architects George Dance and Thomas Henry Wyatt, W. B. Yeats, and, more recently, albeit briefly, Bob Marley – when Marley wasn't dead, to begin with.

This district, adjacent to the Inns of Court, abutting onto Holborn, Soho and Clerkenwell, and developed by the Russell family in the seventeenth and eighteenth centuries, can hardly be described as a 'suburb' for all that it is, undoubtedly a 'little world', one of innumerable 'worlds' in London, as distinct from its neighbours as it is from, say, Pasadena or Montmartre. Culturally, historically, socially, it is singular. Architecturally similar to many other sites in the city, it nonetheless remains other, its difference felt and perceived, rather than known, rather than definable. And what makes Bloomsbury singular, like all those other singularities from which it is distinct, is that it has no definite boundaries, officially. The district, recorded in the *Domesday Book* as having had vineyards and a wood for one hundred pigs, did not receive its name until the land was acquired by Guillaume de Blemond at the end of the twelfth century, who, lending his name to the location, entitled it Blemondisberi, the manor or bury of Blemond. London folklore has it that the area, specifically Russell Square itself, was originally a village, Lomesbury, but this is largely discredited. So, a porcine grazing ground, a manor or borough in the old sense of that word, a village, a fashionable demi-monde. Never, though, a suburb in the conventional sense.

To begin the definition provisionally of 'suburb', acknowledging that the word arrives from Latin via French, the obvious can be stated by saying that the suburb is neither the urb, the central area of a city, nor the exurb, a term coined in the 1950s by Auguste Comte Spectorsky, to describe the wealthy, semi-rural areas beyond the conformity of the suburbs, or otherwise, with reference to London, the commuter or dormitory towns that fill the home counties, from Chalfont St Giles to the Winnersh Triangle. Or, to put this in another way, to define the suburb, we have to find somewhere between Bloomsbury and Russell Square on the one hand, and Woking or Abinger Hammer on the other. This should give us plenty of scope, until it is acknowledged that what in one generation is a suburb becomes by the next part, if not of the centre, then at least, the greater area of the metropolis. Indeed, whilst speaking of definitions, it may be an act of determining the difference between a metropolis and a megalopolis by insisting that the latter can be perceived for its enormous energy and appetite. The megalopolis has that unstoppable ability to swallow and incorporate suburbs into its always heterogeneous and hybrid identity, an identity marked as much by difference as it is by sameness, by the endlessness of its auto-iterability as much as by the apparent continuity of its repetitious pulses, refractions and mirrorings.

At the same time, however, the megalopolis, in its rapid acquisition, its hungry appropriation of the suburb, tends to leave the suburb with its own identity. London as megalopolis is not interested in making the suburb over in its own image. Thus it is, we might suggest, that the suburb is recognizable not least by the fact that it retains a double identity, that it is in effect two places, one the palimpsest of the other, one part belonging to London, the other retaining a definition according to the county it was, and remains, located in, when it was consumed or subsumed. This is most immediately readable in the persistence of postal codes, which deny London affiliation while maintaining a kind of paraph or cryptic signature that announces county status, and from that, the implication of an alternative ontology: 'Surrey man'; 'Men of Kent'; 'Essex Man' or 'Essex girls'; and so on. There is here a kind of journalistic mythology in this shorthand, which registers various significations and implications in much the same way as the phrase 'home counties', though with a little more specificity. What is interesting is that Middlesex has no discernible type, whether positive or negative in perception. Perhaps it is anonymity that defines the inhabitants of Middlesex. Even now, they might be in our midst, and how could we tell?

Every time, however, that we come back to, or look up, the question of the suburb, we meet statements that say, in various ways, with an infinite variety that exhausts the reader, the boundaries or borders are not fixed; they are flexible, porous, invisible; the suburb is protean, malleable, a shape-shifting, amorphous entity, which, as soon as you try to pin it down or look at it directly, it vanishes. With regard to London, so great is the power of the mystical suburb that while there are home counties, and something vaguely called 'Greater London', the County of London as distinct entity was abolished in 1965. Greater London took over, as if London were, itself, greater than any possible act of naming or boundary marking could comprehend. In all senses of the word, London comprehends that which it gathers to it, but like the myriad suburbs out of which it has overflown, London cannot be comprehended in its entirety. It is as if the suburbs have, like so many parasites, consumed the host that sought to consume them. London is nothing other than endless little worlds, countless sub-urbs (and here I introduce a hyphen momentarily, in order to begin the redefinition of a sub-urb). And the sub-urb is everywhere and nowhere, underneath our feet and the pavements and parks of the capital, as the prefix *sub* implies: *sub urbs*, under the city, below the city, an imaginary agglomeration of netherworlds; *Suburbio*, as it is today in Spanish or Portuguese, perhaps a fourth, and missing volume to accompany the *Inferno*, *Purgatorio* and *Paradiso* of Dante's *Divina Commedia*.

Something strange takes place in the suburbs, they are crepuscular places, twilight sites. The very word is strange, for, if we go back to the *OED*, the dictionary informs us that it can be both a collective plural and a collective singular, if not a singular collective. And its eerie, disquieting quality is captured, by chance, in the earliest printed usage given by the *OED*, from John Wyclif (c. 1380), who remarks that they 'hadden subarbis to fed ther the beestis that schuld be offred sacrifice to god in the temple'. It is perhaps for this very reason that as recently as 1993, when signing a contract on an apartment in Kew, a suburb to which I will return, that I noticed a clause indicating that livestock to the number of two sheep, and one milch-cow, could be kept on the local green. No mention of pigs was made, but then, there was always Bloomsbury for pork. And around six years after Wyclif's observation on suburban practices, we also have Chaucer, whose commentary hardly does anything to reassure us: 'In the suburbes of a toun. Lurkynge in hernes and in lanes blynde, / Whereas thise robbours and thise theves by kynde / Holden hir pryvee fereful residence'; (*The Canterbury Tales*, 2008; Canon Yeoman's Prologue; ll.657–60). This is a sentiment echoed as recently as the beginning of March, this year, when the Metropolitan Police issued a 'warning' that criminals were more likely to be found hiding from justice in the leafy lanes of

Twickenham than in Soho's dens of iniquity. From the fourteenth century, then, to Nigel Williams's twentieth-century Wimbledon poisoner, the suburbs are dangerous places.

II

Nowhere is the perception of danger more strikingly realized in the representation of the suburbs than in Richard Marsh's fin-de-siècle Gothic, *The Beetle*. Its first narrative is that of the out-of-work and homeless clerk, Robert Holt. The London the reader encounters in Marsh's novel abounds with elements recognizable from many other *fin de siècle* mysteries, a number of which we have already addressed. It is an inhospitable, largely nocturnal city, where darkness and adverse weather conditions, make possible, while simultaneously hiding, criminal and transgressive behaviour. However, Marsh's London is not purely this. For the novel begins with representations of the city that, while partaking of tropes recognizably similar to those that construct the images of the city in the works of authors such as Conan Doyle, R. L. Stevenson, Bram Stoker, and Oscar Wilde, belong to more realist and naturalist fictions, such as those, for example, of Walter Besant, George Gissing, George Moore or Arthur Morrison. In presenting the narration of the tramp Robert Holt, homeless and wandering the streets of West London suburbs in search of a night's accommodation in the Casual Ward, Marsh offers the reader a glimpse, however fleetingly, into the wretched existence of the capital's poorest inhabitants, the conditions of whom are a by-product of the city. What is all the more startling about the particular image of Holt is that he is not from the working classes but had been a clerk until his dismissal. Furthermore, Marsh stages the initial scene, not in the East End of London, as is commonly the stereotypical setting for late Victorian Gothic, but in the upper and, as we have remarked, largely middle-class districts of West London, from Kensington to Fulham. In small, subtle ways, therefore, *The Beetle* is available as staging an alternative, possibly estranging vision of the city for its readers that is unveiled from the contest between the tropes of *fin de siècle* sensation and those of the text of social realism, while displacing narrative events belonging to both genres from their already clichéd sites in the 1880s and 1890s, East London.

Admittedly, Marsh's acts of what may be described as cultural and literary revision are not sustained in any significant way. However, what is effected in this manner is a disruption in both the literary codes of urban representation and the narratives that are informed by such codes. The city's identity is made to tremble, as are its ontologies and epistemologies of representation. Not only this, but it is not impossible that, in such gestures, *The Beetle* invites one to reflect on the identity of literary models beyond their diegetic codes or mimetic commonplaces. Events occur in places that they should not, borderlines are crossed both in the imagined topography of the city and in the modalities of genre. London in this particular guise is therefore the 'same, yet not the same', to borrow Holt's words (words he borrows from Tennyson) once more. Identities are mixed and thus confounded.

The Egyptian Beetle of the title is only ever encountered secreted away, largely unobserved, in an unassuming 'villa' in a West London suburb, its own cultural marginality doubled by the middle-class topographic margin of the villa. From here, it unnervingly intrudes or dispatches its agents to penetrate into the private houses of the English ruling classes. In a parallel structure it is found also working its hypnotic way into the minds of the English, in a series of what Roger Luckhurst has defined succinctly as trance-gothic encounters (Luckhurst 2000, 148). The novel makes clear that it is the Beetle that introduces the trance condition in Holt, through an act of mesmerism. Holt's loss of self is, however, mapped onto Marsh's representation of suburban streets, so that loss of personal and urban identity conjoined in late nineteenth-century suburban anxiety. The endless serial reiteration of rapid terraced expansion of domestic dwellings in West London suburbs had begun in the 1840s and 1850s, and had continued its creep throughout the following decades, moving continually West. London was becoming, by the time of Marsh's novel, 'radically, even aggressively suburban' (Porter 1994, 307), as is noted early on in the text. Roy Porter provides exhaustive detail on the suburban transformation of London in his comprehensive social history of the city, much of which of course takes place in conjunction with the spread of mass public transport and electricity. While Porter offers historical and sociological analysis of the suburban phenomenon, what can be added is that technology and sprawl support each other's flows in a manner that defies strict regulation or comprehension. It is as if urban – and specifically suburban – planning give way before modes of deterritorialization and the tele-technological erasure of specific boundaries. In other words, the suburban is defined by flow rather than coherence and containment.

Suburban spread is charted in literature from the 1870s and 1880s, through to the 1920s, as anxiety, exhaustion and the erasure of self appear to maintain their effects. Arnold Bennett gives his readers an indication of just how enervating the London suburbs can be for some, when he writes of Mrs Arb in *Riceyman Steps* (published the year after *The Waste Land*), that she 'abandoned . . . Fulham, where she had been desiccating for two years, and flew to Clerkenwell in an eager mood of adventure' (1991a, 30). So lacking in apparent interest are the suburbs that almost anywhere is an improvement. Anonymity, placidity, ennui as the constituent elements of suburban London identity arise through repetition. So does another condition for the subject, however, in his or her encounter with the unidentifiable, which is the apparently identical: a kind of quasi-mesmeric disorientation brought about by incessant recurrence of architectural form. These are the streets of the capital's suburbs to be found in the novels of H. G. Wells, W. Somerset Maugham, Arthur Machen, Amy Levy and many others. Consider this passage, from Levy's 1889 novel, *Reuben Sachs*, which text is discussed at length in *Writing London Vol. III*:

> The Walterton Road is a dreary thoroughfare, which, in respect of unloveliness, if not of length, leaves Harley Street, condemned of the poet, [Tennyson, of Wimpole Street, in *In Memoriam* 7.2] far behind.

It is lined on either side with little sordid gray houses, characterized by tall flights of steps and bow-windows, these latter having for frequent adornment cards proclaiming the practice of various humble occupations, from the letting of lodgings to the tuning of pianos. (2006a 82–3)

Though a different district and rendered in more detail, Levy's London suburb is essentially the same as those described fleetingly by Robert Holt. The quiet oppressiveness of the fin de siècle suburb is expressed as repeatedly in literature as it was to be found in the last two decades in the capital. Such numbing repetition may well account for the relative lack of detailed description of London street scenes in many later novels of the nineteenth century staged in London, and not a few of the first decades of the twentieth.

Coming back to *The Beetle*, Robert Holt's appearance, homeless amongst the fast developing suburbs with their newly constructed or unfinished 'homes' for those not unlike Holt, is an uncomfortable image, to say the least. Despite the taint of the Gothic, there is a documentary nod, however cursory, on Marsh's part towards a lower-middle class version of the poverty stricken worlds of the working classes in Gissing and Morrison. Of the house in which Holt takes refuge in the first chapter, he remarks: 'It was one of those so-called villas which are springing up in multitudes all round London, and which are let at rentals of from twenty-five to forty pounds a year' (Marsh 2004, 46). That figure 'all round'; it is readable in two ways. On the one hand, it suggests a totality of coverage, of a spoor-like manifestation throughout and everywhere in the city; on the other hand, it intimates an encircling belt, surrounding the centre with a suburban stranglehold. The novel's fleeting impression of suburban areas such as Hammersmith and West Kensington in the midst of rapid transformation is later supported by remarks of Marjorie Lindon (2004, 217) and those of Miss Louisa Coleman, who compares the new erections of 'high-class mansions' with those already in existence in 'Grosvenor Square – no shops or public houses, and none of your shanties' (Marsh 2004, 271). The suburb is thus a minor imitation of urban grandeur; it is also resolutely non-commercial, and thus not given over to baser commercial interests. Architectural reiteration, planned similarity and, with that, anonymity or at least the erasure of district-specific identity, is implied in the historical vision of suburban development encapsulated in Miss Coleman's remark. The singularity of identity dissolves – and this is what takes place in Holt's rapid transport across West London, cited above – even as London spreads like a mutating coral reef (to borrow a favoured metaphor for urban sprawl in the 1890s).

As the city is remapped, so the novel in the last years of the nineteenth century redefines its focus away from the City, as if to provide a mediation of its own readers' identities, and to make the adventures of London relevant to a suburban middle-class, whose world was becoming more parochial and circumscribed, in no small part from the sense, however fallacious, that the traditional centres of London and the City were too dangerous, too filled with adventure. That adventure is found in the suburbs at all suggests a desire for the alien and foreign amidst the endless repetition of the self-same, in a petit-bourgeois manifestation of abjection.

III

But if the suburban world is one of threat, where robbers hide out, and animals are kept for ritual slaughter, it is also a place of whimsy and other small, unexpected outbursts of individualism, moments of petty revolt against the conformity of the semi-detached and the terraced house, or otherwise the comic affirmation of one's own smallness. This is what we find in the parody of self-interest, insularity and complacency provided by George and Weedon Grossmith in the caricatured figure of Mr Pooter, the city clerk, in *The Diary of A Nobody*, which first appeared in *Punch* in 1888, and in volume form in 1892. Spiritual father, perhaps to Eliot's clerk carbuncular, Pooter lives on 'Brickfield Terrace' (1999, 11). The very name of the street is blatantly suggestive of the unending sameness, especially in that oxymoron of a brick field. The house is given a name, 'The Laurels', presumably this being the only way to distinguish one's house from all the others in the street, and also to hint at a clichéd sylvan paradise. Aspects of the rented house are small and pleasant, unthreatening. There is a '*little* front garden', a '*little* side entrance', and a '*nice little* back garden' (1999, 11). Mr Pooter goes to the expense of 5d for a 'capital *little* book' on gardening (1999, 22). 'Enlarged and tinted photographs' on the walls look very *nice*', especially when Mrs Pooter, Carrie as her husband's diminutive reminds us, adds silk bows to the corners of the frames (1999, 92; this and the previous four emphases added). Pooter's mode of reference is very telling, for, apropos of nothing, ('By-the-by') he draws attention to the photographs for the sake of displaying the Pooter aesthetic sensibility. The Pooters have just one servant, except when they hold their first party seven months after moving in, when their son puts them to the – to Pooter Sr. – unnecessary expense of hiring a waiter for the 'half-dozen of champagne' (1999, 91); and there is, as in this comment, a constant concern with value for money (the garden backing on to the railway tracks brings about a reduction of the rent by £2; 11). Though the couple suffer 'no inconvenience' over a crack in the garden wall, yet inside the house 'there is always something to be done' (1999, 11). The reader is then afforded a catalogue of domestic adventures: 'a tin-tack here, a Venetian blind to put straight, a fan to nail up, or part of a carpet to nail down'. Chintz covers are ordered to be made, 'for our drawing-room chairs and sofa to prevent the sun fading the green rep of the furniture' (1999, 21). The woman 'called in' to make the covers is recognized by Mr Pooter, proving reassuringly 'how small the world is' (1999, 21). The most distressing event in Mr Pooter's life is the unavailability of good sausages, accompanied by anxiety over a small investment (1999, 137). Faced with this, one wonders whether it might not be better to be abducted, if not by a supernatural creature then by aliens; and this in turn leads one to speculate on the reasons why H. G. Wells wrote *The War of the Worlds*.

Pooter's problem, which is to say the problem of the suburbs, is that, like Forster's Leonard Bast, he tries too hard, too self-consciously, to be different, and so makes himself more like everyone else around him. *The Diary of A Nobody* is a novel in which narcissistic ego is so much larger than life because it insists on drawing attention to itself in all its mundanity, and the obviousness of its tastes. Pooter

For Rickie, the suburb is not a home; indeed, despite this representation being one of twentieth-century culture, there is, in the suggestion of suburban villainy, echoes of Milton, Chaucer and Wyclif, in their assessments of that which is disorderly or disreputable. But then, Forster seems to be suggesting, neither is it homely for those who make it a place of temporary residence. As with Leonard Bast in *Howards End*, or, for a while, the Schlegel sisters, the condition of modern identity is to be homeless, whether spiritually or materially; modernity deterritorializes with a vengeance, and the suburbs provide only provisional shelter, dependent on the flows of transport and economic exchange, under the force of which one is kept disorientated.

V

Against this, however, there still remains that other suburban experience, given focus by T. S. Eliot in a short fiction, 'Eeldrop and Appleplex', first published in two parts, in *The Little Review*, in May and September 1917. In this, Eliot points towards the 'atmosphere' of suburbia:

> The suburban evening was grey and yellow on Sunday; the gardens of the small houses to left and right were rank with ivy and tall grass and lilac bushes; the tropical South London verdure was dusty above and mouldy below; the tepid air swarmed with flies. Eeldrop, at the window, welcomed the smoky smell of lilac, the gramophones, the choir of the Baptist chapel, and the sight of three small girls playing cards on the steps of the police station.

The impressionism of the passage lends itself to identifying the whimsical sub-genre of suburban phantasmagoria. Though not named with any particularity, we know this exotic area to be South London. Eeldrop, 'learned in theology' and 'a sceptic, with a taste for mysticism', gives himself up to the sensory experience of suburban dissolution. As an otherwise unidentified suburb, the district in this story is, not unlikely to be, cousin to those suburbs of *The Waste Land*, that 'undo' one, Richmond and Kew with their conscious echo, in Eliot's poem at least, of Dante's *Purgatorio* (ll.293–4). Determinate geography leads to indeterminate selfhood. Loss of self, dissolution of consciousness, whimsical apprehension: anxiety or nirvana are the choices suburbia appear to offer between the 1880s and 1920s. Perhaps it was in anticipation of anxiety that Ezra Pound ruthlessly purged *The Waste Land* of four lines, which spoke of Richmond and Kew. To the Midwesterner, Surrey is unthinkable; to Virginia Woolf, Kew Gardens is captured in 'layer after layer of green-blue vapour ... and in the drone of the aeroplane [there is caught] the voice of the summer sky murmured its fierce soul' (Woolf 1991, 95). Woolf's evanescent image of impressionistically blurred people trailing the botanical gardens, momentarily standing out as blots of colour, before 'wavering' and 'dissolving like drops of water in the yellow and green atmosphere' (Woolf 1991, 95) grasps, perhaps most effectively, that which the suburb offers: a phenomenal vision that discloses itself with an intensity matched only by its brevity, before retreating once again.

Returning to Forster in conclusion, though not expressing the freedom of the Chilterns, Surrey – to which Kew belongs – offers impossible visions. It is a place where police-traps for speeding motorists are at their worst, according to Margaret in *Howards End*. But it is also where Leonard Bast visits under cover of darkness, with Richard Jeffries and Robert Louis Stevenson, when the 'cosy villas had re-entered ancient night' (2000, 103). Whatever Leonard does or does not find, that Forster admits of both the police and archaic England as the possibility of Surrey, suggests a possible definition for suburbia, intimating as he does the imagined conjunction of incompatible worlds. Such whimsical resonance is captured nowhere more acutely than in Forster's short story, 'The Celestial Omnibus'. Departing from the statement of an address, 'Agathox Lodge, 28, Buckingham Park Road, Surbiton' (2001, 30), Forster's narrative opens onto a depiction of the Surbiton Road captured in the setting sun, a road and a representation in which 'the inequalities of rent were drowned in a saffron afterglow' (2001, 31). The boy, who Forster places as the narrative's principal protagonist, finds for himself in a cutting the emergence of 'desires for something just a little different, he knew not what, desires that would return whenever things were sunlit, as they were this evening . . . till he would feel quite unusual all over, and as likely as not would want to cry' (2001, 31); which desires, in turn, find an answer of sorts on the transcendent omnibus of the title. Ending, and yet not quite, ending with the word 'Telos' in Greek, Forster provides, almost an afterthought, a notice 'From the *Kingston Gazette, Surbiton Times* and *Raynes Park Observer*', which announces the discovery of the mutilated body of Mr Bons, as if he had been 'hurled from a considerable height' (2001, 46). Here, as elsewhere in Forster, the intimation is that the suburban gives access to visions if one can see, while those who are too materially of the suburbs are damned. Despite this, there resides the hope that there may be disclosed to one those little worlds within the one world projecting anachronistic, impressionistic or, just simply, whimsical visions everywhere and nowhere, and nowhere moreso than in the imagination in its desire for the possibility of the impossible.

6

Professions: Of English Diaspora?

I

'Therefore', Jacques Derrida remarks, in a strategic inauguration of an otherwise unjustifiably historicized position

> I am starting, strategically, from the place and the time in which 'we' are, even though in the last analysis my opening is not justifiable, since it is only on the basis of *différance* and its 'history' that we can allegedly know who and where 'we' are, and what the limits of an 'era' might be . . . If the word 'history' did not in and of itself convey the motif of a final repression of difference, one could say that only differences can be 'historical' from the outset and in each of their aspects. (Derrida 1982, 7, 11)

That we do not know who or where 'we' are intimates quite urgently a crisis of subjectivity, and with that, the subject's sense of historicity – or lack thereof. Inhabiting a place where one is unknowing, where one cannot say, marks the subject as abject, without place, and so, without cultural identity. At the same time, though, a 'people without history', observes T. S. Eliot, '[i]s not redeemed from time, for history is a pattern / Of timeless moments' (Eliot 1963, 222). That pattern of 'timeless moments', or the concatenation of produced, productive differences, is only ever available to the witness, the one who responds and, bearing witness, is also the one who takes responsibility for all of 'history's differences', those traces, voices and, ultimately, lives that are dispersed, displaced, silenced and erased in the name of 'history'. Yet, this is not all of 'history'. As is acknowledged in Eliot's poetry, history is subsequently revealed indirectly, in the failing of the light: 'On a winter's afternoon, in a secluded chapel' in the village of Little Gidding. History is thus 'now and England' (Eliot 1963, 222). That 'now', irreducible to any present maintains itself each time one reads, and so it suspends knowledge of 'who and where "we" are, and what the limits of an "era" might be' (Derrida 1982, 7).

Eliot's observations raise certain questions: if the English are a people without history; if those of us who consider ourselves English are a people who, though touched everywhere by our histories, are incapable nevertheless of being aware when history befalls us unless belatedly, how and where might we hear what our histories, histories of the land and the timeless patterns into which we have been interwoven, have to say about who we are? How might we 'only connect', especially when we cannot escape the fact that, as Daniel Defoe put it, 'a true born

Englishman's a contradiction', a 'Het'rogeneous thing'? (Defoe 1889, 195, 194).
The very idea of heterogeneity is not counterintuitive to notions of identity; rather,
it introduces a difference within identity. That difference is, in effect, the trace of
the other, within us, in our voices, and in every utterance that is made in the name,
and in the name of Englishness.

Imagine, then, if you will, a fictional public event.[1] You are invited to hear
someone speak, to attend to a single voice. That lone voice is, however, curiously
impure from its very inauguration. On hearing this voice, you have the sense that
the voice is unassignable and irreducible to a single source. More than one, it is
many, innumerable. A Capella, yet, you find it presents itself and is presented to
you in two guises initially: as *coryphaeus*, one who directs a chorus, and *diaskeuast*,
someone who, through interpolation, engages in the work of invention, recension
and transmission. The voice is one through which a chorus of voices is edited and
transmitted, translated and broadcast. Your apprehension arises from the very first,
when that apparently single voice says to you:

– I have only one culture; it is not mine.[2]

The phrase is chosen deliberately; it is intended to interrupt, to introduce
interference, thereby drawing attention to itself. It is a performative speech act,
the purpose of which is to announce someone who affirms their existence within
and yet excluded from a culture, which they cannot properly claim as theirs. As
John Clare might have put it, the 'now is past' (Clare 2000, 342–3) when a sense
of belonging could have been both expressed and experienced. Affirmation takes
place only in the meagre act of resisting accommodation or incorporation. What
constitutes the statement as a performative resides in its slight illegibility, that
which cannot be carried over or translated fully. There is a local excess not subject
to accumulation or calculation. Sense and meaning are dispersed within an affirmation that, broadcast, speaks of ontological, cultural and historical privation and
dispossession. Dispossession itself, this is what haunts the voice. You know the
words, they are English; but they arrive as if some stranger to English had failed to
master the use of idiom. The phrase interrupts for, inasmuch as it eludes unequivocal comprehension, it also, and as a result of its having escaped your understanding
in part, speaks not only of its own subject's exclusion; it excludes you also. You are
thus, in imagination at least and for one brief moment, aligned in some degree with
that anonymous subject who says 'I' but who can do so only on the condition that
subjectivity is acknowledged through the confession of privation and dispossession
or displacement within 'their' culture as the very condition of their historical and
material being. Listen again to this statement, to the disquieting, unquiet paucity
within its profession, a profession of diaspora:

– I have only one culture; it is not mine.

Hearing this, one might not unreasonably question what it might mean to
profess, questions arise concerning what it means to be a professor and one who

claims to profess, to profess as part of a profession, as well as being a professional, within a profession or institution. It gives rise, doubtless, to particular queries: what is someone, supposedly a professional, doing by interrupting the inaugural event, doing so, moreover, in acting out the role of a professor, by uttering the not-quite-intelligible phrase, 'I have only one culture; it is not mine'? Moreover, what might such a profession or, perhaps more properly, confession, have to do with an English diaspora?

Before we get too entangled in such questions, remember that the place from which they issue in search of an addressee is *just* a fiction. The fiction is that of a voice or voices, which on any given day and in specific situations can arrive, making itself or themselves heard. One might hypothesize that the affirmative resistance of such a voice, in offering a countersignature to what is required in any profession – to proceed professionally, to make a profession which is clear and clearly stated – functions by 'interrupting the weave of our language and then weaving together the interruptions themselves, another language [arriving] to disturb the first one. It doesn't inhabit it, but haunts it' (Derrida 2007, 152). As a fiction, such utterance attests of course to the function of all literature. For fiction or literature, 'can always respond (or refuse to respond) by saying, that was not me speaking as myself, but as an imaginary personage in a work of fiction' (Miller 2005, 284). One has to take literature at its word, but that word is always already implicated in a weave of tongues, always already underway, always already interrupted.

Fiction and, by extension, literature has, as its principle, the right to say anything; but its responsibility is equally, if not more, one of affirming resistance, a 'refusal addressed to sovereign . . . powers' (Miller 2005, 284) such as those embodied in a profession and the institution that grants both literature and the professor their identity and purpose. This refusal takes place and is enacted because of 'a higher obligation' (Miller 2005, 284), in this instance an obligation to all those voices that remain to be heard and to be given place on their own account. If one is to be more than merely professional, if one's profession is not to retreat into that infelicitous mechanical delivery that merely affects or pretends an obligation, then one must speak in such ways that make possible the interruption of business as usual. The one who professes must risk a profession of faith, opposing 'always-illegitimate sovereignty' (Miller 2005, 284) with an affirmation or admission, a confession if you will, of unconditional freedom, that freedom, which, John Wyclif tells us, belongs by right to the voice: above everything else voice is free (Wyclif 1869–71, 75). And this requires, or, better yet, demands opening oneself to the unconditional admission of the other's voices. In this opening, voice does not present itself in the guise or as guarantor of a presence. Rather, in opening itself, and in being opened to those traces that reside within it, it admits itself in its impurity and as *mnemotechnic* as that which bears 'memory, history, and an archive of confession' (Derrida 2002b, 80).

My fiction therefore includes an acknowledgement that a professor is one who, today for example and in a local, unprofessional manner, makes professions of faith by acting 'as if he were nevertheless asking your permission to be unfaithful or a traitor to his habitual practice' (Derrida 2001a, 34). A contest is inaugurated between event and machine: between, on the one hand, the public, institutionalized avoca-tion, which, with its repetitive, somewhat mechanical drive, implies or runs the risk of falling into insincerity or falsity; and, on the other hand, that articulation within the professional voice, which confesses as a profession of faith, and in so doing, acknowledges in itself, always uncertainly, that passively and submissively, it 'obeys a call or command. All we can do' in this case, J. Hillis Miller affirms, is to 'profess faith in the call [of these other voices] or pledge allegiance to it' (Miller 2005, 285). If one professes faith in the possibility of such a call, then one's response might be to suggest that the professions, of which my title speaks, have less to do with the professor or professional who speaks to an audience than with those professions which have disappeared or become marginalized over the course of a thousand years or so as a result of the effects of diaspora. Imagining that one hears those voices emerging out of different experiences and epochs of diaspora, all of whom are gathered in the phrase, 'I have only one culture; it is not mine', I admit their revenant apparition, And they, in turn, demand that I bear witness.

II

Where I live, on Sunday mornings in spring and early summer I can hear two sounds, one natural, the other technological: sheep, lambs and church bells com-bine, in rhythmic and arrhythmic canon and counterpoint. It is an aural image, unchanged more or less for several hundred years. It is disrupted only by the inter-ruption of an incoming cut-price flight, making its final descent into East Midlands Airport. However brief the access to the sempiternal is, it remains, nevertheless, as if a moment in time were both opened and suspended, as if I were witness to the voices of a cyclical, communal temporality, voices which have a ground, and which give ground to identity and a sense of being in the same location. In hearing this, my momentary conceit is that I am joined to all those, living and dead, who have heard something similar, and who have therefore been marked by, and have left their otherwise anonymous marks on, location. Neither a moment of unbroken continuity nor one of sundered discontinuity, but instead an instant in which, *through which*, there is the analogical apperception of a ghostly contiguity.

In such gatherings of sound, or in other remnants that persist, any given place is marked as a site of memory, location as archive, being both witness and recording of the times. Such sites exist, and are revealed in their true condition, 'as arenas in which lives are lived . . . [and] as images of how private and communal life could be conducted' (Davie 1998, 243). In these and other *aletheic* instances, those modalities of truth's unveiling, the articulation and apprehension of other identi-ties are made available. Dissenting or alternative English identities emerge, given representation through their impression on the landscape, as if they were horses' hoof-prints awaiting translation. Unable to read such signs completely, we may perhaps gain insight into a mode of registration for cultural memory: that which passes leaves its traces to be read by future generations, and its 'dissent' remains to be read in the memory work of oral forms and the occasional literary manifestation

– Michael Drayton, John Clare, William Cobbett, Gaskell, Eliot, Hardy, Mary Butts, Ronald Blythe – as the gathering of the signs and voices of some other in danger of occlusion or obliteration. The dissent is, at its most neutral, simply the affirmation that 'I do not belong' and 'I no longer belong' in the historical and cultural transformation of social and cultural determinations of identity. This affirmation registers as the remainder that survives.

Dissent may of course be just the registration of an alternative identity that apprehends its no longer having a home, the expression of a voice at variance with the times, the voice as both contretemps and countersignature. Thomas Hardy gives early expression to this in *Under the Greenwood Tree* most directly in the words of Michael Mail, who delivers the opinion that 'times have changed from the times they used to be' (Hardy 1998c, 22), a sentiment echoed somewhat more polemically in a song by our most famous composer, Anonymous, 'Hard Times of Old England'. As with all such songs, this has travelled down to the present day, given a lyric pertinent to a present in which villages are gentrified, post offices closed, and farmers are no longer able to sell crops as a result of 'agribusiness' and agribarons, in a recording called *The Imagined Village*. In this survival, we can trace nearly two hundred years of diaspora. Almost a century after Thomas Hardy wrote *Under the Greenwood Tree*, and wrote of enclosures that 'the landlord leases land more & more frequently to capitalist farmers' (Hardy 2004, 3), Ronald Blythe records similar sentiments throughout *Akenfield*, the chronicle of a Suffolk village which charts loss and dispersal. One voice especially stands out, Sammy Whitelaw, a farrier and church bell-ringer, who, by his own admission, was 'bell-mad' (Blythe 2005, 77). Sammy's memory of ringing changes – that singularly English practice, where tuned bells are rung in a series of mathematical patterns or changes without the production of a tune – includes the recollection of having to climb the bell tower to strike the bell with a hammer, the ropes being out of commission. This was done so as to mark the death of Billy, 'one of the old people', Sammy says, 'who have gone and who have taken a lot of the truth out of the world with them' (Blythe 2005, 78). As in other villages, the bell was rung so that 'all could hear the passing and take note' (Blythe 2005, 78). At the same time, Billy's wife went to the bottom of the garden to tell the bees that Billy was dead; for, this rural practice has it, if the bees are not told of the death of their keeper, they die also.

Change ringing connects Sammy Whitelaw in 1969 to 'Eight Carriford men and one stranger' (Hardy 1998a, 401) who occupy the belfry of Carriford Church on Midsummer Night, 1867. Carriford is the fictive name for West Stafford, a village midway between Dorchester and East Lulworth, just south of Tolpuddle. In this scene, the epilogue to Thomas Hardy's first published novel, *Desperate Remedies*, the nine bell-ringers are represented in the act of ringing changes, which performance is presented by Hardy in present tense (Hardy 1998a, 401). Captured in an endless 'now', as if representation and witness were conjoined in a singular and ineluctable performative and represented through a 'blue, phosphoric and ghostly' illumination (Hardy 1998a, 401), this is just one of countless midsummer nights. The narrative acknowledges the cyclical, iterable moment, in the affirmation that this has been 'music to the ears of Carriford Parish and the outlying districts for the last four hundred years' (Hardy 1998a, 401). Such bells may have been heard in 1593 by an ancestor, Avis Woollfris, when she married George Turbervill(e). And Turberville, in turn, might have been one of the ghosts Hardy had in mind, when he wrote in his *'Facts' Notebook* the following entry from 21 July 1883:

> Families of the ancient Saxon & Norman race – either extinct or reduced to lowest fortune – Could one of those illustrious shades return to earth he might behold one of his descendants dancing at the lathe – another tippling with his dark brethren of the apron . . . a fifth poaching upon the very manors possessed by his ancestors (Hardy 2004, 3–4).

Whether or not, from Michael Mail to Sammy Whitelaw, Hardy to Blythe, and back, and so, from this, across four hundred years: shared customs are remembered, voicings of communal experience marked by their historicity, and with this a sense of place is marked in passing, mourning, ritual acknowledgement of seasonal rebirth, and so on. These are the ghostly contiguities of which I spoke.

Like Thomas Hardy, this has gone on, I imagine, and will continue, in the words of Hugh Lupton, 'though dynasties pass, to mark and circumscribe our lives'. As Lupton has put it so eloquently, 'we walk this world in music' (Wood, 'Walk this World', *The Lark Descending*, 2005). And every voice, from John Barleycorn or John Ball to Michael Mail or Sammy Whitelaw, is both counterblast and broadcast: a cry affirming its meagre existence in the face of that which would deny it, move it on, displace it or silence it for ever; a voice transmitted, spread and scattered, unknowing of where its traces might take root, or which ears will receive it. Everything is risked on *and* in the voice, in the fiction of a single voice, imagining a single voice that carries the burden of innumerable others. Dissenting always from accommodation within European impositions and the forces of Enlightenment, in such a song chronicling the seasonal cycle inextricable from the cycle of life and death, the verdict of the English voice is heard as it broadcasts an affirmation of itself and what Hélène Cixous has called 'Anglo-Saxon penumbra' (Cixous 1998, 172).

With all such shades and what they might have to whisper in mind, the more one looks and listens, the more one finds evidence everywhere, in historical detail and event obviously, but most insistently through the very weave of language itself, in particular words but also in those voices testifying in so many singular professions, of an English diaspora. Despite their having being broadcast, these diasporic voices are still on the air. The voices clamour for attention, demanding a concerted, yet disconcerting inauguration, which also gives access to revenance through an act of remembering. One finds oneself haunted by their revenance gathering force under the heading of a diaspora that one could speak of as 'English', and of which one might speak in response to the many and various identities captured in singular attestation of different experiences of being English. The voices appear to me all the more insistent because they have never been spoken of in terms of diaspora, they have never been gathered within a shared if occluded ontology, whilst retaining the traces of their singularity, and marked by their differences from one another.

Such voices spoke in their times – and they continue to speak, remaining to be heard – from sites, from different grounds which gave to those voices a place and a meaning and which place and sense was at one or another historical moment irreparably transformed. Now, of course, there are names for the many historical events and irreparable acts of violation and dispossession of which I am thinking, names that serve as short-hand for the barbarity, oppression and displacement that makes up so much of English history and what it means to be English. Of course, the very word 'history' bears in it 'the theme of a final repression of difference' (Derrida 1982, 11). What I hear in this in the very silence or avoidance of speaking of diaspora is just this repression in the name of history. Diaspora bespeaks a heterogeneity and dissemination, which gathers in chorus the 'inscrutable [voices] of the long dead' (Lee 2005, ix) along with, inside, the still living one which roars, as George Eliot might have said, the other side of silence. It is, thus, the one name one never hears, amongst the many names of historical event. Yet, with regard to the various different English identities marked by loss, what *diaspora* professes is all too important to leave unspoken, addressing as it does histories and testimonies, as Iain Chambers describes it, of 'mass rural displacement' (1994, 16); and it must be said that there is more than ample historical fact, data, statistics and research already pursued in a professional manner which authorizes me to speak, and to speak this name, diaspora.

However, on the one hand, while it is always necessary to remind ourselves of particular historical events, on the other hand, one must risk everything on the voice. For, contemporary 'testimonies' of the voice have the ability to 'interrogate or undermine any simple or uncomplicated sense of origins, traditions, and linear movement', which, conversely, academic history risks reconstituting, thereby damping down the disturbance that the voice might introduce (Chambers 1994, 16–17). Furthermore, through that which voice bears in its impurity, 'we are inevitably confronted with mixed histories, cultural mingling, composite languages … that are also central to *our history*' (Chambers 1994, 17; emphasis added). Through its force, voice solicits from within any 'abstract ideology of a uniformity stamped with the seals of tradition, nation, race and religion' (Chambers 1994, 17). In this, the voices of our others, those diasporic traces, have the capability to awaken a 'sense of belonging' marked by difference and alterity. The 'myths we carry in us … linger on as traces, voices, memories and murmurs that are mixed in with other histories, episodes, encounters' (Chambers 1994, 19).

If one is to speak of voices therefore; if one is to speak of lives, the very traces of which are borne on the resonances of those voices and which, in turn, in having become fragmented, frayed, partially erased, or muted have become hard to hear and to receive, as if there were some indistinctly heard group of wassailers outside your door; then facts, data and statistics can never be enough. Although the itinerary inaugurates directions for research, it is insufficient to speak, for example, of the Harrowing of the North, Hinderskelf, Peterloo, Orgreave, Speenhamland, the Swing Riots, Tolpuddle, the Enclosure Acts, The Poll Tax Riots, the SUS laws, Clause 28, the closure of village post offices and so on. Such names, and the facts or statistics that accompany them, all such merely empirical evidence, however irrefutable as a series of names gathered in an itinerary which promise to begin the thinking of diaspora, will never make us feel. Though necessary and important, merely professional 'academic history writing', Robert Lee observes, 'cannot always capture' the voices. It can fail to apprehend with any immediacy or sympathetic resonance the voices of those convicted for poaching, allegedly, in, say, Rufford Park; or, for that matter, those convicted of the Clippesby Skimmington (1868), in which, as a court reporter for the *Norfolk News* reports on 29 February, five young men paraded an effigy of gamekeeper John Mumford, around the neck of which effigy was a sign stating 'no friend to the poor man' (Lee 2005, 141–2). Poaching is, of course, a symptom, not only of enclosure, but anywhere where common land is cordoned off, denied and transformed into private property, as happened with the clearance of villages and parishes under Forest Law, in order to create the New Forest in 1079 for William. With the displacement of inhabitants the area also lost its Anglo-Saxon name, Ytene. Presumably the death in 1100 of William Rufus in the forest at Canterton Glen, was the forest's way of exacting a somewhat ironic vengeance. Perhaps.

Understanding the problem in a merely professional historical account, knowing that the harrowing of the North laid waste to the majority of Yorkshire particularly, all crops and livestock destroyed, a scorched earth policy pursued, if narrated as mere facts organized after the event, is therefore insufficient to a true testimony and equally a true verdict, an act of speaking truly. Similarly, understanding that 7000 enclosure acts between 1700 and 1850 were passed gets us no closer to the life of one person. Providing names such as James Loveless, George Loveless, James Brine, James Hammett, Thomas and John Standfield may help to give individual shapes to the past, but we still have little chance of hearing the dead speak. And if you do not know these names, their voices cannot speak to you, and so remain mute. However, every name bears in it both memory and promise, even as it raises another difficulty. For – and again this an empirical problem, a problem, that is to say, with the assumptions of empiricism and the repression it instigates – a single name or voice does not necessarily connect. It can be observed that oral history projects are all very interesting, but where does one voice, one name gathered in the archive get us? The difficulty resides in empiricism's ideological and epistemological inability to apprehend either connection or invention. Every time a name appears for the first time, it countersigns an inauguration, it marks a beginning, as Alexander Garcia Düttmann argues, and 'as such it is intimidating'. Its intimidation resides in our apprehension concerning what we may come to hear, if 'we hear the name of the other for the first time . . . [yet] have no memory of that name' (Düttmann 2000, 127). The singularity of the other imposes on the living a responsibility to bear witness, to invent a network that maintains difference. The name is therefore analogous to the voice; bearer of memory, encrypted archive, it promises the delivery of that memory, even if we do not know what that is, or what unlocking its secret will demand of us. This, in short, is the gift of language, the gift of an apparition in waiting.

Acknowledging then, the historical itinerary, the various events of which authorize me to speak of an English diaspora, yet knowing such an itinerary to be inadequate, it has to be remarked that this remains a merely professional gesture, a calculated and measured act within the economy and constraints of institutional form, but haunted by a lack, the lack, specifically, of a single voice, to make you see, to make you feel, to borrow Joseph Conrad's formula. The responsibility to make one feel is, perhaps, the greatest responsibility of literature, especially in the face of the occlusion of oral cultures. Literature can present the trace of the voice, not as if it were a presence, but as if, having been broadcast, its trace, its seed and signal, reaches us with a touching immediacy, as in the following lines of John Clare's voice in 'The Fallen Elm', a poem that speaks of Enclosure:

> To wrong another by the name of right
> It grows the liscence of o'erbearing fools
> To cheat plain honesty by force of might
> Thus came enclosure – ruin was its guide
> But freedom's clapping hands enjoyed the sight
> Though comfort's cottage soon was thrust aside
> And workhouse prisons raised upon the site
>
> [...]
>
> The common heath, became the spoilers' prey.
> (Clare 2000, 167–9)

The fatal consequences of what Clare calls the 'fence of ownership' in another poem, 'The Mores', which opposes the freedom of memory to the experience of enclosure, are caught by Oliver Goldsmith, just over a generation before:

> Ill fares the land to hastening ills a prey;
> Where wealth accumulates and men decay;
> Princes and lords may flourish, or may fade;
> A breath can make them as a breath has made;
> But a bold peasantry, their country's pride
> When once destroyed, can never be supplied.
> (2008, ll.51–6)

Here, yet again, a single voice stands in for all those silenced and dispossessed; more than that, those otherwise mute voices gather in the poet's verdict and profession. Though not the voices of that peasantry, Goldsmith nevertheless makes an emotional demand in a voice that bears witness to the experience of what otherwise remains the clinical and objective account. In this, he anticipates a problem that haunts radical critique especially today, captured in questions from a 1926 letter by Antonio Gramsci. Gramsci asks, 'how many times have I wondered if it is really possible to forge links with a mass of people when one has never had strong feelings for anyone ... If it is possible to have a collectivity when one has not been deeply [touched] oneself by individual human creatures' (Gramsci 1991, 147). Without this, everything is a matter, as Gramsci continues, of 'pure intellect, of pure mathematical calculation' (147). Literature as a network of traces has the power to exceed calculation. It can always remind us that the ethics of witnessing and profession 'will not', as Jacques Derrida puts it in response to Francis Fukuyama, 'be a matter of merely accumulating, as Fukuyama might say, "empirical evidence," it will not suffice to point one's finger at the mass of undeniable facts that this [or that] picture could describe or denounce' (Derrida 1994a, 80). Across two hundred years by chance, note how Goldsmith and Derrida are linked in their critique by an undisguised animosity to all that is borne economically and ideologically in the term 'accumulation'. A resonance is caught between the two, as one voice oscillates in the weft of language.

III

At an absolute limit, the diasporic English voice is marked as abject. The abject witness, who is neither singular nor plural but *both* singular *and* plural simultaneously, articulates material, cultural and ontological destitution.[3] The subject is, at the extreme, dispossessed of ground or world. It is this we hear, or receive, in John Clare's affirmation, 'I am – yet what I am none cares nor knows' or, alternatively, 'But now I only am – that's all' (Clare 2000, 311–12). Other voices, not yet forced to such extremity, nevertheless chronicle the experience of becoming dispossessed of the cultural and material ground from which one's being and one's voice has been formed, and which, through song, story, practice and tradition, has served to give voice to one's being. They remark the becoming-destitute that resonates within the diasporic voice. Suffering history we might say, here are two such voices, the first 'fictional', the second 'real'. The first, from the Midlands, is that of Timothy Cooper, an agricultural labourer and minor character in *Middlemarch*, and can be dated to the late 1820s and early 1830s:

> I'n seen lots o' things turn up sin' I war a young un – the war an' the peace, and the canells, an' the oald King George, an' the Regen', an' the new King George, an' the new un as has got a new ne-ame – an' it's been all aloike to the poor mon. What's the canells been t' him? They'n brought him neyther me-at nor be-acon, nor wage to lay by, if he didn't save it wi' clemmin' his own inside. Times ha' got wusser for him sin' I war a young un. An' so it'll be wi' the railroads. They'll on'y leave the poor mon furder behind. (Eliot 2003, 560)

The second voice, that of John Copper, is from Sussex, recorded in 2006:

> When I come to think about it, old Jimmy Copper, my granddad, he was a lucky man, 'cause he worked in a place he really liked to be in, up on those old chalk downs; there's one spot, just in the valley near 'ere, Saltdean Valley, where he liked to be so much when 'e was up there workin', and he used to sit on the boundary stone eatin' 'is lunch, where 'e could look down through the valley to the sea. That was 'is favourite spot. Yeah, 'e liked it so much that 'e asked dad if, after 'e died,

'e'd sprinkle 'is ashes up there; and that's what dad did. 'n I bin up there with 'im many times, to visit the place. You 'ave to 'ave a good imagination now to imagine it like it was when Jim was younger. In fact, when 'e made a recording for the BBC back in 1951, 'e put it quite graphically; 'e said, 'I still do like to walk up on those old 'ills, where I was a shepherd boy; but they've changed today; they're all different now', 'e said . . . but now, you look down there 'n' all you see is 'ouses, 'ouses, 'ouses on the land that we used to plough [. . .] 'Ouses, 'ouses, 'ouses. That makes me prostrate with dismal', 'e said. Yes, there's only one thing he thought 'ad come down from the old days unchanged, and that was our old songs. (Copper and Chandra 2007, ''Ouses, 'Ouses, 'Ouses')

Whether fictional or real, as soon as such voices are taken up or registered, they enter into an iterable field and the mark or sign disseminated becomes what we call literature, in a singular negotiation between orality and writing, event and machine. Literature thereby enables in its recording technique the staging of a 'historicity without history – historicity without direct references to actual occurrences but only direct exposure of its field' (Fynsk 1996, 223). Of course there are more or less direct references in both voices, which give to those voices, to make the point once more, the very ground that is subject to erasure. That ground however, the historical details and empirical facts, constitutes the speaking subject, through what Gilles Deleuze, after David Hume, describes as 'the flux of the sensible, a collection of impressions and images, or a set of perceptions. It is', Deleuze continues, 'movement and change without identity or law'; and coming to appear, to give voice to experience in a 'particular set or a particular collection . . . an animated succession of distinct perceptions' (Deleuze 1991, 87). Hume's empirical comprehension of the giving of ground to the subject might sound strange, closer to phenomenology. But this sensory empirical flow is, nevertheless, that which gives to voice and being its form and the singularity of its affirmation in a given place. Such voices as those just quoted, or that of John Clare, serve to produce testimony of loss and dispossession through the oral ability to give place to the subject. Experience is thus registered as one voice affirming the experience of many, as in the examples given, in spoken word or song.

Timothy Cooper's testimony comes from *Middlemarch*. The second voice, that of John Copper, a member of a family of agricultural labourers and collectors of traditional song who can trace their family back to 1593 in the Rottingdean area. In both, and between the two, voices from more than a thousand years of English dispossession resonate. In shared oral cultures and the communities of difference they signify, what comes to be registered is not simply, if ever, history after the event. Instead, it has always been, and still remains, a living archive, history from the inside, a history that speaks itself every time a song is taken up. In such voices, between them and beyond in the intimation of countless other voices, an affirmation of shared cultural experiences of dispossession is heard. Difference of dialect and accent intimate all those communities of difference suffering the erasure of 'freely chosen alternatives' under the imposition of 'hegemonic rules of exclusion' (Smith 1994, 93, 94). In the supplement of the voice what we thus hear is not simply history after the event. Instead, the supplementary eruption of the trace marks itself and 'so lives on, *at once* translatable *and un*translatable' (Derrida 1979, 79), as a living archive, history felt from the inside. In their singular fashion such voices, centuries later, take up the crisis of nationhood that informs Michael Drayton's *Poly-Olbion*, which is a crisis of people and a land represented as 'fragile and mutable, eroding and deforested, riven with political contest' (McEachern 1996, 139). This is historicity of experience, if you will, of those who attest to the truth beyond distinctions between the fictional or real that 'one can be inside [a culture] without being inside ... there is an ... outside in the inside and this goes on infinitely' (Cixous and Derrida 2005, 5).

In relation to the idea of an English diaspora, the voices of Clare, Copper and Cooper profess the precarious condition of being liminal to the main currents of history and national identity. Their voices also aver that 'as with any displaced people the stories and songs which explain who we are, are locked up in the land'. If we have forgotten this, or indeed never known it, this is because, as Chris Wood has argued, 'unlike the people of Scotland and Eire, the people of England have never been allowed to mourn the loss of their land through enclosure'.[4] Professions of English diaspora then; these are voices of spectral survivals, admitting those who suffered dispossession, displacement and destitution, and with that the loss, if not of life, then certainly the ways and means of existence that connected them with their ancestors.

As is well known, the Napoleonic Wars and the Industrial Revolution conspired with Enclosure and the building of the railroads of course, albeit with a cruel and coincidental historical irony, which ensured loss and silence, the erosion or devastation of communities. It seems to me though a somewhat disingenuous, merely professional, and perhaps pernicious argument on the history of Enclosure, which accounts for experience through the statistics and evidence concerning the extent to which people were 'really' impoverished. This is the state of academic writing on Enclosure in recent years, as articles play with charts and numbers, accumulating evidence from parish records. Wages in some cases – the case of agricultural labourers in the Parish of Helpston, John Clare's home – may well have risen during the period of intense enclosure between 1809 and 1820, as some historians argue. However, this misses the human amongst so many calculations, so many privately pursued acts of displacement. The voice is muffled, silenced. As John Barrell has remarked, not a little while ago, 'such evidence as there is suggests that in strictly economic terms the poor were better off after enclosure; but the unmeasurable factors – the loss of customary rights of common [grazing], and the others – could conceivably have been important enough to counteract this apparent improvement' (Barrell 1972, 215). Loss, in these terms, is beyond calculation. For it is loss not only of freedoms but also the real communities of village and parish, in the name of an imagined national community, all differences suppressed. Cultural memory erased, future generations lose touch with their older other selves, and there is no accounting for dispossession.

A sign of the truth of this speculation is that Scottish and Irish folk cultures have thrived for quite some time, as already remarked, whilst in England, not only song, but practices such as mumming and other ritual, irrational, seasonal celebrations such as morris or molly dancing remain, like the politician's reference to God, just a little bit embarrassing, odd, something apparently one should never try. The bad reader, who rushes to such a judgement – I can imagine him –, betrays historical ignorance, despite his presentist avocations of political correctness. Doubtless the morris (the earliest recorded mention of which is 1448, in the inventory of Caistor Castle, Norfolk) and other folk practices suffer in no small part because we have lost or had wiped vital cultural memory and experience of their purpose and significance. Indeed, as Verity Sharp observed on St George's Day, 'a lot of people think of the morris as all a little bit flippant and jovial. But you just have to listen a little bit closer and you'll find all kinds of messages . . . in both the dance and the music'.[5]

Morris dance or mummers' play, such acts attest, in the words of Athena Vrettos, to what it means 'to be "saturated" with human memories' (Vrettos 2007, 199). Act, song, voice: all are so saturated, and mark us in the reception of displaced memories with transferential phantoms. Such traces are phantasmic, inasmuch as they have no other appearance of being, save for their appeal to us in performance. Song and act, ritual and practice thus take on the form of what Gayatri Spivak terms a 'transactional reading'. That is, in bearing witness to history and experience, transmitting themselves from singer to singer, culture to culture, generation to generation, and across various imagined and interpretive communities, all such manifestations of voice leave themselves provisional and open. In this they offer 'active transaction[s] between past and future in a manner that official histories cannot do' (Spivak cit. Niranjana 1992, 42). Hardy gives us yet another example, this time with the Christmas mummers' play performed for winter solstice, the origin of which, scholars now agree, is in pagan ritual. In presenting the performance in *The Return of the Native*, Hardy's narrative is interpolated with lines taken from particular Dorset versions of such plays:

At this moment the fiddles finished off with a screech, and the serpent emitted a last note that nearly lifted the roof. When, from the comparative quiet within, the mummers judged that the dancers had taken their seats, Father Christmas advanced, lifted the latch, and put his head inside the door.

'Ah, the mummers, the mummers!' cried several guests at once. 'Clear a space for the mummers.'

Humpbacked Father Christmas then made a complete entry, swinging his huge club, and in a general way clearing the stage for the actors proper, while he informed the company in smart verse that he was come, welcome or welcome not; concluding his speech with

'Make room, make room, my gallant boys
And give us space to rhyme;
We've come to show Saint George's play
Upon this Christmas time.'

[...]

> Being wounded, the Knight fell upon one knee, according to the direction. The Doctor now entered, restored the Knight by giving him a draught from the bottle which he carried, and the fight was again resumed, the Turk sinking by degrees until quite overcome – dying as hard in this venerable drama as he is said to do at the present day. (Hardy 1999, 133–5)

Not only is there the oscillation between the *now* of narrative witness and interpretation interspersed by the lines of an anonymous, possibly collective author. Hardy's brief, ironic fillip in the last line, referring to contemporary events in the Balkans effects a rupture in the membrane between literature and history. As with the narrative of the bonfires at the beginning of the novel, here a single articulation stands in for countless others, *now* torn asunder with the admission of every other temporal instance in which are registered similar events. As Hardy puts it in the bonfire scene, conjuring the force of the fictive voice and what it is capable of articulating, 'it was as if these men and boys had suddenly dived into past ages and fetched therefrom an hour and deed which had before been familiar with this spot . . . [to recall] the flames of funeral piles long ago kindled . . . Indeed,' Hardy concludes, 'such blazes as this . . . are rather the lineal descendants from jumbled Druidical rites and Saxon ceremonies than the invention of popular feeling about Gunpowder Plot' (Hardy 1999, 20). Hardy offers us a forgotten truth, breaking up the merely mechanical repetition, like some literary Tolpuddle protestor. Every time such events recur, and voices brought back, they bear in them the voices of others, various English ghosts, who in being remembered return as I have suggested before. The dead live and, in Hugh Lupton's words, 'we are inhabited by the dead every time we speak'.[6] Possessed, you might say, by the dispossessed, it is thus that a voice can address you by saying, 'I have only one culture; it is not mine'. And this is what I imagine is written on every map, in village names such as Cottenham, Afpuddle, Froxfield and Aldbourne, or any village name you care to substitute.

A double remembrance and survival – double in that, on the one hand, the dead speak to us and through us, while on the other hand, they affirm dispossession – is captured in the acts of bearing witness already voiced, and in many others also. So too is it with literature, at least in principle, which is perhaps why one professes literature, professing faith in what literature can give us to hear. Literature does not merely record empirically, but in its textual field gives voice to experience, and places me before its profession of otherwise dispersed signs, giving to me the empirical and perceptual experience of a collection, a flux momentarily suspended, *as if I were there* in the moment from which the voice speaks to me. And this takes place every time a voice arrives, impurely registered thus. One witnesses, therefore, the effect of literature's direct exposure, of what literature lets happen, which is to say the possibility of the impossible, through the revenance of some ghostly trace. It is this return, placing me before it as if I were witness to such exposure and to such events that literature makes possible. It is this which is literature's profession, through the encryption of so many historical signatures, otherwise occluded in their becoming scattered or spread in the alluvial deposits of English cultures from the eleventh century at least to the present day.

Such profession is also the work of song in oral cultures, providing a particularly significant, often-acute form in which the trace of the eyewitness to history becomes remarked through the fiction of the single voice. What Antonio Gramsci calls 'popular song' is significant 'in the context of a nation and its culture' in 'the way in which it conceives the world and life, in contrast with official society'. What oral culture and folklore reveal, Gramsci argues, is that 'the people themselves are not a homogeneous cultural collectivity but . . . numerous and variously combined cultural stratifications' (Gramsci 1991, 195). Voice is thus always already impure, orality marked by the traces of its other voices. As Jacques Derrida has observed 'orality is also an inscription [*frayage*] of the trace' (Derrida 2005c, 1). It is a mode of recording and inscription, which, though largely oral throughout its history, nevertheless bears within itself and from generation to generation, across different voices the traces of its cultures, and with those, the signs of particular pasts. 'Voice', Derrida's affirms, 'always stages itself, or is staged' (2005c, 1). Whether in song or in those commentaries already quoted, voice in song does not merely observe; it is not separate from, nor does it stand apart from, that which its traces re-present. It enacts the experience, as if it were taking place – to me – for a first time, and every time the song is sung.

Thomas Hardy, to whom the songs of Wessex were familiar, is clearly influenced by the power of the single, impure voice, as it opens from within itself to testify to larger histories. He attempts to capture oral immediacy, seeking to re-present the past and capture that performative, staged effect implicit in the voice in as haunting a manner as possible in *The Trumpet-Major*, a romantic comedy set against the Napoleonic Wars. Hardy is at pains to disrupt fictional closure through the narrative of historical consequences, and, in so doing, opening to the reader the transmission of the experience of historical rupture and violence, through the experience of history's others, people such as John, his brother Robert, and Anne Garland who have no historical voice in conventional, broad historical accounts of war. Additionally, Hardy then goes on to recount how, of 'the seven' who take their leave of Anne on the night mentioned in the final chapter, 'five, *including the trumpet-major*, were dead men within the few following years, and their bones left to moulder in the land of their campaigns' (Hardy 1997b, 300; emphasis added).

Hardy thus offers us a vision of what I am tempted to call a diaspora in death. As Daniel Bivona has it, in Hardy 'the history of the individual enacts the history of the race' (Bivona 1999, 98). The titular protagonist leaves for his death, a death already having occurred by the time the novel is written two generations later. Hardy re-emphasizes the destruction to come in the last paragraph, as, seemingly needlessly in an excess of repetition, death returns once more for John. His face is seen briefly by candlelight, as he backs across the doorstep into the 'black night; and in another moment he had plunged into the darkness, the ring of his smart step dying away . . . as he . . . went off to blow his trumpet till silenced for ever upon one of the bloody battle-fields of Spain' (Hardy 1997b, 301). The reiteration of this irreducible event breaks the frame of any mere narrative recounting, for it takes up the burden of an ultimate dispossession, to be reiterated in every reading. Furthermore, in taking up the burden, its iterable manifestation takes on the shape of a chorus, its echoes resounding, to drive home the account. Of course, in this, there still remains in place that mediation of place we call the narrator. In this example, at least, a voice from a subsequent generation stages a voice, risking everything on iterability, and leaving this missive open to reception. The narrator acts as a transmitter between past and future, sending out a signal, recording a voice, and posting it, to be heard by those who remain to come. Hardy's narrator thus assumes the subject position implicit in every song that bears witness to the experience of material hardship, displacement and loss.

What, in effect, Hardy does in the conclusion of *The Trumpet Major* is to register the historical event, as if, on the one hand, it were still yet to happen, while, on the other, tracing the register of it in the living memory of those who survive, marked as it is by the trauma of loss. One voice, speaking for nameless others. Of course, to risk a speculation, had John Loveday survived, he may have found on his return from war that milling was no longer a professional option. As in the narrative of a song such as 'Four Loom Weaver' (which tells the story of a veteran of the wars who, having returned, has found what we would call his cottage industry replaced by factory work or starvation as a result of unemployment), Loveday may have found a way of life on the verge of disappearing. This is a narrative that appears in a number of songs, with numerous variations, speaking of the loss of a cultural identity, and suggesting that the experience of enforced diaspora can be worse than death. Through the fiction of the single voice, there is that which, akin to the effect of what Antonio Gramsci calls 'popular song', takes on an historical significance 'in the context of a nation and its culture' in 'the way in which it conceives the world and life, in contrast with official society'. What oral culture and folklore reveal, Gramsci argues, is that 'the people themselves are not a homogeneous cultural collectivity but . . . numerous and variously combined cultural stratifications' (Gramsci 1991, 195). As such, it becomes the responsibility of the voice, in narrative and song, to bear witness and maintain the political and historical significance of what, otherwise, would disappear.

IV

This sedimented and testamentary stratification is taken up by Kazuo Ishiguro. English song, he remarks:

> . . . is this kind of treasure chest you have sitting in front of you, and if you were American or . . . Irish you might have opened it by now, but because you live here it probably hasn't occurred to you to do so yet. Well, I would urge you to open that thing up . . . because you'll find there a . . . vision of life in the British Isles as it has been lived over the last few centuries; and it's the kind of vision that you can't readily get from the works of say, Dickens or Shakespeare or Elgar or Sir

Christopher Wren. If you don't open that treasure box I think you are going to miss . . . a whole dimension of cultural life in this country.[7]

Often that vision begins with a single voice or song, which interrupts our knowing habits, calling for our attention. A single song, passed from voice to voice, from county to county, across the decades, is altered, amended, remaining itself whilst becoming displaced, subject to translation. Subsequently, the voices that gather together in the songs and narratives of the oral tradition '. . . weave together, intertwine, replace each other' (Derrida 2005c, 1). Songs thus make explicit what is immanent within the apparently lone subaltern voice. There is 'always more than one voice' in any voice. These are the professions of an English diaspora. In the face of this I must respond beyond any calculable responsibility, letting the traces 'resonate with differences in pitch, timbre, and tone: so many others, men or women, who speak in me', who speak to me and, in effect, who speak me. In this profession, it is

as if I ventured to take responsibility for a sort of choir to which I should nonetheless render justice. In countersigning, to confirm, going with or against the other, that which comes to me from more than one other (masculine or feminine). Other unconsciouses also intervene, or the silhouettes of known or unknown addressees, for whom I speak and who let me speak [*me donnent la parole*], who give me their word [*me donnent leur parole*]. (Derrida 2005c, 1)

Giving place to those who give me their word and let me speak brings with it the possibility, in the words of Roger Ebbatson, of chipping 'away at the marmoreally institutionalised surface' of English cultural identity, as this is legislated for, recorded historically, or given support through the notion of a received or standard English (Ebbatson 2006, 1).

Dialect, accent, idiom: all resist the full institution of a common tongue, bespeaking a vital alterity. In this, they connect being and identity to ground intimately. Local rather than national identity is thus professed, self and earth connected. Dialect or accent admit in the voice a spectral profession of identity – spectral because voice, being neither material nor immaterial, has the uncanny power to touch one with an intimacy nearer than any merely material evidence. A single voice, carrying as its burden the countless voices of similarly dispossessed people, and travelling over countless years to arrive at this moment, may touch you therefore, finding in you its addressee for whom it was destined. The difference of the other affirms itself in my hearing; I cannot refuse the voice. Finding oneself thus possessed and haunted, it is little wonder, as Brian Doyle has observed, that dialect was seen as 'linguistic perversion', whether it was the '"debased dialect of the Cockney" or the "perverted Lancashire dialect of the towns"' (Doyle 1989, 36–7). To take the example from *Middlemarch*, the inscription of dialect 'performs' aesthetically a refusal in the 'early nineteenth century [to be] humanised and be contained by ruling groups' at least figuratively, as Roger Ebbatson argues (2004, 114). Dialect or accent, regionality, each contaminates; this has been the anxiety of those who govern us, at least since the introduction of the great-grandparent of

Standard English, Chancery Standard.[8] Dialects refuse translation though, even as their professions make the host impure, as they stake claim to specificity of place, and with that communal histories.

Of course, and I can imagine this already, someone might say 'the phenomena, events and effects of which you speak are indisputable, historically proven and recorded. Do such effects and the events that produced them require describing as diaspora? Is the use of this term not merely a way of drawing attention to what is already known?' My response, in part, would be to say, yes. Calling that of which I am speaking as diasporic is, within certain conventions, unnecessary. But convention and pragmatism should not be permitted to dictate a true profession and with that, a response which gives voice and name. For this is what I am speaking of, the act of naming, an excessive and inappropriate naming but one which is dictated by both a poetics and a politics of alternative, heterogeneous, and heterodox identities. And I risk the small, if inappropriate gesture of naming the very idea of an English diaspora; if I give a name to a kind of quasi-concept, an endlessly transformable series of contiguous but non-synonymous phenomena definable by this motif 'diaspora', it is as a means, not merely of drawing attention to historical fact or empirical evidence, these being already available, present, beyond dispute. It is also to give place to that which is felt, lived, experienced, and left to us as revenant traces, the oscillations of which remain in vibration. One does not have to be physically removed from where one dwells to feel dispossessed. Anyone who has felt a stranger in his or her own land under Thatcher or Blair will know this.

The very idea of professing an English diaspora then enfolds and encompasses within it a recognition, to take the example of English song once more, that here are voices, which, because they have no name, hover on the verge of disappearance, always under threat; and yet affirm more than one voice in themselves. Having issued from the signature 'anonymous', traces are sent out indiscriminately, not with the presumption of an audience or auditor, but to whichever addressee might chance to become the recipient of the innumerable 'testamentary utterance[s]' (Derrida 2008, 144). They arrive as the spectral filaments of 'men or women, who speak in me' (Cixous and Derrida 2005, 2), who speak *to* me, *and* who speak me; they are in effect sedimentary and testamentary. One song speaking out against the imposition of diaspora has an author, but speaks for others nonetheless.

As a result of the erasure of cultural memory, and the concomitant loss of hearing acutely what the voices have to say, we might find we come to inhabit a culture that is not ours, whilst having a culture, which is also not ours, to which we have no access. Unable to receive the dispossessed we find ourselves displaced. As a result song, folk practices and rituals are abandoned and caused to wander. Of course, in suffering this *destinerrance*, this poetic and historical errancy, chance opens to a destiny that cannot be predicted or programmed, either because there is no 'proper' address, or when, despite the apparent specificity of address, that which is sent out is not received, goes awry, or, if received, is either only partially apprehended or not apprehended at all. Hence, a diaspora, registered and borne witness to in the voices in and through which I speak.

What I have sought to acknowledge through the question of one's non-relation

to a language and a culture as that which is always already inescapably and ineluc-
tably contaminated *and* diasporic is as follows: language and all that it attests to in
narrative, in song, through literature and oral cultures, is marked by a dispersion. It
is haunted by an 'evil worse than evil since what' particular presentations of voice
may 'lack' is the 'horizon, or even the hope of their very dispersion ever receiving
a common meaning' (Derrida 2001b, 223). It is the responsibility in any act of
profession beyond mere professionalism to respond to this lack, and to imagine a
horizon in the 'heterogeneity of phrases' and voices that have been left abandoned.
In this, the obligation on the one who hears, the one who becomes the addressee
of such voices, 'whether singular or collective', is to 'link onto the chain' (Lyotard
1988, 99), to paraphrase Immanuel Kant on the law of obligation, the chain of
identities, peoples, cultures that serve in the maintenance of cultural memory. Such
an obligation opens one onto a Kantian 'ethical time'. This 'time' is immeasurable
and irreducible to history, to past, present or future. It is incommensurable with
any marking of time that would fix the moment about which I speak 'in time'
(Lyotard 1988, 126), as it were. Like memory, ethical time is always now and can
always happen now, hence my insistence on attending impossibly to a heterogeneity and multiplicity of voices within any one voice. Ethical time is such because it
resides in 'the now of the phrase'; that is to say, when I speak in another's voice,
when I speak as the addressee and witness of others, I present, and so profess both
my obligation and the one who obligates me. The politics of such a mode might
seem remote to some, Marxists of a certain sort for instance; *The Guardian* edito-
rial writers perhaps, or late-show journalists, many of whom believe themselves to
be radical thinkers. Thinking language, thinking voice *before* and as the necessary
precursor to thinking questions of historical and social formation, rather than the
other way around, is a necessity, however. It intervenes in and interrupts a certain
institutionalized political thinking on the representation of history and literature,
which, in averring the importance of the material world, misses the fact that it can
only do so *through* consciousness and *through* language.

Here I turn in conclusion to Max Adler's Kantian rethinking of Marxism, which
offers, 'an intervention' with a 'number of liberating effects'. It breaks, not least, with
any 'naturalist conception of social relations' and opens the door – providing you
wish to step through – onto a conception of cultural infrastructures as a 'terrain'
dependent 'upon forms of consciousness, and not upon the naturalistic movements
of the forces of production' (Laclau and Mouffe 1985, 28). The terrain of English
diaspora, with their invisible horizons, invites us to break with habits of materialist thought, through presenting us with specific, singular forms of consciousness.
They give place to a chorus of voices, all of which return in the ethical time of a
now, rather than a present, every time I read, on the contingency that I listen, that
I remain open to the different voices and the difference of voices. Oral culture, and
alternative regional cultural practices such as the annual parade of the Whittlesea
Straw Bear, morris or molly dancing, traditional song and other events and 'per-
formatives' all open within the present the enactment of this ethical time focused
through forms of consciousness irreducible to naturalist conceptions of social
relations and forces of production, even though they do speak of such matters.

They remain and endure, even today in their diasporic maintenance, perhaps the 'most imposing figures of spectrality, of spectrality itself'. In this, many elements of English oral tradition strike us as at once 'near but far away, not alien, for that would be too simple, but strange, fantastic, and phantom-like' (Derrida 1998a, 42). We have to learn to live with our ghosts, the ghosts of our others. Forgetting is easier than confessing, and in the words of Chris Wood, ironically enough from an article in the *Journal of Music in Ireland*, 'I am among those who believe that England's highly developed adherence to political correctness stems from a sense of guilt, that it is a sign of cultural disarray, and that the time is approaching when we must move towards something more meaningful'.[9] If we learn how to listen once more, we open the possibility that we can move toward something more meaningful, recovering and inventing a culture that has never been ours, finding what has always been there, as the word *invention* suggests. In doing so, there is the most fragile of chances that we no longer have to remain outside on the inside, no longer professing that 'I only have one culture, and that culture is not mine'. To recall Daniel Bivona's words, 'the history of the individual enacts the history of the race'. The voice of that individual subject, shot through by the traces of his or her material experience and historicity, along with all those other dispersed voices of English diaspora, avers that history is not done, and there is always another perspective to be heard, to be received, and so to be broadcast, scattered abroad in the hope of professions of faith, professions of diaspora – as if, from the very first, the inaugural word.

7

No, Not, None, Nothing, Nobody: Place, Pattern, Death and Narratives of Negation in *Dubliners*

Modern civilization suffers not only from its own flaws and myopia but also from the failure to resolve the entire problem of history. Yet the problem of history may not be resolved; it must be preserved as a problem. Today the danger is that knowing so many particulars, we are losing the ability to see the questions and that which is their foundation.

Jan Patocka

I

While, in the last chapter, I speculated on what remains of voices and the traces of those displaced culturally, and what, in turn, my relation to such traces might be, it is the purpose of the present chapter to consider other traces of historicity, of identity and the possibility of bearing witness to those, which might be read as being encrypted elsewhere, specifically in the short stories of *Dubliners*. If history is a problem to be preserved as such, that is to say a secret to be retained, to what extent does James Joyce confront this 'problem' in *Dubliners*? Are Joyce's Dubliners trapped, held in stasis everywhere because they have no access to a properly historicized comprehension of their identity? And does the idea of being modern cut Dubliners off from older identities, which return to haunt them, the purpose of such haunting being apprehended in only the most impoverished of fashions? Such questions motivate this reading of *Dubliners*, which will argue that Joyce structures his stories through iterable patterns of negation and limitation, border, boundary and threshold, in order to give access to other cultural forces.

II

In reading a collection of short stories, it may or may not occur to you to wonder how we begin to speak of them. Do we, in fact, speak of a 'them', that is to say, a collection, as though the collection were a collective of sorts, having some governing logic or being otherwise and in some fashion homogeneous? To ask the question from another angle: in addressing a collection of short stories, any collection, but perhaps especially a collection of modernist tales, with an implicit, if not explicit emphasis on fragmentation, multiplicity of perspective, fracture, and so forth; is it legitimate to speak of themes, recurrent motifs, or repetitious images and narrative interests, or might we not more reasonably, and so more modestly, begin without the assumption of collective similarity and to talk of those elements or aspects of form and structure, which, by virtue of their iterability, force their recurrence and transmission on our consciousness, if not our comprehension? This is the point from which I begin, observing a series of seemingly contiguous tropes, having to do with negation of one kind or another.

Negation is, of course, an often observed aspect of modernist textuality, its insistence throughout Henry James's writing or Joseph Conrad's *Heart of Darkness* being perhaps the most immediately obvious and visible of examples. Describing something through the expression either of what it is not, or affirming that one is unable to say anything except to say that one can say nothing is common. But, as I hope to show, the persistence of negation's many manifestations and translations underpin and articulate the structures of the stories that make up *Dubliners*; and they do so, more to the point, in a manner that is singular. That is to say, whilst in other modernist works, the articulation of negation or the impossibility of representation – language stepping forth to confess a limit to its powers, litera-ture confronting its own silence in the face of that which is beyond its efforts to refigure – such manifestations take on a somewhat metaphysical aspect, regarding existence itself, in a negotiation between modernist aesthetics and what I will go on to discuss as a negative theology: speaking of God or the Other, an Other, though only in the most indirect of ways. Joyce's negations are not simply negatives, there-fore, admissions of literary inadequacy in the cause of a fractured modernist mode of representation. Instead they serve to construct articulation and so bear witness albeit provisionally; they give place, in one way or another, to Joyce's narratives, and the events that serve in the compositions of those stories, gesturing towards the ineffable and the unknowable. In doing so, they constitute an insistent, if often invisible patterning to the various facets of the everyday in narratives of Edwardian Dublin where the mundane materiality of the quotidian admits glimpses of some-thing beyond, something other; in doing so, they demand our attention.

That being said, before considering Joyce's negatives and negations I want to turn back, briefly, to my initial question concerning how we speak of a collection of short stories, and also to address the matter of iterability, which I have already raised, as opposed to mere repetition. Having asked if one can speak of a collec-tion, I wonder in passing if 'collection' is the best, or most appropriate collective noun for a gathering of such stories. Without falling into the trap of assuming homogeneity, we can begin by resisting this, if we note the title of this collection, *Dubliners*. Each of Joyce's stories is, in effect, named as a different Dubliner, a different group of Dubliners, whose lives, as we know, overlap with one another, intersecting on the streets, in public and private places. Many, we are aware, turn up in *Ulysses*. From 'Two Gallants', there is Lenehan. From the same story, there are also Corley and Holohan. The Mooneys, Bantam Lyons and Mr Doran: all, first appearing in 'The Boarding House', return in *Ulysses*. Without pausing unnecessar-ily to adumbrate schematically all the returning characters of *Dubliners*, which is to say all those Dubliners who come back, often on several occasions, it is enough for now to observe that, aside from the characters already named, another twenty of the *Dubliners* either put in a brief appearance, several appearances, or are otherwise referred to in passing conversations throughout the various episodes of *Ulysses*. There is then, it might be said, risking a somewhat weak Joycean pun, a doubling, and redoubling of Dubliners; this might be our collective noun: *doubling* – not a collection but a *doubling of Dubliners*. Weak humour aside, however, my invention of a new collective noun for Joyce's short stories has this virtue, a double virtue in fact. On the one hand, it names a certain frequency, a network or pattern, without the assumption of sameness or even similarity, save for the observation that Joyce's Dubliners – both the characters and the volume bearing their name – are all living in the same place (to echo a well-known line from *Ulysses*, in which Leopold Bloom defines a nation). This relative proximity, along with their experiences of living in the city – 'the "second" city of the British Empire' as Joyce called it in a letter to his brother, Stanislaus – is what touches on them. Chance geographical and historical concatenation and the possible sharing of events is what serves to provide a map and structure within which they live out their lives, and which lives in turn, in their motions and acts, come to inform us both about Dublin at a given historical moment, and about the meaning of being a Dubliner, of belonging to a particular epoch, an epoch which, by the time the stories were published was already a decade at least away, and so passing away as lived and felt consciousness and experience.

Place and time determine and so give sense to Joyce's *Dubliners* and Joyce's Dubliners therefore. This is, you'd be forgiven for thinking, stating the obvious. Yet, it is so obvious that it often goes unremarked or at least downplayed. This brings me to the second of the two 'virtues' of my collective noun, a noun that, as I have just argued, names community without implying anything but the most fundamental unity. If *doubling* identifies, on the one hand, pattern, network or frequency, it signifies, on the other hand, not merely repetition but iterability. Although the difference between the two terms will be familiar to some, that difference bears reiterating, so to speak. For, while repetition, the idea or concept, implies recurrence without change – pressing, for instance, the repeat button on iTunes, third from the left, on the bottom left of the iTunes window, the button with the two curving arrows seeming to chase one another in endless revolution – the notion of iterability implies repetition with a difference: in repeating, something alters, and so difference both informs the repetition, the form or variation it takes and the difference one notices. While Jacques Derrida has systematically articulated the theory of iterability, the very idea is hardly new. Beyond Derrida's specific example, we have only to listen to compositions such as Bach's *Das Wohltemperierte Klavier* or *Goldberg Variations* to apprehend the work of iterability and difference. Thus, Joyce's writing finds an aesthetic mode already familiar in non-representational art, adapting this to fictive representation. *Doubling* names, therefore, spatial and temporal recurrence and return, through which life and experience are apprehended, not through representation of empirical event and objective perception but in their many flows, fluctuations, and interweavings or interanimations, as subjective perceptual apprehension itself. Without sharing anything other than place and time, Joyce's Dubliners trace patterns onto the city that gives its name to their movements, dictating the directions they take in turn. Place and pattern are closely intertwined, and assume through the narration of individuals' lives, experiences and, equally, if not more importantly, consciousnesses of those experiences and events, what it means to be one more *Dubliner*, both singular and plural. But if Joyce's Dubliners remain fundamentally singular, what if anything in their conscious reflection on being Dubliners might be said to stitch or chain them together? What, for Joyce, justifies calling the disparate group of characters *Dubliners* beyond location and historicity? As my title indicates, and as I will now continue to explore, it is consciousness of being determined by, being the addressee of, modes and motifs, tropes and traces of negation.

III

'There was no hope for him this time: it was the third stroke' (Joyce 1993, 1). This, the opening line of 'The Sisters', first completed in 1904, subsequently revised in 1906, and the first story of James Joyce's collection of fifteen short stories, *Dubliners*, sets the pattern for the author's first published book. Its inaugural negation – that signalled absence of hope serving, if you will, as a death sentence – acts as a place holder, one side of a frame or threshold, over which the reader steps, into a world of stories and an Edwardian-Irish world of decaying Dublin sensibility. This is a death sentence in two senses at least: for, on the one hand, it remarks an imminent demise; on the other hand, to risk a strong reading, this is a sentence of death imposed by Joyce on Dublin and its inhabitants. The impending death of a solitary priest heralds a series of concatenated provincial dramas and commentaries, many, if not all, in some manner, having to do with, and reflecting, on eschatologies of different kinds; and which immanence and anticipation will reach an apotheosis in Gabriel Conroy's belated consciousness, swooning at the sound of snow falling 'through the universe and faintly falling, like the descent of their last end, upon all the living and the dead' (Joyce 1993, 225).

Semantic negations are persistent throughout the fifteen stories. 'None' appears a modest seven times, 'nobody' twelve times, and 'no one' thirteen'. 'Nothing', however, calls attention to itself somewhat insistently, putting in fifty-seven appearances. 'No' forms and informs more than one hundred locutions, as does 'not', whilst 'never', with almost as insistent a frequency, imposes itself on eighty-five occasions. This leads by way of a kind of cognate or quasi-cognate analogy, back to the first line of 'The Sisters', and to the very idea of Death, and with that, dying, and, of course, 'The Dead'. Death, name for the ultimate negation perhaps, is more sparingly mentioned, a mere eighteen references being made. Yet that infrequency should not delude us into thinking death of little importance. It is, undoubtedly, the relative paucity of allusion or acknowledgement, within the patterns and motions of negation, which should concern us. Three occurrences in 'The Sisters', eight in 'A Painful Case', two in 'Ivy Day in the Committee Room', one in 'Grace', and four in 'The Dead': death is only directly mentioned in one-third of Joyce's stories, and of these, only one, 'The Dead' employs the noun metaphorically, as in the moment when Aunt Kate, unconsciously anticipating Greta Conroy's later reminiscences concerning Michael Furey (1993, 223), remarks that 'Mrs Mallins will get her death of cold' (1993, 207). (This does raise the question, of course, as to whether one can die of shame, as it is suggested in 'A Painful Case', and therefore whether this is metaphorical or literal, or indeed, whether something slips here from one register to another, from the semantic to the philosophical.)

The question of metaphor and more generally the figural and tropic effects of language is not unimportant, for it raises the question of reading, interpretation, the matter of evidence, and so a distance, already opened, is remarked, *différance* at the heart of translation always already in place being that which traces a space between oneself and death. This is clearly remarked in 'The Sisters' when the narrator is finally 'persuaded', as he puts it, of the priest's death, by seeing the card pinned to the door: 'The reading of the card persuaded me that he was dead and I was disturbed to find myself at check' (1993, 4). Related to death inevitably then are the noun and adjective 'dead', and, by extension, the verb 'to die', as well as other possible euphemisms and cognates, such as 'fail', 'falling', 'cease to exist', or 'end', all of which are place holders of negation, eschatology and border in *Dubliners*. But note, before we leave that last quotation, how the card, pinned to the crepe on the door – itself a form of border or threshold, the card reduplicating that boundary – announces the double limit of life and death, placed at this symbolic and architectural liminal location, the door, the very reading of which suspends the reading subject, who finds himself 'in check', at a threshold, physical and material, and metaphorical, caught in the disturbing stasis of having to confront the aporia of comprehension. If the opening sentence of 'The Sisters' announces and installs the question of borders, boundaries, limits, thresholds, and so forth, as I began by suggesting, then such gnomonic indices are everywhere throughout *Dubliners*, and we must return to them, even as we have not yet left the vicinity of the limit-term 'death'. Returning to the word 'dead' and its twenty-nine instances (not to mention twenty 'dies'). There may be no deaths in two thirds of *Dubliners'* stories, but in 'Eveline' alone, Eveline's mother is dead, as is Tizzie Dunn and Eveline's brother Ernest (1993, 29, 31). Mrs Mooney's father is also dead, in 'The Boarding House' (1993, 56) while Parnell is remarked as being dead in prose and verse, in 'Ivy Day', until finally we get to Joyce's last story, the tale which ends this narrative series obsessed with cultures of death, endings and negations, 'The Dead'. (In the light of all these dead people, it is a grimly ironic coincidence that, in the making of the film of 'The Dead', director John Huston, who was terminally ill at the time, was insured by the production company, with standby director Karel Reisz, ready to assume duties, should Huston expire before shooting was completed.) 'The Dead' completes our catalogue of the dead, culminating in Gabriel's emergent, disquieting consciousness of the dead: 'He was conscious of, but could not apprehend, their wayward and flickering existence. His own identity was fading out into a grey impalpable world: the solid world itself, which these dead had one time reared and lived in, was dissolving and dwindling' (1993, 224–5).

I will return to this image, of Gabriel feeling himself to be disappearing physically before the overwhelming realization of an invisible immaterial world that begins to impinge, leaving him staring into the dark, a darkness at once material and immaterial, of this world and yet also of another, as the place of the here and now gives way, its threshold breached, to a place that is no-place, a utopia, if you will, of all those others we call the dead. However, in leaving Gabriel standing there, we should observe that he stands at a window. A window is a form of boundary, a frame or border, separating worlds. It acts in Joyce as a material reminder of the separation between mind and body, inner and outer lives, private and public, the individual and all the rest. As such it is a threshold, as well as a frame. One may look out, as if one were looking through the eyes of a building (a commonplace in English is of course the remark that the eyes are the windows to the soul), but then, standing in a window, looking through it, one is also framed, caught in a space of representation. The frame gives out onto a world, and so constructs a sense of place in relation to one's gaze, but one is also, reciprocally, placed; one's being is given a location. One of the most resonant, and frequently critically addressed windows in *Dubliners* is that at the beginning of 'Eveline':

> She sat at the window watching the evening invade the avenue. Her head leaned against the window curtains and in her nostrils was the odour of dusty cretonne. She was tired. (1993, 29)

Eveline is captured here, trapped in the endless days of domestic ennui, given by Joyce the ironic name of home, which at that moment Eveline believes she is about to leave but which we know she never will. The window thus figures a limit, it is a sign of being caught, and thus, as a threshold before which Eveline is stalled, the limit marks the negation of an individual's future possibilities. This, sitting, remaining in the window, is, for Eveline, all there has been, all there is, and all that remains. She is framed, so to speak, not by Joyce (or not simply by Joyce) but by the culture that determines her identity. And as if to re-enforce that limitation, the negation of possibility, and the framing of Eveline within cultural, historical and material place-markers, whilst at the quayside Frank rushes 'beyond the barrier' calling 'to her to follow', and join him on the boat to Buenos Aires, Evvy 'set[s] her white face to him, passive, like a helpless animal' (1993, 34). Her window is, in effect, still there, replaced this time by the barrier that separates her, and by inference every Dubliner, from the rest of the world. The barrier marks one more moment of impossibility and negation. Whether a window or a door, barriers and frames delimit the Dubliner, the Dubliner in turn being defined by stasis. (And notice in passing how words such as de*term*ine and de*fine* remark the limit, the end.) Of course, windows and doors are markedly different and we should not overlook this: a door keeps one in or out, it gives access and egress; it marks, and remarks itself as, the keeper of the law, the economy of the house and all that this implies, implicitly negating freedoms. The window, however, is more tantalizing, ambiguous: it appears to *present* the world as it is (though simultaneously mediated), to provide through its transparency, an opening that is also a barrier.[1] Through such liminal structures, however, and passing over their differences, the negation of possibility is structured through such devices belonging to a particular economy of representation, and 'Eveline' is not the only story to present us with such a poignant moment. At the conclusion of 'Araby', the narrator, lingering before a stall, slowly turns away, before being halted, recalled by a voice. Like Gabriel Conroy at the window of the bedroom in 'The Dead', the narrator of 'Araby' remains suspended at the formal limit of the story itself, its last sentence, its final paragraph, 'gazing up into the darkness' (1993, 28).

Once more we find boundaries across which Joyce's Dubliners cannot cross, either physically or in thought, and, in every case, such framing devices serve multiple purposes, being indicative of the constitution of place and with that negating physical movement and the motion of the imagination or consciousness. From the opening sentence of the 'The Sisters', Joyce peppers *Dubliners* with such images, in fifteen stories that begin at night, in the darkness, and end there, via the various frames and thresholds. In addition to the windows already mentioned, there are more than forty others; of doors there are nearly one hundred mentions. These are just the material verges, and it would be the work of a book-length study at least to address the various mental limits, edges, margins, which serve in the construction of Edwardian Dublin life, especially as these pertain to the expression of negation and the impossibility of bearing witness to anything other than the constant confrontation of limits. It is as if *Dubliners*, written before, though not published *in toto* until after Irish Partition, cannot step beyond its own thresholds, politically, historically, temporally or geographically.

Such a hypothesis, it might be argued, is suggestive of the reason why all Joyce's subsequent fictions are placed before partition, even though written afterwards. Dublin, it might be said, figures as a topographical site for the negation of Ireland's future possibilities – or at least, this, Joyce might be forgiven for thinking, is how it seemed in the second decade of the twentieth century. Joyce's temporal division, the temporal, historical and aesthetic limit he places on location gestures towards that which Jean-Michel Rabaté describes, apropos *Dubliners*, as the 'moral and political perversion of Ireland . . . thereby suggesting the possibility of deducing negatively, *a contrario*, value judgements which at least expose the roots of symptoms' (Rabaté 1991, 15). Negation is one such symptom, the threshold in its many expressions another, and death is thus inscribed in relation to such symptoms as the only figure that heals up what Rabaté identifies as 'perversion', which is in his reading, following Hegel, the 'split consciousness' of Dublin and, by extension, Ireland's inhabitants at the beginning of the twentieth century (Rabaté 1991, 15). Only death closes the rift, the split consciousness, thereby curing the symptoms of perversion.

IV

With fifteen stories, I can do little more than make sketchy gestures such as I have been doing; doing justice to Joyce, I have to admit the impossibility of pretending to a reading which would presume to encompass everything about his work. I can however remain with just the opening of one story, 'The Sisters', and the end of another, 'The Dead'.

Without the erasure of difference that would produce for the reader a sense

of *Dubliners* as undifferentiated collection and community, the tropes of negation, impossibility, death and the boundaries that serve to mark materially the
various symbolic thresholds between absence and presence, past and present, self
and other, living and dead, incomprehension and apprehension, we discern, in
Jacques Derrida's words and 'lacking any better term', the '"gesture," the "strategy,"
the "manner" of writing, of speaking, of reading' (Derrida 2001b, 192). Derrida
hesitates here over the right word, indicating the lack of the appropriate phrase,
for expressing the register of what he calls 'an irreducible difference . . . a difference
"more profound" than a contradiction'. Speaking thus of another's writing on death
and the anticipation of the negation of the self, Derrida offers us an understanding
of that difference which slips across all the boundaries of the various binary pairs to
which I have just alluded, so that we come to perceive in Joyce beyond any dialectic
– between, say, negative and positive, the living and the dead – an affirmation – and
so a responsibility – *in* the inscription of negation and impossibility. 'There was no
hope for him this time' is not simply a negative statement. It affirms the truth of
negation and, specifically, the truth of death, that irreversible passage which arrives,
ahead of itself, in phantom form, to the consciousness of the initially nameless
narrator of 'The Sisters', as the inescapable, ineluctable singularity of death. Death
arrives before it arrives in 'The Sisters'. It steps up in advance of itself, giving to the
protagonist, the unnamed 'I', the apprehension of another's death. Death is 'common' to use Hamlet's word, but paradoxically unique, singular.

So Joyce begins *Dubliners* with the anticipation of a unique death, but one
which, in coming to be anticipated through the conscious awareness and mediation
of the narrator, one who is not yet dead, arrives as if it were the telepathic transmission from beyond the threshold, signalling down through the fifteen stories,
until it arrives finally as anticipatory consciousness, if not full comprehension, for
Gabriel Conroy of all the living and the dead, every Dubliner doubling every other
Dubliner, and yet each remaining wholly and completely other, singular though
iterable. We begin in consciousness of anticipation, and with that the recognition
of the power of fiction, the power of analogy, what Kant calls the *als ob*, the *as if*. For
it is the case that, in coming to an awareness that there is no hope and that doubt
is therefore removed unequivocally, the narrator of 'The Sisters' has affirmed for
him, through the interpretation of signs such as the lighting in the window, that
death, in being read, appears before it appears *as if* it were his own. The logic might
not be transparent here, but we can explain it thus: in arriving at an awareness of
another's death, Father Flynn's, through interpretation rather than physical presence, through phenomenological decoding rather than empirical verification, our
narrator receives, as it were, a posting from the other side of the threshold, in this
case, the material structure of the window with its hitherto unchanging lighting.
This posting or transmission effectively produces a narrative: 'There was no hope
for him this time'. The narrator – and it is important to insist on his initial name-
lessness, for in being anonymous he becomes, by absence of the name, a figure for
each and every other Dubliner, he doubles every other one, however momentarily
and provisionally – whether he knows it or not, receives a fiction beyond any mere
truth or falsehood, and this is fictional because borne in signs and their analysis and

translation in the absence of empirical proof, to stress the distinction once more; the signs – those subtle differentiations in lighting to which the narrator refers – are readable because they are iterable, and have assumed significance in their iterability. Beyond the narrator's immediate apprehension, what we are therefore given to read is a narrative that articulates itself out of a culture of death. We have placed before us a narrative of the way any death arrives. Impossible as it is to experience another's death, the reading of the negation of being as indirect structural revelation affirms how the narrator's – and therefore our deaths – will in turn come to be received: never by ourselves (this is impossible also) and only by others as a narration of an event at once unique and yet one more in a series, 'all those uncommon ends' as Derrida affirms, in the same 'generalization', that is to say, death, dying, negation, all of which tropes are links in the chain of 'serial singularity' (2001b, 193).

Serial singularity: this is what is named in Joyce's title and his subjects, *Dubliners*/ Dubliners. A series of parallel motions are inscribed. From Father Flynn to Michael Furey; from the unnamed to Gabriel Conroy; from youth to maturity; from 'I' to 'he'; from the illusion of full consciousness to mediated consciousness; from read- ing, anticipation and fiction therefore to historicized consciousness, revelation and memory – with every singular event, another sign is inscribed in the serial fiction of Dubliners' identities as Joyce reads these. Dublin for Joyce is an archive, if you will, of affirmations. As such it is also written as an 'immanent system . . . constantly overcoming its own limitations, and then coming up against them once more in a broader form' (Deleuze 1995, 171). This last remark is made by Gilles Deleuze on the matter of the Marxist analysis of capitalism. But it is also, I think, a com- mentary that pertains to the Joycean gesture, strategy, or manner of reading and writing Dublin. The solid world dissolves as Gabriel Conroy comes up against the limitations of thinking in a merely empirical and materialist manner. He is a subject of a world and a system, produced by these and forced to confront the immanence of his own fading consciousness. Apprehending, and being touched by Gretta's grief over the death of another, Gabriel's cosmopolitan modernity is overcome; he receives a fiction of death, the story of Michael Furey. This address, becoming Gabriel's own, presents him with a limit – he is 'conscious of [the presence of the dead], but could not apprehend', you'll recall – which limit overcomes him in anticipation of death because he is unable to overcome the threshold against which he is precipitately thrust, 'his soul . . . [approaching] that region where dwell the vast hosts of the dead' (Joyce 1993, 224). As if this metaphysical confrontation and erasure were not enough, Joyce doubles the metaphysical boundary in the process of dissolution with the stark reminder of the material frame and border of the window, between the warm domestic scene and the cold dark exterior, to which Gabriel is called by 'a few light taps' (Joyce 1993, 225).

And so it is, he remains at the window, his consciousness filtering out, swarmed by the dead, in a negation of self that causes his soul to 'swoon', as Joyce's poetic image has it. In this, Gabriel, like Eveline, like the narrators of 'Araby' and 'The Sisters', is marked by an 'intensely solitary, yet shared experience' (Nolan 1995, 36). Gabriel is overcome, emotionally affected, and the conscious self becomes ecstatic, displaced from itself by its phantasmic other, its spirit or soul, in a conjunction or communion with the impossible. With that erasure the last threshold is overcome, crossed. We had begun *Dubliners* with the coming to consciousness of the narrating subject, someone saying 'I', who stands in the street, looking up at a window, interpreting but unable to enter. Thus *Dubliners* begins with knowledge and consciousness. It ends also with the indirect awareness, if not knowledge exactly, which leads to negation – and, specifically, negation of the self.

Affirmation and negation are two aspects therefore of one consciousness, flickering in and out. Standing in the dark, we see the light; standing in the light, we apprehend the coming dark – and so *Dubliners* ends almost where it began, a gesture on Joyce's part of serial singularity, a scene almost the same but not quite, in what Joyce at the opening of *Finnegans Wake* will describe as a commodious vicus of recirculation. That *almost* is important, for the locations, the windows and the knowledge that affirm limit and negation are not the same. This is no mere repetition but a subtle iterability reaffirmed in the displacement of subjectivity traversed as the shift from first to third person takes place. Trapped at barriers, behind windows, knowing of other worlds beyond Dublin only as possibilities to which they have no access, and having certain knowledge only of death, Joyce's characters 'enjoy no material access' to any other realm, as Emer Nolan argues. Because of this, they have, as Nolan puts it, no 'real imaginative access . . . either. For them, modernity *is* mythological' (Nolan 1995, 31). Thus it is, *Dubliners* illustrates the 'impossibility' and erasure or negation of what Nolan terms the 'grand universalist ideals' (Nolan 1995, 31) that much other modernism touches on, coming to resemble a collection of folktales, 'but with none of its consolations' (Nolan 1995, 36).

8

'A self-referential density': *Glyph*, Fictions of Transgression and the 'Theory' Thing

I HESITATIONS (REHEARSALS, IN SHORT, IN AN APHORISTIC MOOD) . . .

Imagine for yourselves what follows as fragments from an interrupted conversation, not quite epigraphs, this polyphony of voices intrudes, as if gathering, preparing to issue a statement:

> – My thesis, then, is that, as far as personal attributes go, the critic and the creative writer are one and the same. My other thesis is that personal attributes have . . . little to do with the matter . . .
>
> *James R. Kincaid*

> – I assert that no other reading than the one I intend is possible and I defy interpretation beyond my mission.
>
> *Ralph Townsend*

> – Like all stories, any of these I offer here has another side.
>
> *Ralph Townsend*

> – The individual cannot exist *in* language . . .
>
> *Tzvetan Todorov*

> – Has your work been influenced by literary and cultural theory?
> – Sure, why not?
> – I didn't ask you what you *thought of* theory, just whether or not you've been influenced by it. Have you?
> – Sure, why not?
>
> *James R. Kincaid and Percival Everett*

> – . . . doing bad is better than doing nothing.
>
> *James R. Kincaid*

> – And all the rest is literature.
>
> *Paul Verlaine*

II WHERE TO BEGIN (TAKE TWO)

We (all think that we have or continue to) read fiction, whether in the form of novels, short stories, and even journalism or biographies, whether in print or through electronic media. This is the case, even if we are not sure what fiction is, or which fiction we would like to tell about fiction, so as to sound convincing about what we believe to be fiction. Fiction, the *Oxford English Dictionary* tells us, is literature in the form of prose that describes imaginary events and people. It is a fabrication or an invention, in the naïve sense of that word, as opposed to fact. The word comes down to us, via Old French and Middle English, from the Latin meaning 'to contrive'. Produced or generated to entertain, educate, or deceive (none of these are mutually exclusive, you understand), 'fiction' relies on invention. Now, invention can mean two things at least. There is the more obvious, commonly held meaning of invention, what I have already called the 'naïve' version: that is, the production of something new that has never been seen, witnessed or experienced before; something *novel* in short. (Immediately, in what appears to be a pun, you might see a relationship between invention and the new, in this term *novel*. I labour the point because that's what critics do.) There is, however, another meaning to the word invention, something embedded in it, waiting to be discovered, as it were. Invention can also mean to find out or discover. Again from Latin, *invenire*, invention signifies the discovery or recovery of what was already there, but hidden. So, invention can be invented, that is to say unearthed or opened from within itself, so that another meaning, lying fallow, comes to light. Invention invents invention. One meaning crosses the semantic boundary of another and in doing so, transgresses its univocal value. Something *novel* comes (*venire*) into (*in-*) sight or being, through the fiction of invention and the invention of fiction.

Fiction is therefore never entirely new, never completely *novel*. There is no such thing as a novel novel. Furthermore, fiction is never wholly a fabrication, even if it plays with and describes or invents imaginary people or events. However wild, eccentric, esoteric, exotic or just plain odd characters and events in fiction may be, they all have been unearthed from the writer's experience of real events, real people, and so on. Fiction is then never either wholly fictional or wholly documentary or factual. Fiction, in fictionalizing, constantly crosses and recrosses the boundaries or borders between the real and the fictional, so-called. And in crossing these margins, it does not so much invent something new as invent what was there all along: that the borderline is itself a fictional construct which can only be asserted, affirmed and proved in the endless transgression of its own demarcation. The binary opposition established (fiction/fact, fiction/real, and, by extension. real/unreal or truth/fiction, truth/untruth, and, of course, truth/lie) necessary to any conventional definition of fiction, the novel, literature, and so on, is seen to operate, and to be functional only on the premise of a fiction which is neither true nor false concerning the nature of fiction. Thus, transgression, the constant passage, the brief movement from one place to another that exposes the porosity of the border before the margin or horizon closes up, is of the very order of all fiction, and, of course, all story-telling.

What happens though when fiction takes on its own status, when it insists on foregrounding its own transgressive condition? What takes place when a novel takes on the assumptions of the form, those 'engines', if you will, that make the form come into identifiable being and operate for – and on – the reader, and in so doing, lay bare their very operations? Hasn't fiction then crossed a line? Or is it the case that such transgressive motions merely 'invent', in that less-used meaning, what has already been hidden away, kept hidden but working all the time, in all fiction? Isn't it the case that, far from crossing any boundary, such fictions merely redraw the lines, merely remind us that the lines are, if not necessary then, at the very least, inevitable?

This all sounds rather like a magician who, in performing a trick, demonstrates what he or she is doing, and how the illusion tricks you. (As 'proof' of this, I intend to examine in this chapter a novel, which, despite its 'flamboyant graphic and structural gestures', remains, underneath it all, very much, and 'in fact a recogniz-able *Bildungsroman*, and in this respect is a more traditional story' [Russett 2005, 364] than you might otherwise take it for [and no, I'm not going to write about *Tristram Shandy*]). You're left with no illusions as to how a trick deceives, you're made aware of the fabric of the fiction. In a sense, this is what so-called postmodern fictions do. It is part of the very definition of postmodernist literature – where the god or ghost in the machine persists in coming front of stage, stepping out from behind the curtain, out of the wings and from out of the lighting and sound booth, to show you the premises of fictionality. Transgression takes place. Yet, we don't necessarily find that this spoils the effect, do we? After all, that aspect of so-called postmodernist literature has been popular enough that readers appear to want to see how the performance achieves its effects. Not exactly or entirely self-conscious or self-reflective (after all, the narrator is not necessarily telling you about him- or herself, they're only showing you how they produce their effects, fabricate and invent their fictions), the self-mediating metanarrative devices engage in a fiction of fictional demystification through the 'truthful' or 'factual' detailing of *how* fiction invents. Obvious 'examples' of such work – supposing the fiction that one can exemplify, that is to say, erase the differences by which the singular fiction becomes what it is and not something else – include much of the work of Italo Calvino, Jorge Luis Borges, Salman Rushdie or Umberto Eco.

I have hesitated above over the term 'postmodern' because it is so vague, so open to contention concerning its meaning, and employed with such a blithe unreflec-tive acceptance of its historical or cultural truth, that, it seems to me, there is an ironic lack of meta-reflectiveness on the part of those critics who wield it that does disservice to the very ingenuity and inventiveness of the fictions about which they write. This is a much larger argument, of course, and not one I wish to pursue here. So, instead of that fruitless task, instead of speaking in an institutionally approved language of the 'postmodern' – as if we knew what that was – if necessary, I shall talk of self- or auto-demystifying fiction in this chapter that focuses on one par-ticular novel, *Glyph* by Percival Everett. *Glyph*, you should know, combines 'straight narration with surrealistic interpolated episodes' (Russett 2005, 363). *Glyph* is a novel that 'alludes at once to Ellisonian deracination and to the Barthesian embrace of invisibility as the destiny of the modern text' (Russett 2005, 365–6). More than this, it is marked through the aegis of its narrator – of whom there is more to say, and who has much to say for himself – with commentaries on 'the phenomenology of reading' that also 'names a writerly desire', all of which is folded into 'a playful assault on poststructuralism' (Russett 2005, 366).

I take *Glyph* as my focus for two reasons, the first being that a friend asked me to respond to this 'playful assault', knowing me to be positioned, in the eyes of others, if not myself, with 'poststructuralism' – friends being what they are, this is as much as you might expect. The second reason, which emerged after the fact, as is so often the case, I take *Glyph* as the singular focal point, not because I wish to invent (in the more obvious sense) a neologism for a type of fictional endeavour, but because this seems to me the most neutral way of beginning to address and discuss the theoretically transgressive in fiction, the transgressive that *is* fiction, and what, in fiction is always transgressive; that is, its ability to invent endlessly its own forms, demolish its own boundaries, and enter illegally not into some new territory but into the territories that are already familiar to it and so well defined. In this, the transgressive foregrounding of the auto-demystifying fictional form operates in ways that are both complex and simple to be as truthful as possible about *what fiction is or does, or what it can be and can do*. In this then, the self-demystifying fiction transgresses what is perhaps the most cherished shibboleth of humanist and western thought itself: that we can make something unique and original, that we can produce something wholly novel, and never before seen. Fictional transgression of fictional form gives the lie to this, and transgression serves therefore in the affirmation that all we ever do is tell 'the same old story . . . with a difference' as Dickens put it, and that the transgressive is in the *fact* that all fiction is, in the words of Tennyson, 'the same and yet not the same'. Thus, transgressive foregrounding both illustrates and enacts that which is typical in all fiction – and the most transgressive fiction is the one which, paradoxically, is the least transgressive, as we shall see in the reading of *Glyph*. For, while it is 'common practice to assert' that so-called postmodern fiction is formally radical, whilst realism is merely drearily documentary, what is truly transgressive in the auto-demystifying mode of fictional account is the ability to generate in numerous ways the desire for storytelling and the endless reproduction of what Viktor Shklovsky has called, apropos *The Life and Opinions of Tristram Shandy*, 'the most typical novel in world literature' (Shklovsky 1991, 170). Also, transgressive auto-demystification is typical, not in the fact that it rejects authority, institution, convention, and so on, but rather in its gestural play with those very fictions that would deny their own fictionality, claiming their authority to be absolute. In short, transgression names literature *in* theory, literature, in theory; it makes visible, enables a theory of seeing that we call literature.

II FICTIONS OF AUTHORITY

Turning now to *Glyph* and with that understanding of the fictions of authority that transgression in narrative form unveils, consider the two remarks by Ralph

Townsend in the first section of this chapter and, more generally through this, reflect on the work of epigraphs. I have given these citations for a couple of reasons: in miming or 'fictionalising' voice, the gesture of the epigraph gives a chapter, or a book the patina of clever scholarly activity while, at the same time, reminding one that a scene of writing has taken place. There is a calm, almost arrogant certainty in such an inaugural gesture, one which incisively marks the page and demands full attention – a primary narcissism. The epigraph is that device which is employed, conventionally, in order to bully the reader through its supposed authority as a source or indicator of truth, and also to impress her with the erudition of the scholar. Moreover, the epigraph, in providing an authoritative voice, gets things underway for the critic, making it easier to situate an argument, however elliptically. Lazily aggressive, it is thus a double gesture: it announces on the one hand that here – *here* – is my authority, while, on the other hand, it bespeaks authority before writing gets underway. An archive of authority is installed and gestured towards in the inscription of the epigraph. There is none of that hesitation associated, as J. Hillis Miller has reminded us, with the footnote. 'Footnotes', he remarks, 'are often places where an author gives himself away in one way or another in the act of *fabricating* a protective cover. A footnote often reveals an uneasiness, identifies a fissure or seam in an author's thought by saying it is not there' (Miller 1987, 15; notice Miller drawing your attention to fabrication, fictionalizing once more).

So, epigraphs establish a place, they are markedly *there*. (I would say take them or leave them, but then, that's the point, isn't it? You can't leave them.) The two pseudo-epigraphs above, the second and third – I will ignore the others, leaving it to you to figure out their relevance (or otherwise) – above are as good a place as any from which to begin, and I have a feeling that those lines will still have some force by the time I reach the end of this chapter, that they will have refused to go away. Such inscriptions, for all that they are unseemly, intruding themselves before the author can get underway, leave an indelible imprint. They have imposed themselves on me from Percival Everett's thirteenth book, *Glyph* (1999), both lines being spoken by that fictive device known as the narrator, in this case, a first-person narrator.

Now any first-person narrator always performs a tricky balance of speaking about the fictional world from which he comes, showing the reader his role as fictive character in the fictional events and experiences of that imaginary world, whilst at the same time appearing to address the reader in the reader's 'real' world. The reader thus has the 'real experience' of a fictional and imaginary world, and the first-person narrator is situated in a double manner – both inside and outside – along the border. The narrator of *Glyph* goes by the name of Ralph Townsend, as you can see. I will tell you more about Ralph shortly. Right now though, who he is or might be is less important – that is to say, less important strategically, rhetorically, to me, the critic – than what he has to say, particularly what I cite him as saying. Between these two cited remarks, which, on first blush, seem to be somewhat contradictory, something odd occurs. As a result of their pairing a structure appears. I have already said that the first-person narrator is an odd, liminal figure. Not content to rest on the boundary, the function of the narrator is to transgress the very margin in which his voice is transcribed, and from which it moves in two directions. The first-person narrator is a shuttle of sorts, a phantasmic weaving device that stitches together two incompatible worlds, the fictional and the real. Only in that transgressive shuttling is the border at once announced and crossed, re-enforced and ruptured.

Coming back to Ralph's two comments, the structure they produce can be rendered graphically and economically as follows. *On the one hand . . . on the other hand.* This is a figure, which, as we shall see, can be attributed if not to Ralph's 'personality', then at least to one of his favoured forms of argument. We should be on our guard against 'naturalizing' Ralph, seeing him as 'human' and therefore according him a personality, which essentializes. There is no personality here; character is merely a prosopopoeic device for providing recognizable and stable identity to thought, to ideas and conceptualization. Ralph is an effect of writing, one which transgresses repeatedly through rhetorical devices that contradict their own logic, thereby transgressing the limits of the fictive constitution of the human. 'Ralph' enjoys nothing more than the dislocation of the re-mark, of that act of writing which destabilizes propriety and identity, certain meaning and ontology.

But let me pause for a moment. I feel the onset of a digression – a minor instance of Shandeanism in the face of Everett's playful novel, doubtless – born out of nervousness; or perhaps, just call it performance anxiety, which I might always excuse as circumspection. How could I do otherwise, in the face of a narrator or narrating mechanism who – or which – claims to have read 'all of Sterne?' (1999, 17) However, to go back to my hesitation and so to unpack further the point already made about 'personality', signalled beforehand in the use of quotation marks in the last sentence of the previous paragraph.

Narration is of course not 'natural'. It is a rhetorical mode, an artifice rather than a natural representation of voice. It transgresses writing as communication through projecting the illusion – the fiction or novelty – of human presence; it breaks the contract by which writing seeks to communicate across distances. I suspend the term *personality* in scare quotes then because it implies behind it a 'real' human being, as I have already sought to argue. And as we know – don't we? – the self is an illusion produced in fiction, an effect of a web of words. The self is thus *the signifier of a constellation of signifiers*, themselves signalling further networks, constellated arrangements. This is hardly an original remark. The 'self' is merely the axis on which is centred, as a result of certain acts of 'reading', a 'theoretical matrix', which matrix is structured by, even as it engenders the axial determination of 'certain significant historical moments, and . . . certain critical concepts' (Derrida 1976, lxxxix). In certain schools of critical thought, or from what might be called particular theoretical perspectives, the very idea of the self is acknowledged as merely a fictional or formal commonplace. (Though this is not to say that the self does not exist; say instead, the subject is a fiction, a narration without which the 'fact' of the self can have no coherence.) Nonetheless, we accord an imagined life to marks on a page, as these words, and the phrases in which they operate, form little networks amounting to a more or less convincing imitation of 'thought', 'a life', or even – imagine it, the very idea! – a 'real, existent, human being', so-called. We engage in a strangely uncanny act, becoming mediums for phantoms of those who have never been alive in the first place.

More generally, literature, as J. Hillis Miller points out, 'gives access to a virtual reality not otherwise knowable' (2002, 81). Even the most sceptical amongst us likes to enter and to visit the virtual existence behind that bizarre process we call literary fiction, and 'what we call literature in the modern Western sense of the word just happens to be an important form of the imaginary' (2002, 81). This is, after all, one of the reasons that we read literary fiction in a sustained manner and repeatedly, as opposed, say, to the ingredients' lists and nutritional values on all the packages in every aisle of the local supermarket. Or, to put this another way, I read such things on packets all the time, especially when assessing the amount of carbohydrates on the various brands of clam chowder, but I don't imagine behind these marks any particular life, any virtual reality, not even that belonging to the putative author of these irresistible gobbets of information. And it's not simply that I have a limited imagination when it comes to what I perceive as 'literature' as opposed to 'mere' information or that which is not ostensibly the work of the imagination. After all, even reading a novel such as Edwin Abbott's *Flatland* (1998), in which various geometric figures are assumed as 'personalities' within a narrative two-dimensional world, stretches my ability to imagine these figures as real lives, so there has to be a certain 'development', a particular context whether conceptual or descriptive by which I am prepared to accord marks on a page momentarily properties akin to 'life'; and it is in this manner that we come to speak of literary characters not as being formed from the imprint of constellations of letters, words, phrases, idioms, and so on, but as characters in that other sense, as being persons, as having *personality*. Writing, the mark, the very *glyph* itself (about which I will have more to say, count on it), all are made to give way before the power of imagination and the desire for a life other than the one it already has. (Unless, of course, you are a literary critic. In which case I need travel no further along this particular cul-de-sac.)

Well, I said I was going to digress, and if I seem to have done so, and, in having done so gone too far, that's probably not *that* far from the truth – or a fiction of truth, at the least. But, as you'll soon see (or perhaps you've already worked it out), it is a necessary circumlocution. For Ralph 'himself' (and let's face it, there really is no *himself* in a literary work, it's all just a phantasm of the imagination) questions the very nature of the literary fiction of *personality*, along with identity, the assumption of some real, however virtual, behind the page, and any mimetic correspondence between the word and world, or in fact the very possibility – or otherwise – of the word to open to us this world. 'Ralph's' 'personality', such as it is, breaks through the limits of what a 'personality' in fiction should project in order to reveal the fictional conventions by which the illusion of human voice, human presence and psyche or identity are generated. Fiction's transgressive power is just in this: the endless ability to transgress its own articulations, through a transgression that recomposes as it is composed, as Maurice Merleau-Ponty puts it, 'of old elements already experienced ... new relations [becoming] entirely definable through the vocabulary and syntactical relations of the conventional language' (1973, 3).

But, to come back to those pseudo-epigraphs: for a character to be coherent, to take on the guise of being somewhat real, there is on occasion an unwritten assumption, something akin to a contract, between author and reader – of course, in speaking of 'author' and 'reader', 'what is involved', at least as far as I am concerned, 'is an image implicit in the text, not a real author or reader' (Todorov 1975, 20) – that the character and his or her personality be coherent, logically consistent; unless of course the character is in some manner mentally ill, and therefore supposed to behave inconsistently, to be consistently inconsistent. Either that or a character's foibles, the little oddities that we wouldn't accept in so-called real life, are assigned to a genre, such as fantasy. In this manner we rationalize and explain, we naturalize according to the rules of whatever game it is in which we think we're engaging. However, taking those two statements cited above, they are, between them, irreconcilably incompatible, and this is a result of the fact that they are taken to be articulated by the same 'I'.

The assumption at work here is that not only is one I the same I as the other I, even if the two cannot see eye to eye (or so it would appear; and yes, before you say anything, I know the pun is both terrible and obvious; do I look like a novelist? On which, see *Glyph* [Everett 1999, 181], in case you can't wait until I cite the passage in question). But moreover, the implicit postulation is that the 'character' is immutable across the range of the text. To make such an assumption is to cling, however perversely, to the notion of a virtual reality apparently behind the mark, as well as from mark to mark. However, I am still not proposing to treat this 'I' as a person, even though it is attached to Ralph, whoever, or whatever, Ralph might be. Ralph, as I have already suggested in passing and, as I promise, I will come back to discuss, is simply one more sign on the page, privileged it is true in being that peculiar sign, a proper name, but still a sign nonetheless. 'He' admits as much, albeit grudgingly, towards the end of the novel, when 'he' makes a remark about the idea of a 'self', ,which cannot take place or be given place without writing. The fictive status of the narrator is remarked through the action of the sign being given a spooky kind of disembodied voiced-ness on the part of the reader. In effect, in reading 'I', I – the 'I', which I believe myself to be – becomes or is transgressed by, even as I, the other 'I' I tell myself I am, transgresses the 'I' on the page, even though I am not that 'I', and, furthermore, even though that 'I' has never existed *as such* until coming into being as both the uncanny 'I' of the signature 'Ralph Townsend' and yet also an 'I' that I articulate even though it is also an 'I' other than the 'I' I say, when I say 'I' everyday (as, for example, were I to say, right now, here, 'I am not Ralph Townsend'; but how could you be sure?) . . .

Wait. I'm sorry, I got carried away. *I* frequently does, it bears itself away from within itself, in its affirmation as or of the locus of identity. *I* transgresses, constantly, that which *I* serves to remark. It exceeds its own borderline. It bears within itself the very condition of wild, unpredictable transport that *just is language*. In a sneaky way, Ralph admits as much, when he writes, 'Of the letter *I*, I have nothing to say, except where would I be without it and that there is no situation more self-affirming as seeing I to I with oneself. And there is no mutiny as when I can't believe my *I's* . . .' (Everett 1999, 181). You do see, don't you? *On the one hand . . . on the other hand.* (I told you we would get there; you can always trust I to come through, to deliver on its promise.) Self-affirmation *and* mutiny; yes and no, neither one

nor the other, and yet both one and the other . . . The I both is and is not, and yet
it cannot be; though in not being, it doubles and divides itself against and from
within itself, as if to admit despite itself that there is no *itself* except as a fictional
principle or unity. And so again, as I was saying (I has not ceased uttering even if I
has not appeared, even if it tries to mug you with the complacent bombshell of the
cosy, liberal *we*), Ralph admits to the impossibility of assigning a stable location –
or, for that matter, locution – to any self when 'he' writes, towards the conclusion
of *Glyph*, 'But since you have come to this under the pretense of the work being a
fiction, the book being so classified, then even I am or, more precisely "I" is an illusion. I am in exile from my own fiction, which turns out to be my reality, for I may
insist on the truth of the telling only if I acknowledge it as fiction. It is perhaps a
kind of figurative displacement or a resignation to a kind of self-reflexive, gesturing
untruth, which is neither lie nor truth . . .' (Everett 1999, 189).

And yet, though neither lie nor truth, it is both, this statement that sounds like
either the first or the twelfth of the twelve steps of Anacoluthons Anonymous. For,
as will be obvious, the fiction is the reality, it is the only reality that is real, which is
no kind of reality at all, except as the words are said to exist – and this can hardly
be refuted, though what kind of existence that might be in turn is another matter
entirely – on the page, whether the page is that of the novel, any one of however
many were printed, or in their somewhat ghostly return here, in this chapter, on
my computer screen, in whatever format they come to be printed, and so on. Ralph
thus acknowledges that there is that in the notion of a literary fiction, which displaces the self from within itself, that there is no self behind the illusion, except as
this self is not so much behind as it is always the series of skid marks on the surface
of the text. (Indeed, there is nothing but surface to the text. There is no *behind*,
beyond, no *within*, no *meta* – at all.)

And it is this skidding that we witness and read taking place, being staged, in and
between the two epigraphs. For neither statement is any more or less true or untrue
than the other; and the fact that both can coexist quite happily having supposedly
been issued from the same location, given that this location is a self-acknowledged
fiction only serves to show how that which appears contradictory or impossible
is, in reality, the very possibility of the literary. *On the one hand . . . on the other
hand.* Neither lie nor truth, yet both lie and truth. As literature shows us, the self
is nothing but an aporia, and reading is always the encounter with this aporia, it
is always only the experience of the aporetic. Such an experience is everywhere in
Glyph. How can it not be, when we encounter a narrator who says 'I will begin
with infinity?' (Everett 1999, 5) *I* begins every time it is written, every time it is
read; the abyss is the meaning, the undecidable can never be got past, or over, or
through. This means in turn that we can never have done with reading, reading is
never finished, reading always remains to come. Or, to use a phrase that might just
suggest the structure of Percival Everett's novel, *and so on and so forth, etc. etc. . . .*

III THE UNBEARABLE ANTIFRACTIOUS INCISIONS OF EXOUSIASTIC DIFFÉRANCE

(Time for another pseudo-epigraph. Or two.)

> The literary text does not enter into a referential relation with the 'world', as the sentences of everyday speech often do; it is not 'representative' of anything but itself.
>
> *Tzvetan Todorov*

> I had no tobacco can to toss high in the air before shouting, 'The ontological argument is sound', but I did know that my intense desire to see a unicorn was not manufacturing a herd anywhere.
>
> *Ralph Townsend*

Everything has gone horribly wrong. Getting ahead of myself, I have derailed everything, stepping beyond the bounds of a critical reading such as this. You see the impossibility already, don't you? Attempting to write a chapter on Everett's *Glyph*, as a critic to whom the label 'theorist' is occasionally – and occasionally pejoratively – affixed like the tail pinned on the recalcitrant donkey, I find myself somewhat hesitant as to where to begin, or *where* I *might have begun*. *I* cannot have begun anywhere, it is always this fictional invention, the finding of an iterable sign that transgresses me in order that I might articulate myself. Unlike Ralph, I really do not have the luxury to begin with infinity, out of which language emerges the recirculation of its oldest resources, and yet there is no absolutely justifiable starting point. After all, how should I respond to a humorous novel, a large part the wit of which is directed towards the alleged lack of humour in both literary theory and its practitioners? How does one write in response to a text, the very drive or thrust, if not the tone or style of which is parodic, satirical and therefore *transgressive* in the most naked, cartoonish manner? If I were, for example, to take the route of seeking out perceived theoretical 'inaccuracies' on the author's part, a lack of fidelity to argument for the sake of the joke, then I show myself to be as humourless as some of those whom the novel pillories and parodies. If I find the joke funny, do I admit, albeit tacitly, that the novelist has a point, that there is something fundamentally at fault with so-called 'theory'? Or is humour – in this case, seeing the funny side of things when otherwise seriously held hypotheses are rephrased or translated in such a way as to make them resonate transgressively within their own contours – not simply, itself, transgressive? The performative transgression that wit effects in its mockery of the very form or identity on which it depends, from which it parasitically emerges, disarms and disenfranchises the critical argument *avant la lettre*. And Ralph does this time and again as he puts, you might say, the wit in Wittgenstein (and just about every other White European thinker, dead or alive, he lampoons). I'm caught, as they say, between a rock and a hard spot (you'll notice I don't speak of binary oppositions; how could I in dealing with a novel that mocks Roland Barthes?) – a hypothetical rather than a theoretical position,

I'd aver – but then I'll persevere, knowing all the while that I'm doomed to fail, feeling like a parody of some Beckettian narrator.

In the face of being unable to continue and yet forced to do so, I'll backtrack. After all, I am not a critic for nothing, and there's always the time-honoured tradition of the paraphrase or précis as a rhetorical exercise in stalling for time, whilst appearing to narrate in other words. The critical riposte arrives as transgression of transgression, cannibalizing the resources of what is already cannibalized. *Glyph*, for those of you not familiar with it, is told, let me remind you, in a first-person narrative. The first person, as I've already admitted, is Ralph, who eventually, somewhere down the line, becomes Isadore. Remember that line metaphor, it will return, as surely as a Shandeyesque squiggle. The line is everything. The *line* is everything (Everett 1999, 207, 208). Ralph is an African-American infant who is approximately eighteen months old when the majority of the narrative takes place – a series of successively stranger kidnappings and abductions of Ralph – a narrative where Thomas Pynchon meets Jonathan Demme, and in which the reader encounters an eccentric, cartoonish, cross-sectioned view of North America. Caricatures – transgressions of, or deviations from 'normative' identities, a line being crossed in representation to bring out a particular characteristic – come thick and fast, as we meet demented scientists, paranoid, power hungry military figures and their secret service cronies, well-meaning Mexican immigrants, and a paedophile priest. Early on, before most of these figures appear, Ralph remarks, 'I was actually impressed with my imagination and its ability to create so many characters, even if they were stock and repetitive. I thought I knew how it felt to be Louis L'Amour or James Michener or even Dickens'. (Everett 1999, 36–7) Getting over the shock of seeing Dickens compared with L'Amour and Michener, and then realizing the shock has to do with the deliberately provocative nature of the remark (after all, children, being what they are, whatever that is, frequently function through provocation; think of the endlessness of the question 'why?'), we get the sense that the narrative *just is* such a series of stock and repetitive characters, as well as repetitive actions, all of these being so many points along a particular trajectory, which it is the purpose of any reading to trace. After all, the line is everything, you'll recall, even if we have to be reminded that it doesn't move in one direction only (Everett 1999, 6).

This comment on the stock and repetitive is not, I would hasten to add, a criticism. I'm not suggesting that Everett is merely writing a stock, repetitive narrative, filled with stock repetitive characters, even though this is what he appears to have done, or, at least, this is the way I have (quite possibly mis)represented him as doing. I am not suggesting this, really. Although I have to say on reflection, this appears to be exactly what I have done. But then, of course, the novelist and the critic both have a get-out clause, the same one in fact and one, moreover, towards which I have already signalled a degree of wariness, if not suspicion – postmodernism. This is a winner all round. If the novelist is a postmodernist, he gets to have as many stock characters as he wants because that, well, that's self-referential wackiness, the 'stock-ness' or knowing nod to other works depending on the level of your erudition or cool (defined by whether you've read the books on your shelves). The critic, that is to say, me, wins because I get to label the novel as postmodern and therefore get off the hook from having to read it, and can just apply my critical jelly mould. The ontological argument is sound.

But, suspending all this playfulness for a while: why all the fuss about Ralph? Well, though he never speaks, and chooses not to speak (that is, to other characters in the novel he narrates), he is capable of reading, writing and thinking in a self-reflexive, highly abstract manner, often in parodies of what, for convenience's sake, we can call 'poststructuralist' or philosophical discourse. (His impersonations of Wittgenstein have to be read to be believed [Everett 1999, 194–200].) This gradually and shockingly dawns on his parents. His mother, Eve (now there's a name over which we should fall; perhaps *Glyph* is postlapsarian allegory?), is an artist, influenced by Mondrian. She loves the child and his abilities, giving him book after book, including Proust, Wittgenstein, and Harold Bloom's *A Map of Misreading* (which, Ralph admits, he would hurl across the room, if did he not cherish books so much; perhaps it is merely that Ralph is suffering from the anxiety of influence). Once Eve, who Ralph arbitrarily names Mo, convinces her husband of the baby's talents, he wants Ralph analyzed by psychologist Dr Steimmel, who becomes Ralph's first abductor. Ralph, who displays a fascination with the way proper names function that is suggestive of Jacques Derrida, names his father, Douglas, Inflato because, as Ralph puts it, 'he was not a fat man, but he was bloated' (Everett 1999, 6). In fact, as Ralph informs us, 'My father was a poststructuralist and my mother hated his guts' (Everett 1999, 6). There's the ghost of a non sequitur here, but its apparition is not strong enough to dispel the vague unease I have when confronted by the emotional logic of this sentence. As we come to see, Ralph's father is a mediocre academic – the narrative perspective would suggest that, as far as theorists go, such a phrase as the one I've just used might be tautological – who has a hard time getting published, who has never finished his book (the one), and who favours a poststructuralism (whatever that might be) derived mostly from Roland Barthes. The Shandyesque parody of the aspiring, though unpublished, North American academic caught in the tide of discursive and institutional fashion, aside (does Douglas have tenure?), Barthes, by the way, makes a couple of cameo appearances, talking for the most part in a combination of parodic obscurantism and loose allusion, which Ralph helpfully identifies.

So far, so postmodern, or, in the words of Tricky, 'you're brand new, you're retro' (1995). Indeed, the broadsides and sideswipes at 'theory' aside, Everett's novel belongs to a very North American tradition, including novels by Pynchon (despite the fact that *The Crying of Lot 49* bores Ralph to sleep), Coover, Gaddis and Barth, and is marked, like its antecedents, by humour, parody, political satire and 'self-referential density', as Ralph remarks – self-referentially (Everett 1999, 95). *Glyph* is thus most typically a North American novel, and if it is *about* anything, it is about the state of the North American novel in the late twentieth century, its transgressions wholly of a piece with those of its novelistic predecessors. Self-referential density is the formal manifestation of narrative transgression, in that it wears its structural, formal and epistemological framing devices as if they were an exoskeleton. The question arises though, when does self-referential density become just so many acts of tired trading in the stock and repetitive, to recall Ralph's own words? And aren't the stock and repetitive merely more honest names for what some academics, whether avowedly 'theoretical' or not, like to identify, approvingly or otherwise, when defining the canon? One person's 'tradition' may well be another's agent of oppression, but it can be the case that oppression takes place through the peddling of repetitious cliché as eternal verity or aesthetic universal.

Why make this rather snide point? Well, you see, I have this sneaky feeling that Little Ralphie likes to have it both ways. As I have argued near the start of this chapter, he is very much of the 'on the one hand ... on the other' school. (There can be no doubt.) This is why Dr Steimmel, Ralph's psychoanalyst, defines him, with all the discursive analytical precision of her profession, as a 'little bastard' and a 'smart ass', the former of the two becoming something of a dominant metaphor in the novel for the baby (Everett 1999, 34, 36). Yet, if, as I argue above, there is no one beneath the name 'Ralph', then the novel is the 'little bastard'; a self-legitimating-illegitimate collocation of discursive traces, which, in their structural relation, announce not only their parentage but also their historicity – which is also to suggest that the text bears witness, as it responds to, those very forces and phenomena that make it. Like all novels – and this is why it is both transgressive and absolutely typical – *Glyph* is a fiction that bastardizes all the cultural resources of its and other ages available to it, to produce a bastard of its own. Becoming what it always already is, the fiction that is *Glyph* steps across the limits of its form, demolishing them as it goes, in the very process of reforming and deforming its very own bastardy, a bastardy that it shares, though in a wholly singular manner (and that singularity is another sign of performative transgression as the affirmation of the normative and the conventional), with each and every other fiction. To present this in an aphoristic, not to say Wittgensteinian way: the difference of every fiction is its similarity to every other. Similarity is difference.

Everett makes us aware of the political and historical stakes of the matter of density, however, through the inclusion of conversational vignettes, between, for example, Aristophanes and Ralph Ellison – is this the figure for whom the baby is named? – Wittgenstein and Russell, James Baldwin and Socrates, Balzac and G. E. Moore, Merleau-Ponty and Lacan, or Wittgenstein (again) and Nietzsche. All that is missing, to borrow a line of Bob Dylan's from *Desolation Row*, is the image of Ezra Pound and T. S. Eliot, fighting in the Captain's tower. Wittgenstein, though, he gets everywhere, or seems to, in *Glyph*. What appears to be a concern throughout most if not all these conversations is the word and the world – or, to put this another way, representation (by which I also mean storytelling) and reality. If the line *is* everything, how does one represent the world and, how does one represent oneself in the world when we have apparently reached a point when there is so much 'self-referential density'? What is one to do when one's perception of oneself is of a self 'somehow unreal, intangible, a skiagram, a reflection?' (Everett 1999, 120). 'Ralph', having no 'being', as such, is only thrown into relief through the shading and projection of the textual lines, the theoretical matrix, which appears to cause him to become foregrounded, as if he were there. Which causes me to ask: is there a self which, despite being all surface, is not 'dense', not a 'construct', to use a word that Ralph announces he hates, only the result of shadow play and the interplay of lines composing a tightly woven net?

Perhaps yes, perhaps no (on the one hand, on the other . . .), but the density of the self produced by, in, as fiction is not necessarily, if at all, a density with depth. For, as I have just said, all density is on the surface. This is what fiction does, suggesting fathomless reserves through a paper-thin map of words. Ralph suggests this: 'The shadowy figure relaxing in the corner is four years old now, and tucked away writing this. Writing myself into being? I think not. Doing more than surface, novelistic rendering. I think not' (Everett 1999, 16). And then again: 'In fact, attempts at filling in my articulatory gaps with a kind of subtext, though it might prove an amusing exercise, will uncover nothing. At the risk of sounding cocky, my gaps are not gaps at all, but are already full, and all my meaning is surface' (Everett 1999, 31). Which is true, of course, even as it also transgresses the reader/narrator contracts assumed in the formation of many kinds of fiction. Ralph is nothing but words, and 'he' is not about to let the reader forget this, in the presence of every sign: words, words, words, these are the matter, and the matter is 'Ralph', a collection of words on a page, on many pages, so many glyphs with nothing behind them except the author and reader's imaginations (all the authors who inform Everett's work, and all the readers in the world, all those who have read all those authors to whom either Everett or Ralph, depending on your predilection, have alluded to, stolen from, allowed to reappear in whatever manifestation we might chance to find); and which are themselves textual, referring to other signs, and other books, and other . . . well, you get the picture, as it were, metaphorically, and so on, etc., etc. (At the risk of repeating myself.) Or, on another occasion: 'I replaced the *dream* with the *novel*, stripping the stories of my dreams of any real meaning, but causing the form of them to mean everything', to which is appended the footnote, 'And so, I assume, nothing, as no thing can actually mean everything' (Everett 1999, 37). Form *is* meaning, there is no latent content, no subtext. 'A story can tell any reality' (Everett 1999, 199), as Ralph has it in his Wittgensteinian Theory of Fictive Space that concludes the penultimate part of the novel, but then 'nothing is a story but a story' (Everett 1999, 200). Everything is just a series of surface adumbrations, where self-referential density resides in the ability of the reader to notice all the passing references (we're back with that postmodern thing again), the allusions, the parodies and sources, from which Ralph appears, a self-confessed 'illusion' (Everett 1999, 189), and by which method he appears to address us. The act of writing does not produce a reality but a surface of signs gathered in the name of Ralph, or under the glyph of I, if you will. Well, whether you will or not is a moot point. Some of you will, others of you won't. Some of you, like me, will not be able to decide. But this is a moot point because I have just excused myself rhetorically for making the statement 'under the glyph of I'. And there is nothing anyone can do about it.

But there, I sound like a poststructuralist critic, so-called. I have succumbed to an analysis of sorts, whereby the paucity of my process is revealed, a paucity already – always already? – 'inscribed' in the text of *Glyph*; a paucity always already a density. As I mentioned before, Ralph appears to like to get his own way, which is in two directions at least. For, if this is a novel that aims to dismantle theoretical pretensions through what fiction can give us to understand about the truth of hypothetical propositions which disguise their fictionality in their presentation as hypothetical truths, it is also, I cannot help thinking, a theoretical exploration of the exhaustion of narrative or, at the very least, an exploration of the fact that all narrative proceeds in the same way, and yet every narrative is singular, and it is the repetitive procession that allows access to the iterability of singularity. Transgression transgresses its own transgressions in the establishment of norms and conventions of transgressive articulation. If this is not a novel concerned with the death of the author, it is, perhaps, a novel about the death of the novel or, at least, the dearth of really interesting tales to tell. Yet *on the other hand*, perhaps the most interesting story there is, is the endless mutability, the endless difference of narrative, the endless difference *that is narrative*.

Ralph's world – and his words – are marked by a self-referential density, but everything is on the surface, everything about the convention of narrative is in plain view. As Ralph tells us: 'we were Möbius surfaces, our topologies defined by the fact that we can never get around them to the other side, but are always there, both on the other side and staring at it confusedly . . .' (Everett 1999, 177). Narrative, *Glyph* can be read as intimating, is only ever such an infinite surface movement, engaging repeatedly, after the first section, in an endless rerun, where Jacques Derrida and Wiley E. Coyote prove that iterability and cartoons are not mutually exclusive. Indeed, the cartoonish impulse – or should that be drive, *trieb*, *pulsion*? – *qua* iterability is marked and re-marked in the constant return of the various subtitles which serve to subdivide the sections of the novel. Perhaps it is simply the case that Freud is merely the Walt Disney of the imaginary. Thus we read '*différance*', 'incision', '*exousai*', 'anfractuous', 'Mary Mallon', and so on, over and over again. What do they 'mean'? you might ask yourself. Why are they there? Titles, even subtitles, or section titles, are supposed to 'mean'. They're supposed to act as signposts, and here is – presumably – Everett flaunting convention, transgressing even the most minimal textual practices and institutions. Consider briefly what we do have.

Mary Mallon, also known as Typhoid Mary, was identified as the first healthy carrier of typhus. Knowing this, however, does nothing for the reading of the novel, unless, of course, wherever the trace of language resides, it is there as a virus, transmitting, infecting, transmutating. I speculate, of course. 'Anfractuous', meaning full of twists and turns, or tortuous, might just be referential. Whether it refers to the novel itself or to literary theory, so-called poststructuralism, or even postmodernism, is entirely up for grabs, or, as I like to say, undecidable. The *OED* does not list 'exousai', but that doesn't necessarily mean it does not exist. What the dictionary does list is an adjective, 'exousiastic', from the Greek, *exousia*, meaning of, or relating, pertaining to authority, to exercise authority. This is a joke, isn't it, and a very serious one at that? Where is the authority in this text? Whose authority is at stake, given that Ralph spends quite an inordinate amount of time debunking authorities, authors and institutions. Ralph is the transgressive little trope that, responding to all kinds of authoritative text, undercuts authority – and because he is so well read his transgressions are, well, not to put too fine a point on it, authoritative in their incisive (there's another of those words) intervention in all forms of conventional, institutional authority, all of which are perhaps outmoded, as dead as Attic Greek (and the attic is the place they should be put, doubtless), in the face of Ralph's disruptive line-crossing and challenges to the presumed presence and unquestionable identity behind whichever authority, figure or discourse, he chooses at a given moment to demystify, disturb and decentre. Which brings me to . . . 'Différance', which, as some of you, many even, are no doubt aware is Jacques Derrida's neologism, a term by which Derrida, specifically in and through writing, seeks to define a broader sense of writing than mere inscription on a page or computer screen, in order to yoke notions of differentation (spacing) and deferral (temporality) in a single word, and to insist on the singularity of meaning (semantic, ontological, etc.) that différance as inscription, as graphic or *glyphic* makes possible, and without which no meaning, no identity, no presence could have its illusory 'being'. How does Derrida conjoin the concepts and insist on the graphic over the vocalic, writing over voice, difference over autohomogeneity, absence over presence? Through the use of *a* rather than *e* in the spelling of *différance*. Why? Because, when spoken in French, *différance* sounds precisely the same as *différence*. Thus, the *a* that marks difference and 'announces' it silently, risks everything on graphic differentiation and displacement, rather than implying that a voice or presence, a source, is available as the place from which the siglum, the glyph if you like, has been transmitted. And keeps on being transmitted.

And again. *Encore une fois.* But each title, though the same is yet not the same, to recall not some dry-as-dust theorist but that crotchety, cranky Victorian poet to whom I have already alluded. Each changes, yet remains *as the remains* of that which we can never reassemble; each is transformed, transmutates and transgresses its function and meaning in its being iterable. Each figure remains, clinging to each section to which it is appended as though it were some lunatic aphoristic epigraph, thereby becoming a link in a chain of possibly epigonic self-referentiality, where the density is increased, supplemented even as it is divided, doubled and disseminated. And all the while, nothing builds to anything other than what it already is in the, I hate to say it, first instance. Everything that narrative is, is here, yet everything is in ruins. (*It always already was.*)

But remain, if you will, with that phrase, 'self-referential density' a while longer. Here is the remark in its immediate context:

> From morn to noon, from noon to dewy eve, I was carried by my parents from here to there and back, was tossed into the air, had heads rubbed into my belly while suspended above the ground, was handed to strangers on whose shoulders, if I could, I would spit up my mother's nourishing but only adequate milk, and suffer through mindless compliments from mindless onlookers and my mindless parents. I had no legs, but I moved about, not because of a defiance of gravity, but because of a sickening, malignant, imposed and necessary dependency. And it all sat on me like a weight, a kind of self-referential density, as it was the case that whenever I was in the room, I was the object of attention, if not discussion. (Everett 1999, 95)

Of course, this is what happens with babies, or most of them in any case. They are placed, for a while, at the imagined centre of some universe simply because *they are*. One might say this is the existential nature of *babyness*. But for a baby to have knowledge of this – and not merely that tyrannical pre-linguistic consciousness that assumes centredness, with the world as an endless series of satellites pertaining to a largely unreflective, machine-like being – this conveys that very sense of being's burden expressed here by Ralph.

Yet, strictly speaking, in reality (to speak in metaphors), a baby should not be able to articulate this. But this is not reality of course (at least not reality in some limited brute material form); it is a story, a narrative, a fiction, a novel; in which case, it is the case. Therefore, that phrase which is exercising me so much takes on another resonance. Given Ralph's insistence that form is meaning, that meaning is on the surface and that surface is everything with no subtext (and furthermore, as you will have seen, I am in complete agreement), it has to be said that this is not a secondary resonance lurking beneath the more obvious sense pertaining to *babyness*. Indeed, that Ralph is articulating his condition, his reflexive *thrownness*, suggests that he is enacting a kind of being-in-the-world. Such a condition of being is also a condition of constant becoming, everywhere and at the same time, as is evinced through iterability, the awareness of the surface nature of articulation, and the fact that Ralph apprehends the dilemma of being through the admission that the line is everything, which the incision of *I* can only momentarily mark.

However, this is to digress. To come back to the question of resonance: there are at least two oscillations here, operating simultaneously. *On the one hand on . . .* Even as Ralph is speaking of the unbearable babyness of being-baby, he is also commenting, in that mode we have already addressed, first-person narration, not on the ontological condition of the character (who is also the narrated narrator), but on the trajectory and momentary suspension of the 'I' as narrating narrator, through whom every referential sign, every allusion or citation, every parody, is mediated in the act of reading. This amounts to that totality we name 'novel'. And Ralph knows – and admits – as much, despite his jibes, his little-bastard-smartassishness. Thus Ralph proves his own being as that which dismantles ontology, leaving all in ruins; and, in drawing a line or two – placing the ontology of being and any mimetic illusion of stable identity under erasure – through that ontology and the assumed reality of character, he places invisible, yet undeniably powerful citation marks around himself or, more precisely, 'himself'. His being is only ever a becoming, a passage of and in writing that crosses, transgresses a line between non-being and fictional existence, in the becoming of the motion of the glyph, and the difference that gets the motion underway always and everywhere. And of course, though this is *just* a fiction, it does announce, however slyly, the truth, the fact, the case, that I, you, all of us, 'become' with every utterance, becoming ourselves and becoming other.

IV BACK TO THE BEGINNING

This needs to end, so perhaps another epigraph, sort of:

> I *want* the reader to trouble herself over structural analysis . . . The
> shortest distance between two meanings is a straight ambiguity.
>
> *Ralph Townsend*

I seem to be back where I started, with those two quasi-pseudo-epigraphs. Or, at the very least, I have returned to a place from which I've never really departed – the undecidable location around which I cannot manoeuvre, the shortest distance, the straight ambiguity (Everett 1999, 106). The line is everything, after all. Or perhaps that should be: the *line* is everything, as Ralph prefers to write it the second time, as the final line of the book. I like that emphasis in the second citation, the insistence on line, a little graphic law enforcement in the final words of the book, in a performative gesture delivered both through *and as* the last line, a line which announces in its free-standing autonomy, without voice, without presence, without subject, and yet also with some kind of aphoristic sneer, that *the* line *is everything*. Everything – and all the rest.

Ralph's narrative is then not so much an autobiography as it is an auto*glyph*ography. (Knowing the kind of critic I am, you were just waiting for the neologism, weren't you? *Glyphography* is, though, a 'real' word, so there.) *I* is only the cut in the surface, the groove or symbol. It is only ever a momentary hiatus in the difference of language, and all language, in that motion that takes place because of difference, is always the mark, the trace, writing in its broadest and most radical sense. Far from being some privileged affirmation of the stable *locus classicus* of the self, subjectivity, identity, being, what you will, *I* marks a spatial and temporal anomaly that only serves to prove by difference that it is one more glyph *comme les autres*. For in its endless tracing of the line, this narrative must ceaselessly re-mark itself, all itselves, through the constant recourse to *I*, even though *I* is never stable, never definable even if we were to assume the narrative as belonging to some fantasy paradigm which allows us access to a virtual reality where babies, little bastards or not, think in complex, textually dense and allusive ways. Ralph writes himself into – even as he is written into and by a narrative network, a textile weave, over which he has less control than he likes to think. His *I*, initially myopic, is forced to concede, often in the most opinionated manner possible, that *I*, taken as a stable referent or some ontologically coherent being, is an illusion, brought about by the suspension of, and intervention in the endless Aristotelian motion of the line, along which there may be marked *now* and *now* and *now*, but none of which, in the end, amount to a present or a presence. Selfhood, subjectivity, identity, being: all come face to face, not with an abyss in the place of meaning but the abyss *as* meaning, with the abyssal surface which makes it possible for Ralph to ask: 'Am I Ralph or *Ralph*?' (Everett 1999, 105)

On the one hand . . . on the other hand indeed. The question cannot be answered. Or rather, it can be answered but only by answering that the answer is, and remains, undecidable. Identity in ruins, endlessly deferred, doubled and divided. For, on the one hand, I is Ralph, or at least a series of Ralphs; while, on the other hand, everything is *Ralph*, this text of lines, Ralph's, Percival Everett's, and all the other authors in whatever guise in which they appear here (and here, and there), but *Ralph* is merely that glyph which announces shorthand that the line is everything. So, I is both Ralph and *Ralph*. (Ralph, I am tempted to suggest, is just a *glyph*, whose singular articulation is in that 'Ra', the Ra-Glyph, Sun-God and 'creator' of all life: a little ray of sunshine, 'he' makes the world, a world of words, images, texts, writing, and so on . . .) And yet, I is neither just Ralph nor *Ralph*. Neither . . . nor, and yet both. I am reminded of those foreign-language text books, where you see on the page the grammatical structures left hanging around, waiting for you to fill in the blanks, and in that idle suspension affirming the waywardness of the written mark, not yet stabilized through the phallic insertion of the stable subject. *Glyph* may be read as offering the reader – it only appears to offer something for no text does anything unless I make, *I* makes, it do something – such a structure, while acknowledging that *this is the only structure there is* or, structure is all there is if one wants to say 'this is': a structure of play and difference, through which, though the point may be whole and complete (Everett 1999, 207), 'a story represents itself' and nothing else (Everett 1999, 200). So Ralph is right. He is so right, in fact, he proves that he both does and does not exist as such. In doing so, he undermines the very authority that he comes to articulate and figure, even as, in figuring such authority, he does so, once more, in such an authoritative manner that the act of undermining is itself undermined, transgression itself transgressed in a little return of convention and the fiction of the normal. Little Bastard.

9

'Theory' & the novel (and The Novel?)

I

'Theory and the novel': this title makes me not a little uneasy; for one thing it sounds like an imaginative analogical substitution for 'death and the maiden'. In my scenario, the novel becomes the innocent victim of some predatory and ultimately fatal force, a force that it is the fate of the novel in all its virgin purity to suffer. This is not entirely fanciful, as you'd realize had you heard, as I did, 'Start the Week' (Radio 4; 31 March 2008). Novelist Maggie Gee spoke of what she saw as the problem facing students of English in terms of the amount of 'dead' and 'abstract' language that they were expected to read. From those buzzwords you'd be forgiven for imagining, initially, that Gee was referring perhaps to Aristotle's *Poetics*, certainly something Greek and philosophical, but no, 'theory' in all its gory glory was the phantom shaking its grizzly locks in the novelist's overheated gothic imagination. Misha Glennie, another of the guests and author of *McMafia* – a book on organized crime – observed that students were expected to read theory before reading 'actual' works of literature. That word, 'actual', is quite nice, isn't it? It hints at something solid, material, real, not imagined, airy-fairy or virtual. (But wait a minute: isn't 'actual' literature, in no small measure, composed, quite literally, from the imagined or virtual? Isn't every novel a virtual reality, a *virtuactuality*?) Maggie Gee responded that with the introduction of theoretical materials 'something hideous began ... this mad language of ...' Such violence did theory do, apparently, that it left Gee nearly speechless, like Kurtz trying to describe the experience of the heart of darkness, or a new contestant on *Just a Minute*. As she was searching for the word 'poststructuralism', Andrew Marr gleefully interjected 'structuralism' like a journalistic Mr Jingles, or Mr Toad shouting 'Poop-Poop!' (these are two references, by the way, from 'actual' literature, allusions to two of the greatest comic novels in the English language), which splutter sounded as if it had an exclamation mark after it, if not being spelt in capital letters. Having found her word eventually, Gee then remarked that theory was the Emperor's new clothes, described it as mad once more, and confidently proclaimed 'it will disappear' as if this were, if not fact, then a performative utterance intended to conjure its own desire; at which point Marr uttered the phrase 'completely bonkers'. It was as if a David Lodge novel had suddenly broken free of its parallel universe and stepped into mine.

Whilst some teachers, or indeed 'actual' students instead of Gee's and Glennie's imagined cohort, might find such an exchange bizarre and/or irritating – but also *extremely* funny, to paraphrase the title of an article by Jacques Derrida – this does illuminate what is symptomatic about the assumptions which often underlie attempts to talk about the subject of 'theory', as if there were such a thing. The forced identification of similarities within form or process that allow for the imposition of meaning, name or identity, such as 'theory' or 'novel' notwithstanding, there is also at work a set of assumptions concerning how one is authorized to think, or proscribed from thinking, about 'literature'. This is no small matter, given the multiple differences and singularities that such forcing imposes quite violently in conventional intellectual and academic practice. Not least of these is that, if there is 'theory', *a* theory, singular and homogeneous in its ontological self-sufficiency, and that 'it' can be taught as a set of theorems and procedures, as a series of systems of propositions or principles vis-à-vis its presumed object or subject, then this is to be pursued quite separately and often prior to, the 'proper' business of reading and interpreting the novel. Once we have understood and come to terms with the 'theory' so-called, with so-called 'literary theory',[1] then we can put it behind us, and get on with the business at hand, informed as we now are by a set of theorems, little metaphorical spanners and wrenches, which, taken out of our institutional tool box, can be applied to literary analysis of a given form, such as 'the novel'.

Can we talk about 'theory *and* the novel' then? Let me confess that I find the idea problematic, quite genuinely troublesome. There's a fall here, a retrenchment or relapse into a static binarism grounded on the supposed notion of absolutely static and therefore knowable concepts, institutionally defined phenomena, discourses or entities. To borrow an argument of Jacques Derrida's, where he affirms a resistance to a false distinction between literature and literary criticism, while, on the one hand I 'wouldn't distinguish' between 'theory' and 'the novel', on the other hand, I 'wouldn't [simply] assimilate all forms of writing or reading', for, instead, distinctions, such as we can make with all due care and rigour, ought, in any case, 'to give up on the purity and linearity of frontiers'. And this should be aimed for, because the novel, for all its radical impurity of discourse, should teach us that 'good' theory, like 'good' criticism, 'the only worthwhile kind', must invent 'an act, a literary signature or counter-signature, an inventive experience of language, *in* language'. 'Theory', if there is such a thing, so-called or not, must risk an invention, 'it' must invent that which belongs 'to literature while deforming its limits' (Derrida 1992a, 52).

Some would say that's just me being, if not 'theoretical', then, a 'theorist'. After all, so received wisdom would have us accept, we all know that there is 'theory' and then there is 'the novel'. Well, yes, and no. (It strikes me at this moment that I sound just like Ralph, from the previous chapter.) Institutions, universities, colleges, other places of higher education, teach modules on 'theory' whilst also teaching modules on 'the novel': 'introduction to the novel', 'the novel in the nineteenth century', and so on. 'Theory' appears in similar ways on course handbooks and web pages. In one example, just found by googling 'literary theory module', I came across a description of a plan of studies in which the student is expected to take one or two core modules on theory, which would serve as the conceptual framework for the historical study of literature. This is far from uncommon, and the practice in departments of literature is to make material the 'theoretical' assumption behind the very idea of 'theory'. Institutionally, 'theory' is placed, located and given an identity, as (a) preliminary, coming before the study of literature-proper (as if there were such a thing); and (b) therefore revealed as being contextual, secondary, supplementary, and so on (though without the ghost of supplementarity haunting the use of the term 'supplementary' by those who would define, and have determined, 'theory' as this; of course, we know, don't we, that you cannot lay this ghost to rest). 'Theory', institutionally speaking, is just this propaedeutic material, serving as preparation rather than as something in its own right.

However, as I shall go on to explore here, the situation of 'theory' as propaedeutic and utilitarian contextualizing model is untenable, if one reflects rigorously on the identity of 'theory'; that is to say, if one pauses long enough to construct and consider a hypothesis concerning the constitution, misrepresentation and, finally, use of 'theory'. In such an approach, 'theory' is ill-served – and so too, as a consequence, is the student of literature. This is especially so if that which is gathered in the name of 'theory', if the various discourses, disciplines and modes of thought that weave the meshes of 'theory', are treated as merely contextual and only preliminary *as well as supplementary*, as at once prior to and coming after 'the novel'; and also if this 'it' is seen as solely for the purposes of mechanical and repetitive application, then applied solely as support to the proper work of reading literature, which should be historical and aesthetic. What follows then is a critical reflection on how this might be avoided and, with that, the possible benefits to student – and teacher – of re-thinking, or let's just call it beginning to think, what it is to read with theory; or let's just say *what it is to read.*

II

I will continue then with a second anecdote concerning the relation or non-relation, perceived or real, between 'theory' and the Victorian novel, this particular collective manifestation of 'literature' having taken up much space in the first part of this book. I do so because, by chance and at the point I began to think about writing the present chapter, the example I am about to present imposed itself on me. I should immediately qualify the foregoing remark by saying that what I am about to narrate is not intended to expose anyone's resistance to, or lack of comprehension concerning, 'theory', so-called. Rather, it is to identify a central concern in this chapter, which has to do with how little 'theory', so-called, has been accommodated on 'its' own terms, or the extent to which 'it' has become habituated or habitual (or, as it was recently put to me, 'we're all theorized now, more or less'); or, to push the point further, the question is one concerning the fact that multiple and different modes of thinking, having been reduced to and so neutralized by this catch-all identity 'theory', have been positioned institutionally and found, if not a home, then a lodging place with greater or lesser shows of hospitality; a home, one might add, in which, being kept on a tightly reined leash and made to perform in given ways, 'theory', so-called, having been neutered, nonetheless remains

under surveillance, policed in the very place it has been taken in and allowed
to dwell.[2]

I begin with this narrative account in order to eschew a 'theoretical' beginning
from which one departs conventionally in discussions such as this, to take on a
reading once the 'theory' has been exemplified and dispensed with; to talk first
about 'theory' in theoretical terms (what it is, what it does, and so on) in a chapter
on 'theory (or "theory") and the novel' would, quite simply, reproduce the 'first
the concept, then the practice' model of which I am critical. But I begin with this
anecdote also to respond to empirical events. I place myself in the wake of the
occasion, and respond, as responsibly as possible, to a situation which demands
that I answer this particular event. At the same time, I am also responding to the
request to write on a particular subject, already defined in principle, and with
certain assumptions at work, which I have sought to unfold. Both responses, the
double reply, oriented in different directions, are taken up therefore in order to situate and disturb any simply accepted or cosy consensus underwriting the very idea
of 'theory and the novel'. Anecdote and empiricism, *mere* narrative recounting of
events without hyperbole: what could be further from 'theory', or closer, perhaps,
to what constitutes the novel in the nineteenth century, and to the narrative realism
that constitutes, in many cases, such novels?

So, the anecdote: in a departmental meeting, the subject of a forthcoming
visiting speaker was raised, and a colleague inquired as to the title of the visiting
speaker's talk. Another colleague replied that the talk concerned the Brontë sisters,
and gave the precise title. The title contained words like 'phenomenological', 'meth-
odological', and 'deconstructive'. This raised a slight laugh from the colleague who
had made the enquiry, along with some additional smirks and knowing, complicit
looks from others. At the risk of interpreting this moment, I would imagine the
mirth came from what was seen as a combination of what, for some, would be
jargon or theoretical buzz-words (even now, thirty to forty years after 'theory' was
first imported into departments of English), and the sense on the part of those
who were amused, that such an approach to the Brontës was inappropriate, anachronistic even. Anachronism is here read as the untimely 'application' of particular
modes of thought and inquiry to texts which – the argument would go – are inappropriate to such forms of analysis because the texts were written historically prior
to the development of those modes of philosophically inflected consideration. Put
more simply, a phenomenological or 'deconstructive' approach to the Brontës is
wrong because the types of discourse identified as 'theoretical' belong to a period,
or periods, after the Brontës wrote. Such a reading gesture could not take account
of the contexts of production (social, cultural, political) and so removed itself
from a 'properly' historical account. Such an argument, the one I'm assuming to
be implicit in the event described, is flawed on several accounts.

There are many things to say about this scenario, and I will try to be as brief as
possible without resorting to crude reductiveness. First, it has to be asked, can one
ever recover the histories that make up a text, is it ever possible to reconstruct the
totality of history out of which a text appears, and which that text then mediates
through its own encoded signs of its historicity? I believe the answer is no; not only

is a totality impossible, there is also no direct access to another period, the forms of its thought, its cultural practices, and so on. However dogged my research, however much I may believe my approach to be empirical, I can only ever read, I *do only ever read* from within the complex matrix of cultural forces and historical practices and discourses that make up and inform – inscribe – my own subject-position. This is not to say that one cannot recover at least in some translatable and provisional manner the traces of a history, which manner betrays even as it recovers, ruining as much as it reassembles, but that one must always recognize that such traces are themselves immediately translations of event and experience, and that furthermore, my interpretation of them is not neutral, however naïvely I may assure myself I read, but is positioned and overdetermined, in possibly innumerable ways.

As this might give you to understand, there is not one history but multiple histories for which one must account; concomitantly, there is more than one way to address the historical, and the assumption that a theoretical approach is ahistorical or unhistorical, not only bolsters itself unthinkingly with the notion that there is just one right historical approach is deeply problematic and erroneous. Different texts, being singular, speak of, and to, their histories, in differing, singular ways from one another. No one historical approach can account for this, and, what is worse, to make comparative judgements between texts, extracting 'evidence' selectively from them in order to promote a single historical thesis, generated from a monolithic historical overview of a moment in the past is a gesture that is both politically and ethically suspect, not to mention an act of violence.

Second point: whatever objections there may or may not have been to the research paper when it was presented, this always has more to do with how cogently and coherently the speaker or writer presents the reading of the poetry, novel, or whichever text is being read; that is to say, criticism of a particular approach or paradigm must begin from an informed judgement that suspends its own herme-neutics of suspicion and knowingness concerning 'theory'. Before we can even come on to the matter of 'theory', it has to be stated that no 'theoretical' reading is, necessarily, inappropriate as such. There are only good readings and bad readings; or, to refine this somewhat, there are readings of texts that are more sensitively handled and less sensitively handled, if we understand and agree as a premise from which to begin that every text is different from every other text. This being the case, it follows therefore that, in its singularity, every text is other than every other text. In this, it must necessarily also be the case that any and every reading must always begin not from a fixed intellectual position imposed on that – and every other – text. Instead, every reading begins only as a response to the singularity of said text, starting in response from a recognition that one is not imposing a read-ing but instead articulating, finding, a reading dictated to you by that text in its singular difference, and then articulated or translated by that which takes place in the event of reading between text and reading subject. Of course, it is necessary to pause here, if only to acknowledge that what one calls a text to which one responds relies on the assumption, as Derek Attridge puts it, that the text exists only as 'a set of coded signals', which become a novel in 'a specific reading', and 'within which [process] the reader too comes into being' (Attridge 2004, 87).

If this involves a recognition of particular forms of representation or modes of literary production as being comprehensible according to one's own apprehension of philosophical or political discursive models, the work of scholarship and the act of critical reading might – and only might – generate what Attridge calls a creative reading of the text. What I have called the critical reading is what Attridge terms a 'literary reading' (2004, 86–7). The 'literary reading' is that process by which, being 'embedded in the culture of which literature . . . [and a particular literary form such as a novel] is a part, one . . . deploy[s] one's familiarity with the conventionalized routines of the literary institution'; and this, Attridge argues, involves one in a 'great deal of patient labour [which] is unavoidable if a responsible reading is to be achieved'. However, such routine, patient and hopefully rigorous scholarly work is still only the 'foundation' of a creative reading (Attridge 2004, 87). The creative reading, being 'both passive and active' (Attridge 2004, 85), involves one in the effort of doing justice to the singularity of the text (as Attridge has it; 2004, 85), whilst also letting that singularity, the otherness of the text in all its 'strangeness' or anomalous difference 'happen' to one, thereby experiencing the text in its otherness (Attridge 2004, 85).

Without wishing to raise a laugh from academic colleagues similar to those in my own department who laughed at the title of the research paper to be given, and so to escape any accusations of using 'theoretical' (so-called) 'jargon' (so-called), the alterity, the singularity, the strangeness experienced in the event of reading might well be the sign or trace of the material or historical; this is not something, however, that one can guarantee before one's encounter with the text. Certainly, however scholarly an approach grounded in a particular epistemological paradigm may be, in its responsibility to the text it must always be prepared for that which it cannot be prepared and address that as it is, as it arrives. The textual anomaly, the odd image, trope, scene, that which opens a gap in logic and comprehension, or that about which a text remains silent whilst, nevertheless, drawing attention to its silence which affirms itself against the vast and mobile army of metaphors (to paraphrase Nietzsche) that direct one to read in a certain direction; this is what remains to be read, and to which one must attend.

III

The resistance to certain manifestations of 'theory' and the privileging given to 'theoretical' readings favouring the historical and the material can perhaps be traced to the reading history of the novel in universities, and the justifications made for reading the novel. For a number of years in literary study the novel was seen as a poor relation to poetry or drama. However, Since 1948, with the publication of Leavis's *The Great Tradition*, and subsequent works by Wayne Booth and Dorothy Van Ghent, the attempts to articulate, if not a 'theory', then a poetics *of* the novel have demanded that we take our formalized and systematic commentaries on the ontology of the novel somewhat more seriously. However, as an adjunct of what is part polemic, part apologia, the justification for reading the novel has been on some historical ground or other. To invert an argument put forward by David Carroll, because literature, and the novel especially, is representational, it is taken as producing figures; which figuration or representation offer the reader beyond the immediate event or experience being presented in prose:

> ... a particular and recognizable historical, social or psychological reality or, in a more abstract manner, a figure of an ideal, mythical, metaphysical 'reality' – when it presents or makes visible the 'essential' or 'characteristic' traits of some 'outside', of a space or context other than the 'strictly literary'. The 'outside' is assumed to exist before its representation and thus to be the origin of representational literature, to be present in itself before it is represented in literature – which means that this 'outside' is defined by other means than 'strictly literary' ones and assumed to exist in itself before it is 'figured' and recognized for what it is in literature. (Carroll 1980, 201)

The Marxist or quasi-Marxist dismissal of theoretical models of reading other than those explicitly materialist and historicist, allied to the empirical assumption that what is on the page is a representation of the world and that it is our job, as critics, to read the world, has to do, I think, with a sustained effort (one which becomes mechanically repetitious) to justify one's own reading act by turning to the 'outside' of the text – the very idea, as if such a thing were possible; for, as the good reader will already know, there is no outside-the-text. History, society, culture: all are terms, conceptual totalities, assuming homogeneous and stable ontological forms given material expression in the world.

There has been a degree of inevitability or predictability about this type of read-ing. One might almost say there has been an historical necessity dictated to leftist, pseudo- or quasi-leftist critics from the publication of Gyorgy Lukacs' *Theory of the Novel* onwards, in which the difference of novels was reduced to a totality both formal and historical in nature. When Lukacs wrote that the novel was the epic for disintegrated civilizations and disenchanted worlds, his postlapsarian inflection led him to remark that the novel 'thinks in terms of totality' (*TN* 56). Nothing is less the case in fact; novels, especially but not exclusively novels in the nineteenth century, are vast, densely woven irregular matrices of heterogeneous materials, irreducible to a totality. It is only a certain type of critic who, incapable or unwilling to think in anything other than terms of totality, sees totality everywhere, and sets out, Quixote-like, tilting at ontological and historical windmills of his or her own making. Like 'theory' though, the novel is irreducible to ontological determina-tions which hold; both are, in reality, chance concatenations of lines of flight, singular or individual manifestations which come about by the chance of historical and material forces. As such, literary language is 'theoretical', to the extent that, comprised of differing and heterogeneous discourses, it weaves a mediated network even as it invites us to attend to language as language, the purpose of which is, in engaging with the historical moment, to generate not merely a representation but a rhetorical reading of material conditions, translated into the literary, and therefore available as ideological critique of the materiality of history. 'Theory' makes the 'rhetorical' reading of the nineteenth-century author's own rhetorical reading available because, in treating language as language, it asks the student to take seriously the power with which language is invested.

IV

Though everything I have observed thus far addresses implicitly the question of teaching in general, and teaching the nineteenth-century specifically, I have refrained from discussing teaching as such. Having been asked to address a few questions concerning teaching, I will respond to those in a moment, but first there remains this apparent 'avoidance' of discussing teaching. There are a number of reasons for this, not least that – and I'm sure this is quite an unfashionable, not to say anachronistic, comment in the recent and current institutional and governmentally driven climate (can one 'drive' a 'climate'?) – there is an ethical component at work here, beyond or before institutional demands. Teaching is and remains a singular practice: singular in the sense that one person's practice will, inevitably, differ from another's, whatever the similarities; and singular also – or it should be – in that the teaching 'event' (to risk sounding pompous, which is not the intention here; but then you cannot control the reception of what you say, ever) should involve a degree of unpreparedness. Certainly, much teaching involves careful preparation, the acquisition of knowledge, an understanding of analysis and argument, and so forth, on the part of the teacher. At the same time, however, in entering a formal space, such as a classroom, sticking to the programme is not the best plan. Indeed, the plan should only ever be constrained by the possibility that the plan might be abandoned. One has to risk not staying with a script. More importantly, there has to be the chance that an event, something completely unpredictable, inventive, and involving sudden unforeseen decisions, has the merest possibility of taking place.

Thus, while nine out of ten seminars will proceed by the book, as it were, there might be that tenth seminar where one is open to what arrives, in the form of a question, a commentary, a reaction, which transforms both the students' and the teacher's understanding of what is taking place, the text being read, the material of the course as a whole. No amount of preparation can prepare one for this happening, and no such event can be programmed. It might be asked, what about lectures? The same is true, though in different ways. Do not be prepared merely to go off-script: do away with the script altogether.

Such reflection might appear mere avoidance. Again, I cannot control reception of what I'm saying here, and I have to take that chance. I find myself compelled, though, to say, in a paraphrase of a remark of Peggy Kamuf's, that before the student-teacher relationship (that is, before any institutionally situated and pre-scribed hierarchy), there is always the face-to-face with the other. Additionally, the other is not ever just or simply the group of students. Every student is an other; every student is different from every other student, and the teacher is just one more other in this situation. Admittedly, the teacher has a privileged position institutionally in this structure. However, one must always seek to teach as if an ethics of the face-to-face with the other, in which I must be open to response to each and every other, rather than seeking to determine or impose my position, were possible at all times, even though, and in advance of the experience of teaching, I can never be sure that this openness, this response, this attentiveness to the ethical recognition of the singular encounter or event, can be guaranteed. In fact, I know that it cannot, that I must always in some manner betray this ethical injunction. I am thus required to commit myself, with the sure and certain knowledge that I cannot maintain such a commitment, to an ethics beyond ethics in teaching. Hence the refusal, not the avoidance, of setting out a 'here's what you do' guide in the act of teaching.

I realize that this chapter raises questions of practice, and I will come to those shortly. For now, though, it has to be said that in the face of this ethical question, a dilemma arises. Another anecdote, this time from my own teaching practice: in a class on literary theory, an 'introduction' placed somewhat idiosyncratically in the senior or fourth year of a North American institution, and placed there also as one of two quasi-compulsory courses (*quasi* – because you had to take one or the other; there was a limited choice through a kind of institutional get-out clause, making sure students could avoid encountering 'pure' theory if they so chose, or thought they chose), in being asked a question, I found myself having step back every time I tried to frame an answer, to open on to broader, and more complex frames. There was, though, never any stepping beyond or outside the text; there was no outside-the-text. The question, a two-parter, had to do, perhaps ironically, with the reason for theory at all, the student having asked something along the lines of this: if theory is important, why is it only introduced to us in our final year? And, given that we are all English Majors, who apparently know how to read very well (having got high scores in high school, and gained access to a highly selective private university with an international research reputation), why do we need to be taught other ways of reading? This question arose at the beginning of the seminar, that moment when one or two people are still coming in, others are switching off mobile phones, a few are finishing a conversation, and so on; or, if not at the beginning, then in that curious margin slightly before the beginning but after the point where the seminar has begun, which was positioned rhetorically by the student asking the question, in this way: 'before we get going with this week's reading, I'd like ask a quick question'. The question may have been quick, in that rhetorical formula involving an apologia, which students use regularly, but the answer was anything but, taking over the seminar and lasting forty-three minutes. This left five to six minutes in which to discuss 'this week's reading'. But what is one to do?

I take it seriously, therefore, that on the one hand, one has a responsibility to the other, which exceeds any institutional regulation, any mere programming. On the other hand, to respond to an other in this manner means that one is not doing what is required of one according to certain laws, rules, and so forth, and that therefore one is neglecting or giving short shrift to every other. Any attempted balance cannot be programmed either, for if one seeks to do so, one retreats from the ethical into a merely economic consideration, one makes a calculated strategic gesture, recuperating oneself into the machinic and the programmed. Business as usual. It has to be recognized, therefore, that one can always be faced with a situation which remains undecidable; one encounters an aporia at the heart of institutional logic, in the face of which one cannot decide through simple choice but also one cannot abnegate all responsibility, and avoid decision, remaining in the aporetic moment. Before any calculation, one encounters a 'crisis' and one is forced to decide in response to the undecidable; or, as Jacques Derrida remarks, 'I am responsible to any one (that is to say, to the other) only by failing in my responsibilities to all the others . . . Whether I want to or not, I will never be able to justify the fact that I prefer or sacrifice any one (any other) to the other . . . What binds me to singularities, to this one or that one . . . remains finally unjustifiable'. Or as he puts it rather more directly: 'How would you justify the fact that you sacrifice all the cats in the world to the cat that you feed at home every day for years, whereas other cats die of hunger at every instant?' (Derrida 2008, 71) Teaching is not the same as feeding cats (although there are many aspects of institutional work resembling herding of said animals), but the principle governing what is ultimately unjustifiable is a matter of degree, rather than kind. There is thus always that in excess of the programmed which can erupt in the true choices or decisions one makes, beyond those calculations, those choices where one can weigh the situation.

Of course, I can imagine someone observing, 'well Wolfreys could have just told the student to come and see him in office hours and they would discuss the point'. The very fact aside that one cannot be prepared for what arrives, what calls on one, and which transmission or communication makes one into the addressee to whom it was destined, it also has to be said that such a comment is itself an institutional formula, which, in emerging, forestalls the possibility of an event, because it corrals and polices itself within and according to the impersonal dictates of the law, the institution, and so forth. It reintroduces, in the specific example of teaching I am giving – and again this is only my own singular situation, in a singular moment, responding to a singular other – the protocol and hierarchy of a machinery, and this, while it might be effective time management, is not teaching. Then again, in another fiction of anticipation, I can hear someone say, this is all very Derridean but . . . (or worse yet, I can imagine the bad reader saying 'can't we do away with deconstruction[ism], after all it's just a theory to be applied . . .' [the -ism, by the way, is optional, I'm merely signalling degrees of bad readership]).

The point here is that there is, in teaching, always the possibility of an excess that erupts from within, that which throws a spanner in the works, where the works rely for their smooth operation on a production-line assembly mode of knowledge acquisition, as one fits or equips the student. However, to go back almost to where I began: theory and practice are inseparable. If this particular section of this chapter is 'Derridean' in its ethics – and I would like to believe it is, but not for the reasons I imagine haunt the objection I've invented, above – this has to do not with a theory and a practice of teaching, or even a theory and a practice of teaching theory, a theory and practice of teaching theory in relation to the nineteenth-century novel, etc., and so on, and so forth . . . This section emerges itself as a response.

I have therefore begun a response – I'm not finished yet – in a manner that unjustifiably seeks to do justice to the question of addressing teaching directly. I am thus attempting to perform here (in the sense of a performative speech act) a response that is marked by, and produced from, the very ethical responsibility about which I am talking, and which I take to underpin a true teaching. If this overruns the word count, the possibility is that much of this section will have to be edited out (hopefully with a footnote put in its place, with a much briefer indication of what was said; of course, you won't know that this has taken place, if this has to be cut, and I have to add the note explaining what is not there). But, it has been my intention in what comes at what was to have been the end of the chapter and as a preface to the next and final section, not simply to convey what might take place in teaching but to 'teach' through the example of the singular and excessive response as a necessary ethical gesture.

V

Which leads me back to the request to address particular questions. Because I have already taken up too much space here, I must necessarily be somewhat schematic, and risk doing violence to what is central here, the question of teaching 'theory' and, that is to say, in correlation with, the nineteenth-century novel, the one insinuating itself in, and thus unfolding, the other (though in which direction this should head is another matter entirely: 'theory' reads the nineteenth-century novel or the nineteenth-century novel reads 'theory', not forgetting all the difficulties already announced). The questions asked of me are:

• For those in the example set forth early on in the chapter who snickered at the subject of a speaker's talk, how would you justify the kind of reading put forth in this chapter as valuable for students of nineteenth-century fiction?
• What would you say about what students gain from such an engagement with 'theory'?
• How do you recommend teachers convey such readings to students?
• What kinds of questions should teachers ask in class discussions?
• What kinds of background knowledge should they be taught to enable theoretical applications?
• What sorts of writing assignments should be given in order to prompt this kind of analysis?

Let me address each of these in turn:
   First question, first response: For those whose reaction indicates perhaps a discomfort with the proximity between the language of 'theory' and that of 'the nineteenth-century novel', I would suggest initially that they reflect on the extent to which any novel of the nineteenth century is always a mix of much stranger languages. In this, one might consider also the hostility and incomprehension that made itself manifest in criticism of Thomas Hardy's novels, not least in F. R. Leavis, but elsewhere also, where the abiding assumption was that Hardy's fictions were, despite their popularity, aesthetic failures when held up against particular critical

criteria concerning form, representation, appropriate levels of discourse, and so on. While Dickens's characterizations can always be explained away aesthetically as belonging to the grotesque, the satirical, the caricature or otherwise, assigned to different forms, genres and literary traditions, and while George Eliot maintains the illusion of omniscience through the rhetorical disguise of position, ideology and so forth, Hardy makes language strange by forcing its relations, thereby calling into question, albeit as an indirect after-effect, the efficacy of any criticism-grounded assumptions of aesthetic wholeness or organic unity of form. The point here is that language is a powerfully estranging medium, which encloses us, makes us feel as though we belong, or otherwise excludes us. 'Theory' has been only the most visible form of such articulation in the last few decades, and this can be more clearly seen if one reflects on the dialectical battles fought in the name of the more overtly political of 'theories' such as Marxism or feminism.

Putting forward a justification for a 'theoretical' reading of a nineteenth-century novel, and recognizing all the while that there is no justification, any more than one can justify any practice, I would have to say that, first, but on every subsequent occasion, one must always strive to investigate one's own language, and the conceptual frameworks that dictate one's own rhetorical and ideological, as well as aesthetic, assumptions. In short, ask questions of yourself about those very practices of thought where you don't think, where habitually you take something as 'read', or that you assume something 'goes without saying'. If something goes as read, and without saying, its mute inscription is all the more pervasive. Ask why do certain forms of language – the language of 'theory' – make you uncomfortable, and avoid the immediate fall back into the obvious answers. Also, consider the fact that in other disciplines, one is expected to master certain discourses or language praxes – mathematics or physics, for example. Yet, with 'English literature' or 'literatures in English' we are doing professionally what we do anyway (the phrase 'reading for pleasure' springs to mind). There is, behind whatever implicit assumptions are at work here, the idea that there is something 'natural', 'inevitable' and 'self-evident' in what we do and how we do it, when we're doing reading or when we're doing what passes for reading but which is, already, a programme by which we are written as liberal humanist western Europeans or North Americans, the parameters and protocols of which we all share, more or less. Even – or perhaps especially – political criticism shares the same, or similar, often humanist values, and justifies its own departure from the 'normative' or 'conventional' mode of reading, out of political necessity, the demands of demystification, and so on.

One aspect of 'theory' is to question fundamentally what it is we think we're doing when we read, and having to learn a new language with difficult concepts behind it, appearing, from an unthought-through aesthetic position, unnecessary at best, pernicious at worst. Students of nineteenth-century novels can gain much from 'theory' however (as can students of any literary form or period), for the following reason: it is not a question of learning a theory so that 'practically' they can 'apply' something 'useful' to a novel, as though the novel were soft jelly being poured into a mould, or as if 'theory' were a template, into which the novel could be made to 'fit' once 'theory' had rubbed off its rough edges. Rather, the close and patient reading of 'theory' can serve to illuminate ideas already at work in the novel, which, in the drive for narrative content, the student might otherwise overlook. Equally, the novel can be shown as a medium for the exploration of philosophical ideas in particular cultural and historical moments, which ideas are given shape and form, or given face – what in classical rhetoric would be called prosopopoeia – through characters, the worlds they inhabit, and the interactions between those characters in those sites, at specific historical moments, and in relation to the local materiality of the singular world they exist in and serve to define through their experiences.

Second question, second response: students gain a great deal from the engagement with 'theory', not least the ability to reason in complex ways that challenge habits of thought and assumptions about their world and the world depicted through novels. In being hybrid and heterogeneous, 'theory' exposes the student to a complexity of different disciplinary modes of thinking, including historical and ideological discourses, discourses of contemporary science, practices in linguistics and an understanding of otherwise silent and unconscious modes of thought as revealed through psychoanalysis; and, additionally, there is the encounter with the discourses of philosophy, often those developing out of ontology and phenomenology, as well as aesthetics, which place at centre-stage questions concerning the meaning of being and the ways in which the human subject perceives and so interprets the world. Were one to advocate 'theory' in its own right (again supposing such a thing existed, and one could speak both of an 'it' and an 'in its own right'), such concerns should be more than enough, if not to justify 'theory' then at least to explain what is important, urgent even. However, what can also be said here, through analogy, is that the nineteenth-century novel in its many guises and through the various modes of realist presentation that are assumed in the novels of Dickens, Trollope, Gissing, Thackeray, the Brontës, Gaskell, Oliphant and so on, is, though different, not dissimilar to the web that goes by the name 'theory'. The same and yet not the same, it too asks questions of history, ideology, politics, language, questions of value, both economic and aesthetic, what laws define a society, what gives meaning to human life, how one interprets the world, and so forth.

Third question, third response: this question is much more difficult to answer, in no small part for the reasons I have attempted to trace concerning an ethics of teaching apropos singularity and the other. What I would suggest, however, as one possible practice is that small passages, no more than a couple of paragraphs, be given over to close reading, in seminars, and in written exercises. If possible, find a passage in a given thinker (Lacan or Kristeva, perhaps, or indeed, any critic or 'theorist' you might employ) and compare it with a passage from a novel in which the subject is, if not similar, then, at least, in some way discernibly related through its different modes of representation and the play in which these modes engage. Where, for example, Kristeva speaks of abjection in relation to coroporeality, *jouissance* and violence (Kristeva 1982, 10), consider as a contrast the passage in Gaskell's *Cranford* where the story of a cat being forced to take an emetic is shared amongst a group of genteel ladies (Gaskell 1998, 125–6).[3] And this passage, in turn, might be turned towards a discussion of analogy, catachresis, modes of signification and, in short, pussy vomit as a model for *pure* literary production, for what Derrida calls a 'non-exchangeable productivity in terms of sensible objects or signs of sensible objects (money for example)' (Derrida 1998, 271). Conveying that the function of artistic and literary activity 'is essentially *parodic*' (Eagleton 1978, 51) Gaskell's narrative of fabulous regurgitation, a metaphorical regurgitation of the narrative and the displacement of vomit into narrative iterability coming back and up over and over again, admits of 'neither . . . use-value nor . . . exchange value' (Derrida 1998b, 271).

Another way to approach the two passages is not to simply find overlaps or analogous resemblance but to read both passages rhetorically or 'poetically', considering tropes, metaphors, other figures of speech, and how they operate in the extracts in question. One might take, again to give an example, a passage from Lacan's well-known essay on returning to Freud, 'The Agency of the Letter in the Unconscious or Reason since Freud' (Lacan 1977, 146–78). In the second section of this essay, 'The Letter in the Unconscious' Lacan offers a 'definition' of 'the topography of the unconscious' in relation to the signifier and, by extension, chains of signification expressed in writing, as this 'topography' is to be expressed as an 'algorithm' (1977, 163). Why, we might pause to ask, is this figure of 'topography' appropriate? Is it appropriate, and what is Lacan doing in 'representing the unconscious through the figure of a map and then substituting that trope with another, this time one from the symbolic logic of mathematics? What is the relation between topography and writing, mapping and other forms of inscription? What does thinking the unconscious as a map, or thinking a literary text as a map for that matter, change in our perception of literary form, the supposed linearity of narrative, structures of literary representation and so forth? Already the Lacanian excerpt throws up all kinds of questions that we can ask of literary texts. It enables a different thinking, a thinking of difference in relation to our habitual practices of reading the literary. But to take this further, one should observe how Lacan's text is a series of interplays between linear text and algorithmic diagrammes, thus (1977, 163–64):

> It is a matter, therefore, of defining the topography of this unconscious. I say that it is the very topography defined by the algorithm:

$$\frac{S}{s}$$

From this point, Lacan develops a series of increasingly complex algorithms, qualifying their presentation as symbols through discussion of metaphor, metonymy and metonymic structure (1977, 164). Against this, one might read, or seek to unravel the symbolic and metonymic logic at work, in an extract from Thomas Hardy's *Far from the Madding Crowd*. In this, Gabriel Oak and Jan Coggan, in pursuit of Bathsheba Everdene, stop to decode different forms of horse's hoof-prints (Hardy 2000, 184–6). There is more than mere similarity here between the Lacanian and the Hardyan world of symbol and signification, though this is undeniably significant and worth exploration. Both texts, more significantly, are available to us as explorations and plays with the limits of competing epistemologies and modes of representational logic. In *Far from the Madding Crowd*, in its first volume edition at least rather than the Wessex edition, Hardy introduces diagrammes of the prints. Coggan stops before some tracks, of which the narrator records that 'the footprints forming this recent impression were full of information as to pace: being difficult to describe in words, they are given in the following diagram' (Hardy 2000, 184). On the page before the reader, appear two parallel, hand-drawn lines within which are shapes resembling horse's hooves at different distances. Hardy reproduces such prints several more times (Hardy 2000, 185–6), each set developing, like Lacan's algorithms, yet remaining resolutely at the limits of legibility. In these pages Coggan deciphers the tracks, both for Oak, whose knowledge is scanty and of the most general kind at best, but also, importantly, for the reader. Not only is the pace translated, so too is the fact that the horse being tracked is recently shod, and that it is lamed eventually. Such is what we are given to read in the 'mystic charactery' of the hoof-prints (Hardy 2000, 186). Whether it is the late Victorian novelist remaking on the difficulty in expressing verbally the significance of the signs, or the Freudian-structuralist analyst elaborating on the function of the subject in the work of signification, each passage offers important insight into that which is, for want of a better word, 'theoretical' at the heart of narrative discourse, and with that, the epistemological historicity of a given text, which remains as encrypted as it may be said to give up its meanings. More than this, they offer an analogy between the structure of the unconscious and the structure of a novel, which itself not only speaks of but engages in a performativity through the very different examples – for both texts do the very things about which they speak, in, as it were, so many signs of their times.

Fourth question, fourth response: the teacher should always ask questions that are dictated by the singularity of the text. Making a statement based on the assumption or assertion of 'realism', so-called, as a quasi-universal, self-evident determinant grounded on only the vaguest or most general of observations about what novels do, is reductive, stupid and wrong. It is all of these for the reason that every text is singular; every text differs from every other and no text can be made to stand as exemplary of a few, many or all the others that are supposedly like it. The question should be formulated as a response to the text, whether 'theoretical' or fictive, as if the text were asking a question, in response to which another question is demanded as answer *and* question. At the same time, the question should focus on that which in representation or narrative goes unremarked. Much time in seminars is taken up with talking about character motivation or psychology as if the character were not a construct of language. This is then extended to the reading of narrative trajectory. Call such a reading to a halt and focus on *how* a passage produces effects in a reader. Ask, for example, why Dickens in *Dombey and Son* allegorizes train travel as some manifestation of Death, and why that manifestation is itself quasi-anthropomorphic or prosopopoeic; or, to take *Bleak House* as the example, consider the powerful passage where Joe, the road sweeper is found to be dead. What takes place in that strange and disquieting instance of parabasis, where Dickens addresses the nation, Queen Victoria herself? Ask if this is realism and what is going on in such a gesture? As a further example, take a small passage such as that in *Middlemarch*, where George Eliot introduces Timothy Cooper, a labourer. Why is he allowed to step forward, to speak for himself? What is the function of voice as witness? If there is a fundamental question one might ask, this would be to invite students to consider why something anomalous appears in a novel. Why, for instance, is there endless reference to optics and vision, visibility and visuality in *The Pickwick Papers* when, ostensibly, such references in all their frequency have little to do either with narrative or representation of a given scene. Asking the student to notice a network of figures, which often persist for no immediately apparent reason, can produce very important 'theoretical' discussions, which reveal much about a novel beyond what it has to tell us on its surface.

Fifth question, fifth response: in attempting to answer the question of what kinds of background knowledge students should be taught to enable theoretical applications, I have to call a halt here because it strikes me that the angles from which the question comes are somewhat in error. For all the reasons I suggest throughout this chapter, it should be clear that 'theory' is not something one 'applies'. 'It' is a series of modes of thought and critical engagement from multiple and diverse intellectual locations (the metaphor of background is problematic not least because it suggests material of greater or lesser importance), which cannot all be made to fit together in the neat package 'literary theory'. But many people know this. Instead, the question ought to address the kinds of conceptual thinking, which students out to be introduced to, so that they can be enabled to formulate appropriate questions for themselves. Given that the novel works through the medium of a narrator or 'narrator-effect' (for there is no narrator there, only what Colin MacCabe calls a metalanguage, a language commenting on the language and behaviours of invented characters), it is, I believe, important to introduce the student to notions of ontology, the meaning of being, and how ontological definitions are formed, and, equally, it is important to introduce the student to matters of perspective *as* perception. Even in the most seemingly omniscient 'voice', interpretation based on a subjective interpretation or translation of the material and empirical world takes place, and as a reader one is thus always subject to a phenomenological filter, even if the writer might believe he or she is simply presenting the world as it is. This in turn can lead to the student being introduced to the subject of how language as a structural system operates, why a word or group of words produces an effect or meaning, and which other synonymous and non-synonymous substitutions do not. And, once more, such attention to perception, ontological construction, phenomenological interpretation, the role of seemingly purposeless meshes of metaphors and tropes, and linguistic or rhetorical devices: all direct the student to the historicity of the text. Thus, the student need not be introduced to 'theory' as such but to that which 'theory' is grounded in: the investigation of conceptual frames and structures and the historicity of their production.

Last question, last response: There is no *one* writing assignment that is appropriate; again this is a question of one's response to the other. Students should be

10

Ghosts: Of Ourselves, or, Drifting with Hardy and Heidegger

... 'tis not to married couples but to single sleepers that a ghost shows himself when 'a do come. One has been seen lately, too. A very strange one.

The Return of the Native

I thought you were the ghost of yourself.

The Return of the Native

We shall go away, a very long distance, hundreds of miles from these parts, and such as this can never happen again, and no ghost of the past reach there.

Tess of the D'Urbervilles

I

As my three epigraphs indicate, the idea of the ghost has a certain frequency, if not a currency, for Thomas Hardy. I shall come back to Hardy as 'ghost-writer' of modernity shortly and the manner in which he complicates our notion of what it means to be haunted, but it is necessary to address, albeit briefly, Hardy's significance regarding his perception of the role of the ghost, and of spectrality as literary and *theoretical* – that is to say speculative, specular, visionary – trope. Hardy is our first example because he remains the writer of spectrality *par excellence*. Hardy is the author, more than any other, whose writing shifts, or makes possible, the reorientation of thought apropos haunting, the phantom or phantasm, the apparition, the revenant, and the ghost in relation to questions of subjectivity and historicity, as well as to the relation between writing and the past. This is what one is given, read in even the most fleeting consideration of the epigraphs. A briefly adumbrated reading of the spectral trope in these citations opens for us a mobile, provisional epistemology of haunting as it is received in the last decades of the nineteenth century. In retrospect, and perhaps more significantly, it might also be said that Hardy reveals that which could not have been anticipated in the thinking of haunting. He admits to fiction the coming of a spectral future that could not have been envisioned.

Though each of the epigraphs name ghosts, each has a different time. The first epigraph admits a spectral convention framed folklorically as a narrative of received, shared wisdom. Doxical knowledge offers insight into traditions of haunting. The second epigraph resonates differently, suggesting the experience of the uncanny, an apprehension – a *frisson*, the touch of which announces the countersignature of phenomenological reception – of the self as other, the self received as the doppelganger, the living as dead. The ghost thus arrives before it arrives, it 'returns' unexpectedly as the anticipation of a future, from that future, as that which is to come. The last epigraph's 'ghost', mere metaphor as it seems, admits to a number of modern conceits: on the one hand, it appears to suggest psychological burden, that which is written on subjectivity and the subject's psyche. On the other hand, it bespeaks a certain historical psychic weight, wherein memory and history, the personal and broader cultural or material events might coincide. It remarks a desire for a different place for the subject, as if place itself were – perhaps fetishistically – haunted. It also intimates that a ghost cannot leave its given place, whilst, perhaps naïvely, expressing the hope that if a ghost is a thing of the past, it also remains outside memory and conscience, *not really* inscribed within the subject. And, of course, finally, for now, this last epigraph, in its phrasing – *ghost of the past* – determines haunting as a matter of structural figuration, whilst signalling that, in the words of Jacques Derrida, the 'age already in the *past* is in fact constituted in every respect as a *text* . . . [as] such the age conserves the values of legibility and the efficacy of a model and thus disturbs the time (tense) of the line or the line of time' (Derrida 1976, lxxxix–xc).[1]

This is not to deny the past, of course. Only the most perverse misreading or avoidance of reading would assume such a thing. Instead, it is to acknowledge that the past *as such* can never be present in the present, and that to acknowledge this is to acknowledge also that what we name the past exceeds any mere present moment by virtue of its being legible, by leaving legible traces and inscriptions, the very persistence and revenance of which disturb both structure and history, as Derrida's chiasmus gives us to comprehend. That chiasmus places the absolute separation of text and context, word and world, under erasure. In this crossing through, an unsuturable fissure opens, and the ghost of modernity appears. Its apparition causes us to comprehend how being is written. More than this, however, being, in being apprehended, as what Derrida terms *l'être écrit* (1967, 31; the being written/the written being) is written as being haunted: subject to the traces of historicity, and to those disquieting eruptions that remain all too legible, one's being – if it can be expressed thus – is never on time with itself, its presence and its present always already disturbed by the ghost of itself, and also the ghosts of all its others. Any ontology of being is therefore always already ruined from the start. The house of being is a haunted locus, and Tess's naïve desire to escape the ghost of the past fails in its tragic comprehension to appreciate the extent to which the ghost remains with us, as that which we cannot admit determining who we are. Tess's desire cannot comprehend how, if the past is ghost, then so too is that which is to come, and that the future, irreducible to a programme by which we can anticipate our 'future anterior', is the apparition of 'ce monde à venir et . . . ce qui en lui aura fait trembler . . .' / 'that world to come . . . and that which will have made [or caused it to] shake' (1967, 14; translation my own).

II

Such shaking or trembling is caused to take place temporally, as well as spatially. It has to do with the opening of a gap, and so, with that instant of sundering, the appearance of a double, an other. Despite the different times of the epigraphs drawn from Thomas Hardy, what one is given to see is an otherwise inaccessible image, imagined as, or through the perception of another. Jacques Derrida apprehends the appearance of any spectral form as a condition of technological or written reproduction, and so, implicitly, to traces a link to matters of repetition and representation: 'When the very *first* perception of an image is linked to a structure of reproduction, then we are dealing with the realm of phantoms' (Derrida 2008, 61). As soon as there is image, and perception of that, there is both the material objective form, and its phenomenal counterpart. What this always comes down to, though never in exactly the same manner, is the eerie efficacy of the spectral as an inescapable condition of the forms which we inhabit, literally or metaphorically, and which we need to get along, at home, at work, and in the sense of ourselves in relation to the world. The 'architecture' of every form, everything we understand as 'reality' – whether it be that of a house, a town, a novel, the notions of subjectivity or being – is traced by a double, an incorporeal phantom or phantasm, a 'gap', to use Nicolas Abraham's word. Abraham remarks that 'what haunts are not the dead, but the gaps left within us by the secrets of others' (Abraham and Torok 1994, 171). As we see from the epigraphs, perception admits the other within the structures we mistakenly believe to be unities, complete, whole and undifferentiated.

Yet, haunting is irreducible to the apparition. The spectral or uncanny effect is not simply a matter of seeing a ghost. The haunting process puts into play a disruptive structure or, to consider this another way, recalling the idea of the phantom or phantasm as 'gap', a disruption that is other to the familiarity of particular structures wherein the disruption is itself structural and irreducible to a simple, stabilized representation. The disruption of the familiar is clearly marked in the three epigraphs. In the first, the familiar *is* the unfamiliar, folkloric convention being that the ghost appears to single sleepers. What opens from within this, though, is a question of competing knowledges, differing epistemological frames that are irreconcilable. While the speaker firmly adheres to the apparition and reproduction of an image as a 'familiar' encounter within a given culture, the 'ghost' that appears to a single sleeper is also readable as a phantasm, which, as Peter Schwenger points out, 'is both a ghost and an image in the mind' (Schwenger 1999, 5). As Rodolphe Gasché remarks of the idea of the phantasm, 'the phantasmatic "structure," puts in play not the phantasm itself – there never could be one – but one of its figures . . . the phantasmatic is the space in which representation is fragmented' (Gasché 1997, 172). The efficacy of haunting is in its resistance to being represented whole or undifferentiated, or being 'seen' as itself rather than being uncannily intimated.

To 'see' something is, however precariously, to initiate a process of familiarization, of anthropomorphizing domestication. The spectral or haunting movement which opens the 'gap' already there is far more troubling because, despite the apparent fact of perception, the estranging materiality of the spectral persists in its disturbance, even though we can only acknowledge its effect at the limit of comprehension. What is all the more perplexing, to make this point once more, is that the phantom or the spectral is not alien to the familiar space, even if it is other, but is as much at home within the architectural space as we are (if not more so), wherein its motion causes what Mark Wigley describes as that 'uncanny internal displacement' (1993, 162), which belongs so intimately to the domestic scene. We may inhabit the spaces and places in question (whether we refer to our sense of identity or our homes, which indeed we also comprehend as belonging to a sense of selfhood), but the spectre, though incorporeal, is incorporated into the very economy of dwelling, even as its otherness both exceeds and serves in the determination of the identity of place. What remains as its haunting possibility is the unexpectedness of its coming, as the epigraphs tacitly acknowledge, the final epigraph seeking to forestall such an event through flight.

III

The question of the unexpected arrival that catches one unawares, so that one's response cannot be calculated or anticipated, is central to the thought of the other's haunting of the subject, whether that other arrives from the past or a certain future. In this scenario, the subject's unpreparedness defines the modern condition. Apropos the subject's awaiting the other, it is arguable that 'ambiguity and incompletion are indeed written into the very fabric of our collective existence rather than just the works of intellectuals' (Merleau-Ponty 2008, 81). The ghost is thus not only, no longer, a thing of the past, it is no longer containable, on the one hand, to a realm of investigation and research, or on the other, to popular narratives and genres, communities of oral transmission, or folkloric traditions – if it ever was. What we name 'ghost' acknowledges no boundaries, other than to mark their porosity, as is well known.

If Hardy – of whom there is more to be said – signals the modernity of the apparition, he is not the only writer to do so. In an appreciation of the modernity of Henry James's writing, Virginia Woolf observes, in a well-known and frequently quoted passage on what might be registered as the epochal shift from the Gothic to the psychoanalytic, that:

> Henry James's ghosts have nothing in common with the violent old ghosts – the blood-stained sea captains, the white horses, the headless ladies of dark lanes and windy commons. They have their origin within us. They are present whenever the significant overflows our powers of expressing it; whenever the ordinary appears ringed by the strange. (324)

Marked as it is with a tacit, and almost imperceptible, admission of the uncanny, Woolf's reading of James has the effect of dating – if such a thing is possible – the interiorization or incorporation of the ghostly and spectral. Consigning the 'origin', or finding at the very least, inventing the return of a phantasm always already at work but hitherto unavailable to apprehension, such disquieting forces us to acknowledge an otherwise inexpressible significance 'within us', Woolf acknowledges James as a writer whose work moves across, or through, a boundary, on one side of which lie narratives about the ghostly, and on the other, manifestations of 'ghostly narrative', to borrow a fine and significant distinction drawn by Nicholas Royle (2008, 1). What Woolf admits into the discourse and experience of the ghostly is, most obviously, a psychological dimension, one which, in writers of the nineteenth century, was, if not 'explained', then at least narrated through tales of mediumship, uncanny foresight, visions, and so forth. What marks James's writing, or, perhaps better said, the difference by which James's text remarks itself as being haunted, is that explanation is inevitably found wanting, as James's ghostly narratives do not so much close as they remain open to the undecidable, the possibility of the impossible, and the experience of the other.

This is entirely appropriate to any hauntological event, for, to recall the words of Jacques Derrida, '[g]hosts always pass quickly, with the infinite speed of a furtive apparition, in an instant without duration, presence without present of a present, which, coming back, only *haunts*' (Derrida 1989b, 64). What Derrida's appreciation of the spectral – as the phenomenal flickering of the trace of the other – shares with Woolf, after a certain fashion and, differently, with James, is the apprehension of the unexpected related, on the one hand, to eruption or overflow and, on the other hand, to duration or frequency. Derrida continues:

> The ghost, *le re-venant*, the survivor, appears only by means of figure or fiction, but its appearance is not nothing, nor is it mere semblance. And this 'synthesis of the phantom' enables us to recognize in the figure of the phantom the working of . . . the transcendental imagination . . . whose temporalizing schemes . . . are indeed 'fantastic' – are, in Kant's phrase, those of an *art hidden* in the depths of the soul . . . the art of memory and . . . the memory of art. (Derrida 1989b, 64)

Irreducible to mere representation, that which is approximated as a quasi-ontological quasi-being, the ghost, is nevertheless *only possible* through a tropic, fictional *coming-to-pass*. Inasmuch as it can be said to take its passage, its significance is only ever perceived, if at all, belatedly, as Woolf's affirmation of 'the significant' that overflows. What comes to overflow only becomes available as 'the significant' after the event of its having come to pass, and having retreated in its becoming, leaving behind the trait that one attempts to read as the signature of 'the significant'. This phenomenon, that which discloses itself in coming to light and so shedding light in those places where we have no direct expression for the experience, is both the art of memory and the memory of art, to reiterate Derrida's words. To conjure the ghost of Hegel, art, it has to be said, therefore, 'is a thing of the past' (Derrida 1989b, 64).

If that which survives beyond any mere existence returns through a phantasmic and phantastic revenant temporal scheme, whether through the memory of art or the art of memory, then this is to admit, in the most ghostly terms, that memory and art stage the phantoms of history, in a performative projection of the trace of historicity. Yet, it is just this opening to historicity's ghostly remnant, its rem(a)inder, which is not acknowledged in Woolf's psychoanalytic and phenom-enological appreciation of Jamesian modernity. The ghostly trace of historicity must then be acknowledged as the supplement to that which is already supple-mentary, the haunting opening of modernity's narratives. To become modern one must open oneself to those manifestations of 'a past which has never been present and will never allow itself to be reanimated in the interiority of consciousness' (Derrida 1989b, 65). This admission takes place, if it occurs at all, 'through writ-ing, the sign, *tekhnè*, with that thinking memory, that memory without memory' (Derrida 1989b, 65), which narrative has the possibility of enabling. Thinking this, we are opening the thinking of narrative as a form of *tekhnè*, a *mnemotechnic* to be precise, 'whose movement' and operation as an exteriorized, archived, and prosthetic survival of memory without memory, marks it as a phantom machine – both a ghostly mechanism constructed out of nothing other than writing, the sign, and so forth, but also a machinic medium the purpose of which is to conjure and project its singular-collective of phantasmagorical traces 'whose movement carries an essential affirmation, a kind of engagement beyond negativity . . . which is mourning itself' (Derrida 1989b, 65).

Arguably – and this is to make a claim that I cannot hope to support here – such mourning does not concern James; or, at least, it cannot, is not to be admitted. Similarly with Woolf's reading. So 'modern' is the Jamesian interiorization of the spectre in those characters who Woolf takes to be figures of analogy with 'us', whose powers of expression have momentarily failed, allowing the upsurge of the phantom, that it is, in effect and in fact, dated, past its sell-by date. James's is an old-fashioned, even a quaintly anachronistic modernity, a modernity in which is written the anticipation of a modern*ism*, the very coming of which would always already have dated it with the trace of an historical moment, the tragedy of which is that it is without the fortune to have become anachronistic, or to have been countersigned by a necessary affirmative anachrony making it other than its times. James's 'modern' ghostly narrative becomes dated precisely because it gives no access to 'the immemorial or unrememberable, with an archive that no interiorizing memory can take into itself' (Derrida 1989b, 67), by which a text might announce an 'affirmative . . . an amnesic fidelity' with the 'dead being that will never itself return, never again be there, present to answer to or to share' (Derrida 1989b, 66) what amounts to a faith, keeping faith with a past that can never be present. To open in a proper fashion to that which memory cannot take into itself, and so risk everything on the invention of a historicity at once *more* and *less* modern, we have to turn back to Thomas Hardy.

IV

Hardy's interest in haunting addresses a concern for which we have to take account: what it means to *have* a world. As Jacques Derrida reminds us, apropos Heidegger, the human has world, while, problematically, seemingly paradoxically and admitting to a 'logical contradiction', the animal 'does and does not have a world' (Derrida 1989c, 51). As Derrida is quick to point out, the fault – or let us call it limit to thought and to be thought is not with the ontology of the animal, animality, and so forth – is with the thinking of 'world', specifically the concept of world rather than its material counterpart (to think for a moment the unthinkable, in imagining, in theory and as some fictive projection, the separation of the two). The question thus becomes one of *spirit*, for this, and 'Heidegger insists on this, is the name of that without which there is no world' (Derrida 1989c, 51). To have a world and not have a world according to the apprehension of a spirit to which one nevertheless has no access is, I would argue, that which presents Thomas Hardy's characters – and the narrator of certain of his poems – with their own abject being-in-the-world. They are marked as human animals, either through a poverty of spirit and perception, or through knowing themselves to have that 'theoretical' vision, from which imagined world they are excluded. Oddly, uncannily, the Hardy 'being' or, if you will, the Hardyesque expression and, therefore anticipation of, *Dasein*, anticipating as it does phenomenologically the Heideggerian project of determining the Being of beings according to thrownness, en-worlding, en-knowning, temporality, care and death, is somewhere between the fully human and the animal. This, we might wish to speculate, is the very sign of their historicity. Becoming-human, and, therefore, reminded of his or her materiality, his or her belonging materially as a mortal to the earth and shut out from spirit, the being Hardy perceives is one he or she can never truly become; it is as if I perceive barely the phantasm of a truer self, which my material being apprehends as being always inacapable of gaining.

Hardy's characters are haunted by the spectre of a humanity to which they will never have full access because, on the one hand, they are excluded from a future and the becoming-culture of modern England, which can never be theirs, whilst they are also expelled, compelled to wander and drift, and so are haunted also by the traces of a past that inform their being but, again, which remains unavailable to them. Hardyean subjectivity is thus placed as the axial locus naked before a world to-come, and incapable of understanding those traces of the past by which they are haunted. The most poignant figures for this are of course Tess and Jude: the former stooping in a field picking vegetables, and seen from some god-like vantage by a narrative eye who compares her with an insect on the landscape; the latter standing on the Ickeneild Way, looking towards Christminster (Oxford), but neither fully able to enter that spiritual life (as is figured cruelly by his inability to grasp Greek), nor to turn back to a rural community or spirit which, historically, he has outgrown. Thus, Tess, Jude and other Hardy figures are haunted by the impossibility of their temporal condition, an impossibility remarked through their perception *and* their lack of access. In this, they lack spirit. More than animals, they are less than human. They become the figures of a spectral liminality, the product of a modernity that marginalizes historically and materially, and leaves without access to future or past. They become thus phantasms of modernity itself, in their having been sacrificed in this manner.

Thomas Hardy's novels are notably free of 'literal' ghosts, even as particular human beings have their being put under erasure, crossed out but maintained as a material reminder of the possibility of one's becoming anachronistic and surviving only to haunt where one both is and is not, leaving in the wake of this crossing-out or crossing through, only a 'benumbedness' (Derrida 1989c, 54), a condition which closes one off whilst simultaneously leaving closure open, remarking an access through which the figure cannot go. It is this hovering on the threshold that marks Hardy's characters in their spectrality, announcing that spectral condition, a *becoming-spectral*, as a modern symptom of being anachronic, belated. The ghost in Hardy, or rather, say, the phenomenon of becoming-spectral is thus tied to an existence that is neither of a world touched by spirit (and so not fully alive), nor one in which one's death is absolute, unconditional, without doubt. Hardy's characters exist as mere, poor beings who hover, as if they were dead.

Where the term *ghost* does appear in Hardy's text, it is, for the most part, as metaphor or simile – at least on the surface. Objects and characters momentarily assume the guise of the ghostly for others. There is superstitious speculation on the reasons for ghostly visitations, as we have seen in the first of the three epigraphs. But across fourteen novels, there is not one ghost *as such*. It might be thought, therefore, that to write of Hardy's ghosts as if there were ghosts in the text of Hardy, is a little odd, not to say perverse. Certainly, ghosts, phantoms and other modes of apparitioning take place in the poetry, and there are ghostly effects, unexplained phenomena, and uncanny occasions to be found in various short stories. However, regarding the novels, it is this very absence which might give us pause, and, from that, a place to begin again in drifting. What can be said is that, at a certain point towards the close of his novel-writing career, with the publication of *Jude the Obscure* and the revised version of *The Well-Beloved* a small, almost imperceptible change in the work of the spectral trope is to be read. Here are two examples of ghostly disturbance from Hardy's two final novels:

> Knowing not a human being here, Jude began to be impressed with the isolation of his own personality, as with a *self-spectre*, the sensation being that of one who walked but could not make himself seen or heard. He drew his breath pensively, and, seeming thus almost *his own ghost*, gave his thoughts to the other *ghostly presences* with which the nooks were *haunted*. (Hardy 1998b, 75; emphases added)

> The evening and night winds here were, to Pierston's mind, *charged with a something* that did not burden them elsewhere. They brought it up from that sinister Bay to the west, whose movement she and he were hearing now. *It was a presence – an imaginary shape or essence* from the human multitude lying below: those who had gone down in vessels of war, East Indiamen, barges, brigs, and ships of the Armada – select people, common, and debased, whose interests and hopes had been as wide asunder as the poles, but who had rolled each other to oneness on that restless sea-bed. *There could almost be felt the brush of their huge composite ghost as it ran a shapeless figure over the isle, shrieking for some good god who would disunite it again.* (Hardy 1997, 186; emphases added)

Arguably, neither passage takes part in the conventions of the ghost story. Something quite singular, possibly novel, is at work here; certainly Hardy invents the phenomena of ghosting in a disturbing manner. The passages are disquieting precisely because they touch on the experience of being haunted, as if the reader were to find him- or herself in the place of the narratives' subjects, Jude Fawley and Jocelyn Pierston.

Taking each in turn, if we observe the opening of the chapter from which comes Jude's uncanny sense of self and the place in which he finds himself, we will find the aura of the spectral already at work. In the opening sentence of the first chapter of Part II, 'At Christminster', it is remarked that 'he appeared gliding steadily onward through a dusky landscape' (Hardy 1998b, 77) on his way to Hardy's fictional rendering of Oxford. The time of day, that liminal and crepuscular instant of transition, a 'between times', as it were, is given somewhat indistinctly, in being 'dusky'. The image is hardly made any more solid by Jude's appearance of gliding. There is something ethereal, barely of the material world about this initial representation, even though Hardy does attempt to ameliorate the phantasmic perception in the next but one paragraph, in which the author seeks to make Jude more materially there through detailed representation. Yet, in commenting on his being a stonemason, Jude's hair and beard are shown as having the traces of stone-dust still upon them, at least implicitly. If such 'whitening' does not make Jude ghostly exactly, it has the odd effect of making him appear older than he is. From this, the reader is informed of a photograph belonging to Jude's aunt, which, despite his asking for it, his aunt had refused to give, the consequence of which being that 'it haunted him' (Hardy 1998b, 78). Arriving in Christminster in the evening, and exploring the streets, Jude 'saw nothing of real city in the suburbs' (Hardy 1998b, 78). Anything he sees which is not in 'harmony' with the medieval college buildings his eyes do not see. Following the tolling of a bell, 'fewer and fewer people were visible, and still he serpentined among the shadows', maintaining that barely physical motion, with which he had been introduced to the reader at the start of the chapter (Hardy 1998b, 77). And thus he finds himself in 'obscure alleys, apparently never trodden now by the foot of man, and whose very existence seemed to be forgotten, there would jut into the path porticoes, oriels, doorways of enriched and florid middle-age design, their extinct air being accentuated by the rottenness of the stones. It seemed impossible that modern thought could house itself in such decrepit and superseded chambers' (Hardy 1998b, 79). And so it is, we arrive, with Jude, at that experience of being a 'self-spectre', his 'own ghost', surrounded by the haunted material of college buildings. Much here has to do with Jude's own perception, of course.

It is Jude's openness to the phenomenological impression of place that Hardy registers so carefully throughout the opening paragraphs of the chapter. What is significant, however, is that the registration takes place in the narrative, and so is turned towards the reader. The writing takes up the spectral trope, in order to assume its own haunting force and to pass beyond the merely constative or descriptive, objective act, to enter into a performative dimension, doing in words what it seeks to convey concerning Jude's own psychic faculties. We are witness to a phenomenology of the spectral here, a *hauntology* rather than an ontology. Indeed, that the spectral manifestation is implicitly of a phenomenological kind suggests that the ontological cannot be determined as stable conceptual frame. Fiction thus becomes haunted by the work of thought and perception, turned simultaneously towards representation of another's state of mind on the one hand, and, on the other, towards the very interiority of the reader's imaginative projection.

Regarding the passage from *The Well-Beloved* Hardy again, typically, presents the reader with a perception on perception, particularly turned towards that which is at the limits of, or just beyond, representation, visibility and articulation. Borne on the wind, there is a *something* that appears indistinctly to Jocelyn's mind. This spectral manifestation takes on the condition of imaginary presence, shape or essence. Hardy's language pursues the chase of Pierston's psyche, which moves not after the form as such, but after a term appropriate to giving shape to the trace of the spectre, as that belongs in turn to all the dead who appear to make themselves felt through the unnerving touch of a 'huge composite ghost'. Yet, this is still unavailable to any direct representation, for we read of the spectre, indirectly revealed as a shapeless figure, a flow of energy or force desirous of being dismembered. Like Jude, Jocelyn is confronted with the phantasmic apparition that he can barely comprehend. In each singular event, the spectral touches as intimately as it announces exclusion from fully human apprehension. Both men experience the traversal of their internal worlds, behind which is the revelation of being that lets itself be known to perception. Being and meaning are aligned, though with this distinction: both Pierston and Fawley gain momentary access to a perception of being that can never be theirs, as if, in their material exclusion they are shown to be not fully human. In this poverty, they are perceived as somewhat ghostly witnesses to humanity's historicity through a fracturing of being. And this fracture – through which perception of the spectral other arrives – announces the secret of modernity's arrival, for the fracture of being is also, and at the same moment, the fracture of the present and of pure presence in which phantasms 'hover like anxious shades' (Appelbaum 2009, 48). As in the entirety of another Hardy novel, *A Laodicean*, the two scenes – two events – from *Jude the Obscure* and *The Well-Beloved* bracket the present with shades of the past and the future, leaving the modern subject to assume responsibility for its vision of its time 'as it faces the singular' manifestation of the other (Appelbaum 2009, 48), and with that, the ghosts of the past and of the future.

V

The spectral and ghostly thus admit to a relation, without relation, of past with future, wherein consciousness, 'seeing the phantom of being-in-itself vanish before it' and encountering also to itself the 'disappearance of an essence that exists only for it, for it qua specific consciousness', gives place to a truth concerning the subject's apperception of its historicity, 'which is both in-itself and for consciousness' (Hyppolite 1974, 228). The spectre of modernity thus enables the momentary 'reconciliation of the history of thought with thought itself' (Hyppolite 1974, 228). Such reconciliation is scant comfort, however, a brief and illusory apprehension of transcendence; for reconciliation is the place where the spectral announces itself to consciousness, only as consciousness, subjectivity or being apprehend themselves in relation to being other. Thought is always this affirmation of the other within the self, whereby the self is revealed to itself as an other. What Hardy makes clear then is that there is an inescapable uncanniness by which the modern subject is caused to suffer, through the self-reflection of thought that dwells on the relation between thought and being, and the revelation to being's consciousness that the self is at the axis of past and future, with the responsibility to decide on the meaning of being in the face of the undecidable. With this consideration of the uncanniness of being in mind, we should turn to Heidegger.

On a number of occasions, Martin Heidegger had recourse to think the uncanny. Reflection on the uncanny appears in his lectures, seminars and texts, from the 1920s to the 1960s, not least, in particular, passages of *Being and Time* and in the work immediately preceding – and in some senses rehearsing – Heidegger's most famous interrogation of the question of Being, *History of the Concept of Time: Prolegomena*. Elsewhere, the uncanny surfaces as a topic for rigorous meditation in correlation with the thinking of Being in lectures dedicated to the text of Parmenides, on the one hand, and Hölderlin, on the other. In every case however, regardless of the local orientation of Heidegger's theses, the uncanny is woven into the philosophical mediation of the question of Being, the Being of beings, and the question of home, the homely, unhomeliness, the hearth, and, of course, the question of what it means to dwell, that topic broached in some of Heidegger's most significant essays produced in the post-war years ('Building, Dwelling, Thinking', '. . . Poetically, Man Dwells . . .'), after the alledged 'turn' (*die Kehre*). Though Heidegger uses terms such as homely, unhomely or hearth, and does not refer to 'dwelling' in the earlier works (with the obvious exception of certain somewhat rapid sketches in *Being and Time*, particularly H61–63, where Heidegger gathers 'dwelling' together with 'looking-at' and 'perception', apropos what one might term provisionally the un-homely technicity of being),[2] it is nevertheless the case that the thinking and questioning of being *qua* dwelling arises directly out of Heidegger's readings in Parmenides and Hölderlin among others.

Those already familiar with such discussions will know that, though Heidegger's uncanny touches on aspects of that topic, which overlap with Freudian thinking, the philosopher's consideration has more profound, even radical implications apropos the nature of what we take to be uncanny. Sharing with Freud an insistence on semantic and etymological considerations, Heidegger departs from the psychoanalyst by rejecting the uncanny as 'impression' or 'effect' that arises in particular situations. In doing so, the philosopher perceives the uncanny as being of the essence of being itself, of the Being of beings as he would put it. In such a fundamental and, again, radical reorientation, Heidegger steps beyond all the impasses and aporia, up against which Freud repeatedly finds himself in his famous essay of 1919, without resolving or doing away with the essential uncanniness of the experience of undecidability. In this, the uncanny appears as both radically interior to being and yet also of the world and thus the trace, however undecidable or unreadable, of being's materiality, its historicity. And it is precisely because Heidegger privileges the uncanny in its many manifestations, its 'manifold' essence, that he is able to overcome the psychologistic limit imposed on what is, for him, of the most crucial importance. While, for Freud, the problem of the uncanny is that it cannot be determined, for Heidegger, undecidability is of the essence and so not a problem to be resolved or reconciled. If James had been merely modernist in relation to a Hardyean modernity of subjectivity and being, then, in a different fashion, the same relation between Freud and Heidegger may also be posited.

Given certain commentaries on Heidegger, though, which do not stress this word, *unheimlich*, is it wrong or even a little perverse to give such significance to the uncanny, the un-homely, to be more precise and following Heidegger's own distinction, on which he insists in order to move the thinker away from the misperception of mere effect? Take the following commentary by David Farrell Krell. 'Heidegger's thought', Krell insists correctly, 'circles about a double theme: the meaning of Being and the propriative event (*Ereignis*) of disclosure'. Krell continues:

> *Sein* and *aletheia* remain the key words, *Sein* meaning coming to presence, and *aletheia* the disclosedness or unconcealment implied in such presence ... [However] Coming to presence suggests an absence before and after itself, so that withdrawal and departure must always be thought together with *Sein* as presencing; disclosedness or unconcealment suggests a surrounding obscurity. The propriative event is always simultaneously expropriative. (Krell 1993, 32)

Sein and *aletheia*: Being and modalities of truth's disclosure or unveiling. Heidegger's keywords announce the ghost, although its force is never nominated as such. That motion of coming to pass, of retreat, of absence and obscurity from which the disclosedness emerges and into which it retreats: these are the very motions of the spectral, all the more uncanny for being so forcefully announced and yet never named. As an introduction to the thinking of Heideggerian being, Krell's commentary strikes at the very heart of what motivates Heidegger, and situates in its own terms both the thinking of temporality – withdrawal and departure – *and* spatiality – the place, as well as the event, of disclosedness and that 'surrounding obscurity'; – without which we cannot begin to appreciate the *topos* of being as the place of a certain experience of haunting; and which in turn lends to the Heideggerian notion of *Dasein* its historicity and groundedness (without which there would be the risk of a retrenchment back into just another mode of German idealism). It is this very temporal placedness, this being-in-the-world, the material self-conciousness that comes to one as a complex relation, at the nexus of which is the thinking being, which makes possible the thinking of dwelling in the lectures of 1951 already mentioned.

Yet, such a thinking would not be possible without earlier investigations on Heidegger's part into Parmenides. Parmenidean reasoning holds that it is impossible to think what does not exist. Even if, like Thomas Hardy's characters, I imagine something which has never been seen 'in person', because I can visualize that 'something', it exists, even if its existence is of a phantasmic rather than a material order. (As we have seen, this is not a binarism, so much as the one is always already the haunting double of the other, the locus of such haunting being my being, and my perception of the other apropos my being.) True enough then, its existence is of a different order than, say, a chair or table. Nevertheless, its non-existence in the world as I inhabit it is not, for Parmenides, a true non-existence; for were this 'it' not to exist, I could not have thought it. It is this that the following fragment encapsulates: χρὴ τὸ λέγειν τε νοεῖν τ' ... [It needs must be that what can be thought and spoken of is {Saying [i.e., the letting show itself] and [the thus occurring] perceiving are necessary ...' [to take up]}] Parmenides (Fragment VI, 1). Furthermore, there is no thinking without being, and, conversely, there is no being save for thinking: τὸ γὰρ αὐτὸ νοεῖν ἐστίν τε καὶ εἶναι [The same is thinking and being / For it is the same thing that can be thought and that can be {'perceptual mean-ing and being are the same'}] (Parmenides Fragment I, 3). The logic here develops from the fundamental understanding on Parmenides's part, concerning the inextricable interrelatedness of thinking and being, and so discloses to us the Heideggerian thinking of the *unheimlich*, for, as immanence belongs to, or 'is said to be of the region of consciousness', so '*immanence* implies, first of all, to be in another' (Heidegger 1985, 103). Lived experiences give access to this uncanny reflection 'insofar as they are a possible object of an apprehension through reflection' (Heidegger 1985, 103).

Crucially, the haunting experience of immanence – which can be most immediately understood through the example of the imagination apprehending the experience of an other – is perceived not for someone in themselves, but as that which marks the space between, and consequently the relationship of being between entities, as Heidegger describes it. Being, apprehended as an other in the immanence of the apprehension of the other for the subject, is what gives determination to being, rather than being as such, or in itself (Heidegger 1985, 103). I am thus doubled, as it were, phantasmically in my access to the other's experience – and this of course, is that, in principle, by which we might define the work of literature. For immanence gives to my apprehension the phantasmic experience of that which has what Heidegger calls the 'peculiar nearness of something coming but not yet on hand [that] constitutes the structure of the encounter' we call uncanny (Heidegger 1985, 286), while also maintaining an 'indefiniteness', 'a nothing worldly', though constitutive of '*being-in-the-world*', and 'nothing definite' (Heidegger 1985, 290).

The trace of such thinking stretches across Heidegger's work. In an early essay from 1912, 'The Problem of Reality in Modern Philosophy', Heidegger expresses a similar notion. 'All being [*Sein*]', he argues, 'is being-conscious [*Bewußt-Sein*]. The concept of consciousness includes both the conscious subject and the object of consciousness, but these two moments are only separable by abstraction. The result of this is the inextricable concatenation of thought and being' (Heidegger 2002, 42). In 1928, in the lecture course published as the volume *The Metaphysical Foundations of Logic*, Heidegger takes up Parmenides's claim on the correlation between thinking and being. Doing so in order to counter misreadings of idealism in Parmenides, Heidegger observes how '[t]here were attempts in the nineteenth century to claim [Parmenides's] statement for ... "the first glimmerings of idealism," as if Parmenides had held that the subject is what first posits beings as beings, or as if ... objects order themselves according to our knowledge' (1984, 142). In a comparison between the nineteenth-century misreading of Parmenides and a similar misperception of Kant, Heidegger continues, accepting that a kernel of truth exists in the misreading, inasmuch as – and here he acknowledges the statement made in my first epigraph – 'being is related to the subject' (1984, 142). However, in turning to the semantic play in the Greek, Heidegger argues that there 'is no causal ontic dependency' and that 'interpretations of Parmenides' thought as "realism" are equally untenable' (1984, 142). In order to clarify the error, Heidegger states categorically that:

> The point is not whether the subject posits beings or whether it, as knowing subject, directs itself towards beings, but the point is rather the way in which the human being as such understands anything like being at all. (1984, 142–3)

Failing to perceive this, one fails to grasp what is at stake with, as Heidegger has it, 'sufficient radicality' (1984, 143). The 'basic problem', as the philosopher sees it, is not at all a problem of epistemology (1984, 143). Such interpretations remain within traditions of thought that do not fully perceive that which constitutes the disclosedness of Being to beings.

At Freiburg, in the summer of 1942, Martin Heidegger presented his final major lecture course on Friedrich Hölderlin (Heidegger 1996a, ix). In these lectures, the philosopher devoted considerable attention to the human being as the 'uncanniest of the uncanny' (1996a, 51ff.) and, as a consequence, proposed the uncanny as the 'ground of human beings' (1996a, 68 ff.), as this in turn relates to the home and the homely, and so to the question of the relation of one's being in relation to dwelling. In those lectures, Heidegger addresses uncanniness as it pertains to looking. Looking is not merely the gaze, the act or ability of a human to see, and so to know, the world, as sight gives to the human the representation of that world. Looking distinguishes humans from other merely existing animals because looking gives access to 'the Being of beings'. Looking, remarks Heidegger, 'shows [that] Being itself is not something human but belongs to the essence of Being itself as belonging to appearance in the unconcealed' (1992, 104).

Yet, what is perhaps most uncanny about the look – which is to say, the fundamentally and primarily *theoretical* orientation of the being towards the world – is that it cannot give us to comprehend in any unmediated manner the truth of being. Jude looks along the road; Pierston looks over the bay; each has disclosed to them the haunting experience of being unable to access the truth of Being, and pauses to dwell on this, on the condition of being's dwelling. This is also witnessed in the well-known moment of apprehension from *A Pair of Blue Eyes*. Henry Knight, hanging from a cliff-edge, observes embedded into the cliff face a fossilized trilobite, eye to dead 'eye' with him:

Knight was a geologist . . . his mind found time to take in, by a momentary sweep, the varied scenes that had had their day between this creature's epoch and his own. There is no place like a cleft landscape for bringing home such imaginings as these.

Time closed up like a fan before him. He saw himself at one extremity of the years, face to face with the beginning and all the intermediate centuries simultaneously. (Hardy 1998d, 214)

This 'face to face' with the other leads Knight into a self-reflective consideration of temporality and mortality, and the place of the self in the universe perceived historically. Here is the trauma of becoming-conscious of one's historicity and being up close. Knight's experience of a radical, destabilizing anachrony, with its simultaneous phantasmagoria of past moments, in which he apprehends his own becoming-consciousness as just one more in a temporal sequence, takes place precisely because he is written into history at this moment. The historicity of his being is traumatically unveiled to his consciousness, because apprehension involves the phenomenological reflection – and anticipation – of his moment of modernity as being immanent in its own passing away. Despite his theoretical knowledge of geology, he cannot anticipate the sudden apocalypse of 'sensuously accessible *phainomena*' (Seel 2005, 22) that project themselves 'in the ephemerality of this . . . presence of appearing', which is the result not only of his personal education but also as the historical result of much scientific research in the nineteenth century (Seel 2005, 20). Knight's training in geology has not prepared him for the aesthetic mode of sensuous apprehension by which self-reading comes to takes place, and its arrival, the unveiling of the truth of being retreats almost as soon as it has unveiled itself, in the disclosedness of its singular modality.

Being's spectral disclosedness retreats, then, in the moment that I perceive its having returned. We have no sustained or direct access to the essence of truth, Heidegger tells us, because 'we neither comprehend the essence of truth nor do we comprehend ourselves, and we do not know who we ourselves are' (Heidegger 1992, 162). The implication of this is that Knight, like Pierston and Jude Fawley, remains outside the immanent revelation, and thus are haunted by its impossible nearness. It is, however, 'good to know this ignorance', Heidegger continues, and this at least is what we read in Hardy's tragic figures: being's historicity, its haunted modernity, is revealed but this no more gives them to know themselves than it gives them access to truth. The 'truth' of haunting perceived by Woolf, and read in James, is merely one revelation of a certain historical experience. For Hardy's figures, what haunts – even though they do not fully comprehend it – is that the 'being and non-being' of 'historical people' and 'European culture' remains 'undecided, unquestioned, and even forgotten' (Heidegger, 1992, 162). Thus it is, Hardy's characters remain haunted, trapped epochally in the experience of the unhomely, which no psychoanalysis can resolve. Whether it is Jude on the road, Jocelyn overlooking the bay, or Henry Knight hanging by his fingers on the cliff's edge, humans remain on the verge, at the limit, always homeless. Without the 'truth of Being, beings are never steadfast' (Heidegger 1992, 162) but remain haunted by an apperception of 'the destination toward which' one is always 'underway, namely the home' of the truth that in the very idea of *Aletheia* (1992, 162–3), to which one is always on the way, but which one cannot reach. The home 'also directs the course of the thinker's genuine experience', but, conversely, brings back that sense of being haunted in being *unheimlich*, without home, 'from which all history begins' (Heidegger 1992, 162). Hardy's language thus expresses that which remains inaccessible to his own characters, albeit that their experience gives access to the disclosure of Being; but, in a different way, it confesses that which remains unknowable also to James or Woolf; Hardy's language articulates and affirms 'the essence of history, and history, because it is the sending of Being and because Being only comes to light unexpectedly, is appropriated always in the unexpectedness of the primordiality of the beginning' (Heidegger 1992, 163).

V

That history is, or might be read as, the sending of Being suggests history as a spectral postal service, or perhaps a tele-spectro-technics causing being to appear, as a phantom – coming to light – unexpectedly. Thus, wherever Being comes to light, without warning and as this apparation affirming the historicity of being, it does so with the uncanny, haunting arrival of the knowledge that whatever is originary is always that which presents itself in the event, thereby disrupting presence and the present. Hence, history as a sending, which can be illustrated with a return to Hardy, or Hardy's return through that passage concerning the auto-spectral revelation of Jude to himself. Jude appears to himself, and is enlightened as a *self-spectre* you will recall. He is made aware of his own occluded, obscure subjectivity in coming face to face with all that fails to perceive him. The historicity of this revenant transmission, the structure of which is profoundly complex, is marked in the event of becoming self-aware; Jude has revealed to him the spectres of other anonymous ghosts, the traces of other historical moments, events and experiences. His own coming to consciousness concerning his bare existence and the paucity of his being for others, opens to Jude the analogical apperception of those countless others whose traces constitute a spectral history. Paused, suspended in his own reflection, Jude finds himself on the verge of disappearance. Always on the road, but without destination except the revelation of his own finitude, Jude encounters the spectral not-self at the obscure heart of being. Jude apprehends his destiny as only an 'avenue to himself' and that 'there is no himself without "them"', those others already spectral that serve as the historical traces affirming Jude's own 'isolation of personality', as Hardy puts it. If it is the case, then what can be thought is this: if being is given to apprehension, as Parmenides suggests, and if, furthermore, if perception opens to one, and so presents the condition of being, then Jude's uncanny access to knowledge of the self is that which admits the other at the limits of selfhood.

VI

Do we know where we're going? Are we, like Jude, under the illusion – up to a point – that we know the direction we are taking? Is the idea, that one knows where one is headed, true, strictly speaking or ever? Of course there is always death, we are all beings toward death; and in this anticipatory retrospect, in our 'future anterior' we are vouchsafed the most uncanny of 'dwellings', an inescapable authenticity in the negation of being as its ownmost inevitability. I can imagine myself, no longer the 'myself', when I am no longer even a body without organs, merely a without, without knowledge of this. Yet, it is important to acknowledge that in knowing where we are going, nothing in fact could be less certain. For while death is that which is inescapable, that which is the future therefore, and one of the few events to which one can, properly speaking, give the name 'future' as opposed to speaking of that which is to come (that which may one day arrive but which cannot be anticipated or programmed), nevertheless, I cannot experience what I call 'my death'. The Authenticity of futurity is always already haunted therefore by its own inauthenticity, except in the fiction of the *als ob*, the as if; it is haunted by the impossibility of knowing ahead of time, ahead of the absence of all time, all world, and, therefore, all consciousness of dwelling. It is haunted by the impossibility of knowing either ahead of time, in time, or on time. When death arrives, it does so in a manner where time is not, and can never be the issue at stake. Ultimate anachrony, all time gone. Dwell on this: untimely death. If what haunts authenticity is inauthenticity, that from which the former cannot escape, then the felicity of a performance is always troubled, spooked, we might say, by the very possibility, the *eigenartigkeit*, the strangeness and singularity of infelicity, the *Heimlich, Heimisch* as *unheimlich, unheimlisch*. Heidegger apprehends as much in those movements that he traces of the uncanny, the *unheimlich*, as the self flees the self in the face of being's ownmost authenticity.

So there you have it, suspended for a moment and all time, in no time, a solitary figure, his back towards you, as if he were about to walk away, stepping off in meditation through the forest, on no discernible path. We cannot get away from Heidegger, even though he appears to be wanting to get away from us. Think of that well-known photograph, in which the philosopher is caught, walking away, his cane held behind his back, thumbs aligned along its uppermost surface, his hat not a little reminiscent of Buster Keaton. No path, just the leaves, the trees, and a vanishing point into which he will become as nothing. A future forestalled, home deferred indefinitely, whereby a locale comes into existence, only by virtue of what lies ahead, but *in which* he will never witness himself, or be capable of retreating from; therein is a space and becoming suspended, an image as the impossible time, representing the inauthenticity of being in the oncoming face of the authenticity of a line of flight, mapping the unmappable becoming of *Dasein*. Thus, in the photo, within representation, we attain a glimpse of what we do not see, indirectly we have made known to us, in temporal suspension 'the boundary [as] that from which something *begins its essential unfolding*' (Heidegger 1992, 355–6). The silence here in the woods may well be deafening, as Heidegger gets off the beaten path. Heidegger walks without path, in the experience of that which cannot be interpreted *as such*. In this gesture, which many attribute to bad writing, obfuscation, an obscurantism, and so forth, he institutes the becoming of what, invisibly, is already underway, on the way, without a map of the way: that is to say, an 'inceptual thinking in the other beginning', which 'en-thinks the truth of be-ing'. This necessary gesture, a leap of sorts, will nonetheless fall into the machinic; this is always its risk, thereby forcing an 'opening of the still undecided decision unto the grounding of this truth', even, and especially, when authenticity always retreats before inauthenticity, the felicitous recuperated in the infelicitous, resulting in 'the failure to enact the grounding . . . [as] the necessary destiny of the first beginning' (Heidegger 2006, 55). But where does dwelling remain? Dwelling is always *aletheic*, indirectly revealed through a movement, a becoming which is also, and simultaneously, an unbecoming, haunted by its own ineluctability, and as that which might arrive, which remains to come, but which remains undecidable, and all the more ghostly and haunting for that; in becoming other than myself, as the limit of myself, across that limit, there remains the trace of the self always already on the way to death. This, at least, is what is perceived in our thinking of the ghost – the spectre of the other. Neither immaterial nor material, there, a *there* irreducible to any here, a past or future irreducible to any present or presence, haunting takes place; but always at borders, between all those 'ones' and 'others' – alive and dead, present and absent, there and not there, visible and invisible – the pairings of which serve to map out, in a kind of spectro-t(r)opology, the spaces in-between. If there is apparitioning, taking place is 'its' condition in its disclosedness, and giving place in its having come to pass, the experience of that which, though no being as such, touches me most intimately.

11

The Reiterable Circularity Of Being: Poetics, Selfhood and the Singular Witness that is 'I'

The poem has always hoped ... to speak also ... *on behalf of the other*, who knows, perhaps of an altogether other.

Paul Celan

The heavens [have] no diversitie or difference, but a simplicity of parts, and equiformity in motion continually succeeding each other; so that, from what point soever we compute, the account will be common unto the whole circularity.

Sir Thomas Browne

Only a being ... 'has' the word

Martin Heidegger

I ONE IS (NOT)

Nonetheless, metaphor. This will have returned, therefore.

II PASSAGE, TRANSFER

Though not a discussion of metaphor as such, this chapter nevertheless relies on the notion of the 'I' and of 'one' as metaphors of, and for expression of, or reflection on, the self, being, subjectivity, and so on (whilst not assuming that such terms are synonymous). More than this, however, in talking of circulation and circularity, return, economies of motion and other related 'metaphorical' substitutions by which one 'comes to terms' with consciousness, often without reflection, I am drawing on what is already inscribed within the very idea of metaphoricity, this being the idea of carrying over, transport, transfer, and so on. Elsewhere in this chapter, I refer to the ancient Greek root of the term 'metaphor', but the modern Greek, μεταφορά, is also pertinent, used to signify transfer, as in the transference of money from one bank account to another. There is, thus, an economy of the transfer, but an economy haunted, nevertheless, by the possibility of displacement or loss.

Whilst 'I' and 'one' are metaphors to the extent that they substitute in singular situations for the otherwise unrepresentable notion of being, the figural as the ruse of the ontological, language as that which clothes and gives form to otherwise invisible being, they are also geometric points within a structure that is both linguistic and material, historical and phenomenological. As such they are not merely substitutes, but also figures of transfer, and so operate according to an economy of semantic structure; they transfer or carry over the same to the not-same, inscribing in iterable manner a (self) conscious re-marking of the self as itself and its other; in this carrying or transference the economy of circulation, the circuit, and the circle is marked by the fact that transference, in reiterating what is constant or quasi-constant in the subject, comes to be marked by a difference, but is still comprehensible as 'self' to itself, the same and yet not the same.

This apparent paradox is understood in relation to the notion of singularity, which can only be 'known' to be singular through its iterable transference and is, therefore, both a closed and open system. The figure, or trope, of the circle is appropriate as a metaphor, if not an example of catechresis, signifier of a signifer without relation, because, in moving over itself, it completes itself, and so intimates completion and full sameness. However, at the same time, in passing through its own motion, it becomes a palimpsest of itself, a reinscription, which is also, partly, an erasure, an over-layering and occlusion.

III FICTIONS OF 'I'

When I speak, when the 'I' I believe myself to be, positions itself, implicitly or explicitly through thought or enunciation to others, is this an originary moment, an opening? Or is there, in that 'I' which presents itself nakedly or hides itself as the subject-position from which articulation apparently comes, a return, a revenant appearance, something myself and not myself, a seemingly still point in a moveable world, and yet, in its recurrence, having more to do with the provisional opening that metaphor admits? Is 'I' a metaphor? Am I, nonetheless, metaphor? And if metaphor, from the Greek *metapherein*, means to transfer or to transport over or beyond some fixed place, what in the articulation of being is the something, if anything, being carried over? From the other side, what is carried over from, and what resides or remains, in 'I'? I bears in itself the trace of itself as an other. I, therefore, nevertheless, metaphor, within a circulating economy, an economy and geometry of the circle: what goes around, comes around (albeit with a difference, as we shall see).

Where does *one* begin though, with circularity? Does *one* begin at all? These are not idle questions, especially when one notes that Sir Thomas Browne has already done away with any pretence for beginning, observing as he does that *the account will be common*, wherever one is (in) this figure. Wherever one is, there is where one begins. Write this in a number of ways, more than one: one *is*; *one* is. In a certain manner this is to say, and yet not to say, I am; to say it without saying it, in fact and in principle. To present the simulacrum of a subject, to play on the verb of being, without giving face to the singularity, groundedness, or being of (a) being – quite. In this, the verb doubles that which is already stated in the number. *One. Is. Is* announces nothing other than that which *One* has already staged, after a fashion. Whether posited in the form of question or assertion the remarking of the apparent fact that *one is* – a predicate of sorts – says without quite saying that 'one exists'. It implies or perhaps whispers from within its articulation, as the other of the ostensibly disinterested observation of the self in *and* as an other location, that one has access to the circular reflection of one's existence in the act of saying that one exists. This is, of course, not the same as existing, not the same as being the existing one who says that one exists; though not the fact, it figures an analogy for the fact that announces both the fact and the principle. Though neither *the fact* – as in the commonplace phrase *the fact is* – nor *as such*, but available through that testimony of apprehension, the fiction of the *as if* that the work of analogy enables.

Circularity, circulation, circumlocution, reiteration and return: all announce that where one is, there, already, always, *there* – and *there* – are two. *One* begins only as the return of the consciousness that one is, as that consciousness returns to *one*, returning to one the idea that one is in fact one and is expressed as one in the remembrance that is also a forgetting of the circulation of being that divides the self against and from within *it-self*. Thus to risk periphrasis: one is; *yet* one is not. One is-not *in* the very affirmation *one is*, the circular return against and from within. And this takes place as the return of (the other in) itself in its articulation. It cancels the unity of the *itself*, crossing through and erasing in the very instant of coming-to-being, in the illusory event of the becoming-one (that one both is *and* is not) by that doubling *and* division remembered and forgotten, remembered and dismembered.

Articulation, then – and as disjointing. Such circular propositions imply a temporality having to do with *anamnesis* as the very possibility for any reflective, yet displaced and displacing, effectively *self-differencing* statement of existence. However, what is the nature of this temporal condition? It cannot be claimed with any certainty or assurance that what returns is simply a prior moment as such, a fixed precedent or conceptual *one*, an ontological *O* that encircles as it *de-scribes* and thus gives ideal form to the concept of being *a priori*. What returns is what already is *and* was and yet which never is, if the verb should be taken mistakenly to indicate the figure of the sole subject. But what *was* is inseparable from what *is* (even though it always remains other), from the *one is* that is *more than one*. There is here a simultaneity that is impossible *in stricto sensu*. One is thus announces the very possibility of the impossible, figuring impossibly this impossible possibility that is *one's* (self-) consciousness to itself.

Aspects of this conundrum are spoken of in one of the papers of Immanuel Kant gathered in the collection called *Opus Postumum*. Kant makes the following remark on the effective manifestation of the *cogito* given in the words *I am*. 'This act of consciousness (*apperceptio*)', argues Kant, 'does not arise as a consciousness of something preceding (as, for instance, if I say to myself: I think *therefore* I am) for otherwise I should presuppose my existence in order to demonstrate this existence – which would be a mere tautology' (Kant 1993, 200). Of course, Kant does not draw our attention here to the circular nature of thinking consciousness, his purpose being, instead, to illustrate how we cannot place ourselves outside the (conscious) thinking of consciousness, without, and in some manner, entering into a 'structural fantasy'. Whilst this is not necessarily implicated in the circularity of thinking, or the thinking of circularity, of thinking the self as involving oneself in a motion that is both circulation and circularity, nevertheless by that acknowledgement of the tautological, a closed economy – one of repeating the same – the circular logic is invoked, however indirectly. Haunted as it is by the ghosts of Leibnitz and Descartes in the traces of the *apperceptio* and the *cogito*, the Kantian proposition traces the circle of conscious reflection that marks and re-marks a distinction between mere perception and apperception. One is conscious of one's own existence and of one's own perceptions, not least those perceptions concerning one's own consciousness. The announcement of consciousness, which is always a self-consciousness, is not of something preceding the act of coming to consciousness. It is not informed by a presupposition or an *a priori* constant outside the circulating reflection of the act that returns to itself as its own first principle, deconstructed-in-itself.

The difficulty here is that one risks inscribing oneself in a solipsistic unity, circumscribing oneself in a continual self-affirmation. There is, it might not unreasonably be argued, little room for manoeuvre. One comes back to 'I'. 'I' returns to itself as a return to the experience of the aporetic – unless, that is, 'I' is discerned as metaphor, and moreover a metaphor for metaphoricity in general, for that metaphor which names nothing as such, *being* (as will be made clear shortly). 'I' is the singular event of being stepping beyond itself, opening itself and letting itself be opened as witness to event-ness and the singular historicity of an event, which then returns through the narrative mode of presenting and presencing – in truth, phantasmic and metaphorical – given in the articulation of the subject. Returning and turning back on itself, believing itself to remain the same however, 'I' nevertheless fails to apprehend how, according to the myriad and micrological operations of difference that score the 'I', it returns as the same but with a difference, difference bearing or carrying the sign of being's historicity.

However, before one can arrive at this possibility, one must return to Kantian tautology. Kant's critique reveals the extent to which one apprehends oneself through that apperception which is always already a misperception, expressed as 'the knowledge of oneself as a person who constitutes himself as a principle and is his originator' (Kant 1993, 213). This misperception is not, however, a flaw. It appears (as) a necessary, ineluctable process, an apparent first step in the structuring of consciousness. One *must* orient oneself. One must orient the *itself* even if with such orientation comes the motion entailing one's own disorientation. The structural motion of the circular logic of being's apperception to itself is a necessary, and indeed perhaps inevitable detour – the *detour* that makes possible the *retour* – so that one has the possibility spatially and temporally to 'orient oneself in thinking', as the title of another of Kant's essays has it (Kant 1996, 1–18). As Kant expresses it in spatial terms that also acknowledge the temporal *retour* of memory, 'in the dark I orient myself in a room that is familiar to me if I can take hold of even one single object whose position I *remember*' (Kant 1996, 9; emphasis added). The figure of *retour* that I have called up is important here. This hardly used, somewhat archaic English word expresses the necessary spatial and temporal conditions of that return that in returning disrupts even as it makes possible the articulation of *one is*. One traces and retraces the completion of a circle already inscribed, and with that the return to any supposed starting place always and in a particular, apparently paradoxical, manner that is inescapable. This gesture announces in the performance of its own articulation its own division, which in turn and *by analogy* allows indirectly for one's perception or intuition of the other as being other and yet the same. I stress *by analogy* in order to alert the reader to a circulation that escapes the purely logical in the movement of the analogical as the temporal deferral and spatial differentiation. Figurally, correspondence, relation, agreement come to take place. They come to pass *where one is*.

In returning to where I am, where one is who both is and is not the 'I' of *I am*, the motion of *retour* as the movement of conscious reflection affirms the other within the one – correspondence occurs as both agreement and communication or intercourse. *Retour* has also certain juridical senses relating to propriety and property, in the sense that what returns to one is what is properly the property, what is proper, to that person. But what we see returning to one, what is properly one's own, what one has the right to, is, properly understood, improper to oneself; the *is-not* is the only proper condition of that which *one is*, the other is the most proper-improper aspect of one's self. To make the point once more, orientation in thinking is disorientation, but disorientation is the necessary, if circular act of tracing if one is to apprehend the others that *one is*. Thus there is communication and correspondence. And yet this communication fails to arrive properly in its arrival. What inscribes or perhaps circumscribes the necessity of disorientation in and yet other to orientation? What makes the proper improper? It is, as Kant admits, 'a *subjective* ground of differentiation' (1996, 9). The subjective ground of differentiation that comes to appear is, however, groundless. In being announced as subjective, the ground gives way. This is not to say that the effect of differentiation – and, we would argue, deferral – is not there, not experienced or perceived, but rather that the subject projects the simulacrum of a ground in order to give ground to the groundless differentiation. If there were a ground to subjectivity it would not be of the order of a foundation so much as it would be a motion, a figure recircling, turning back, folding itself upon itself in its rhythm of unfolding – as if it were a ground bass in fact. Difference is that motif, the musical recurrence of which gives to the subject the illusion of a structure. Difference moves over the ground only to erase the very idea in tracing and reiterating it. That which comes to appear in fact reappears. It is always already marked, and re-marks the it-self, as reappearance. It returns in its circular fashion, to articulate that which is properly improper to the self. Neither self nor not-self, it arrives to reappear as a *revenant* trace in memory revealing the *one is* and the *one is-not*, and playing between the two. We thus apperceive the apparition to the self of the trace of the other, apprehended as 'appearance, intuition, immediate revelation, or whatever else one wants to call such a presentation' (1996, 15).

IV CARRYING, LEAPING (GETTING AHEAD OF ONESELF)

The problem, therefore: Why is it difficult to discuss being without (re)turning to metaphor or analogy? If it appears that the other is maintained under the economy of the self or the same in an iterable circularity of being, it is a salutary reminder that 'human existence can be viewed as *being*, which cannot be objectified' and the 'proper task' of being 'is the event of letting-be what emerges into the openness of being' (Boss 2001, x). Sufferance and witness conjoin ethically. In such a Heideggerian mode of thinking, being is no longer to be thought as the appearance of an object within the world. The apparent leap from Kant to Heidegger here is justified, inasmuch as Kant returns in Heidegger's thinking of being, even as Heidegger returns to Kant (if one can say that he had ever left Heidegger). In order to understand the question of metaphor that disturbs, it must be noted that for Kant, and Heidegger after him, 'Being is obviously not a real predicate, that is, it is not a concept of something, which could be added to the concept of a thing'. If not a predicate of something real – and Heidegger in the passage cited goes on to stress this matter of the real as the stake of thinking Being – then of what? Heidegger, following Kant, moves from signifier (being) to linguistic function (predicate) to concept, and from there to object, noting as he does so, somewhat implicitly, that because Being is not properly speaking a conceptual term (it is, *stricto sensu*, a quasi-concept), it only appears to signify a metaphysical or transcendental ideal. Its apparent function fails, and so there is, implicitly, a return to the mesh of the materiality of the letter. Being remains – and as such, undoes all Platonism on the one hand, whilst resisting an empirical materialism on the other. Being is, thus, as sign of itself, only ever apprehensible as metaphorical signifier, and metaphorical, inasmuch as it can be given expression either as this ruined quasi-concept (we apprehend its function because we cannot escape metaphysics, not because it is a metaphysical term), or comes to be exemplified through the metaphorical substitution of 'I', 'One', and so on. The singular articulation of the subject, given ground through the individual expression of being, operates on the principal of a substitution of the grounded for the groundless.

Moreover, because being is not a real predicate, indicating a concept that indicates an object, the thinking of being is, as a result, merely a positing, a supposition that is, at the same time, an acceptance, to use Heidegger's terms (Kant 1963, 504). The 'evidence' (*e-videre*: out+to see; to show oneself, we might say, or to step out; being shows itself in its unconcealment) for being resides only in the 'I', in its return, its recirculation, and in the metaphorical circularity that it apparently rewrites every time it is enunciated, even as, in letting oneself 'be seen' or 'showing itself from itself', the 'I' emerges – and this, as metaphor *par excellence*. Without ground, having no substance as such, but not without history, 'I' is what Heidegger terms, apropos being, as the 'highest kind of grounding [*Begründung*]' (Heidegger 2001b, 5). We return to metaphor – metaphor returns to us, as us, as that groundless orientation which nonetheless opens itself, as a grounding, to the very grounds of history. This apparent paradox (groundless/grounding) is already implicit, or at least finds its analogy, in the equally apparent paradox that either everyone is the same or that we are absolutely singular. However, positing such a static binarism fails to account for the metaphoricity of being as it is expressed in each and every singular utterance of 'I'. 'I' never speaks itself in the abstract. 'I' is always subject to the forces of differentiation, even though everywhere it appears as the same. To say 'I' is to say 'I am there', and one resorts to analogy or metaphor because it is only through the force of such tropological deployment that 'I' in my singular circumstance can convey to another 'I' by analogy how the experience of history – or the political – can be presented. If 'I' takes itself as truth, it denies its subjectivity as being subjectified. Admitting not to its illusory but groundless condition – being is not a real predicate, a predicate, that is to say, and to remind ourselves of the Kantian proposition, of the real – 'I' admits, opens itself and lets show its historicity and contingency, on the grounds of its being just this recurrent metaphor.

V OSTINATO

An interlude.

Kant's apparent rush in the passage cited above – *whatever else one wants to call* . . . – is as amusing as it is instructive. He seeks to dismiss the problem of naming the phenomenological apperception of that which is nothing as such, and which as such is irreducible to any properly oriented naming in the impropriety of its slippage along a spectral chain of ghostly analogical signifiers. Naming is everything and yet nothing. Its very articulation only communicates its failure, its spluttering, stuttering inadequacy in the unformed, potentially endlessly reformulated subjectivity. *One must name.* This is the imperative, and yet no name will do. *One* appears to name. In its appearance it appears to name. It seems as if it names in its appearance; it appears as the name, by analogy. And one must name. Here is the directive to being, to a being conscious of itself as itself, as corresponding with *and* to itself. Yet, again, and in every inflection, there is the failure to communicate finally. So the philosopher's resources are exhausted, as that *whatever else* admits. Every term gestures in the direction of the naming of the meaning of being while at the same time pointing us in another direction, in other directions that might be seen simultaneously as either towards or away from that which resists identification; hence orientation as disorientation in the very act of perception itself. Thus, we might say that the philosopher becomes impatient in the face of the other's obstinacy, in coming face to face with the iterable *ostinato* of being. The basis for reiteration, the *ostinato* informs being as the rhythmic pulse of being. Yet even in that affirmation, an affirmation of difference and the difference that is affirmation – *yes, yes* (see Derrida 1992b, 253–309) – there is a performative resistance or, perhaps better, obstinacy to becoming fixed. The presentation of being is *obstinate*: it appears, and in appearing appears to gesture both towards and away from itself. It takes a stand (*stare*) towards and against (*Ob*), and this disorienting duplicity announces itself in the undecidability of the prefix (*ob-*) that orients the stance.[1]

It could be argued that the *substance* of being is just the instance of this *obstance*. And in this double, and thus undecidable, gesture, being slips away and returns. Circulating endlessly, the *ostinato* of being varies within itself as not-itself, as not-self in the performance of a difference that *différance* makes possible. Moving in a continuous-discontinuous weave that produces the illusion of a ground, of a finite subjectivity – *one is* – *ostinato* projects the illusion of closure in order to open to another reiteration that announces once more the 'becoming-space of time, and the becoming-time of space' (Derrida 2005b, 38). *Ostinato*, therefore, forms no true ground at all but a ground only in a perceptual sense, in other words, as 'substance' of being. And it is this forming/deforming that informs Kant's remark. For, in admitting the inability to name finally the ground, Kant's sentence provides a performative illustration of perceptual motion as that very possibility of its own utterance and articulation. Such performative irony is where *one is* in circularity and where *one returns* in the circularity of being.

VI CORRESPONDENCE (CIRCULATING POSTCARDS)

The *retour* of the poetic.

Two comments in three languages, at least, concerning where *one is* (the emphases are added):

Da	There	Then
war ich	was *I*	I still
noch ganz	yet whole	Was whole
(Celan 1995, 111/112)[2]		

and:

Il faut redire en altérant le même / *One* must repeat while altering (it all) the same. (Deguy 2005, 84/85)[3]

Notwithstanding what Paul Celan has called 'the inalienable complexity of expression' (Celan 2003, 16), with reference to a certain necessary responsibility that persists in the articulation and attestation of post-holocaust German poetry – and which phrase is applicable to either of the above quotations – we must take responsibility for what appears to be reiterated in the two locations. Despite their different languages, something circulates between the two citations from, respectively, Paul Celan and Michel Deguy. Something of the circularity of being appears here and there, now and then *as if* there were an attempted communication, as if something were passing, were coming to pass, were appearing between the *one* and the *other*, without admitting of any precedence or priority on either hand. If anything at all can be said of what *comes to pass* between both reflections on the subject, of the coming to pass of being as it announces its own passage, then it is undeniably a matter of temporality, and perhaps also tempo. It appears *to be and as* – a question of tempo because both mediations of being mark time – the time of a being's reflection on itself; and within that, the motion, the *retour* and *ostinato* of the not-self, of an other. The matter of temporality is nothing, as such, yet it is everything here.

For the self does not reflect on some exterior temporality. What might come to be seen and read here is that the subject's reflection on itself does not admit of a fall into any vulgar concept of time, thinkable as being external to the subject.[4] Both remarks serve to illustrate the 'originary temporality' (Derrida 1989c, 27) of being and with that, the circulation of that temporality, inseparable from being, in a motion 'from time to time, one time into another' (Derrida 1989c, 28). In this, being is read as a 'becoming-temporalization'. This is a 'becoming-temporalization' that always already *is*, and which, in this paradoxical though nonetheless inescapable and possibly unbearable condition, puts 'itself' invisibly, repeatedly under erasure as the erroneous assumption of its being the sign of *where one is* – hence the deconstruction of a unity that the Kantian perplexity reveals.

In the case of the second citation from Michel Deguy, time is the time of a necessary repetition as the sign that iterability transfigures any movement into a *now* which is to come and which is irreducible to the *now* of the one. In Deguy's apprehension of being, time is both continuous and discontinuous. It is simultaneously the motion of time and two temporal punctuations – *now* and *now* implicit in the acknowledgement of the inescapable iterability that proves singularity. In the case of the first quotation, from Paul Celan, the subject is apprehended, re-membered even; and perhaps mourned also in that apparent nostalgia for an impossible unity that has never taken place, and yet which haunts the language of subjectivity, being, and ontology. The subject is recalled nevertheless, called to and remembered in a single location that is already, irrevocably doubled, split. The division announces itself; it performs itself, from within the single word, and does so spatially – *there* (*da*) – and temporally – *then* (*da*). But this takes place also, always belatedly; it thus reveals the *itself* as subjected to, subject of the experience of *Nachträglichkeit*, that moment of coming to consciousness as an *après coup*.

(Of course, to pause for a moment, it is somewhat misleading to suggest a simple equivalence between the German and French, even though the French is the translation of the German in psychoanalytic discourse, introduced initially in the work of Jacques Lacan. In considering Freud's use of the term in his work on the Wolf Man in 'The Function and Field of Speech and Language in Psychoanalysis', Jacques Lacan defines the *nachträglich* as that process identified by Freud as a 'turning point where the subject restructures himself [according to] events [that] take place . . . at a later date' (Lacan 1977, 48). For Freud, therefore there is a deliberate reorientation of the self, as the self rewrites and apparently escapes the circularity of being, through the revisionism that later events in one's life make possible in relation to earlier determining moments. There is thus a structural relationship for Freud between a significant or traumatic event and the later determination of the event with significance. A problem arises with the Freudian notion in that it is difficult, if not impossible, to say whether the early event has significance and is thus deterministic, or whether the later event or 'restructuring' is a mode of retrospective narrativization. However, one can put forward the supposition that the past, whether deterministic or revised, has in it the trace of the other, about which I knew nothing at the time, and about which I know nothing now in my 'restructuring' or 'resignification'. The other thus rewrites me, and in coming belatedly to this knowledge the *après-coup* arrives.)

That simultaneity of space and time undoes itself and remarks itself from within itself. Pierre Joris's translation of '*da*' as 'then' is certainly reasonable, justifiable even given Celan's repeated use of '*als*' earlier in the poem to indicate a prior temporal moment. However, I have chosen 'there' as indicative not only of the temporal but also the spatial dimension of being's reflection on itself. Thus there becomes readable, as the merest possibility, nostalgia for the notion of a previous unity to identity, which the subsequent spacing and reflection of the 'I' emerges from, and disrupts irrevocably. *Then* is a time past. *There* on the other hand is both a sign of that moment lost as such; but it is also a sign of the place where that moment has taken place.

There are other troublesome resonances at work in the passage apropos the circularity of being. While '*ganz*' obviously means whole, entire or complete, it can also mean 'quite' depending on context. '*Noch*', meaning 'yet', 'still', 'just', or 'even', would seem to share a partial semantic resonance with the more occluded trace in '*ganz*', and the temporal disturbance inflicted by reflective consciousness on the temporal recognition of being is perhaps signified, however slightly, in '*noch*' and its function in particular words such as *nochmals* (once again), *nochgeschäft* (option to double) or *nochmalig* (renewed) indicative of iterability. Finally, the word order in German of the declined verb of being – *war Ich* – evinces for the English reader of German a sense of the temporal and spatial placement of an *I* (hence my emphasis). Whilst Joris's translation is perfectly idiomatic, a strong reading, and one not unmindful of Heiddegger's insistence on the grounding that *da* gives to *da-sein*, might be proffered that the emplacement of 'I' is what is forgotten in the native speaker's utterance. Celan's German admits of a subject position discrete or quasi-discrete, and therefore discontinuous, from as well as other than the *I* who recalls its other self to itself.

The second of my two quotations is available to different readings, if *one* risks forcing the translation; which it has to be said is demanded by the line itself. Such an unavoidable forcing of the subject takes place for us to read. In a sense this is what *one* does within the line itself. Moving on from the reflection on being's becoming-conscious to itself through the example of Kant in the first part of the essay (and yet remaining with it), I wish to turn to the circulation of this becoming-being and being's becoming in its/their always dissymmetrical singular iterability as such disfigured figures are articulated and disarticulated in two poems. It should be stressed at this juncture, this *turning point in the circle that we are de-scribing*, that the present chapter does not amount or aspire to a reading of either of those poems by Celan or Deguy. Rather, both Deguy and Celan are taken to offer felicitous examples of the circulation of being's consciousness to itself in the poems in question, and the significance – to reiterate and extend one of the citations already given – of the 'interval or the gap, of the trace [of being] as gap [*écart*], of the becoming-space of time or the becoming-time of space' (Derrida 2005b, 38).

But to return to Deguy's meditation on being's iterability, its revenant motion of becoming other in the return of becoming itself to itself: *Il faut redire en altérant le même*. Key to this forcing is the phrase '*en altérant*'. Both the work of the preposition and the various meanings of the verb must be taken into account. Take *en*. One must repeat *when* altering the same. One must repeat *in* altering the same. One must repeat *with* altering the same. This of course leaves out any acknowledgement of where a particular pressure arises, in that *one*, in *must*, in *one must*. As for *altérer* – to impair, to affect, to spoil, to mar, to alter, to change, to fade, to distort, to falsify, to adulterate. There is an alarming alterity to *altérer*. The condition of transformation or translation is intricately interwoven in a matrix of possibilities to do with the circulation and circularity of the one, of the ways in which it folds back on itself in coming to a consciousness of itself, but only in that structural condition of distorting and change, of alteration and falsification.

At the same time, as Deguy's phrase admits in the copula of the preposition, *One* not only repeats *in* altering (or falsifying, or distorting, and so on) the same; one also speaks again; *one* reiterates itself in itself and from itself, as both itself and not-itself, as the simultaneous trace of self and other within the repetition that one names, thereby giving the lie to unity, ontology, and a subjectivity undifferentiated either spatially or temporally. Taking this further, as the line already does, it is to be observed that one arrives and comes to speak once more (*re-dire*) *when* and *where* one alters, where the alterity of *one* arrives *in the re-speaking that is repetition as reiteration*. *One* thereby announces, as we have already indicated, the *itara*, the other, within the circling enunciation of consciousness to itself as not-itself in naming it-self. And this despite the apparent in-difference that is assumed, silently evinced in that figure (*all*) *the same*.

However naïvely, or, however one assumes the posture or performance of a strategic naïvety for the purposes of opening the circularity of being's articulation to itself, as this is dictated and marked by its own necessary difference in its articulation and repetition, it might be asked, even parenthetically – as if the very question would not bear the weight of the inquiry it demands – '*comment l'un «traduirait»-il l'autre?* / 'how could the one "translate" the other?' (Deguy 2005, 108/109). Something is missing in the given translation, the appended reflexive subject, that 'it', possibly 'itself', so that allowing this silent graphic mark to return, one would be given to read: *how would one translate it-/one-self the other?*

Clearly I am once again forcing the translation, to open the problem of recirculation and *retour*, to bring into plain sight the frustration of an impossible communication that takes place, and which, in taking place, gives place to being. All of which is unravelled and wound, folded and unfolded, over and under, in this, the last citation from Michel Deguy, this time the poem *Catachréses* (Deguy 2005, 102/103):

> *Retournant l'endroit et l'envers, tournant à l'endroit l'envers: ce qu'il attend n'est pas là – visiblement: ce qui n'est pas, ni l'endroit ni l'envers.*

First Wilson Baldridge's translation, then my own:

> Turning outside to inside over and over, turning the inside out: what he is waiting for is not there – visibly; that which is not, neither the outside nor the inside.

Returning, turning again, the right side wrong side, turning (towards) the outside inside: that's what he's waiting for, what is not there – visibly: that which is
not, neither right nor wrong, out nor inside.

I have, once again, forced open the translation here quite unreasonably. I have
risked this, however, in order to stress, to enflame and irritate the catachreses of
circulation *and* iterability, being here staged and thus displayed as neither absolutely continuous nor discontinuous, and yet figuring an uneasy and paradoxical
interweaving of the continuity and discontinuity. At the same time, what also
comes to light here is the sense of circulation as not merely a matter of a relatively
straightforward or 'progressive' temporality, however much traces might remain
in play, however 'overdetermined' by the ghosts of one's past selves one's present
self reveals itself to be. What we see here at play in Deguy's Moebius matrix is a
circulation of apparent surfaces. In this play is the appearance of that which is
not – not nothing exactly, even though it is not something, not the absence of
some thing; and which therefore in not being either something or nothing is not
nothing. This is what is not there – visibly: being, circling around and returning,
appearing/disappearing in the very gesture of turning outside inside and turning
inside outside.

VII ECONOMIES OF BEING

A circle is round, it is a round; but a round is not necessarily circular, at least not
simply. As with the idea of a musical ground, for example the *ostinato*, the round,
the idea of a round, announces series and sequence, and also cycle. The circular
thus opens out from within its own structure, moving beyond its apparent closure
or foreclosure. It does so via a succession, chain, or cycle of gestures that, while
appearing to mimic that seemingly closed, 'first' figure, remain the same and yet
move on, in the enactment of 'the becoming-space of time and the becoming-time
of space' of being's being. So: the round as the insistence on the impossibility of the
stability of any ground. Ground is placed under erasure in that gesture of mapping
that takes place. What goes around comes around.

As Rimbaud knew, and wrote repeatedly, 'I is an other' (Rimbaud 1957, xxvii,
xxix).[5] There is both a luminous obscurity and an obscure luminosity to this phrase.
Its brilliance blinds even as that illumination keeps the secret safe, in plain sight.
At the same time, or nearly the same time – which is as much as to say out of all
time with itself, not with itself in confessing its alterity, the location of the other as
dislocation of the self – the true light remains secreted also, only to be captured in
afterglow. For as much as it has been read or not read at all, misread, it announces
with perfect economy the abyssal topography of a being, which always where it is, is
nevertheless nowhere as such, other than in spatio-temporal *différance* that one can
glimpse as having always already been shadowed in those motion-signs of *becoming*
and *between*. Thus *one* always becomes other again and again, and this takes place, to
reiterate the point, *where one is*. This is where one is in circularity, in the question of

circularity. *One* is placed, *one* takes place, in the staging and framing that circularity *de-scribes*, in the (ana)logic of which all surface and depth, exteriority and interiority, originary ground and the myth of temporal fixity give way. Or, rather say, *give place* in the limiting-delimiting of the inherence of being's circular recursive revenance. I am never myself, as such, but neither am I the transcendent possibility of past moments of I that I might recall when *I* was, yet whole, quite complete.

Supposedly.

If every 'being-there is a being-in' (Lacoste 2004, 9), *where one is* is always traced by, even as it enacts, both the poetics and 'logic of immanence' (Lacoste 2004, 10). I comes to be disclosed as *an other, as every other and wholly other*, as *I* is simultaneously placed and displaced in the taking place of this immanent othering, this radical ecstasis one names being.

This is what a poetics of being discloses, what it reveals as it suspends the intuitive and steps momentarily 'outside *one*'s ordinary mode of seeing' (Gosetti-Ferencei 2004, 238; emphasis added), as is glimpsed in Rimbaud, in Celan, in Deguy, and doubtless in many other poetic locations. Poetic modes of staging being as the performance of a simultaneous 'disorientation and clarity' (Gosetti-Ferencei 2004, 238) admit the phenomenal contingency of that reflective apperception of being as *where one is*; but such staging is never merely a commentary upon the experience of being. It is the very trace of being returning, always, in other words, as the attestation of the unbearable circulation of being that the literary makes possible. This is where one is in the circularity, the circulation that is named, variously, the literary or the poetic, before and beyond, circling around any merely philosophical logic, and exceeding that logic repeatedly.

This is where one is.

And this is where one begins in circularity, a circularity that, in writing itself, erases itself, tracing over the palimpsest, substituting in the process another self. And this is why one must admit (to) the force of metaphor, analogy, the trope, submitting oneself to this revenance.

Again and again. Being, not being a real predicate, metaphor (is all that) remains. This is revealed in the emergence, or what Heidegger calls the uncon-cealedness (*Aletheia*) of the truth of being. Insofar as thinking the self unveils the truth of being to itself, truth as its own recurring unconcealedness, one returns to a beginning, a beginning which also returns to one. Truth, the truth of being, is this circular motion: it directs us home (to use Heidegger's term) and figures the point of departure in thinking (the) truth (of being); and 'Truth dwells in everything that comes to presence' (Heidegger 1992, 163). Yet such reiterable circularity of being is far from being solipsistic and groundless. For, in order to be expressed, there is language, language being the medium through which being reveals itself, and this language, remarks Heidegger, 'expresses the essence of history, and history, because it is the sending of Being and because Being only comes to light unexpectedly, is appropriated always in the unexpectedness of the primordiality of beginning' (Heieddeger 1992, 163). Language, moreover, the language of the Occident as Heidegger has it, 'expresses the beginning . . . the still concealed essence of the truth of Being' (Heidegger 1992, 163).

This is where one is. In metaphor, so to speak – and in a structural geometry of being's consciousness to itself, through all those metaphorical and metonymic ruses, such as recirculation, replacement, displacement, doubling, supplementarity and iterability, all of which motivate and are motivated in that motif of difference, that differentiation of which Heidegger spoke as the 'infinity of the I'. Here the circle closes in on its ever-moving point, and so opens itself to itself, within itself, continuing without end:

> Consciousness becomes aware of the *I* which differentiates itself from itself and thus knows that it is not differentiated from itself. Consciousness knows consciously of the inner difference, since consciousness is consciousness of the I and of the self – is self-consciousness . . . by saying I, I is posited as I:I = I. But I 'equals' I is just the difference which has to be made, solely in order basically not to be a difference. Since this inner difference has the character of an I [*ichlich*] and since the I posits itself, it differentiates itself at the same time from the not-I . . . With this there *opens up* for the I as I a realm of encountering this or that being which has the character of a not-I. (Heidegger 1988, 124–5; emphasis added)

As soon as there is difference, there – *there* – is *I*, the I as not I, and yet I also, in relation to myself, (fiction of) auto-differentiation, by which *I* stands over against the self and yet also as that which guards the self from the not-self, admitting to the not-self, however, in its own demarcation.

VIII

Samuel Beckett captures this – or at least, let us say, he apprehends the displacement of the I that gives place to I's possibility of affirming itself, in confessing its difference to itself. This is the crux, the axis perhaps, of that which is unnamable, *The Unnamable* itself. At the limits of the readable, the self between readability and unreadability, Beckett posits the I, I saying I, 'unbelieving' (Beckett 1979, 267). In the face of all the impossibilities, 'I have to begin. That is to say I have to go on' (1979, 268). In a beginning that is always already a continuance, a supplement to the self, there in that phrase – that is to say, *c'est-à-dire* – is the economy of transport, transfer, displacement and the motion of the one to the other. But in beginning to reach a conclusion, there comes the recognition that 'it was never I, I've never stirred, I've listened . . . I haven't stirred, that's all I know, no, I know something else, it's not I, I always forget that, I resume, you must resume, never stirred from here, never stopped telling stories, to myself . . .' (1979, 380).

Although in motion, I have never been moved on; in hearing myself speak, in having opened to me the I which differentiates itself from itself, I realize – there's no getting away from it – that I have come, if not full circle, then back to where I began, that is to say, having to continue, even though 'it won't be I, it's not I, I'm not there yet' (1979, 377). 'I' thus places itself in Beckett as that which returns to itself, conscious of itself, in a circular gesture of revenant awareness, by which, in coming to itself, it recognizes paradoxically that it has forgotten it cannot be that 'I' in any pure, full or simple sense. There is no being to 'I', it remains, speaking of itself, as 'a thing that divides the world in two, on the one side the outside, on the other the inside' (1979, 376). In this, 'I' is merely the 'constitutive difference' a 'between' (Szafraniec 2007, 130) a disjunction and yet, simultaneously, copulative conjunction, marking a double boundary: 'I'm the partition. I've two surfaces and no thickness' (Beckett 1979, 376). Neither subject nor object, 'I' has already entered the game, is in the looping play. 'I' names a resonance by which it is heard, and hears itself, a double differentiation, confessing finally that, as a result of 'all the old stories incomprehensibly' that 'it will be I, it will be the place, the silence, the end, the beginning, *the beginning again*, how can I say it . . . you must go on, I can't go on, I'll go on' (1979, 380, 382).

And this is where one begins, and where one is, and is not.

12

Teaching Derrida: 'but just a minute, before we begin, a preface of sorts (after the event), a defence, apologia, apologue . . .', and other responses in the face of (yet another) programmed avoidance of reading

---

[But wait, just a minute, before we begin, an apologue, that is to say, a fable, or story of sorts, which is also, as a response, an apologia, both words – apologue, apologia – the same and yet not the same, from the Greek απο [*apo-*] off, away, + λογος [*logos*] speech, and also απολογια [*apologia*], signifying defence, speaking in defence [of a topic, subject, oneself] . . . To apologize and to mount a defence therefore, indirectly, through a narrative, a fiction, the contours of which are already well-known, that the force of the fable comes from its familiarity and the inevitability of its arrival, *one more time . . .*

An email arrives one day. It invites you to write an essay. The essay should concern itself with a reflection on the question of 'teaching Derrida'. I will get into the difficulties such a title presents shortly; be patient. From some place, the request arrives. What do you do? This is an impossible situation in which you find yourself, because you know the request comes with an already programmed desire, however well intentioned. What that might be does not necessarily come from the person sending the email. In a sense the transmission takes place *through* that person. So, do you decline, or do you accept, knowing, in the words of the song, 'there may be trouble ahead'? To paraphrase someone or other, you only have two choices, both of which are incorrect . . .

. . . the 'trouble', already pre-programmed because pre-dating anything you might write, and being, therefore, both ahead of you and always following you, returns once you've written what you take to be a careful, considered, patient response, the only one you can give, based, in part, on the experience of teaching in general, and 'teaching Derrida' in particular; that is to say, teaching seminars to both undergraduates and graduate students, in which you attempt to explore some line of thought in a text or two, published in the name of Jacques Derrida. The problem is that, once you send the essay out, it arrives, out of your control, at a place where reading doesn't take place, and where, as you have it filtered back to you, there is no reading, no openness in response, merely the same, inevitable avoidance of reading, yet again, in the name of a programme, or the desire for a programme. The programme, which is also a mode of judgement, a form of law, in the face of which, and despite everything, you must speak for the defence, wants everything its own way. It hands down its judgement: things begin by being slippery, not easy to pin down. Despite that fluidity, though, or perhaps because of it, the judgement is also made that you are speaking in a 'patronising *de haut en bas* tone', and certain sub-topics within your principal subject – supposing that one knows confidently how to separate and hierarchize – are difficult, too hard to warrant inclusion. Additionally, there is also the judgement that, on the one hand, you don't need to tell others (the judgement implicitly includes the idea that the place of its issuance also has the power to determine the audience, that the law knows the audience or projects the audience more than you can; in short, that it knows more about your subject and your audience than you do, even though you have been asked to write something on this subject) what you do tell them, while, on the other hand, you're not telling your audience what (someone else says) you need to tell them, and so on . . .

So, the last first: the programme, the law, issues contradictory remarks, such as, 'we don't need telling *X*', and 'why don't you show us how to do *Y*'. This forms a contradiction in as much as, if you really don't need telling, then you wouldn't be asking to be shown something, which, mistakenly, you think (without knowing in the first place, otherwise you wouldn't ask this) is that which I'm trying to tell you, and which you say you don't need telling, while, almost at the same time, you want me not to show you anything other than a programmed response to a programmed desire for a process that runs like clockwork, as if the machine were fixed ahead of the event, and as if no event could take place, but that, in the place of reading, a programme is run, the icon having been 'double-clicked', and the sausage-maker's software generates one more packaged 'deconstruction' (so-called). That being the case, what I think you want is *this* text or *that* book, this critic or that introduction. I am expected not to do what I do, but to do what someone else does, even though someone else hasn't been asked, and so on . . .

That I am writing this lengthy parenthesis at all means that the fiction I've just spun has taken place. That I need to write this at all means that a spanner has been thrown into the works. The software has a virus. We're off the rails.

You may think that I am adopting a 'patronising *de haut en bas* tone' here. You may think so, I couldn't possibly comment. I couldn't possibly comment because what is written is irreducible to a single tone, and tone is as much, if not more, a matter of how one reads or misreads, or doesn't read at all, as it is of writing (if a text, in fact, has a tone, or several, innumerable tones). The phrase – 'patronizing *de haut en bas* tone' – is not mine. I appreciate the interjection of French. It assumes something of a grand manner, doesn't it, a little of patrician *hauteur*? Or am I perceiving a 'tone' or 'style', in saying this? *De haut en bas*: from above to below. Then, 'patronizing', to treat with an apparent kindness that betrays a feeling of superiority. This is the *OED*, by the way, not me. Again, it is a question of tone, or style. But a message can be sent out and have unintended consequences, as I have already implied. It may be that someone – not you, or you – perceives themselves as being patronized, talked down to, for a number of reasons, not least being that one which says there is a programme, and all one needs is to have the operations of the programme explained, objectively. Anybody not obeying the law will be judged, the judgement being handed down from above onto the subject not obeying the law, the subject becoming positioned below automatically in the act of the judgement; which judgement avoids doing justice to the other, and thereby avoids reading. That person, who presumes to speak in this authoritative voice for everyone, on behalf of everyone, inverts assumed positions. That person, having assumed the law is being handed down, has usurped the position from which they believe, imagine, me to be speaking, taking up the position for themselves. Except, I was never in the position of the law in the first place. A call came, a command, to write. Mine was always a subordinate position, as one subject to the law, of whom it was demanded – in the guise of an invitation (what is more threatening, more patronizing, more an act of kindness masking its superiority) – that I write. So, never having been in the position of the law, I am not displaced. The one who would displace me with accusations of slipperiness and 'tone' is already – always already – in the position of the patron, the patrician, the patriarch; nothing is overturned.

What I would suggest has taken place here – and this is idle speculation, all part of my apologue, my apologia, the defence which is also an act of storytelling, and, at the same time, an act of speaking away from the subject, by which, in not seeming to speak of the subject about which it is demanded that I speak, I am in fact addressing that subject, speaking in those tongues, those languages, without speaking them, *in other words*, as the idiom has it – is that my essay is sent out and comes to arrive at a 'reader'. That 'reader' feels patronized because he or she does not want to be told that there is no such thing as a 'programme' when it comes to being taught Derrida. That person already has an idea of what it means to teach Derrida, and they mistake, in their impatience, my careful, reflexive explanation, my caution over how something is said, as having this 'patronizing *de haut en bas*' tone'. In short, they feel somewhat troubled by being reminded of something that, deep down, they have known all along: which is, that it takes time to read Derrida, that they have not given enough time to reading Derrida, that they desire a short-hand Derrida, that which goes by the name 'deconstruction', in the place of doing the work.

You'd be forgiven for thinking I am making too much of this. But when such responses arrive, coupled with observations to do with the assumption that a thinker such as Edmund Husserl is 'hard' or 'difficult' (again, not my words), something is troubling someone, somewhere. The implication behind such a remark is that Derrida is not 'difficult', so why complicate matters by referring in passing to Edmund Husserl? Were you to look at that part of the essay where I mention Edmund Husserl, you will see that, in what I take to be an appropriate scholarly manner, I refer to Husserl because I am referring to a work of Derrida's, *Speech and Phenomena*, in which, as I go on to remark (forgive me for citing myself, ahead of myself, though also after myself, given that I am writing this *after* I have written what remains to come), 'Derrida is responding to, and elaborating on, the founder of modern phenomenology Edmund Husserl's (1859–1938) discussion of the role of language in the expression of Being'. I then continue with an all too brief explication of Husserl on language and being, before quoting that line of Derrida's, which – and here I will anticipate that part of the essay by quoting myself, again, quoting Derrida: 'Derrida . . . remarks of Husserl's analysis and comprehension of meaning's relation to Being that "[t]he prerogative of being cannot withstand the deconstruction of the word", following this almost immediately with the question, apropos the verb "to be", "[b]ut why does using words get mixed up with the determination of being in general as presence?" (1973, 74).' The point here, one which, clearly, the reader could not read, was, is and will be, to begin an elucidation of the problematic word 'deconstruction', a word which, perhaps more than any other, is associated with the work, the thought, and the text, of Jacques Derrida. Shortly before that, I had briefly remarked on the necessity, following Derrida's own commentaries over a number of years, of disabusing the reader of the idea that 'deconstruction' was a methodology, a programme for reading. In order that the reader not simply take my word for it, I then cite an example, an early example, of Derrida's usage of the word, a use which is not indicative of an application. In citing this passage, I felt obligated to explain, in a limited manner, a little context, without exhausting that context, or suggesting that it is either the only context or that a context can be finite; I repeat, I felt obligated to explain, in order that the reader – whoever the reader is, student or teacher – not fall into the assumption that Derrida is simply playing with words, is 'deconstructing' language, is speaking in an obscurantist fashion, and so on . . . What I try to do here is show how Derrida exposes a crucial relation between, on the one hand, the philosophical thinking of the question of being, the fundamental question of that branch of philosophy called ontology, and, on the other hand, the work of language. Being is understood as a concept. It is thought, or perceived, to be whole, absolute and coterminous with itself in a spatio-temporal way. The assumption that underpins the notion of being (a concept disguised as a context) is that of what Derrida would call full-presence. Language, however, is the means by which one articulates one's being. There is no immediate presentation of being as such. Language is structured through the work of difference, through differences that both defer and differ, which displace temporally and which also demonstrate or show themselves as different spatially. This work of language, specifically, the word, by which Being is articulated, in being always already spaced and spacing, temporally construed, effects in its motion, its mere utterance, the 'deconstruction' of being. I could go on, but perhaps thinking this is hard, difficult . . .

So, what happens? Someone – here's the fiction, again – feels bothered by being confronted with something that does not conform to their *a priori* assumptions about how one begins to approach Derrida; and because it does not conform, and raises the possibility of a responsibility to read 'outside their comfort zone', simultaneously, they go on the defensive *and* on the attack, remarking on matters of style and tone as if these were matters of fact, or epistemological significance. Such a rhetorical device on the part of the bad reader assumes no responsibility; it eschews the very kind of commitment to thought that reading Derrida requires; it is the very signature of an avoidance of responsibility, the responsibility good reading imposes and demands. Such a response struggles to make accusatory gestures in a manner that implies it does not have to deal with the content or form of what is being presented for consideration because the language in which the essay is written is 'hard', 'slippery' (with words such as these, I could accuse the reader of being a phallocentric pornographer, delivering his/her judgement in a 'patronizing *de haut en bas* tone'. In short, the response seeks to let itself out of having to consider what is different or other in that which arrives. If we take the example of Edmund Husserl, the philosopher of phenomenology and teacher of Martin Heidegger, as well as the author of a work, 'Origin of Geometry', to which Derrida wrote a lengthy introduction as one of his earliest publications, is the real difficulty that Husserl is 'hard' or 'difficult'? Or is it that the anonymous reader, who, along with allegations about my 'tone', sees Husserl as problematic because there might just be the assumption that if Derrida is at all 'useful' to literary critics then we have to keep the philosophy to a minimum, maintaining the institutional fiction – much more prevalent and pernicious in the UK than in the US; at least, in the US, where Derrida is misread, he is still read, after a fashion; in the UK, however, avoidance of reading and non-reading are indicative symptoms of a rush to judgement without evidence; this is, laughably, almost a default position, really – that Derrida is merely a punning nihilist, someone whose work has a strategic usefulness for playing around with words and formal aspects of semantic generation and construction. The last thing any critic would want to do is to have to start reading difficult material outside their own discipline, unless of course it's obviously 'political'; there's always the excuse of necessity and urgency; but what's the use of, well, philosophy, unless words such as 'moral' or 'political' are attached as prefixes?

All of which is to reach the point, before I begin, whereby the following can be said, as a preface of sorts (after the event), a defence, apologia, apologue ...

I ANTICIPATIONS

Teaching *Derrida.*
  Teaching Derrida.
  Teaching, Derrida ...
  Teaching? Derrida.
  Teaching. *Derrida?*
  Teaching: Derrida
  Teaching? Derrida?

II ABSTENSIONS

[... *but just a minute, before we begin, a preface of sorts (after the event), a defence, apologia, apologue ...*

In his most recent – as I write – publication, Fielding Derrida: Philosophy, Literary Criticism, History, and the Work of Deconstruction (2008), *Joshua*

Kates points out that many readers of Jacques Derrida get Derrida wrong, as it were, because, in wanting Derrida to be exclusively a literary critic, and/or the inventor of a methodology in which skepticism is the motivating force, they exhibit all the symptoms of poor reading and misreading that have dogged some of Derrida's readers from the first. Kates identifies the problem through a close reading of Jonathan Culler and Christopher Norris as typical of the first generation 'deconstruction is a method of criticism' approach, grounded in skepticism. As Kates argues, contra *the canonical misreadings of Norris and Culler, 'Derrida always wished to keep a distance from all forms of skepticism, and . . . he repeatedly turned to [Edmund] Husserl's phenomenology in order to do so' (2008, 3).*

Both Culler and Norris produce misreadings of Derrida, in effect, because they fail to understand or take account properly of the philosophical ground of Derrida's work, located in Derrida's responses to Husserl. However, Derrida's 'Introduction' to Husserl, is, observes Kates, 'clearly the decisive text for all . . . matters' regarding the development of Derrida's thought (2008, 37). Part of the problem, then, in the transformation of Derrida into skeptical methodologist of deconstructive critique, has to do with a failure to engage seriously on the part of some with the philosophical locations, to which Derrida's work is a response and an invention. In the English-speaking world, those Kates calls the 'first-wave' of Derrida critics have skewed the reception of Derrida through passing over Derrida's earlier work on Husserl in favour of a focus primarily on Of Grammatology, *in order to produce and portray deconstruction 'in popular representations of Derrida's thought' (2008, 11). 'Taking deconstruction as the center of Derrida's thought', Kates maintains – and I cite him here because he sums up the problem I seek to resist in this chapter – 'the first wave, in a nutshell, claims that deconstruction (1) introduces a new way of reading; (2) focuses on writing and language; and (3) draws negative, or skeptical conclusions about philosophy, reason, and truth' (2008, 11–12).*

Inasmuch as 'deconstruction', thought as such a critical programme, has remained the horizon of misreading, the errors of the first generation are not only repeated, they're compounded. It is, therefore, partly the purpose of this chapter to avoid such repetition. What you will have read, then, will not have offered you a method for literary criticism. It will not have kept a 'literary' Derrida separate from a philosophical one. Furthermore, it will not pretend to stand outside Derrida's work, providing an objective critical commentary on what Derrida's work is or does; neither will it presume to show or tell you 'how to do criticism' after Derrida.

Beginning with a performative reflection on the first part of my title – teaching Derrida *– I seek to navigate a passage between predictability and the imprescribable, an open response to the alterity of the text and any exercise of intellectual mastery, as those aspects of pedagogy which repeatedly confront one another in the experience of teaching, without resolution. I reflect on certain ways of approaching the teaching of Derrida, which, if not the most efficacious, are the least violent in their* translation *of Derrida. I refrain from giving detailed descriptions of how such teaching takes place, as this would run the risk of transforming this chapter into a programme for reading. That risk is already there, and that cannot be avoided. And of course, there is also the irresolvable problem that, even in the most scrupulous or rigorous effort to remain* *open, one falls back into a series of programmed responses.*

Were I to present here a syllabus or seminar plan in the guise of this chapter (and I would not describe even these as typical, *inasmuch as I try not to repeat the same process, I try not to return to the same book or essays, I avoid having carefully planned notes or a fully scripted lecture), the present article would be very much shorter than it is. Possibly, it would look – and this is merely one hypothetical scenario, a fiction of sorts – like this:*

> We will examine how Derrida reads another's text. We will read a single work by Derrida and will also read those works or work that Derrida discusses. Taking a text by Derrida, such as *Edmund Husserl's Origin of Geometry: An Introduction*, we will begin by reading Husserl's work, which is included in Derrida's volume. There is no guarantee that we will get very far with this process, because the approach to a reading will be dictated by the involvement of everyone in the seminar. This means that the seminar cannot have a fixed syllabus, and that we have to be prepared to move at different speeds, going over and returning to the text in different ways. Should we reach a point where everyone can agree that they feel they have a sufficient understanding of Husserl's text, then we can move on to Derrida's introduction, with the same *caveat* as before.

Such would be the chapter, all of it, with a footnote appended – in all seriousness – that this is only one possible way to teach Derrida. No true pedagogy can be reduced to a formula, even though every act of teaching runs the risk of falling into the programmed, the institutionally constrained, gesture and structure. Before any teacher-student relationship, there is always the face-to-face with the other, and this remains the case, whether I am speaking to another person, or whether I am reading a given text. In my explication below, there is, doubtless, an element of the formulaic, the pre-programmed, and this, in no small measure, comes about because I am responding yet again to a demand that I produce an chapter which inscribes business as usual, and because I am put in a position of having to respond in a manner that replicates and reiterates the fiction of response, as if it were the first time, as if we were beginning, the first time, every time . . .

III PRETEXT

Starting, then, from the beginning, as it were, there are quite a few ways that the first two words of my title could be read. To take just two: on the one hand, the phrase 'teaching Derrida' suggests – foolishly – that one could teach Jacques Derrida, were he still alive. What a notion, the idea that one could teach Derrida anything, so comprehensive his knowledge, so astute, so finely tuned, his thinking and his analytical and reading abilities, his powers of reasoning, his sense of how the finer and more occluded nuances of any form of thought or text are. How absurd, then, to believe that one could or would attempt to 'teach Derrida'. Having dismissed this patently ridiculous idea, the other reading of the title – one other reading of the title – is that someone, possibly me, though several or even many others, might try to *teach* (you how to read, and so learn from) *Derrida*, that is to say the texts that are signed in his name. (Before going any further, you should not assume that the proper name is anything other than a shorthand for the texts, in all their multiple complexities and rigorous arguments. You should never allow sloppy thinking of the kind that says a person's life or some aspect of their public persona, their private psyche, or, for that matter, their choice in ties somehow indicates a shortcut to understanding the work they produce.)

So, on the one hand . . . on the other hand . . . I have begun by drawing your attention to something – in this case my title – which is conventionally a mode of shorthand, a signpost at best, and not always given over therefore to the close scrutiny of reading that the text 'proper' is delivered. In doing so, I have complicated your comprehension of both the conventions of what it is proper to read, and also how one reads a title. In doing so, I have asked you to submit the marginal element, the title, to a double reading, both of which – despite what I say about the absurdity of assuming that one could teach Derrida anything (and clearly there were those who did, as is reflected in Derrida's immense learning, and also in those proper names he acknowledges as having learnt from, being in love with, apropos their texts and thought, and so on) – are equally valid readings of the semantic content and structure. On the one hand, then, teaching *Derrida*; on the other hand, *teaching* Derrida, my italics being added in order to reiterate through graphic stress where meaning resides in the otherwise undecidable written sign.

In doing this, in a very small, local, and highly simplified fashion, I am trying to orientate you through my act of reading, in what I would like to call the performative gesture of my reflection on the title by which my reading does not simply comment on its subject but actively does what it is talking about – that is to say, to teach through the illustration or example of a reading – to a particular approach to analysis. This approach is, you'll note, dictated by what I am reading, in this case, the language of a title, and its singular form. This is not a method of reading, for the reason that, inasmuch as I am responding to the singularity of a given textual form, I have to shape my reading according to that form or structure. It is only the attention to textual form or semantic content that I can carry from the brief discussion of a title to, say, the consideration of a line of poetry, or the work of particular metaphors in a novel, play or short story. A method would assume an absolutely repeated programme of analysis grounded in the first place in an a priori methodology or theory of reading. This, clearly, cannot be the case. This singular approach or, instead, say, the approach to singularity (which, appearances, to the contrary, is not the same), is one I have developed from reading Derrida, and which I take to be just one minute, very localized dimension (certainly not everything), not extracted from or illustrative of a 'Derridean theory of reading', so-called (as if there were such a thing), so much as a learnt mode of attentiveness the contours of which take place from time to time, on this occasion or that, and which, at best we might describe, idiomatically, as *what Derrida does*.

What this comes down to, therefore, is that, from the unpacking of the title in a movement that reads *on the one hand* and *on the other hand*, I have moved towards a third reading available in the title. For the title is one which eschews, albeit indirectly, any idea that the texts of Jacques Derrida can be reduced to or read, if faithfully, so as to produce, a method, theory, or programme of reading, critical analysis or exegesis. The third reading, one which I have been taught, I believe, from reading Derrida, is one that says 'teaching Derrida' is just that: what Derrida does, in writing or, putting this slightly differently, *Derrida teaches* (this inasmuch – and this is much – as Derrida serves to illustrate the forms of that which he opens to the beginnings of an exhaustive reading). Derrida is the one who teaches, the text that is signed by the name of Derrida is, first and foremost, in its patient readings or gestures towards a reading that is never completed, a teaching text. The writing of Jacques Derrida is not merely a text for someone to teach from (though it is also, and very much that), but principally a text that teaches, if you read it carefully and patiently. So, I cannot teach Derrida anything, but Derrida remains to teach me, and all who would be good readers, how to read in his wake.

Where does this leave us though, in an essay which claims to be about 'teaching Derrida', in the sense that, situated [in its original, shorter version] as this essay is in a collection called something like 'teaching theory', it has already been claimed that the notion of theory is suspect, at least as this term, theory, and the ideas that underpin the use of such a term, are problematized as soon as one speaks of Derrida? I am already underway here, I am in the midst of trying to explore or reflect on what Derrida might be able to teach you, or, putting this a little more baldly, *to teach you Derrida teaching, to teach you (teaching) Derrida*. I put 'teaching' in parentheses here, by the way, for if it is admitted that Derrida does nothing if he does not teach, then the proper name says it all; it already announces that teaching is taking place, whether or not you're receiving that.

So, how to proceed? I must be highly schematic here, if I am to begin even to gesture towards how one teaches, or hopes to teach Derrida. (1) I must first dismiss the notion – I've already begun this – that 'what Derrida does' can be produced as a theory, methodology or programme. Part of this is to ask you to dissociate for yourselves the association of the proper name 'Derrida' with the notion or quasi-concept bandied around in Departments of English and elsewhere of 'deconstruction', as if this term were the name of a theory. (2) I must then illustrate for you how, disabused of the notion that what Derrida does can be transformed into a theory or is already a theory, you might attempt to begin a reading of Derrida that teaches you not only how to read Derrida freed from the search for a theory, but also to read so as to be taught by Derrida. This I will attempt here through two alternative approaches.

Before I describe these approaches to reading Derrida, I should add another caveat here. These are far from being the only ways one might orientate oneself to Derrida, and so allow Derrida to teach (in truth Derrida never ceases teaching; but whether we learn, that is another matter). What I can say, however, is that both approaches to beginning the reading of how Derrida reads, how Derrida teaches and how reading Derrida reading can teach you how to read after Derrida, have proved not ineffectual in teaching Derrida (as opposed to teaching deconstruction; if you want that, look somewhere else, stop reading now; of course, if that's what you do want, I'd have to say that you've already stopped reading or, in fact, you've never begun; you're simply avoiding reading – and therefore thinking – at all costs, and I can't help you). So, two approaches to Derrida, approaching Derrida, as if for the first time: (3) the first approach is to take a single text by Derrida (even one essay or chapter in one of Derrida's publications might well prove overwhelming, but one has to start somewhere), and to read this alongside the text or texts that Derrida reads. In short, read Derrida reading, follow along with Derrida, and listen with Derrida to what the other text has to say, because teaching always begins with listening. (4) The second approach involves taking a small passage from an essay by Derrida and unpacking it line-by-line, word-by-word, letting it dictate to you, leading you in different directions. This is what I propose to set out here, in teaching Derrida.

No pressure then.

IV DENEGATIONS

The first part, consisting of, let's call it, clearing the ground or, to employ a word used by Derrida as the title of an essay, denegations, should not take up too much space here. Denegation, by the way, is not a neologism; this is the first denegation. I halt almost immediately here before getting underway for the reason that, as with the word 'deconstruction', denegation is one of those words that some bad readers of Derrida claim is a neologism, something Derrida has fabricated, allegedly needlessly. This is just ignorance, if not stupidity, a kind of verbal chauvinism, the perpetuator of which being unable or unwilling to imagine there are more words in heaven and earth than are dreamt of in a given person's lexicon. Denegation is taken from the verb *denegate*, a now obscure word used in its earliest sources, like 'deconstruction', in largely legal contexts, derived from the Latin *denegare*, meaning to deny or refuse to grant.

But, to denegate: deconstruction is not a neologism coined by Jacques Derrida, any more than is 'deconstructionism', which the *OED* inaccurately claims, very unhelpfully, to be 'the theory or practice of deconstruction'. That idiocy aside, which, unfortunately, is not confined to the dictionary, 'deconstruction' is still not, nor was it ever as far as Derrida was concerned, what the *OED* defines as 'a strategy of critical analysis . . . directed towards exposing unquestioned metaphysical assumptions and internal contradictions in philosophical and literary language'. There are, to be fair, a few grains, if not of truth, then at least resemblance to a much dried-up kernel extracted from Derrida's writings by many commentators, pro- and anti-, on Derrida's work. This is not the place to go into these, especially as I intend to do no more here than deny that deconstruction, so-called, is a methodology or 'strategy of critical analysis'. The argument is too large, too complex, but Derrida's resurrection of a very old French – and, subsequently, English – word, was only ever a strategic resuscitation for the purposes of local translation from German, specifically German philosophical, *phenomenological* discourse found at work in the text of Martin Heidegger, in particular philosophical contexts. It did not give a name to a practice or theory; neither did Derrida ever claim this, nor did his use of the word equate with the analytical procedure he followed in those places where the word 'deconstruction' was employed, whether in its first uses by Derrida or subsequently, in those texts where he spoke either of the impossibility of defining it, thus or at all, or when he repudiated or denegated its association with a programme of reading or literary theory. Over the years, from the late 1960s, when the term 'deconstruction' first surfaced in his writing, almost until his death, Derrida made a number of statements, usually, but not exclusively, as responses in interviews, and with increasing frequency, to the effect that deconstruction was not a method or mode, and, whatever it was, he explained, that he employed the term for, with all kinds of philosophical rigour and attendant caution, these uses were provisional, strategic, and above all incommensurable with any sense that 'deconstruction' was what one did, that someone could 'deconstruct', that there was sufficient evidence in Derrida's writing which one could extract, combine, and put to work as a method of repeatable critical intervention in texts (as implied in the *OED*'s definition; for some of Derrida's remarks *contra* deconstruction as methodology or programme, see the following: 1984, 124; 1985, 273–5; 1996, 218; 2000b, 288, 297; 2001b, 18–19).

V TO BE DONE WITH DECONSTRUCTION

So, to be done with 'deconstruction', the word as nominal indicator of a method for reading; it remains, perhaps, to give one example of Derrida's cautious usage of the term against the more widespread misrepresentation, and unpack it in as careful a reading as space will permit. The quotation to follow is taken from one of three publications of Derrida's in 1967, translated subsequently as *Speech and Phenomena*. Here, Derrida is responding to, and elaborating on, the founder of modern phenomenology Edmund Husserl's (1859–1938) discussion of the role of language in the expression of Being. Husserl had departed from dominant trends in philosophical and scientific thought by stressing the significance of subjective experience in our orientation in and translation of the objective phenomena that make up our worlds. In communicating that experience and the impression left on us – whether to ourselves or others – Husserl drew the distinction between the subjective production of meaning and the object or phenomena being deter-mined. Thus, for Husserl, and subsequent philosophers such as his student, Martin Heidegger, language and related semantic structures were crucial to the subject's apprehension of itself and the nature of its being. Derrida thus remarks of Husserl's analysis and comprehension of meaning's relation to Being that '[t]he prerogative of being cannot withstand the deconstruction of the word', following this almost immediately with the question, apropos the verb 'to be', '[b]ut why does using words get mixed up with the determination of being in general as presence?' (1973, 74). (A small but necessary parenthetical observation: *être* in French, *sein* in German; both are indicative of the verb, 'to be' and the condition of being, the point being that, unlike in English, the separation between meaning and being is not absolutely separated, except through the varying contexts within which one uses such terms.)

By indicating what he calls the 'prerogative of being', Derrida signals the privilege given to our being, literally the right accorded in discussions of humanity and existence to being's ontology, the sheer *being* of being, if you will, or, as Heidegger would have it, the *Being of beings*. It is as if, in this privilege, what constitutes being is a given: life, consciousness of existence and therefore self-consciousness ('I think therefore I am'), and the apparent, self-evident presence of one being to another, or the assumption of presence. Yet, as Derrida remarks of this presumptive understanding, the very idea of such a prerogative must immediately give way before the word, before language, articulation, expression, inscription. The word giveth life, we might say, but the word – not another being but language itself – deconstructs. Putting this another way, as soon as there is language, presence, meaning, being – all are subject to an articulation that divides and differentiates, which marks a difference between being and non-being, one being and another, and which, moreover, marks the difference both spatially (I am here/I am not here; he is here/she is there) and temporally (I was not here/I will no longer be here). Language serves to announce being. But it also undermines the absolute presence and permanence of being (hence Derrida's question, following on from the assertion, which I also quoted). It should also be pointed out that Derrida's phrase 'the deconstruction of the word' is available to a double, self-differentiating reading. It operates as if it were a double genitive. On the one hand, it is the word that 'deconstructs' pure presence, pure identity. In giving meaning to being by announcing 'being', 'to be', 'I am' and so on, it differentiates, it doubles, divides, displaces, and defers, one from another, endlessly. On the other hand, the word – that is, the symbol or signifier that bears and apparently guarantees the unicity, the univocity, of meaning, the undifferentiated meaning of being and the being of meaning – is deconstructed. It deconstructs itself. How can this be so? The meaning of any word is never intrinsic to itself. It is always reliant on the context in which it is found or in which it finds itself, and its meaning is also dependent on the time it takes for it to be understood. Meaning, like Being, is never given, self-sufficient, but only produced through the interrelated and differentiating structures of space and temporality.

Let's pause. There is a lot to take in here. I'm asking you, indirectly, to think about matters apparently beyond the limits of literary criticism. Yet, if language as that which gives meaning and identity to otherwise undifferentiated being – indeed, if it names being itself as differentiated through an act of naming and giving meaning – well, is this not what literature does? Literature gathers together language in various ways, heterogeneously informed and hybrid in presentation, in which one reads and so discerns what one takes to be the meaning of beings, in other locations, with identities other than our own, from different cultures and historical periods, or from cultures distinct from those by which we define ourselves.

That being said – and it's much, a large question and equally broad claim – if you return to my discussion of that one sentence of Derrida's, you will notice that I have anticipated what I had said would be the final part of my essay, in however diminished, small or local a manner. Recall: I argued that one way one teaches, and indeed learns from Derrida, is through the close reading of a given word or passage, being attentive to its contexts. To this, I have to add the caveat that one must realize one cannot limit oneself to a single context, and nor can one suppose that contexts can be either exhausted or that they are exclusive. That said, in starting from the departure point of challenging the claims concerning deconstruction as a methodology, I have had to resort to the kind of detailed close reading of phrase and word I had promised would conclude this essay. What is more, I have also had to point, in establishing a context, to how Derrida produces this particular line as, itself, a response, if not a reading. Let us remind ourselves that Derrida does not simply make the claim concerning language, meaning and being, but instead situates his commentary as a commentary *upon* a particular philosopher, Edmund Husserl, and a specific text, or texts by Husserl, about which I have somewhat violently summarized and sought to encapsulate in a reductive nutshell, in order to address *what Derrida does*. In, again, a small and local fashion, I have therefore also exceeded my schematic order, leaving it somewhat in ruins if you will, by sketching the kind of teaching that I advocate as another approach to Derrida. Without being able to keep to my order, I have already done what I have said I would do. Teaching Derrida involves such risks. It is impossible to stick to a path, not from any lack of discipline but because one is directed from some other place in the act of seeking to be as faithful as possible to the manner and spirit of Derrida's textual interventions and inventions.

VI INVENTIONS

This last word – inventions – interests Derrida greatly, as it does me also, having come to my attention through reading Derrida. As Derrida has occasion to mention, there are at least two meanings for the term. On the one hand, invention, conventionally, means to make something new that had never existed before. On the other hand, buried as a secret within its etymology, invention means to find that which was already there. This sense is far more radical than our more conventional use. To invent means to unearth or let in that which was there but invisible, hidden away yet always imminent, capable of arriving, of coming to pass. This is what the Latin *venire* means, signifying what is to come, what arrives, what can turn up, or what remains in the future, always awaiting its chance. Reading is thus an act of invention. It is a matter of pursuing patiently the meaning of a given text, whether a word, sentence, phrase, paragraph, institution, identity, or being, seeking for, and yet not expecting exactly, what is both there and not there, what is unavailable but in place nonetheless, and which may come to reveal itself – or not. Reading invents, it finds, and invention names this act of reading. In fact, following Derrida in this apprehension of invention, this is what I have just illustrated. Reading invention, I have invented ('found') invention's other meaning. I haven't invented that meaning; I haven't created it out of nothing, but I have invented it. I have invented – or dis-covered, uncovered – a reading that was awaiting my act of reading. I have therefore engaged in a performative speech act. Far from merely commenting on my subject, my language has acted out or performed the very thing I am talking about in the present paragraph. It is for this very reason that a patient reading, the kind which teaching Derrida can teach us, or which, let us just say, Derrida can teach us, can undo, disorder, ruin any anticipation of an order, a schema, a programme for reading, or even a methodology of repeatable procedures.

VII CONTINUANCE

Continuance: (a) the state of remaining in operation; remaining in a particular position or condition (b) a postponement or adjournment

So, having paused, turned back on myself, and finding that in my reading of a line or two I have done ahead of myself what I had promised I would do, I can now continue. If we presume that we can take a single text by Derrida, always supposing that we know what a 'single text' might be, how we might define it, and so on, which would it be? A text: what is meant by this? There are innumerable answers to this question, but for the purposes of this chapter, in an unreasonable and quite indefensible gesture (you'll have to take my word for this, I simply cannot go into everything here), I am going to take 'text' to be a non-synonymous term for 'book'.

I should say, however, that book does not define nor delimit the meaning of text. Nor is a text merely that which is 'written' in the narrow sense of marks on paper, papyrus, stone, computer or other screen, or whichever substrate for the remote communication of thoughts, images, representations and ideas you might care to imagine. It is certainly not a metaphor meant to suggest that nothing real exists, as some of the more intellectually bereft or challenged, or those aspiring to journalism have claimed with regard to Derrida or so-called 'deconstruction'. Something can be a 'text' or textual and yet be real, and to claim that everything is textual in no way denies reality any more than it can be taken to mean that there is no meaning or that one can read any meaning one wishes into the object of one's inquiry. If you think of 'textile', you might have a less misleading comprehension of what a 'text' can be: that is to say, a weave in different directions, and with different spatial relations of multiple threads, all of which, though different from one another, nonetheless according to particular conditions of 'weaving', enfolding, knotting, intertwining and so forth, produce a form. That form can change, and the textile weave, the means of producing the form, or let's call this an identity, can also change as a result of forces within the 'machinery' producing the textile. The 'machinery' can be society, historical conditions, an institution such as a government, the textile, the laws or an institution such as a university. The university can also be a machine producing 'weaves' of knowledge, interrelations of knowledge and its uses, and so on. A text need not be a book, therefore, and a book is a product of particular interweavings of cultural, social and political history that may determine its content and its reception at different times. At the same time, however, the ideas of book and author are also particular forms or identities woven out of acutely singular conditions and machineries.

Having said all that, let us remain with the convention of equating a text with a book. Teaching Derrida through particular texts to which he has signed his name is one possible way of being, if not more faithful to Derrida, then certainly less unfaithful to the spirit of Derrida. However, not all texts by Derrida are equally amenable to such an approach. Some remain – for me at least – positively recalcitrant to this. This has less to do with their respective accessibility or difficulty than my own ability to decipher them. That being said, however, certain of Derrida's publications, because of their relatively restricted focus – their ostensible focus – respond in their immediate navigations to fewer texts than others. One such 'text' would be *The Truth in Painting* (1987b), another, *Khora. On the Name* (1995b), a third, *Archive Fever* (1995a), a fourth. Another would be *Demeure: Fiction and Testimony* (2000a), and my last example 'On a Newly Arisen Apocalyptic Tone in Philosophy' (1993). There are many more, and equally there are many essays from which one could depart in this way, rather than seeking to come to terms with what looks like a book. But for now, I'll stay with the five just mentioned, narrowing to one in particular.

Taking a glance at my choices, the first thing to remark is the breadth of coverage here. *The Truth in Painting* discusses, among many things, four key texts (Plato, Kant, Hegel and Heidegger) in the history of philosophy on the discourse on painting, art and aesthetics. Kant's third *Critique*, Hegel's *Lectures on Aesthetics*, and Heidegger's *The Origin of the Work of Art* are the principal texts from which Derrida engages with particular passages, tropes, and what might be called, most conveniently, the assumptions of thinking within the limits of convention. *The Truth in Painting* is not, however, merely a study of the history of aesthetics in the discourse of philosophy, even though it is very much this, in however disguised a form, and into the frame of which Derrida places his own contribution, becoming part of the representation he seeks to frame, for he also situates singular analyses of the work of Italian artist Valerio Adami (b. 1935).

Archive Fever speaks to psychoanalysis and philosophy. Interrogating the idea and structure of the archive from its inception, its relation to memory, and the implications for the physical or material archive in the epoch of hypermedia, virtual realities and tele-technological modes of storage, Derrida pursues various threads throughout the labyrinth of Freud's writings, with a concentration on Freud's *Moses and Monotheism* and a response to that text by Yosef Yerushalmi, in the latter's *Freud's Moses: Judaism Terminable and Interminable*. Thus as a constant location in his exploration of the idea of the archive and memory, Derrida mediates between Freud and Yerushalmi, moving between what is said and what remains unsaid, between what is given Yerushalmi to read, and those blind spots in Yerushalmi's text or, to put this somewhat differently, that which Yerushalmi fails to address in Freud. This manner of approach to the two texts is somewhat similar to Derrida's approach to essays by Heidegger and Meyer Shapiro in the last chapter from *The Truth in Painting*, 'Restitutions of the Truth in Pointing [*pointure*]' (1987b, 255–382). Heidegger and Shapiro provide analyses of a painting by Van Gogh, and Derrida painstakingly works through both essays, examining their assumptions, perspectives, and again, blind spots, teaching us in the process how to read, how Heidegger and Shapiro read, and how they come to the limits of their respective readings because of certain conceptual and philosophical assumptions that unthinkingly govern their readings.

Khora (the title is an ancient Greek word, the meaning of which shifts depending on the context in which it is found) offers the reader a sustained engagement on Derrida's part with Plato, again, and one work by Plato in particular, the *Timeaus*. Exploring questions of space and spacing, in relation to the Greek term that is found at the heart of Plato's text, Derrida's essay unfolds a narrative and structure concerning representation, storytelling and form. *Demeure: Fiction and Testimony* considers the role of literature in acts of testimony and, bearing witness, relating both to the problem of the secret and the notion of the instant. It does so through an extended consideration of a short autobiographical story by Maurice Blanchot, *The Instant of My Death* (Blanchot and Derrida 2000a, 1–13), and provides what is at once a singular and exemplary critical reorientation on the connections and tensions between writing and history. Finally, with regard to the texts, I have chosen to illustrate the possibilities and impossibilities of teaching Derrida (a title I would amend as 'teaching Derrida instead of/before/after/beyond deconstruction', inviting you to consider what takes place in such an excessive and exaggerated title), there is Derrida's essay on Kant, 'On a Newly Arisen Apocalyptic Tone in Philosophy' (1993, 117–73). As with *Khora* and *Demeure*, this essay responds to, pursuing the rhythms and folds of, a single work, in this case, Kant's essay 'On a Newly Arisen Superior Tone in Philosophy' (Derrida 1993, 51–83), in order to investigate the question of 'tone' as a philosophical topic.

This is to give you a, hopefully not misleading, sense of the texts in question. In each, as in most of Derrida's publications, the focus is primarily on a single text, though not without inevitable reference to a vast body of knowledge and reading in passing, as well as to various concepts and quasi-concepts, threads and motifs from Derrida's own immense bibliography. (A small but important matter here: Derrida claims never to have written a 'book', that is to say, a collection of essays begun from a thesis or argument that remains in place in the act of composition. Rather, in writing in response to particular texts, or for specific occasions, Derrida's own texts shape themselves in response to an 'other' [an essay, an event, an institution] in that singular encounter, and subsequently become gathered in those collections we conventionally refer to as books. It is perhaps less important therefore that you read a Derrida 'book' from cover to cover in the conventional manner, than, in reading a particular essay, chapter, or in a number of cases, interviews – always a good starting point with Derrida – you pursue a particular idea, concept, term, focal point, across different texts, moving, let us offer an example, the responses to psychoanalysis from early essays to *The Post Card From Socrates to Freud and Beyond* (1987a), to the collection of essays in *Resistances of Psychoanalysis* (1998c) and of course *Archive Fever: A Freudian Impression* (1995a). Alternatively, reading through those texts that foreground the performative speech act, such as 'Signature Event Context' (in *Margins of Philosophy* [1982]), and *Psyche: Invention of the Other* (2007), will construct a different, though equally invaluable, experience of Derrida teaching one how to read well. This anticipates and recalls, whilst translating, my third signpost, above. There I had suggested the close reading of a small passage, word by word. As I will go on to comment, this takes you in two directions: on the one hand, it will lead you further into the labyrinthine weave of the given passage, deeper into its structures; on the other hand, it will also cause you to pause in the act of becoming entangled, and, thereby, out of that passage to other texts by Derrida, and by other critics, authors and philosophers also. Whilst that model of reading Derrida and teaching Derrida depends on a microtextual patience and attention, and also opens the reader to the endlessness of reading, the fact that a true reading can never come to an end [perhaps the most important thing that Derrida has to teach us, along with respect for the singularity of the other, and the experience of the event of encountering the other on the other's terms and not my own], in my parenthetical detour here, I am indicating pulling and pursuing – ravelling – if not a thread, then a certain skein, whether discursive or conceptual [not that the two are separable or necessarily distinct]. But there, I've got ahead of myself again, exceeded the limit, the order, and the frame dictated above.) How to proceed, then, faced with such texts as *The Truth in Painting* or *Archive Fever*: read – and if you teach, teach – that given text, but also include in your reading those texts to which Derrida responds. The temptation might arise that a secondary source should be included, such as a commentary on Derrida, from which one can fillet the various discussions of the Derrida text in question, but there is more than enough taking place in the interaction between Derrida and, say, Kant, Plato or Freud, and the patient inauguration of unpacking the phantasmic dialogue that Derrida stages will take a great deal of time. *Demeure* and 'On a Newly Arisen Apocalyptic Tone' appear in volumes with the text being read, Blanchot and Kant respectively.

VIII ADDRESSING DERRIDA

But, I imagine someone will say, I haven't shown you how to read or teach Derrida – no, for all the reasons that are embedded throughout this essay. To do this would be to add another layer, to produce a reading or analysis of Derrida 'reading' Plato, Kant or whoever. In all likelihood, it would not amount to a 'reading', that is to say, imagining one possible definition for the notion of reading, a discussion of the entire text. Instead, in being as faithful to the text of Derrida – pursuing patiently just one or two figures or ideas as they impose themselves on me from the vast web of thinking that presents itself in even the smallest of essays – and, what is more, in seeking to be faithful to the singularity of Derrida's 'virtual teaching' (because Derrida isn't present, because he can no longer be present, and that there is no presence except the ghost you imagine yourself to be encountering as you seek to read the text; none of this means that the trace of Derrida doesn't remain in full force, or that teaching doesn't take place) – it would take the consideration of only a word or two, as Derrida does in an essay on Joyce, or as I do with the phrase above concerning meaning, language and being, following the line, and playing out that thread. There is, and can only ever be, the experience of the encounter with Derrida's writing, one text at a time, and to suffer that encounter in the hope that a teaching will take place, will arrive or come to pass, but without the certainty that this will happen. Indeed, it may happen that it does take place for you, in you, in a manner whereby you become the addressee for whom Derrida writes, your being becomes translated through the 'deconstruction of the word'. But you won't know, necessarily, immediately, or immediately after, what you might think of as a first reading. What may have taken place does not equate simply with some facile notion of 'transferable skills'. Derrida's text is not available in this way, and, thought of in conventional pedagogical terms, might be said – and I risk this formula knowing already it will leave me open to charges of misapprehension – to be marked as, simultaneously, radically inventive, inaugural, and yet joyously 'useless'. There is an heroic, epic inutility in every page of Derrida's writing in its resistance to facile adaptation and application (unless one adamantly avoids 'going with the flow' in order to 'get with the programme') that stages an affirmative resistance to pedagogical business as usual, inviting in the process that one stop teaching and begin listening.

IX THE ENDS OF TEACHING, THE BEGINNING OF READING I

This takes me to one of two possible conclusions: first, an approach to 'teaching Derrida', or just approaching Derrida, on the grounds of selecting a small passage, already anticipated, paraphrased ahead of itself. Let me present to you a citation from *The Post Card*:

> You might read these *envois*[1] as the preface[2] to a book[3] that I[4] have not written.[5]
>
> It would have treated[6] that which proceeds from the *postes*,[7] *postes* of every genre,[8] to psychoanalysis.[9]
>
> Less in order to attempt a psychoanalysis of the postal effect[10] than to start from a singular[11] event,[12] Freudian[13] psychoanalysis, and to refer to a history[14] and a technology[15] of the *courrier*,[16] to some general theory[17] of the *envoi* and of everything[18] which by means of some telecommunication[19] allegedly *destines*[20] itself.
>
> The three last parts of the present work, 'To Speculate – on "Freud,"' 'Le facteur de la vérité', 'Du tout' are all different by virtue of their length, their circumstance or pretext, their manner and their dates.[21] But the preserve[22] the memory[23] of this project, occasionally even exhibit[24] it.
>
> As for the 'Envois' themselves, I do not know if their reading[25] is bearable.
>
> You might consider them, if you really wish to, as the remainders[26] of a recently destroyed correspondence.[27] Destroyed by fire[28] or by that which figuratively takes its place,[29] more certain of leaving nothing out of the reach of what I would like to call the tongue of fire, not even the cinders,[30] if cinders there are [*s'il y a là cendre*].[31]
>
> Save [*fors*][32] a chance.[33]

A correspondence: this is still to say too much, or too little. Perhaps it was not one (But more or less) nor very correspondent. This still remains[34] to be decided.[35]

Today, the seventh of September nineteen seventy-nine,[36] there are but *envois*, only *envois*, from which whatever was spared or if you prefer 'saved'[37] (I already hear murmured 'registered,'[38] as is said for a kind of receipt[39]) will have been due, yes, due to a very strange principle of selection, and which for my part, even today, I consider questionable, as, moreover, the grate,[40] the filter,[41] and the economy[42] of sorting can be on every occasion,[43] especially if they destine for preservation, not to say for the archive.[44] In a word, I rigorously do not approve of this principle. I denounce it ceaselessly, and in this respect reconciliation is impossible.[45] It will be seen to what extent I insist on this on the way. But it was my *due*[46] to give in to it, and it is up to all of you to tell me why.

Up to you [*toi*][47] first: I await only one response and it falls[48] to you. Thus I apostrophize.[49] This too is a genre one can afford oneself, the apostrophe.[50] A genre and a tone.[51] The word – apostrophizes – speaks of the words addressed[52] to the singular[53] one, a live interpellation (the man of discourse or writing interrupts[54] the continuous development of the sequence,[55] abruptly turns[56] toward someone, that is, something, addresses himself to you), but the word also speaks of the address to be detoured.[57] (1987a, 3–4)

You will note that the extract is marked. A good part of its lexicon is enumerated. Fifty-eight superscript numbers taking on the appearance of footnotes, but leading to none, address themselves to you. They demand your attention, even though they are not the only choices I could have made. You are expected to read the words on which they hang, and you are asked to reflect on what depends on such words in the text of Jacques Derrida. Were I teaching 'Derrida' (my quotation marks indicate the title of a module or course, of course), I might begin with just such a passage. Taking the words marked – and other readers of Derrida would doubtless choose others still in this excerpt – I would begin, again and again, to discuss the words, how they might touch upon one another, and how they might be said to gesture towards everything that is in Derrida – everything, as Derrida remarks somewhere, and the rest. But this would only be the inaugural gesture, one indicating that we have yet to begin, and that before beginning any reading, there has to be the fiction of an orientation, in this case around a given lexicon, as the words in question suggest themselves to me. This would not excuse one from the act of reading. It would not be a substitute for reading. Rather it might be taken to be the beginnings of a process whereby one might start to think the question of how such words operate in Derrida's text, how each would serve to signify an endless work, the work of reading. The task, as Derrida remarks on the question of questioning a certain hegemony over forms of knowledge (and, one might suggest, over the very question, a politics, of teaching), 'is infinite'. However, 'if the task is infinite', Derrida continues

... it is not only because there will always be more to do ... [B]eyond all the analyses, which cannot but remain incomplete, the task is infinite for a reason

of another order, which, in a certain way, folds or interrupts the homogeneous unfolding of an endless progress – and finishes the infinite. (Derrida
2002a, 65)

In the face of a demand – from that anonymous reader for one – that one 'objectify'
knowledge (that knowledge or those knowledges in particular which is/are signified in the name of Jacques Derrida) in order, supposedly, to 'get at', gain access to,
the 'truth' of Jacques Derrida (and thereby give oneself permission to stop reading
– to stop reading before one begins on the order of objectification in the service of
truth), one's only response can be to take responsibility, in order that one 'leaves
room for a new type of question about this very determination of the infinite
task that retains an essential relation with the process of knowledge as process of
objectification' (Derrida 2002a, 65).

X *THE ENDS OF TEACHING, THE BEGINNING OF READING II: OF DARK SENTENCES AND GNOMES:[2] TOWARDS A READING OF* OF GRAMMATOLOGY

My second 'conclusion', which is really a response to that which opens itself to me,
is that, taking a given text, let us say, *Of Grammatology*, the agreement will be that I
read until a sentence makes itself felt. At once legible and yet enigmatic, it indicates
a problem for knowledge, which requires, as part of a response, thought, opinion,
judgement, as the axes of a reading to come.

Where does one begin in *Of Grammatology*? There must be a kind of 'reading
experiment', a process of construal through the various folds and turns of the text,
which wagers everything on the possibility that something can be invented. What
will I find, this time? Where will it lead? Perhaps nowhere, or to a place where I
return to myself, though different, touched by a difference. I am sentenced to a reading, with which I will never have done, as I follow, sentence by sentence, sentence
after sentence, feeling almost blindly through a labyrinth which promises to open
onto an abyss. Way of thinking, opinion, an authoritative decision or judgement.

A phrase to which I find myself returning repeatedly is '"signifier of the signifier"
["*signifiant du signifiant*"]' (1976, 7/11) near the beginning of *Of Grammatology*,
and the sentence of which it is a part. This phrase is idiomatic, perhaps axiomatic,
in that, performatively, it stages not only its own radical instability, an instability
arising out of, even as it constitutes and so projects, an undecidability; additionally,
it also gives expression and place to the 'truth', if you will, of Derrida's radically
expanded conception of 'writing', summed up by Sarah Kofman, in the observation that '*l'écriture est la différence, l'espacement orginaire de soi avec soi*' ['writing is
difference, the originary spacing of itself by itself'] (Kofman 1984, 20). It marks
that which is, simultaneously, *finite* and *endless*, signalling, countersigning perhaps,
as one phrase has it, the end of the book and the beginning of writing. Always
already underway, always already interrupting, folding back, enfolding, unfolding and cutting into, even as it erupts out of, itself, '*signifiant du signifiant*' marks

that which *just is* writing, the articulation of disarticulation: '*tissu de différences,* [*l'écriture*] *est toujours hétérogéne. Sans identité propre, ouvert sur son dehors*' ['tissue of differences, writing is always heterogeneous, Without proper identity, open on its outside'] (Kofman 1984, 16).

The work of doubling and iterability informs the phrase, but also disturbs logical or grammatical order, as well as sense, and could take up some time here. Doubled in its appearance, the phrase – operating in the manner of an idiom or axiom – maintains its doubling; doubling itself as it itself becomes redoubled before our eyes, it threatens to engulf or overwhelm. I find myself 'adrift in the threat of limitlessness', and in this my experience doubles that of the simple, though enigmatic, form. However, there is an initial sense of paradox. For, while apparently limitless, or threatening illimitability, the expression leaves both reader and idiom 'all at sea', as it were, the expression remains within itself, folding back on itself. Simultaneously, it finds 'itself recaptured within that play' that promises the erasure of limits; and so, in this recuperation, it appears 'brought back to its own finitude at the very moment when its limits seem to disappear' ('inflation', I am tempted to say, in a partial citation, and in an iterable gesture, 'absolute inflation, inflation itself' [1976, 6]).

Its doubling thus reduplicated, the perhaps axiomatic expression becomes replayed in a single page, and also ironized through the introduction of quotation marks, in the sentence where it appears, following the observation that, 'In all senses of the word, [and the word is writing, not *logos*] writing thus *comprehends* language' (1976, 7). Here is the sentence:

> Not that the word 'writing' has ceased to designate the signifier of the signifier [this is already the second appearance of the phrase, the first shortly before the line I am quoting, it being given in italics, its graphic and material condition emphasized], but it appears, strange as it may seem, that 'signifier of the signifier' *no longer* defines accidental doubling and fallen secondarity. (1976, 7; emphasis added)

There has been a graphic play on and of the words in their given form leading up to this particular sentence, thus:

> By a hardly perceptible necessity, it seems as though the concept of writing . . . no longer designating the exterior surface, the insubstantial double of a major signifier, *the signifer of the signifier* – is beginning to go beyond the extension of writing. (1976, 6–7)

So, from '*the signifier of the signifier*' (italics) to signifier of the signifier (without quotation marks, no italics, shortly to be cited in the sentence that frames it), and, thence, to 'signifier of the signifier' (in quotation marks, in that sentence from which I have drawn the phrase in order to begin), none of the differences of which can be heard, save for the abandonment of that first definite article. With a degree of circumspection all too necessary here, Derrida proposes a transformation in the signification of the concept of writing, which, we should recall, is observed in 1967. The historical moment of inscription is worth noting, albeit in passing, given the sudden coming-to-appear, and frequency, of '*aujourdhui*' in the '*exergue*', a frequency a little downplayed by Gayatri Spivak's omission of the first reference to a 'today', and the world or planet *today*, at the end of the first paragraph (Derrida 1976, 3); and from here to the following page, 'But *today* something lets itself appear as such, allows it a kind of takeover without our being able to translate this novelty into clear cut notions of mutation, explicitation, accumulation, revolution, or tradition. These values belong no doubt to the system whose dislocation is *today* presented as such . . . only within a logocentric epoch' (1976, 4). Of course, *today* appears and is always already problematized, erupting within any present moment. Which today is spoken (of) here? What would constitute the *today* that causes Derrida to pause with intense reflective concern about what is taking place, what is coming to take place within an epoch, which, presumably, encompasses that *today* even as, in not being specified, singular and yet without date, *today* is the trace of something excessive, overflowing the limits of (the thinking of) an epoch, or any thinking that is implied by the notion of epochality?

In that sentence where *signifier of the signifier* appears, italicized, it does so no longer as the equivalent of the concept of writing conventionally and traditionally received or designated. In clearing the ground through the accumulation and signification of negation, in a supplementary multiplication, expansion, explication, *and* slippage (as if we were, in fact, still the witnesses, as well as the heirs, of the generative effects of an insubstantial double), Derrida engages in the construction of a sentence in which writing appears to begin to go beyond the mere extension of writing, in its *comprehension* of that conventionally conceived supplementary form. This final phrase, 'extension of writing' also does double work, for, on the one hand, it signifies the extension that writing just is in any logocentric system, the extension or prosthesis of voice and presence, while, on the other hand, Derrida's supplementary iteration extends writing or demonstrates writing extending itself beyond itself in a performative gesture of its own operation and excessive reduplication, without recuperation into a final signified, a presence, or some anterior presence or metaphysical concept. Thus begins the destabilizing effects of a writing which, no longer just the signifier of some (transcendental or metaphysical) signifier, via the ruse or illusion of presence, comes into its own, through the iterable and graphic morphology – graphemorphology or grammamorphology – of the phrase 'signifier of the signifier'.

One could say much more about this phrase, which in its performative play both invites commentary and hints at the exhaustion of that commentary without its having reached an end. However, I am only gesturing towards that as a possible scene of reading. For now, this is what follows:

> 'Signifier of the signifier' describes on the contrary the movement of language: in its origin, to be sure, but one can already suspect that an origin whose structure can be expressed as 'signifier of the signifier' conceals and erases itself in its own production. There the signified always already functions as a signifier. (1976, 7)

The question of that which is questioned implicitly under the sign of an 'origin' in this sentence aside (for the moment at least), it is of course both obvious and important that one reiterates a structural matter here, a matter which, whilst being initially or provisionally structural, is not simply, if ever, merely formal, a retreat into formalism, or symptomatic of any other such misreading.

Clearly, 'signifier^1', that is to say, the first mark on the page in the quasi-idiom 'signifier^1 of the signifier^2', or let us call it, for argument's sake, 'A' is, on the one hand, that which signifies 'signifier'^{2}, or, provisionally, B. On the other hand, A is also that which is being signified by B, signifier^1 being the signified of signifier^2, as if the phrase operated according to the logic of the double genitive. In effect, one could substitute the first for the second, supposing each to be so designated, and the work of expression remains apparently the same. So A signifies B but A is, momentarily in the two-way passage, the signified of B. The logic of the sentence does nothing to resolve the installation of such destabilization. It cannot: for the destabilization or explication, that motion by which the idiom unfolds itself, expanding beyond itself, whilst remaining in its own bounds, is always already there, and on which, the most fundamental semantic coherence is dependent. Meaning is thus structured around the most disquieting and radical undecidability. Indeed, 'signifier of the signifier', as formal phrase, only serves to promote that which is, simultaneously, adrift and recaptured, limitless and finite. If, instead of referring to A and B, we refer to A^1 and A^2, this hardly helps, if one requires help in the sense of a reduction or simplification of the ineluctable motion that is at work. What might be done, however, is to pursue a certain mathematical work within language, that frees language from the assumptions of its representational subordination, while also reminding us of the valency of writing, and why, within the history of metaphysics, writing is read as threat, as dead, exterior, and so on. Logic cannot save us either, for in what might look like a parody of representation or a parodic meditation *chez* Badiou, mathematical logic only tends to the 'end' of proving – as if such a thing were possible – an arche-originary deconstruction as that which is writing in the expanded Derridean sense, and as that which haunts writing as the concept put to work in the service of metaphysics and logocentrism.[3]

But this is only a preliminary step, admittedly, one by which we appear to travel not at all. If there is any meagre merit here it is that, for me at least, the performative work of the phrase inaugurates a double gesture of ravelling, of pulling at a thread, which one might pursue throughout *Grammatology* (see, for example [though to remark, of course, the caution that Derrida issues regarding the problem of exemplarity early on], following a certain clew of one's own discerning, through pages 17, 21, 23, 30, 36, 37, 40, 43, 47, 49, 50, 56, and so forth, and so on, etc. . . . to 313, where Derrida speculates on 'the power of exteriority as constitutive of interiority: of speech, of signified meaning, of the present as such in the sense in which I said . . . that the representative mortal doubling-halving constituted the living present, without adding itself to presence; or rather constituted it, paradoxically, by being added to it. The question is of an originary supplement [signifier of the signifier], if this absurd expression may be risked, totally unacceptable as it is within classical logic' [1976, 313]), undoing particular nodal points in a matrix, even as we weave a particular shape, constituting ourselves as the axis of another matrix, one of our own production but also one which engenders the reader as its subject. (In this, I am referring to Derrida's discussion of 'a theoretical matrix' and the 'axis' of a reading that should free itself from the 'classical categories of history' [1976, lxxxix].) Returning to the phrase, as will be equally obvious, language, that is to say, spoken language and the privilege given that through phonocentric and logocentric assumptions, which seeks in what Derrida calls 'our epoch' to displace and debase writing, cannot escape that which it remarks – in short, saying aloud 'the signifier of the signifier' or 'signifier of the signifier' does not solve the 'problem' of which is which, which signifier signifies which signifier and is the supplement of the other, or indeed the other's supplement, the other as supplement, supplement of the other. (In this, I would suggest, albeit with the benefit of hindsight, we might read an anticipation of the inscription of a much later phrase: *tout autre est tout autre*.) Every time I read the phrase aloud, every time I give voice to the phrase, I only serve to reintroduce writing, the structure and play of which comprehends language, grasping, encompassing, bringing together language in its own matrix, a matrix which reforms itself around the axis of the speaking subject, and, constituting that subject in the process, to the finitude of a limitless matrix 'at the very moment when the limits seem [about] to disappear'. Thus, 'origin', which in the first sentence cited refers not to an absolute origin, or the possibility of thinking such a thing, but instead, an iterable 'origin' that appears every time there is language. Or to put this slightly differently, the axis that I name here 'origin' (an origin that takes place through the articulation I make and *every time I do so*) is constituted, comprehended, in and through the reformulation of the phrase expressed as 'signifier of the signifier'.

Clearly, there is a quite powerful and subtle performative at work in the opening, which one might trace back to the preface and the, for me, interesting phrase 'theoretical matrix', from the first sentence (1976, lxxxix). As we all know there are both immediate and supplementary readings, transparent readings and strong readings to be mined or invented. This phrase is evidence of that, for, on the one hand, the 'theoretical matrix' may well be taken or mis-taken as one which Derrida will propose. On the other hand, whilst Derrida is about to embark on the constitution of a matrix, or, at the very least, the invention of one, it is a matrix generated by a constellation of theoretical models and paradigms. The gathering Derrida undertakes maps an epoch, which remains ours, and with which we are not yet done. At the same time, while Derrida suggests that the critical concepts belong to the matrix, this is not, he cautions, to imply that these are examples, for the notion of the example leads one to think of relation. The example is exemplary of that which, greater than itself, can be deduced or adduced from it. There may be a non-synonymous relation, a 'relation without relation', but that is as much, if not more, a generation that is ours rather than being that which we can assign to another's proper name, or historical moment, as in the phrase 'the "age" of Hegel'. As Derrida cautions, an age already in the past is 'in fact constituted in every respect as a *text*'; that is to say, a matrix is constituted through the assemblage or bricolage of reading, which has as its axis, the reading subject, the subject's historicity, its

being or ontology. In the comprehension of this axis, and through that the constitution of one's own subjectivity and historicity, one has the responsibility to begin
reading *after* Derrida, so as to question, as Derrida has it, the classical categories
of history, as these are informed and serve to inform the hegemonic powers of
logocentrism and phonocentrism, in that epoch within which we find ourselves
remaining, suspended.

To begin to open up such comprehension, this is what it would mean to teach
Derrida, and this is why the ends of teaching must be found in the beginning of
reading, again, and again.

13

'The strong dead return': Harold Bloom's Daemonic Shades

He becomes an echo of someone else's music, an actor of a part that has
not been written for him.

Oscar Wilde, The Picture of Dorian Gray

What able-bodied man . . . does not wish . . . to bedevil his ecstasy?

Marquis de Sade

I REFLECTIONS ON READING

'Theory', that illusory, yet all-too-problematic will-o'-the-wisp amongst critics is,
some of them would *still* have you believe, that which transgresses. It breaks the
contract with its subjects, literature and culture. It is transgressive of art, the text, and
all aesthetic forms available to sensuous apprehension. Is this really the case, or does
so-called 'theory' transgress in another fashion, by confessing what is transgressive
about language in the first place? 'Theory', or, let us say, philosophically inflected language reflecting on how language operates in given discursive and historical frames,
transgresses by breaking the silent accord between word and world, by giving away
the secret of our being: that we are all fallen, we have all transgressed through the
necessity of language (whether verbal or visual, oral or graphic) as the only medium
available to re-present precisely what we have lost in being – becoming – human.
To be human means to have fallen, to have stepped irrevocably and irreversibly over
the boundary between a perception of a full being we believe might once have been
ours, but of which we can never be certain. And so, we write. Or paint. Or make
films, take photographs, carve, create installations, and so on, producing form after
form of 'language' or 'text', to give indirect apprehension and 'poetic' expression to
the truth of being. Being fallen: this is to be, and so to be transgressive. 'Theory', in
theory (as it were), opens our eyes to the fallen condition, and relies on the errant
or literary nature of language in order to trace the fall, the drift, that which disinters
itself from within the very heart of any textual or structural matrix shaped so as to
generate and maintain the illusion of a stable meaning.

That, at the very least, underwrites certain so-called theoretical reflections or
commentaries on what is profoundly disturbing or touching about art. In considering what 'theory' or criticism, criticism interested in asking of itself why it
concerns itself with what remains impossible to define as such, seeks to reveal,
thereby making blatant the transgression that is always already at work in any

mode of representation (that is the very break or rupture that necessitates modes of representation in order to re-present what is no longer available), I will take a well-known, and perhaps misunderstood or misrepresented critical figure, or, to invert this, I will consider the haunting of criticism by a particular figural mode, which inhabits, without becoming reconciled with, the critical perception that it enables without the one – criticism, theory – becoming reconciled with the other – the figural other, figure of the other, other of figurality. The present chapter will sketch a series of adumbrated notes towards a reading of particular aspects of Harold Bloom's well-known theory of poetry presented in *The Anxiety of Influence*. That theory is too well known to warrant reductive paraphrase here. Therefore, these notes are also belated responses in a manner I take to be appropriate to this most obvious and yet enigmatic of critical works. In this sketch, I seek to attend to how the strong dead return, not for poets, as Bloom claims (though I am not debating the accuracy or otherwise of what must remain hypothetical). Instead, I turn to the many returns that haunt – and so structure, even as they cause to bring about the destinerrance of that structure's premise – Bloom's theory, albeit in an admittedly oblique manner, in order to suggest that Bloom's great insight is into the very thing he cannot admit directly: that to write and read critically is to live with ghosts, to be, in effect, a ghost writer, whose uncanny work is always, in one manner or another, an act of doubling and repetition.

II BEGINNING, WITH ITERABILITY (THE FALL)

In the beginning was reiteration and response – or, what I would like to describe as alterity's introjection. Repetition, as a reaction to, and acknowledgement of the other, then: a God perhaps, but in the greater narrative that Harold Bloom wishes to construct as the skeletal structure of *The Anxiety of Influence: A Theory of Poetry*, this other is what he calls '*the poet in a poet*, or the aboriginal poetic self' (1973, 11). Note the juxtaposition, if you will, in a series of interplays here: we read the motion of past and present, certainly. But also absence and presence, and definite article and indefinite article, the latter opening up a movement from generation to generation in the anonymity of abyssal, indefinite substitutions for, incomplete supplements of, the One. Note, too, implicit in Bloom's schema, the counterpoint of material and immaterial, physical and metaphysical, that subject, *a poet*, who merely lives, and the other which lives beyond living, which lives on, outside or beyond any originary selfhood as the spirit that informs and deforms any merely present poetic voice: 'the Spectre squats in our repressiveness' (1973, 24) intones Harold Bloom in a voice not a little haunted by the spirit of William Blake. Here, then, we read Bloom in the process of accommodating a spectraliza- tion of inheritance, the very trace of which informs the motions of his language in those juxtapositions. Bloom, like Freud (of whom more later), lays bare certain hidden forces, as his discourse teaches us – in the words of Nicholas Royle, writing on Freud – to be 'uncertain, to question, to experience' (Royle 2003, 24), even if Bloom is the last person to admit this.

We will not get much further than the prologue to *The Anxiety of Influence*. A repetition in its own right, it is haunted by all that it will seek – and fail – to exorcize throughout *The Anxiety* proper, so to speak, those chapters that assemble themselves around a number of Greek keywords, thereby affirming a desire for a continuity with and a 'revisionary relationship to the dead' (1973, 140), the Ancients from which they are forever cut off, even as there is traced the attempted communing with the dead. The prologue sets off with a gesture of repetition then, in which the aboriginal self has already – always already – retreated, withdrawn, departed and yet left behind it an indelible mark or legacy, after and in the wake of which we struggle. As Bloom translates this elsewhere in *Anxiety*, 'Separation anxiety is thus an anxiety of exclusion' (1973, 58). But it is an exclusion of which we can never be certain. For what reminds us that we are excluded, if not a voice, a presence of sorts, spectral to be sure, but nonetheless *there*, with us and telling us all the time that we are excluded from its presence? What seduces us is just this phantom other. It betrays us with the transgressive promise of a certain crossing of an impossible line or limit. It is 'the shadow or Spectre . . .' It is not some one or some thing but rather, '[a] spectral state' (1973, 24), giving us to believe, whispering from inside us that we are excluded. We are always already in an 'outside' of a spectral 'inside', which it has never been ours to inhabit, but which we inherit nonetheless.

Pursuing its contours, we may see that the prologue recounts as it paraphrases a narrative concerned with memory, and a certain becoming conscious of one's difference, inspired as it is by the spirit of a tale that remarks the institution of all stories as melancholy recollections of ungatherable plenitude. In this telling, and in the subsequent narrative history of misreading that Bloom pursues, difference, specifically the difference of poetry, is always post-lapsarian, and therefore lacking, tainted by the degeneracy of later generations. In part, this is acknowledged by Bloom, not a little contentiously, in a historical observation that 'poetry has become more subjective' (1973, 11). Yet that insistence on the growth of subjectivity within and as the manifestation of poetic form as the reaction to the aboriginal other that haunts all poetry is, doubtless, Bloom's own attempt to ward off in himself 'the melancholy of the creative mind's desperate insistence upon priority' (1973, 15). Without getting ahead of ourselves, we should note how the critic transgresses subject-positions within his own essay, within and across the very formulation of his positions.

So, returning once more to where we began: the prologue tells the reader a familiar story, the narrative of a fall. The fall is a falling away, a separation. As Bloom pursues the dying arc, destined never to reach a bottom, across *The Anxiety of Influence*, so he makes it clear that this falling is always in motion, always taking place. There is no fall, no end to the descent, on which the narrative moments of response and acknowledgement depend. The prologue illustrates this economically. It marks and remarks itself as a departure from plenitude. The prologue tells belatedly and with the melancholy of all retrospective accounts of exclusion, how the poetry voices a continuity of rupture and discontinuity. It announces also, in that narrative and memory of the fall, the loss of language. Language tells the tale of its own loss, that by which it is marked and that which haunts it. Even though 'no quest ends' (1973, 13), Bloom's Viconian world is one in which the endless quest only circles back on itself, coming to, but unable to cross, again and again, the 'Limit' imposed by the other.

III BELATEDNESS

Memory of loss, inscribed in the poignant and elegiac tongue that halts before its own limits, touching on what it no longer tastes – this is the language that remains, and, it might be said, the remains of language. If language is the house of being, it is, as Bloom admits, the place where the dead return (1973, 15). For a later poet, every day is marked as 'dismal or unlucky' (1973, 15; 141). And this is known because only passion reaches beyond the limit to haunt the present time. The poet inherits the daemon other to remind us that we are excluded from 'our ever-potential divinity' that marks us, in our fall, as guilty inheritors and latecomers (1973, 139). Only suffering in the face of loss and inheritance allows the perception of a transgression that connects as it divides across a border shared by two, across which they cannot travel and at which they find themselves halted. Even in those moments where 'he thought he was about to speak . . . the silence continued' (1973, 3). Genesis is always belated falsification then, the critic-ephebe's *misinterpretation*, a *mistranslation*, structured spectrally as what it is doomed to be, a 'dyad and not a monad' (1973, 71).

Genesis therefore as feeble, post-lapsarian afterthought, belatedly told and traced in itself by the ghost of a loss to which it turns, after which it yearns, but of which it can never comment. Anxiety, in this apparition of desire for the trace of what is apprehended only in being taken from us, is thus anxiety over the lack of lack (see Lacan 2008, 57-91 passim). Narrative itself is the transgression, a rupture of the line that one has crossed in order to be able to narrate a remembered plenitude without reserve, the very breach marks one as fallen, as having transgressed, and of which one is all the more guiltily transgressive for being unable to suture the gap. Reading searches feebly after, in the wake of the trace of a transgressive phantom, by which it is doomed to utter, to bear witness, and because of which it can only say that it cannot say, that attestation comes down to a poetics which is also an apophatic affirmation. Harold Bloom's biblical testament emphasizes therefore, as he says of Freud, that 'every forgotten precursor becomes a giant of the imagination' (1973, 107). All reading, all writing, is haunted by this transgressive force, by the strong dead who cross and re-cross the scene of reading and writing, who return in one's every articulation, causing the projection of an 'I' that is never one's own.

It is in this manner that one comes to perceive how 'that shade all things cast whenever the sunlight of knowledge falls upon them – that shade too am I' (Nietzsche 1920–1929, 872),[1] as Bloom's theory of poetic misprision makes terrifyingly clear. For, as Bloom would have us understand, when the light, the enlightenment of an irrecoverable loss or fall, illuminates our sense of who we are, we find ourselves – but we find ourselves haunted, transgressed, by the shades, the ghosts that we have already become, which we have always been. The daemons may lurk and are mute, but 'they lurk everywhere' in us 'quite audibly', as the critic has it of Ralph Waldo Emerson (Bloom 1973, 100), and 'negation of the precursor is never possible' (1973, 102).

IV PERSISTENT CLEWS

What is becoming all too clear in this meandering response, tracing as it does a strand across the weave of Bloom's argument, is the appearance of that somewhat fraying thread that, in its strands, comes at times to resemble an iterable, haunting persistence. This clew, if you will, persists despite attempts on Bloom's part to hold it at bay in the face of what he calls 'the precursor's heterocosm, a shuddering sense of the arbitrary' (1973, 42). What Bloom calls shuddering and arbitrary, we might recognize as the work of the clew itself, the vibrating thread within consciousness, within the subjective dwelling place that the house of being is haunted. The clew does nothing less than countersign Bloom's text as a transgressive trope therefore. The strand in question, woven from a family of traces having to do with ghosts, spectres, revenants and phantasms, is transgressive in that sense of infringing or stepping across boundaries. It steps over the limits, specifically, the limits of any present or separate – that is to say autonomous and free – sense of self or identity, spreading, and contaminating as it goes. That trace of a phantom collective by which one is forever bound upon the wheel as T. S. Eliot acknowledged in drafts of *The Waste Land* reveals itself; it is the haunting strand that transgresses as it insinuates. It plagues, irritates and infects the Bloomian transcendental ego, that supposedly objective consciousness that wishes to construct (a) a symptomatic history of poetic production; (b) a transferable psychobiography for the strong poet; and (c) a cultural account of Western poetics premised on the ineluctable force of misprision in any generational reading as a will to the poetic ego's survival in the face of all those transferential, transgressive daemons.

V THE SPECTRAL

In Bloom's consideration of Empedocles' notion of the daemon, we read how the spectral is always at work, always undermining and yet informing the poetic persona. The spectre is by its condition always transgressive, as has been intimated. Bloom appreciates the extent to which transgression is a determinant condition of the return. His apprehension of poetry and poetic influence is therefore a matter of delineating and so responding in the wake of a spectropoetics, even though, as early as the introduction of *The Anxiety of Influence*, Bloom wants to downplay or limit the force of phantasmagoria in his analysis. Yet, he cannot do so, for anxiety, 'this mode of melancholy', admits us to a haunted place. In acknowledging our anxiety, our melancholic apprehension in the face of all from which we are excluded but by which we are nonetheless plagued, we admit our presence on 'the dark and daemonic ground' (1973, 25). And this spectral force condemns the poet, and the critic it has to be said, to an experience of one's own frustrated desires through coming to an awareness of all that haunts one, those '*other selves*', who speak the truth that the poem, though always other, 'is *within* him' (1973, 26).

Despite his own anxieties however, and as Bloom's language suggests with its reference to the daemonic, the phantasmic, and the uncanny, the ghostly trace in and *as* the poetic is not so easily to be stayed or denied. All attempts to conjure the spectre, to mark the limits of its transgressions in a theory of poetic influence, only lead to further signs of its appearance, thereby producing in the reading subject – and Bloom is the paradigmatic example in this scenario of haunting and double reading – even greater anxiety than hitherto announced. In reading this staging of the very anxiety he would hold at bay in his analytic exploration of discontinuous inheritance and the survival of the daemonic, Bloom appears to transform the critic into a Jamesian governess, prey to all the whispers of the past that circulate and resound in the house of poetry, until it is impossible to tell whether the phantoms are in the mind of the victim of anxiety or are indeed the signs of some revenant persistence. It is necessary therefore to acknowledge the ways in which Bloom turns in *The Anxiety of Influence* to promote particular aspects of a certain Freudian influence on his own work. If there is a turn, however, Bloom, it must be noted, also attempts to maintain a distance from that influence, in his own tracing of the limits in Freudian discourse apropos the reading of poetry.

VI PAPA FREUD AND THE LAW

Freud, we might speculate, is Bloom's true, spectral father. There are many others, as I shall shortly acknowledge. But it may be that it is with Freud whom Bloom will come to be read as being engaged in the bitterest Oedipal struggle, even as he enters into an excessive and incalculable contest with the mystical foundations of authority in *Anxiety*. More than twenty years ago, Steve Polansky noted the indebtedness in the remark that it is from Freud, 'whence Bloom derives the concepts of belatedness, anxiety, the family romance, and his system of defense mechanisms' (Polansky 1981, 227). Polansky specifically notes Bloom's effort to 'rhetoricize Freudian psychology, to take back from Freud ... what [Bloom believes Freud] took from poetry' (Polansky 1981, 234). Bloom's concept of anxiety, 'at once disabling and enabling', is Freudian (Polansky 1981, 234). And it is in Bloom's observation that anxiety 'is something felt, ... a state of unpleasure different from sorrow, grief, and mere mental tension' (Bloom 1973, 57) that the Father's words are heard and encrypted. Despite that effort to rhetoricize Freudian discourse on Bloom's part, however, Bloom's own daemonic trace is given us to read in that *something felt* of his, a confession despite the desire to control through determination within the limits of an already troubled formalism which admits the spectre of the other, admission here being a drive, a *pulsion* or *trieb*, and also, on the one hand, a confession and acknowledgement, and, on the other hand, the granting of a right of entry for that which in any case could never have been kept out.

As should be transparent already, but as the rhetorical torque in this one citation makes plain, *The Anxiety of Influence* is both a double and a duplicitous text,
haunted everywhere by its own procedures, and yet driven – driven, we might say,
and riven – in the very performative act of explaining away a poetics of the spectral trace. It assumes in its doubleness and division the very language of the father
to which it cannot fully admit, nor from which it can ever completely break even
though, also, it will never have complete access. This would be to psychologize the
reading of poetry, to map the text as the apophatic articulation of the inchoate,
inarticulate psyche. But then, Bloom knows that; his *admission* of the *something
felt* confesses as much. (And admission, let me say in passing, is everything in
Bloom, with its postal principle at work, *admittere*, from which the word derives,
meaning *to send*; Bloom leaves his mail everywhere in plain view, careless with it,
allowing us to read, if we give a neurotic's attention to the marks on the page.)
For, has he not already in his prologue, and subsequently, at every turn of the page
and every turn of the screw, admitted to being before the Law? Has he not placed
himself in relation, and in response also, to the foundational violence of the Law,
to paraphrase Jacques Derrida, and a Law the very premise of which places every
poetic subject hereafter in a moment of suspension, that time of an *epoché*?[2] It is
as if, imagine the scenario, Bloom has displaced himself in placing himself on the
couch, and therefore at the centre of the family romance.

Polansky comments on the family romance apropos his reading of Bloom in
the following manner:

> For Bloom, the strong precursor-poet assumes the role of father-figure in this
> rather simplified Oedipal-poetic process, and thus acts as prime inhibitor or
> blocking agent. The belated or new poet, like Freud's son, is interested in becom-
> ing his own progenitor. In Bloom's rhetorical scheme, this is accomplished by
> means of the ultimate trope, or trope of a trope, *metalepsis*, through which
> time, and thus priority, are figuratively conquered and reversed. (Polansky
> 1981, 235)

Polansky's reading is correct, up to a point. But the point is that of rhetoric,
and his assumption that to be merely rhetorical is to invent a 'rather simplified
Oedipal-poetic process' is, itself, rather simplified, especially in that misperception
of the rhetorical turn – in truth a meta-rhetorical turn on Bloom's part, troping
the Freudian trope so as to identify the tropological mechanism of metalepsis in
the first, or, more precisely, supplementary place – as 'Oedipal'. The 'literary' here
is precisely in that evasive and yet persistent motion of manifestation and meta-
morphosis. For while it is doubtless the case that the turn is Freud's, the re-turn
Bloom's, so what returns through Bloom's turn are spectres of Freud, inscribed
in and by the 'Oedipal', that inescapable and ineluctable trope of the father, tied
into the Gordian knot of the son's anxiety. Bloom's rhetorical-performative offers
both the grounds, the foundations for an *anxiety* of influence, and an anxiety of
influence (of which more in a moment), and also plays out the ground, the bass-
note continuo in the cellarage of his discourse, which ghostly counterpoint, in

countersigning Bloom's discourse, shakes the very ground on which a Bloomian theory is constructed, causing its rhetorical structure to come apart, and so let in those spectres of Freud: the spectres, on the one hand, of the Freudian discourse, which trouble Bloom; and those illuminating phantoms, on the other hand, by which Freud, himself, was haunted, and which remain within, and yet not of, the structure of the Freudian text.

VII SPECTRES OF FREUD

To admit Freud when he is already here might seem a little odd, but is warranted nonetheless, even as it necessitates a detour of sorts, in which a few examples from Freud himself will provide us with the illusion of a ground, and so expose what I am tempted to describe as the literary in the work of theory. Implicated in my remarks above is a double reading of that phrase *anxiety of influence*, a duplicity of which I would like to imagine that Harold Bloom the good-bad Freudian he is would admit, albeit in secret. The doubling and division takes on the form of a quasi-genitive, or can be read as such, at least. For, on the one hand, there is the anxiety one feels in the face of the recognition that one is influenced, that one will never escape the father's or the precursor's influence. On the other hand influence is anxiety, its own most secret and improper property. Influence, *influenza*, that influx from the stars, mapping one's astrological chart and determining the 'character and destiny of men' or 'occult force' as the *OED* has it, is what is shared, daemonically and in sublunary fashion, by Freud and Bloom. Influence is, moreover, that 'capacity or faculty of producing effects by insensible or invisible means' (again, the *OED*). Such 'power of a non-material or unexpressed kind' is precisely the uncanny and haunting contamination of the conscious, wakeful self. It is all those viral strains of the unconscious that plague the present subject, leaving one susceptible to 'influence' and therefore *anxious, anxi-us*, or troubled in mind. As Freud knew all too well, even though he never said as much, to be anxious is merely to be aware that something influences, something is felt, but that knowing will not necessarily calm down all the side-effects. When Bloom writes *Anxiety of Influence*, he is doing no more than producing a metalepsis that is named in and performed by the very title of the text. For, *anxiety* tropes *influence*: the same and yet not the same, it replicates, reiterates it, and so admits metaleptic intensification. In this performative gesture, Bloom brings in Freud under the radar as it were, acknowledging as he does that no merely rhetorical exercise will ever exorcize the Freudian spectre. In this very phrase, its troublesome and contaminative work, the rhetorical is admitted *as* no less than the haunting place of psychoanalysis, rhetorical turns being the visible and formal traces of the uncanny and unconscious manifestations of the daemonic and transgressive.

If Polansky had not seen this, a much more perspicacious reader such as Paul de Man had, some time before in his review of *The Anxiety of Influence*. As he begins his review, 'Harold Bloom's latest essay is by no means what it pretends to be' (de Man 1983, 267). As Shuli Barzilai glosses this typically (for de Man) perspicuous

and enigmatic observation, 'this can be read in two ways: either the avowed intention of the author and the apparent meaning of his work do not coincide with the
results, and the author doesn't know it; or the discrepancy in the text is deliberate,
and the author is aware of what he's doing' (Barzilai 1985, 134). Either ... or, or,
either/or and both – and yet, neither, exclusively. In all of these incommensur-
ate possibilities (or, as Leibniz might have it, *incompossibilities*) we glimpse at
work not only in Bloom's title, but everywhere in his text what Freud describes
in 'Screen Memories' as a 'case of displacement along the plane of association by
contiguity or, if one views the case as a whole, a case of repression, accompanied
by the replacement of what is repressed by something in its ... vicinity' (Freud
2003, 7). What, for Polansky, is merely rhetorical is, both for de Man and of course
Freud, the replacement of one example of psychical content with another (Freud
2003, 7), which just happens to be given possible determination in literary form or
manifestation, though strictly speaking this remains undecidable, hence the very
questions of anxiety and influence for Bloom: the anxiety of influence and the
influence of anxiety. What Freud's model of the screen memory reveals in a reading
of Bloom contra Bloom is that it is impossible to decide on the extent to which the
paternal ghost haunts the later poet or critic because the very idea that motivates
the notion of an anxiety of influence could, in itself, be a significant acknowledgement that the reproducible 'memory images' (Freud 2003, 7) are those of the later
writer – or not. As Freud himself argues in the same essay, 'there's no guarantee
whatever' (Freud 2003, 15). As Barzilai observes, reiterating de Man's analysis, an
aporia opens within Bloom's staging of his essay 'between the explicit and implicit
content of *The Anxiety of Influence*' (Barzilai 1985, 135), and while through such
a gap the spectral lure appears, there can be no final accounting for the latter poet's
reading of his precursors as either merely a banal supplement or a strong reading
or countersignature. To put this another way, in light of Freud's observations, this
is what haunts and plagues Bloom the most. Thus, de Man's remark speaks both of
Bloom's text and Bloom's reading of poets and their precursors. De Man reiterates
in a performative observation the very tropological gesture and psychic displacement that plagues Bloom's text.

   In effect then, what I am proposing is that, in no small measure, *The Anxiety
of Influence* is a hypothetical exploration – a kind of theoretical fiction much
concerned with producing a narrative about what remains to be seen in the
work of the literary and turned towards the question of poetic influence – of the
Freudian hypothesis of the 'screen memory', in which a later memory displaces
earlier experience and subsequent memory, thereby covering up and yet doubling,
that earlier trace. The first trace is doubled, and so occluded even as it remains on
the surface of the text, as the shade of the text itself. What for Bloom becomes
the strong manifest text of the later poet is, in truth, only a screen for the strong
precursor-poet, in which a poem, like a memory, has 'value' (as Freud puts it of
the later memory) inasmuch 'its content is connected ... by links of a symbolic
or similar nature' (Freud 2003, 15). And the anxiety arises in the suspicion, only
ever immanent, and yet traced everywhere that what appears 'strong' in the later
poet's work is, in reality, no more than the haunting force of the 'strong dead' and

their return, thereby revealing the later work as the poetic equivalent of the screen. The screen-poem does not so much banish or displace its paternal predecessor as it makes it visible everywhere in seeking to displace and repress it. This is what, with regard to later works such as *Agon* or *The Breaking of the Vessels*, Cathy Caruth describes as Bloom's 'transference model' (Caruth 1983, 1286) and if for Bloom Freud 'underestimated poets' (1973, 8), such blatant disavowal on the critic's part reveals the extent to which he underestimates the draw of Freud in his own work. When, in those later works already named, Bloom criticizes Freud for a fall from the empirical to the daemonic (as Caruth avers; 1983, 1287), arguing, in Caruth's words, that 'Freudian theory creates myths which attempt to measure the immeasurable' (Caruth 1983, 1288), this is, arguably, precisely Bloom's own motivation, in which gesture he doubles and displaces the Freudian model.

There is, in this Bloomian process, the signs of another Freudian essay serving as a route map despite the critic, 'Family Romances'. As is well known, in this essay Freud traces the generational dialectical structure of opposition, rebellion, and once again displacement. The intense desire of early years to assume the parents' place is replaced by doubt (or anxiety) about one's own role in the family and a 'mood of dissatisfaction for the child' (Freud 2003, 37) from which comes criticism and creative misprision. The 'development of this incipient estrangement from the parents' produces the neurotic's talent, as Freud calls it, defined as a 'special imaginative activity' (Freud 2003, 37). The apparent motive of 'revenge and retaliation' that drives the child presents itself in a narrative peculiar to the family romance in which 'the author-hero [the poet, the critic] returns to legitimacy himself... eliminat[ing] his siblings as illegitimate' (Freud 2003, 39). However, as Freud generously admits, the hostility of such a fiction secretly screens the child's 'original affection for the parents'; furthermore, 'the child does not really eliminate his father, but exalts him', this in turn being 'an expression of the child's longing for the happy times gone by' (Freud 2003, 40). As a hypothetical fiction, it is a compelling one, especially in the context of reading Bloom *contra* Bloom. For this longing disguised as animosity, a longing that can nowhere be confessed and so remains traceable only in those eruptions of spectral disturbance and possession, is markedly on every page of Bloom's *Anxiety*. Freud, we might say authorizes Bloom's anxiety, and influences his critical being as only a father can, from the fall onwards. Of Bloom's first disobedience and the fall, one might write, returning in the process to where we began (almost) with postlapsarian reponse ...

But then Bloom knows this, and admits as much in the essay 'Wrestling Sigmund', from *The Breaking of the Vessels* (1982). We move, as Wallace Jackson has it, in an impressively astute review of *The Breaking of the Vessels*, 'between the polarities of displacement and haunting; to dislodge the precursor is to suffer his return, even to commemorate it in such a way that the successor is defined by the recognition and transumptive enlistment of the precursor trope' (Jackson 1985, 92). The problem for Bloom is that even as he affirms this, and even as he bemoans the fact in 'Wrestling Sigmund' that Freud has displaced anachronistically all his poetic precursors to become misread by a generation of critics as the precursor of poets 'while nearly all precedent tropes seem quite belated in comparison' (Bloom

1982, 63), so too does Bloom know his own belated and fallen response is to write in the wake of, and haunted by the ghost of the father to whom he remains indentured in *The Anxiety of Influence*, and by whom he is, in every sentence, re-leased (as old English legal documents have it; and which is, inevitably, no release at all).

VIII OF SPIRIT

But enough of Freud, he is as inescapable as he is inevitable, and as Christopher Beach has argued, Bloom is ironically (and after Freud himself), 'the originator and foremost exponent of the Freudian or "genealogical" model' (Beach 1989, 463). Above, Derrida had caused us to turn to the Law, before which we always find ourselves, unable to pass or get past, as if in every encounter with the Law the experience were that of an encounter with the aporetic. In many ways, Bloom's anxiety over the Law of the Father replicates this aporetic impasse, as if the spectral father were saying either 'remember me' or 'do not forget'. Let us turn at this juncture, therefore, however briefly, to Derrida. Something is always left over in the inaugural sentence of Derrida's *Of Spirit*. Something will always remain to be read in the opening line, with its reference to flame, and its subsequent unreadable remainder, ashes. 'I shall speak', announces Derrida, 'of ghost [*revenant*], of flame, and of ashes' (1989c 1). As Derrida goes on to affirm, his subject will also be the meaning of avoidance, something that Bloom knows all about, even though he is scrupulous in his own avoidance of this very subject, apropos Freud at least, in *The Anxiety of Influence*.

Of course, *Of Spirit* is not the only text to speak of ashes. Derrida also speaks at length about ashes, or cinders in the book of *that* name. But the question here, the one that imposes itself on me at this point, is: why flame? And, we may ask, what – if any – is the relation that can be drawn between *le revenant* and flame? Moreover, what between these two, between ghost and flame, authorizes Derrida to speak of that particular type of ghost, which is known only through its return, its revenance? To put this differently, what remains to be thought between repetition and fire, in the name of spirit?

Harold Bloom provides a possible answer, albeit accidentally, and certainly well before the publication of *Of Spirit*, in Chapter Six of *The Anxiety of Influence*. At the beginning of the final chapter of this book, he remarks that 'Empedocles held that our psyche at death returned to the fire from whence it came'. However, he continues

> our daemon, at once our guilt and our ever potential divinity, came to us not from the fire, but from our precursors. The stolen element had to be returned: the daemon was never stolen but inherited, and at death was passed on to the ephebe, the latecomer who could accept both the crime and the godhead at once. (Bloom 1973, 139)

Note the doubleness implicit in the reading of the 'daemon' – at once our guilt
and our ever-potential divinity. This is the double that is inferred by Derrida's
reading of *Geist*, in its guise as a specifically idiomatic, German spirit, and also
as the very manifestation of evil for which one is guilty. It is what also connects
culture and barbarity, the double and divided spirit to the recollection of which
Walter Benjamin draws our attention, thereby demanding our acceptance of a
responsibility, to which we had always been bound, but which we only come to
apprehend belatedly. In the passage just quoted, that simultaneity of repetition
within the self-same spirit that becomes inherited is repeated by Bloom in his final
image of the latecomer.

The Derridean interruption above acknowledges that flame is the brilliant
illumination, the outward manifestation of a particular spirit, the manifestation of
the spirit that burns in the poetic – and, in the context of his reading of Heidegger,
the political – struggle with the dead who return. As Derrida observes, 'Spirit
returns' (1989c 23), and this burning revenance is precisely what lies at the centre
of Bloom's theory of influence and the anxiety that the theory maps, and by which
it is occasioned. It is in the sharing and exchange, the desire and anxiety that Bloom
calls, apropos of W. B. Yeats, the 'ghostly intensities . . . mixed with a disinterested
enthusiasm for violence' (Bloom 1973, 153) that we apprehend the return, the
revenance that disturbs, decomposes as it composes and orders all poetic tradition
and misprision. And it is most persistently that which remains as the burning heart
of Bloom's own inquiry. For we can never escape that exclusion and the fall – a fall
not, as Derrida reminds us, from spirit to time, but from 'time to time, one time
to another' (1989c 28) of each and every poet – that describes its descent into
ghost-ridden subjectivity.

Speaking of which . . .

IX SCHATTEN

. . . turning to the shades of Nietzsche and Freud, Bloom acknowledges them, however grudgingly, as 'the prime influences upon the theory of influence' presented
in *The Anxiety of Influence*. Yet, he directs the reader to the limits of power in both
his parents (one being the stronger father, as I have hypothesized quite unreasonably). For, as if to distance himself, he observes that though 'Nietzsche and Freud
underestimated poets and poetry, yet each yielded more power to phantasmagoria
than it *truly* possesses' (Bloom 1973, 8; emphasis added). All at once, in this
acknowledgement of the two fathers – and where, for Bloom, we might ask, is the
ever-absent mother? Where is the woman in *Anxiety* who is neither a muse nor
that 'strengthless and female fruit' (Bloom 1973, 3)? Bloom draws the line. This
line or border that Bloom seeks anxiously to patrol concerns the power of the ghost
and the extent to which it properly, *truly*, has the power claimed for it by those
influential fathers of the anxious modern subject.

What is the power of this ghost, these spectres? What takes place? In part I have
already addressed this apropos Freud. In the revenance of the flame, illumination

is vouchsafed. What it illuminates however is the consumption, the destruction to come in its engulfing immolation: 'The strong dead return, in poems as in our lives, and they do not come back without darkening the living' (Bloom 1973, 139). Here we read the essential and singular translation, the distillation perhaps of all those generalized 'anxieties of indebtedness' (1973, 5) of which Bloom speaks. The influence, once again, is there, though invisible, neither presence nor absence as such. It transgresses the border between past and present, living and dead. It returns to induce in us knowledge; it appears to demand our awareness and to institute as conditions of our self-conscious being melancholy and the apperception of loss or absence. We the living are therefore darkened, our lives tainted with the melancholy of falling and, with that, mortality. We become overshadowed by that shade that touches us more nearly for its having taken up, in its revenance, a place *in our lives*.

More than this, we are most directly and intimately found to bear within us, within what Malraux (invoked by Bloom) called the graveyard that is our hearts, the poem of the dead that is *within* (Bloom 1973, 26). So powerful a force is the shade of Malraux, so much is he the exemplar of the strong dead, that his words, the trace of his now forever absent voice, impose themselves in Bloom's text: 'Every young man's heart . . . is a graveyard in which are inscribed the names of a thousand dead artists but whose only actual denizens are a few mighty, often antagonistic, ghosts'. The poet, for Malraux, is therefore 'haunted by a voice' (1973, 26).

Pausing for a moment to reflect on Bloom's chosen voice, or, let us say, voices, in order to recollect without bringing back directly all those 'voices' or their traces at least, which intervene and return across the pages of *The Anxiety of Influence*, transgressing as they wander any claims to order, structure or originality of argument that Bloom might be said to have; halting, loitering by the graveyard, we might come to see how *The Anxiety of Influence* is nothing other (but this nothing is no little thing at all) than the effective dismantling of all critical authority. The critic as host, Bloom bears in him, in the text bearing his name, both the flame of apprehension and anxiety and the traces not only of influence, but also of the signs, the fragments and ruins we name citation (and which he ruins all the more in not providing sources, realizing such an act to be fatuous), as the legacy or gift of the dead others who apprehend what it means to be possessed by spirits.

X TRANSFERENCE

There is what might be termed a *cryptaesthetic* at work in, and haunting Bloom's analytical procedure, whereby the text 'unhinges, in effect, the logic' (Royle 1990, 55) that makes possible Bloom's analysis from the start. The aesthetic of the crypt, defined in some detail by Nicholas Royle through a tripartite reading of Derrida, Emily Brontë, and Abraham and Torok (1994, 28–62), is to give place to, and make felt, another. In his discussion of Derrida's 'crypt', Royle demonstrates how the text 'harbours' a 'foreign body' or a kind of writing that codes or encrypts what appears to be said, and so structures those places where the other comes to be preserved in, and at the heart of, the *corpus* of language – in this case the language of the critic commenting on the author's encryption of another author. As if to illustrate this, and so confess that the critic is the place of the crypt, wherein the voice of the critic is displaced almost from the outside, Bloom turns to Oscar Wilde. Citing Wilde, and so seeming to acknowledge in this not only the paucity of originality in his own argument but also the paternal claims of Wilde as yet another father to Bloom's theory of misprision, Bloom draws approvingly on *The Portrait of Mr. W. H.*, wherein it is remarked that 'Influence is simply a transference of personality, a mode of giving away what is most precious of one's self' (Bloom 1973, 6). This is not all, for Wilde – whose own parent, Coleridge, turns up for Bloom as the ghost in the machine of *The Ballad of Reading Gaol* – remarks of influence that 'its exercise produces a sense, and, it may be, a reality of loss' (1973, 6). This sense, this 'reality', if it is indeed that, is a curious phenomenon. For it is, in addition to being the felt space of what is missing and the articulation of that absence, the internalization as Bloom remarks elsewhere of 'Tradition' as a 'mode of deliberateness' that can operate at 'many levels of consciousness, and with many shades between negation and avowal' (Bloom 1975, 19).

XI THE PLACE OF HAUNTING

The self is thus always transgressed. It returns, revenant trace of itself, always already transgressed, as soon as it commits itself to articulation or inscription. For in those very gestures are acknowledgement and response that the shade too is I. I am transgressed. I remain, in Bloom's theory of influence and the anxiety it arouses, the ruined and haunted site of all that remains of culture, tradition, heritage, all that 'I' bears witness to, but which is never mine. For 'I' is the place where haunting takes place, when I reiterate, translate, and am opened up to a consciousness of both loss and possession. In this seeming paradox, I remains, not having fallen, but always falling, through the ineluctable oscillation of 'an awareness of other selves' (1973, 26).

   But, of course, this is merely an interpretation. As such it is 'thus necessarily a misinterpretation' (Bloom 1973, 43). And with that, Bloom admits to the impossibility of his task, resigning himself to live with ghosts. Language, for the critic or the poet, is never 'free of the one wrought by his precursors' (1973, 25). I am – 'I' is, *I* remains – always transgressed by the aboriginal poetic self, each other and every other, the wholly other. Such crossing through of the self by the other – that, if it happens at all, will always already have taken place, whether or not that which it has left as its countersignature remains wholly or partially secret, secreted in me, this is my final and first anxiety, that I will never have known the extent of the influence – is that to which literature gives place, that by which literature takes place, a certain taking place or possibility of the impossible. This is what remains, this is the flame that, giving light, will transform for those of us in exile, the knowledge that spirit and ashes are connected, inevitably and intimately. Language is the place where the flame bursts forth, where the spirit speaks but where, in the touch of an other's tongue upon mine, I taste the ashes in the knowledge that 'language is the relic of an abandoned cyclic poem'. It is, always, already, a 'language in which poetry already is written' (1973, 25). It is therefore, and also, a language, which, though the only one I possess, will never be mine. In this knowledge, Bloom acknowledges throughout *The Anxiety of Influence* that relation with the other, 'that is to say' that relation, which 'according to the law ... calls us to yield to the other infinite precedence of the completely other' (Derrida 2001b, 207). I – always, *already* transgressed, transgressing the limit of the self, therefore, and transgressing, and so admitting one to a place beyond which I will never have stepped, and yet promising to return. Here, it might be said in conclusion therefore, is the work of literature *in* theory. In theory, at least, this is what literature causes us to see, giving illumination to that which takes place, causing place to take shape, in that work of 'building', which, 'theoretically' we name as the literary. Harold Bloom apprehends this work, and so situates the critic as literature's housekeeper, the one who lives with ghosts and shades, the one who stands, as he has it in the title to the concluding chapter of *A Map of Misreading*, 'in the shadow of the shadows' (Bloom 1975, 193).

14

Face to Face with Agamben or, the Other *in* Love

Seeing something simply in its being-thus – irreparable, but not
for that reason necessary; thus, but not for that reason contingent
– is love.

Giorgio Agamben, The Coming Community

Stand still, and I will read to thee
A lecture, love, in love's philosophy.

John Donne, 'A Lecture upon the Shadow'

Love is found everywhere in the text of Giorgio Agamben. It is that which affirms
through its singular apparitions as the condition by which philosophy reaches the
limits of mere reason. Love thus remains that which, in the house of philosophy, as
other trace, as trace of the other. We should neither confuse nor conflate 'love' with
either desire or any erotism, as I shall go on to explain. Separating what is already
other than these clinical and classical terms, love must be maintained as other to
them. Neither synonymous nor supplementary, love remains in Agamben as that
for which we will have to account in a language that, though indirect, must keep
itself separate from the philosopher's economy. More than merely 'found', as if it
were encountered, scattered like the wind-blown detritus of hastily ripped apart
love letters, love places itself in one's way. The subject in reading is interrupted
by love, as if it arrived to call the reader, to become the beloved, 'in the spirit of
a pseudo-Platonic letter' (Agamben 1993a, 3). It appears momentarily, here and
there, disposing of its traces, in between one subject and another, or as the visible
manifestation for the reader, the 'illumination' of and for a subject otherwise
remaining unrepresentable. Hardly a subject at all, except in the example of
one essay, 'The Passion of Facticity', which perversely and ingeniously speaks to
the trace of love precisely at those places where it is found only *in absentia*, love
remains, nonetheless – and as a trope, a *topos*, a *souvenir*.

– Of what?

Of that which is never present, no longer present, nor available to presence. A
souvenir is kept as memory trace, it can cause one to reflect and so cause the other to
appear, however indirectly. Love in the text of Agamben is, therefore, the souvenir
of the other, as well as the sign under which the face to face with the other might
be possible, however unlikely. Love's trace remains in the place of, thereby giving
place to the other.

– Why *love*?

Without getting ahead of ourselves, it is to be observed that love is the necessary pre-condition of knowledge. In his commentary on the apparent absence of love in Martin Heidegger's *Being and Time*, a lack or silence that has troubled a number of commentators since that volume first appeared, Giorgio Agamben observes that, as far as one can discern for Heidegger, love 'conditions precisely the possibility of knowledge and the access of truth' (Agamben 1999, 186). It not only conditions the possibility of knowledge. In disturbing the time of reading with the demand for a different temporality, it opens a space in the search for truth, and in doing so interrupts the subject as the displaced phantom for the other; and specifically, the Other, as my title has it, *in* love.

     – To my knowledge, Agamben never uses the term 'Other'. Is it the best term to use if you're going to speak of Agamben? After all, Agamben has striven to keep a distance between himself and the work of Derrida or, by extension, Levinas, apropos any thinking of the matter of an 'ethics of the other'.

     It is, I think, precisely because neither the 'other' nor the 'Other' appear, nor do they become distinctly visible in Agamben's text, that I take the work of alterity to be all the more persistent, particularly if we note, as I plan to, and as I have already signalled, the frequency of love. Beyond the obvious distance of Agamben from various philosophers of alterity, if I can put it like that, the very absence of the other signals itself and so demands consideration. What is also striking about such an absence – and this is no more than speculation, the projection of a fiction – that beyond the immediate distance that Agamben wishes to maintain from the discourse of alterity, there might be perhaps, a question of refusing an encounter with psychoanalysis. Philosophy denies psychoanalysis, for psychoanalysis would insist on the other of philosophy, for which the philosopher – and in this term I wish to signal specifically Agamben *contra* both Derrida's psychoanalyzing of the philosophical corpus and Levinas's return to a theological Other – cannot countenance alterity, an alterity that haunts philosophy as surely as does literature. While one cannot give more space to that consideration here, given love's frequency, it would be perverse, if not to discuss otherness, the other, alterity, then at least to acknowledge its phantom presence, the breath of its passage, through the affirmation of its absence in the text of Agamben. The perversion arises because love *is not philosophical. It remains – and as such is unavailable to philosophy, its institutions, its practice, its discourses.* Love is the hauntological sign that plays on the ontological imperative in the philosophical corpus. If love arrives as a trace, interrupting repeatedly any reading, then love must arrive from somewhere – or even some*one*, some *other*. Arrival, interruption, disruption, transmission: all of these are impossible without an other location or location of an other, however occluded or impossible to situate such an imaginary or phantasmatic locus might be. That Agamben does not play down the play of love, that he turns and returns to it, that it returns insistently to him, suggests at least the possibility of the impossible, that is to say an unfigurable alterity within his discourse, that which is so wholly and completely other, that it remains as the unnameable in the text of Agamben and for Agamben.

     It may be also, to insist on this point, that the question has to be why Agamben avoids the term. In this avoidance (if it is one), there is an echo of infrequency, which Agamben notes concerning the paucity of references to love in Heidegger, and which therefore should give us pause, as I have remarked. Is Agamben's silence – how can we tell if it is a silence? Is silence the same as an avoidance? Or does silence admit to an unbearable proximity for Agamben? – itself structural, and is this structure, at once strategic and necessary, informed by the haunting force of Heidegger? But beyond the question of avoidance (and we should not rush to assume this is simply the case, if it is at all), there is also another question concerning the possible relationship to be read between Agamben and any Derridean or Levinasian project having to do with that 'ethics of the other' to which you allude. I am not at all sure I can answer these questions. What I would say, though, is that perhaps – imagine this fiction if you will – that love is the name of the other; love names that which cannot be named, and so it is that naming directly must be avoided, if the wholly other is to remain the secret love of Agamben's text. This is, of course, only a hypothesis. But bear with me, and listen to the title, once more.

You might hear in this title, in passing, what I take to be at the heart of all love's motivations, its numerous *Stimmungen* – all those otherwise untranslatable intonations, moods, emotive states, and even opinions – as these are recorded and move across, thereby *inspiring* the text of Agamben. Whether Agamben writes of troubadour poetry, Auschwitz, a radical reformulation of historicity, or the condition of the sovereign state, the innumerable *Stimmungen* and their pulse is felt. Even where it is not mentioned or paused over, Agamben's writing nonetheless finds its endless motivation, its rhythmic turns, in love. Agamben's is, we might say, a text *in love*, and as such expresses and stages the text that is *in love*, acting out in its patterns and pulses the endless desire that haunt's Agamben's writing of a face to face with the other. It is out of love, love of and for the other that Agamben moves after love, chasing it while proceeding in the wake of love. This flight, never on time with itself, never able to catch up with that which, as revenant spirit, always haunts across multiple spaces, differing discourses, and several centuries, is undertaken in order to begin to 'measure the revolutionary and novel character of a conception of love that despite changes during the passing of seven centuries, is still, with all of its ambiguities and contradictions, substantially ours' (Agamben 1993b, 23). The persistent *Stimmungen* and *souvenirs* of love repeat and transform knowledge for Agamben, and so by the dynamics and tempi of the amorous phantasm the reader encounters, coming face to face, with the unspeakable other in the motions of the text.

– Then it might be said that such movements and e-motions leave deposited across the surface of Agamben's writing the whisper of a phantom breath (*phantasikon pneuma*), as if the merest scent was all that was left in the place one finds oneself. It is as if one recognizes that, the other having departed ahead of one, this leaves the subject with the realization that one is always after the other, one is always *after* love. One trails belatedly in the wake of the other. And this belated reflection, the untimely apprehension of finding oneself traversed and transgressed by the other is what causes Agamben to identify what takes place between one face and another, in the face to face, and in the face of the other, singularly the other *in* love.

Indeed. For it is not only that the other is in love with the self, as Agamben's coyly lyrical text reveals, hesitantly and in sudden, momentary unveilings. It is not a question of there being simply some 'external body' (Agamben 1993b, 23). It is also that there, *there* half-concealed and half-revealed is the other, *in* love, in what is signalled in the name of love. The other who, or which, is in love, might be that other with whom I find myself face to face, facing up to the fact that love takes place, if at all, *between*. But this is not all. Indeed, it is nothing more than mere semblance, merely mimetic resemblance – and therefore not *vraisemblance* – of what remains unavailable to direct perception. This alterity in 'love' . . .

– and also 'in love', for does this 'condition of being' not name an alterity for and of the self, an otherness, which takes one out of oneself, in a 'self-showing' to the subject, to the other of the subject and the subject of the other? Is not this idiom, 'in love', the most transparent and enigmatic of ex-pressions, e-motions, articulating revelation and encryption of the self-transgressing and the self-transgressed?

. . . this name for nothing as such, is, fundamentally and originarily, that which is at the fathomless heart of the revelation of the self to itself in the self-showing of its being, and therefore in the reflexive transcendence of Being, as this is given to one, by the other.

In this chapter, therefore, in having placed myself face to face with what has already fled, and so setting out on an endless quest after Agamben in order to come face to face with that which love gives to Agamben throughout his text, we come to find ourselves, together, in the proximity of a line or two from Giorgio Agamben's essay, 'The Face', the concluding essay from the second part of *Means without End: Notes on Politics* (Agamben 2000, 91–100). In pursuing the tropic and topical work of love in the text of Agamben, we find ourselves in the midst of a clearing. For Agamben's text in its loving engagement constitutes the most sustained, transparent and yet, simultaneously, opaque of commentaries indebted to the phenomenological tradition. And this will lead, as I shall have occasion to argue in conclusion to this essay, with the most profound call for a reorientation to the question of temporality in any hegemonic model of historicity, which currently and in recent decades has informed, not to say dominated, academic, critical, political and philosophical discourses. (See Chapter Four, above.)

Agamben's remarks on love, through which various historical others come face to face with love, attuning themselves singularly in relation to that which takes place in the space between one face and another, constitute a history or, perhaps, genealogy of what he calls in *Stanzas* the 'phantasmatic character of the process [not only] of love' but in its 'heroic-demonic' dimension, that which drives Being's very historicity (Agamben 1993b, 121, 120). Thus, love in the text of Agamben brings us face to face with the grounds of history itself. This singular orientation – of, and *towards*, the face to face – thus serves to remark that which is called in *The Coming Community* 'the multiple common place . . . the place of the neighbour that each person inevitably receives'. Without the reorientation and opening to the 'common place' there can be no reading of the historical nor an apprehension of the necessary deconstruction of the historical in the name of that which is to come, and hence the weak messianic hope of a radical and revolutionary reorientation of Being towards its other. This 'common place', which both takes and gives place, is, argues Agamben, 'nothing but the coming to itself of each singularity'. This, moreover, is an otherwise 'unrepresentable space', an 'empty place where each can move freely . . . where spatial proximity borders on opportune time'. This space or place (and the two are not the same, even though Agamben assumes correspond-ence, relation and a shared familial trait), in which transgression is the free radical condition of the making or taking-place of shared space, and wherein one comes to singularity through the subject's reception of the neighbour, the lover, the other; such spacing is, according to Agamben, that which 'designates' if not 'the very place of love' then 'love as the experience of taking-place in a whatever singularity' (Agamben 1993c, 25). Such statements or observations, on the part of the author, concerning love remark it as a 'topic' (never quite a concept and perhaps more properly the taking-place that a word stages, a phantasm or 'spacing'), although it might be more accurate, giving the motion, the to and fro, appearance and retreat that I am noting, to consider love as tropic . . .

– and as you have noted, such references turn up and are treated throughout Agamben's *oeuvre*; not least throughout *Stanzas* and with less immediate intensity in *The Coming Community*, but additionally such reflections are to be read through the space of a carefully demarcated paragraph in *Idea of Prose*, and in that small but telling essay concerning the apparent absence or, at least, marked paucity of love in Martin Heidegger's *Being and Time* (Agamben 1995, 61; 1999, 185–204).

Once we have been interrupted by love, it is always a matter of turning back, of reflection and reorientation. Whatever the subject, ostensibly, where love arrives as the sign of the experience of a certain singularity, such singularity announces the other *in* love as my title has it. But to continue, this re-encounter, this revenant experience is not only an abstract reflection. It informs the most immediate and materially grounded experiences of one's subjectivity. Here is Agamben, speaking of the encounter with another's face and the taking place that goes by the strange name of love. 'I look someone in the eyes', confesses Agamben. To which gesture, which gaze, there is returned the momentarily equivocal response: 'either these eyes are cast down . . . or they look back at me' (2000, 93). Agamben maintains the equivocation, and with that the maintenance of an opening in the glimpse of another before meaning is given, relation established, in hypothesizing that, on the one hand, 'they can look at me shamelessly . . . Or, they can look at me with a chaste impudence and *without reserve, thereby letting love and the word happen in the emptiness of our gazes*' (emphasis added) (2000, 93).

Something takes place here in the blink of an eye. I am witness to, and the subject of, a transgression, literally a movement across the boundaries of selfhood. What occurs, however, is not in one direction solely; it, moreover, is irreducible to, resists alignment with, any thinking of desire or any erotics. The 'endless joy of erotic experience' of which Agamben speaks in *Stanzas* has nothing to do with love as such, its experience or passage. For such joy would belong to a recuperative and aggrandizing economics of the self-same. Such joy is the place where I can tell myself I master and so silence the breath of the other, where I engage in the ineluctability of the narcissistic loop, trapped always on playback. However, love opens one beyond this; there is a mutual experience of the other within the same, from either side. It happens – and I experience this happening, as it happens to me; I am not outside this experience that I observe – before I can articulate fully what has taken place, before I can name the experience or surround its nakedness and intimacy with the armature of an epistemology. There is in the experience the transgressive arrival of *phainesthai* before *epistasthai*. In this, love arrives; in coming (*venire*), it surfaces within my consciousness, from beneath (*sou-venir*). And this is perceived, as Agamben argues Heidegger perceived throughout the composition of *Being and Time*, 'precisely because the mode of Being of an opening [which is given in the gaze and its circuitous reciprocation] . . . is more original than all knowledge (and takes place, according to Scheler and Augustine, in love)' (Agamben 2000, 187). More original than all knowledge, in this touch of the other an originary interpellation befalls the subject, calling to him or her; in this call or interruption, *there* is the instauration of the phantasmic memory, a memory all the more spectral for having never been mine. The situation of opening in love as the singular condition of that originary coming to pass prior to knowledge is not to be ignored. The open return of the gaze, doubled and displaced, haunted in its very opening, once apprehended in this manner forces on one the recognition that 'love can no longer be conceived as it is commonly represented, that is, as a relation between . . . two subjects. It must, instead', Agamben continues in his reading of Heideggerian Being, 'find its place and proper articulation in the Being-already-in-the-world that characterizes Dasein's transcendence' (Agamben 2000, 187). Being is given, and gives place to the other *in* love, the other *in love*, an other which traverses the one and the other, leaving neither separate or untouched. The very idea of relation as stable is undone.

The question of love is then, when truly considered, irreducible to the stasis of representation, specifically that of a relation between beings. Rather, as its unveiling through the passage between gazes makes manifest, the appearance or *apparition-ing* of love has a temporal and spatial dimension, consisting in its showing of itself (*phainesthai*). Such 'self-showing' or *seeming*, as Heidegger has it '[*Scheinen*]' (Heidegger 1996b, 25) is at the same time revealed and yet remains veiled in the semblance or *phainomenon* of an other, materialized in the *eidolon*, in which, a correspondence having been sent and received, self and other remain themselves and yet other also, without correspondence, without relation. Love is what has been 'let happen' in Agamben's phrase, whereby the reciprocity of the gaze, in opening the self to other, shows the self to itself as the other self-showing, in that self-showing of seeming *and* illumination, appearance as casting or shedding light. 'Let happen' marks the *factical* element in the phenomenology of love that Agamben is tracing, in which gesture he follows Heidegger, bringing to light that which remains for Heidegger the secret motivation in *Being and Time*.

– Love is not natural; it does not spring from out of nowhere, but is of the order of a making. No, from this perspective, love is the most unnatural experience. Uncanny in its intimacy, it is made. Love is therefore what comes to be crafted, not engendered through the touch that is shared between two souls, revealed and yet remaining invisible in the reciprocity, and touch, of the gaze, of eye touching upon eye. Love, as Agamben observes in a commentary on Heidegger's Augustinian heritage, 'is not natural', for in 'Latin, *facticius* is opposed to *nativus*' (Agamben

2000, 187). Furthermore, there is no relation as such, much less anything that one can represent as being fixed in place in this giving-place that allows or lets love happen as a factical making. For the gazes are mutually, sympathetically, empty – it should be noted – as they fall into, enfolding, one another. Falling in love, as the commonplace has it is, in effect, far from common, for it causes to be made known, given out to the self that shows itself in the registration of the appearance of the other in the singular encounter with and experience of the other's gaze, a fleeting apprehension of Being as fallen. Love is just the memory of the originary fallenness of Being, of one finding oneself in the world. Love is uncanny to the extent that it is the memory trace, the encrypted mnemotechnic of the very condition of Being in its facticity, its historicity.

– Yet, all takes place between, or there is nothing. At the same time, however, it is not only love that the gazes let happen. It is also, before knowledge, the word. To phrase this another way (and in order to move on from this in following Agamben): after Heidegger, it is not a question of articulating a phenomenology of love – although this preliminary project may well be what one finds scattered in intermittent traces across Agamben's publications, through little occasions or experiences, what might be termed 'surges' – but rather that love *is* phenomenological. If it can be seen, if it can be understood in its revelation as the semblance of that which the other lets happen, then this is as a phenomenology, a *phainomenon* and a *logos*.[1] Love is just this correspondence and mutual coinage: the intimate touch between the *phainomenon*, the *phainesthai* and the *logos*, the word or communication that carries in it the phantom, phantasm or revenant of Being.

I begin to see in this a missed encounter. It occurs that Agamben has found himself, repeatedly, face to face with Heidegger, but never directly. A séance takes place. What is more, in the name of love and as a result of the gaze that is staged everywhere, this encounter has resulted in those numerous frequencies that score Agamben's text with their commentaries on love, in the midst of so many different and singular critical discussions. Whether these are focused on politics, philosophy, poetics or human identity, there is always a turn on the part of the philosopher, who finds in his turn the return of love, *there* as the secret that, unveiled everywhere, leaving its traces on the text. And all the while, this remains without apparent system or order in the work of Agamben.

This is, for Agamben, the idea of love, which comes down to the following experience:

> To live in intimacy with a stranger, not in order to draw him closer, or to make him known, but rather to keep him strange, remote: unapparent – so unapparent that *his name contains him entirely*. And, even in discomfort, *to be nothing else*, day after day, *than the ever open place, the unwaning light* in which that one being, that thing remains forever *exposed and sealed off*. (Agamben 1995, 61; emphases added)

To live with someone implies a practice, a knowledge, a familiarity and understanding. However, Agamben maintains the unfamiliarity, the strangeness, of intimacy in order to articulate all the more powerfully the 'idea' of love. Such an idea opens, once more, a space, a taking and giving place, which in its staging or manifestation estranges – makes unquiet or unhomely – the phantom effects of love. The other, reduced to a name, resides within that sign, that *logos* as supplement to the self, always exposed by, *in*, the phenomenological light of Being. The coming *logos* that love offers to countersign, itself being traced by the countersignature of the other, this is the only passage, the sole transgressive translation of an otherwise inexpressible existence, 'pure Being . . . which is simply ineffable' unless expressed, and thereby translated from potentiality to actuality, as the singular inscription of the self. In this formula, and in the 'process of acquiring knowledge', *love* is the signature, logos, or 'letter of which you are the meaning' (Agamben 1999, 247)

The experience of love perhaps, then, serves to open expression of, and to, the otherwise, the wholly other and the ineffable that is inscribed in the sign of love, a palimpsest and imprimatur of the opening of alterity. It gives place therefore to the naming of this experience, however indirectly, whereby the *logos* provides the semblance of what remains hidden, invisible, or 'sealed off'; a semblance, a mere ghosting, nothing more, of what takes place and has place, as 'the very taking place of language in the unspeakable experience of the Voice' (Agamben 1991, 66). Such places, such *topoi*, wherein love is unveiled in its facticity, are also *lieux de mémoire*, sites of memory as I have sought to establish. What comes back therefore in the illumination that arrives to the gaze in its being returned is love, once more, as *revenant*, as *souvenir*, the ghostly memory made from the touch between the eyes of the one and the other, the one who is, always already, the other of the other. But this memory is unlike any other memory. For, as I have already implied, it is a memory that has never been my own, or, indeed, anyone's. This is the disquiet of the scenario given above. To live in intimacy with one who returns one's gaze, but to whom one remains as a stranger – here is a forceful dislocation in the affirmation of love. In this manner the self is opened, and uncovers as it discovers in itself an abyss, a radical alterity *in love*. The return of the gaze affords a taking place and a staging of place opening what is between us for the memory of the other – and what is more, the other in love. My eyes 'find' what was already *exposed and sealed off*, as do the eyes of the other in looking into mine. Thus, as Agamben argues apropos the Provençal troubadours, love (*Amors*), in being the name given by the poets to the 'experience of the poetic word', and from which it is to be noted that the word, *logos*, emerges, thereby giving place not to 'psychological or biographical events that are successively expressed in words, but rather, of the attempt to *live the topos itself, the event of language as a fundamental amorous and poetic experience*;' here in this word, in the place and taking place, it marks, there is the mapping of impossible co-ordinates (Agamben 1991, 68): *logos* then as memory of *topos*, in which place the revenant or *phainesthai* has seemed to appear, letting love happen.

– Which suggests a temporal, if not historical dimension, a dimension to the encounter with each and every other, always already haunted by the untimely reminder and remainder that love announces?

Yes, yes; but, it has to be said, this temporal condition is why Agamben is so insistent on demanding a face to face with Heidegger, particularly apropos that which haunts Heidegger's major work, the trace of love, by which Being is marked, and remarks, 'the descent of actuality toward manifestation' (Agamben 1999, 247). That manifestation or apparition is, there can be no doubt, the sign of the other, *in love*. It designates not the 'factual situation' of the relation between beings. Rather it signifies what Heidegger terms 'the "character of Being" (*Seinscharakter*) and "e-motion" proper to life' (Agamben 1999, 190), which is, for Agamben a 'kind of prehistory of the analytic of Dasein and the self-transcendence of Being-in-the-world' (Agamben 1999, 190–1). (A brief digression: Agamben passes over in silence that phrase translated as 'character of Being'. Yet the translation only alludes somewhat weakly to what is in the Heideggerian portmanteau, which is that Being is a 'character' not simply in the sense of personality but also as an inscription, a letter, or manifestation of the meaning of Being.) Such signification, Agamben has us understand, is fundamental to the falling, the 'thrownness' of Dasein, a 'movement [as Heidegger describes it] that produces itself and that, nevertheless does not produce itself, producing the emptiness in which it moves; for its emptiness is the possibility of movement' (Heidegger cit. Agamben 1999, 191). Here, we see – do we not? – in this remarkable expression of Heidegger's, precisely the opening, the spacing and the movement, e-motion, which informs, bearing up in itself, the illumination that *love* offers in the text of Agamben, as it situates itself, again and again, at the very heart of Being in the face of the other. And that it is a movement – e-motion directed towards a falling *ex-stasis* – is itself indicative of the temporality at stake in *being-in-love*, which affirms in its singular experience Dasein's self-transcendence.

One could therefore say, in response to Agamben's prompt, that if 'the structure of Dasein is marked by a kind of original fetishism' (1999, 196; Agamben is at pains to point out the shared etymological heritage between facticity and fetishism) as he claims, then this fetish is to be found precisely in the *eidolon*, the phantasmic image of the beloved haunting my imagination, in the face of the otherwise ineffable alterity which lies in the radically depthless depths of *love*. The other arrives in the guise of love to interrupt me in the midst of my everyday existence, in which I reside inauthentically in a condition of having forgotten the condition of Being. It thus calls to mind the authenticity of Being, and so reminds us that, though forgotten, love, the *sou-venir*, is 'always already present . . . and traverse[s] our Being from the beginning' (Agamben 1999, 198). Along with hate, therefore, love is, for Heidegger as it is for Agamben, a 'fundamental' guise or manner, 'through which Dasein experiences . . . the opening and retreat of the being that it is and must be'. In love, Agamben continues, the being 'establishes himself more deeply in that into which he is thrown, appropriating his very facticity' (Agamben 1999, 199). The subject, opened to memory by the revenance of love, finds himself traversed, transgressed by the temporal e-motion of the other, *in love*.

Love is thus the experience of an impossible face to face, and is transgressive precisely because in being 'the *passion of Facticity* in which man bears . . . nonbeing and darkness', it exceeds mere narcissistic dialectical strife at the cost of the beloved, becoming through its singular experience 'the passion and exposition of facticity itself and . . . the irreducible impropriety of beings' (Agamben 1999, 204). The most authentic experience for Agamben, in that it is the only possibility of the taking place of the face to face (which is the gift, the giving place of the other *in* love), love sheds light, illuminating the lover and the beloved '*in their concealment, in an eternal facticity beyond Being*' (Agamben 1999, 204; emphasis in original). Love is neither mine, nor yours; it is neither proper, nor a property. Love is made and so makes us in its name. That 'eternal' facticity to which Agamben addresses himself and which he seeks to outface in almost every text – thereby bringing its invisible persistence to light – bespeaks in secret the memory beneath the surface of my consciousness, traversing that border, transgressing the limits of consciousness. Always already there, the facticity of love, the only authentic souvenir of Being, promises to return, revenant source of illumination that it is.

– But hadn't you remarked how being-in-love was marked not only by a temporality but also an experience of historicity, of the historicity of beings, which offered to rewrite conventional discourses of historicity?

Yes, it remains for me to address this. So, permit me to recall here that love is the 'experience of taking place in a whatever singularity' (Agamben 1993c, 25). Thus the experience of love is 'invariably accompanied by a certain experience of time, which is implicit in it, [and] conditions it'. While Agamben is speaking of the implication of time within any conception of history, the perception of the singular experience of love as similarly temporal opens to us the different reading of history that Agamben enables. Singularity, understood properly, can only be perceived through the possibility that whatever singularity we address, this is – fundamentally and in principle – endlessly iterable. If love is neither yours nor mine but is made, then there is the temporal condition by which making occurs, repeatedly, yet with a difference. Every time is singular, and therefore other. Yet every time that love returns it is disturbed by its familiar unfamiliarity, by that untimely return, despite the fundamental forgetting that informs Being. Love undoes from within, as anachronic ghost, that model or modality of history defined by Agamben as the 'vulgar representation of time as a precise and homogeneous continuum' (Agamben 1993a, 91). Love therefore admits – confesses and gives entrance to – its own uncanny condition. It enlightens us, illuminating 'the basis of the radical "otherness" of time, and of its "destructive" character' (Agamben 1993a, 93) with regard to history conceived as undifferentiated continuum. A 'destructive' character, love as *logos* scores the unbroken line of history, rupturing its calm surface, haunting and insuring 'Western man's incapacity to master time and his consequent obsession with gaining it and passing it' (Agamben 1993a, 93).

Such incapacity is doubtless caught up with the possessiveness of desire, with the desire to possess, to make property what is improper. It is also the repeated reminder that one is always after that by which one is obsessed; which, on the one hand, one can never catch up with; while on the other, being always placed in a belated relation to it.

– One is never on time, then.

And for a very good reason, time being, like love, always untimely. Hence, as Agamben recollects, the 'Augustinian anxiety *in the face* of time's fleeting essence'. For time's movement is, like love, we feel, 'the thing existing which is not when it is, and is when it is not: A half-glimpsed becoming' (Agamben 1993a, 98; emphasis added). We are back with the gaze, this time from that coy, lidded location of the other, in its provisional response. The other, half-glimpsed, looks us in the face and we are called, interrupted, displaced from the untransgressed continuity of our inauthentic historical Being. Half-glimpsed – and yet 'for everyone there is an immediate and available experience on which a new concept of time could be founded' (Agamben 1993a, 104). Turning to the past, to Aristotle on the one hand and on the other to the Provençal troubadours, Agamben places a hope in the *souvenir*, that which is to come, the heterogeneity of pleasure – heterogeneous in that, as pleasure, it is irreducible to, 'outside any measurable duration' (Agamben 1993a, 104). In history, yet outside its flow, we experience, in the blink of an eye, that which we later remember and which befalls us, 'the full, discontinuous, finite and complete time of pleasure' (Agamben 1993a, 104). And it is this, Agamben demands, which we must 'set against the empty, continuous and infinite time of vulgar historicism . . . [and the] chronological time of pseudo-history' (Agamben 1993a, 105). The other in love makes this possibility an actuality, every time there is love, and every time the other is apprehended as *being-in-love*.

In conclusion, it may be added, love is what takes place between two, as that which gives place to the between, as that which is between-two as ghostly motion of *being-in-love*. There is thus, a spectral life, a living beyond mere existence, with which the figures of love, the between-two, and being-love admits, and which figurality plays on the very impossibility of assigning to love a determining economy or law. Love, in its singular experience and its tropic manifestations, is thus always, and in some manner, a 'state of exception', if I can borrow this phrase. The exception, in the experience of love and in that, which love's tropic and spectral motions constitutes in the event, is exception from one's submersion in that unknowing subjectivity that maintains one as belonging to a culture, a history, a nation, a state – in short, that which otherwise maintains one as a political animal.

In *State of Exception*, which takes its title from a remark of Carl Schmitt's, from a publication in 1922, in which Schmitt defines the role of the sovereign and the sovereign right to decide on the 'state of exception' (Agamben 2005, 1), Agamben, never, to my knowledge, mentions love. On the surface of things, this is hardly surprising, given that Agamben writes *State of Exception* in the wake of legal transformations following 9/11. However, Love's 'state of exception' is just such a state, which no sovereign can determine or decide on, as is realized in that sovereign countersignature and subjugation of the state of politics in the playful troping structured by John Donne, when he writes, in 'The Sun Rising': 'She is all states, and all princes, I, / Nothing else is. / Princes do but play us' (1987 ll.21–3). This 'state of exception' is that state of being-two, being-in-love, and with this the inversion and usurpation of sovereign power that love grants.

Donne's gesture achieves what Agamben in *State of Exception* reads as yet to come; for there is in this countersignature of sovereign power the 'deactivation and inactivity . . . another use of the law', which seeks 'to "play" with it, in the name of love' (Agamben 2005, 64). This is not, however, to come, as Agamben suggests, when he observes that '[o]ne day humanity will play with law . . . in order to . . .

free them from it for good' (Agamben 2005, 64). Such utopian desire is merely law itself, the writing of a law dictating, and so attempting to programme the future. Donne's rebellion, his giving a place to the state of exception, admits (to) what Walter Benjamin calls a weak messianic force (Benjamin 1969, 254), that hope against hope for a justice to come; and which, we might add, is figured everywhere in literature, and as the work of literature, as that which can always arrive, which can appear at any moment. Such appearance, *in* literature, is, *in theory* – it is that which theory *in* literature causes to be seen, arriving in that visionary event which is literature's, in theory.

But, concluding: Love is not a law, and this is what Donne's poem admits in the poet's inability to command the sun, to stop its inevitable rising. It is thus revealed as what Agamben most desires at the conclusion of *State of Exeption*: a pure word, a 'word that does not bind, that neither commands nor prohibits anything, but says only itself . . . show[ing] only itself [as a being-between-two] without any relation to an end':

> And, between the two, [love thus names] not a lost original state, but only the use and human praxis that the powers of law and myth had sought to capture in the state of exception. (Agamben 2005, 88)

Responsibilities of *J*, or, Aphorism's Other: Criticism's Transformation

Our main business in the coming years will be to teach people to read – to read all the signs, including those of the newspaper and of the mass culture surrounding us, as well as those signs inscribed on the pages of the old canonical books. In the coming years an informed citizenry in our democracy will be one that can read and think clearly about all the signs that at every moment bombard us through eye and ear. Figuring out the best ways to ensure the existence of this citizenry will be a great responsibility but also an exhilarating opportunity.

J. Hillis Miller

From J. there is a *demand for narrative*.

Jacques Derrida

My selfbeing, my consciousness and feeling of myself, that taste of myself, of *I* and *me* above and in all things . . . is incommunicable by any means to another man.

Gerard Manley Hopkins

. . . and what if, resonance in this other language still leading you astray, I liked words *in order to be-tray* (to treat, triturate, trice, in-trigue, trace, track).

Jacques Derrida

APHORISM 1: YOU START WITH THE EVENT OF READING, WHICH IS NEITHER ILLUSORY NOR ARBITRARY, BUT IS SOMETHING THAT OCCURS WHEN YOU READ, AND YOU GO ON FROM THERE

You can learn quite a lot about reading from J. Hillis Miller. Among so many things you might learn from Miller, if you attend with patience, diligence, care and responsibility to only one or two threads drawn from the vast weave of more than fifty years of publication, is that, in the act of reading, there is always the singular encounter with the other, with others. Or, perhaps more accurately, there is always the chance of that encounter. One can never be certain, ahead of the event. As Miller's lucid, eloquent, engaged prose makes plain, if otherness is missed in what to all intents and purposes looks like an act of reading, no amount of elucidation after the fact will ever explain it to the reader who has missed that momentary passage. This is true, whether one is speaking of a novel, of poetry, of 'deconstruction', so-called, or criticism in general. Each of J. Hillis Miller's texts are comprised of so many singular encounters with, or experiences of, the other in their acts of reading, but they also comprise, equally, so many articulations of the other, of innumerable others, for which each and every good reader of Miller is responsible. Yet nothing can be more certain than the fact that, in the effort to be responsible, the reader of Miller may have got it wrong.

This is not to impugn the intelligence of the reader; it is though to suggest a certain deceptive and therefore disabling force that underlies the apparent calm of any text by Miller. Were I to seek the appropriate metaphor or image for Miller's texts, it might be the still, shimmering surface of a lake. The tranquillity and composure of that lake remains for the most part undisturbed, offering to those who contemplate it an apparently unruffled play of light and shade, mediating rather than merely reflecting the composition, the structure and form of the text across the surface. Something emerges without warning, however, from the darkness that the surface calm belies, disturbing irrevocably the illusion of placidity and liquid unity. Or, to continue this metaphor, there is that other effect. You are out on the lake, moving across its surface or remaining relatively still at one point (the point is illusory; you only imagine a point in the otherwise unbroken surface). An agitation begins, imperceptibly at first, gradually building to a swell of irresistible proportions, in the midst of which you find yourself thrown around, disoriented; capsized even. To bear witness to this is to become the reader Miller desires, to be translated, *transgressed*, by one's having been touched by the aphoristic pulsing of the other (and this *is* aphoristic, as I shall show). However, supposing one (believes that one) has read aright, even to the smallest degree, this is not to say that reading has come to an end or that the responsibilities entailed in any act of reading have been fulfilled. In recognition of these, I hope my reader will allow me what might appear a brief, perhaps somewhat elliptical, reflection. These will take place through a consideration of what the title of this chapter – *responsibilities of J or, aphorism's other* – puts to work as a means of opening oneself to a dialogue with the others in the text of J. Hillis Miller.

A question arises from the title. I can imagine it: why speak of aphorism at all, let alone address it through this strange phrase, *aphorism's other*, which appears to have imposed itself on me? What is it about aphorism that appears an appropriate figure for addressing Miller's criticism? The second part of my title involves a double genitive. On the one hand, it announces that other, that singular example without example and experience of the other, which we call aphorism. In this sense, the aphorism, every aphorism, is other because it arrives, it *calls* (I will return to the call, below); but the supposed or hypothetical place from which it arrives, the guise, persona in which it comes to call, that which we might want to identify as the 'style', 'tone' or 'voice' of the aphorism's origin (supposing there were such a thing) in order to give location or identity – these are unlocatable, unidentifiable, perhaps even radically undecidable. Every aphorism, it might be said, is different from every other aphorism; every aphorism is wholly aphoristic. It departs from an unlocatable horizon, being other than that, even as it gestures towards the illusion of a horizon, which its inscription inscribes rather than merely describes. Aphorism is thus always already double, and in being double, opens abyssally. It doubles itself for, arriving under cover as elliptical or occluded knowledge, aphorism 'does' something with words, it is performative within and other than its glacial, yet provocative placidity.

On the other hand – there will, by the way, be more than two hands; and these will have been multiple, diverse, heterogeneous – there is remarked the other that the performative we call aphorism gives place to, that which, in the place of the aphorism, takes place. This place, however, is strange, a place, if it is one, concerning the very ground of which one cannot have knowledge, let alone be certain concerning its existence. The aphorism is thus a singular manifestation of the *atopical*, and 'this strange locus is another name for the ground of things ... *something other* to any activity of mapping' (Miller 1995, 7; emphasis added); neither absolutely groundless nor firmly grounded, but *something other*, a ghostly passage or, for want of a better phrase, a 'tropological entity' (Hamacher 2004, 178). What might be considered the appropriate ground then? From which location do I begin, if mapping is impossible? What is the ground on which I build or embellish, in order to produce either structure or counterpoint? And what is it in Miller's work, as so many singular attestations of the other that calls to me, to us, to so many readers over the years? What is it that comes, returns, continues to come unceasingly, and promises to come? What is it within the act of reading in Miller's writing that, as the encounter with an other signals the promise of that which remains to-come? What is that arrives, often with the lightning flash of aphorism or insight, or what Jacques Derrida has called, with regard to aphorism, the *trait d'esprit* (1989c, 123) in a manner that, in being just this compulsive call, is both command and gift? The phrase of Derrida's, *trait d'esprit*, which remains in French in the translation, as if it were some ghostly remainder, some aphoristic other, returning, arriving, retreating, and yet all the while remaining to be read, comes from the following remark: 'Under the brilliant singularity of Valéry's aphorism or *trait d'esprit*, one recognizes those profound invariables, those repetitions which their author opposes, precisely, as nature to spirit'. Appropriately – more or less – at least with regard to that which I wish to situate or, at least, acknowledge as that which arrives from the texts of J. Hillis Miller, Derrida is writing of the certain movement of the *revenant*, the ghost, and spirit of a particular identity, as this comes to be articulated through a series of articles by Paul Valéry. In the same footnote as I have just quoted, Derrida has occasion to cite Valéry's definition of spirit as 'very simply a *power of transformation* ...' It is precisely this power of transformation that arrives in Miller's writing, often with an aphoristic force, with the force of an undeniable command and an excessive gift for which there can never be any adequate acknowledgement or recompense, except the acknowledgement of response and the responsibility which that entails, as I go on to discuss. Miller's writing, it has to be said, is always marked by this ghostly trace, this *trait d'esprit*. The other arrives, aphoristically, from within the calm, considered, measured and rigorous place of exegesis, as that which is given us to read.

APHORISM 2: EACH FORM OF REPETITION CALLS UP THE OTHER, BY AN INCALCULABLE COMPULSION

The *trace d'esprit* is, it may be imagined, the trace of the wholly other. A trope in the place of the trace of the revenant, it is that which is not only singularly atopical, and thereby involved with an undermining of topographical certainties; it is also, in its apparitioning, returning motion, temporally disruptive, announcing, affirming the insupportable times of reading: 'in one way or another the wholly other is ghostly and takes the form of an apparitional promise. The *tout autre* is already there, a revenant from some immemorial past, and yet heralds or invokes or demands a future...' (Miller 2001a, 2). What comes to me from some unmappable locus as the aphoristic remains to be answered. In the face of the other's arrival or return, if such a thing takes place, there is no proper time. It may be that the *trace d'esprit* which countersigns aphorism gives rise to 'a consciousness of temporality', and this consciousness gives us to reflect that there is no proper time, even though we remain attentive to its possibility.[1]

Let me, therefore, as a bare acknowledgement to the glimpse of what I will call provisionally J. Hillis Miller's *trace d'esprit*, single out three words as traces of that which arrives aphoristically, and which calls. These traces set up a particular resonance, and find themselves insistently reiterated, whilst also, circulating, once again, and yet with a difference, in this chapter: *other, performative, topos*. As with the question or, more properly, the admission of a difficulty in the face of the demand of the question, it is not my intention here to analyze these words, to give them much space beyond their having been remarked. That they arrive and return insistently must be enough. But what is remarked here is the recognition that I am called upon by the other. I am addressed by each and every other, in each of these figures, and find myself repeating these figures, a few among many. In repeating, I am obliged to respond, if not to them (for, once again, there is not the space to do them justice), then to what is announced in their arrival. The other(s) arrive(s) to call me by some 'incalculable compulsion' (Miller 1982, 9) to responsibility. Whatever this responsibility is, it is without doubt more than one, even if, at the same time, it is less than this. It is, furthermore, endless, 'forever impossible' (Miller 2001b, 214). Such inescapable impossibility may well reside in the fact that, even in the sketched gesture that is reiteration, there is still to be read a 'search for grounds', which nonetheless 'finds its groundless ground, its *abgründlich Grund*... That thought was there waiting for me (but where is "there"?)' (Miller 1985, 433). Where is *there* indeed, when there is no there *there* as such. I am not sure, therefore, that I can even begin to identify correctly where precisely the responsibilities lie. So, for now at least, it is enough – and also never enough – to locate responsibility in a graphic mark, a sign or trace, as encrypted as it is readable, which, on the one hand, offers a name for responsibility, while, on the other hand, offers to stand in for the impossibility of either limiting responsibility or speaking of a limited responsibility. In this, to hazard a performative gesture (and to risk also the chance that the performativity of the inscription will have been missed), it has to be said that '[t]he moment is, so to speak, its own image. It is haunted by itself as if it were its own uncanny *revenant*. The moment is single, and yet it is imperceptibly doubled within itself' (Miller 1985, 432). Another way to remark what takes place here is to suggest that the critical repetition involves an action whereby the 'second [act of writing] is . . . [the] "counterpart" [or counterpoint of the first writing] in a strange relation whereby the second is the subversive ghost of the first, always already present within it as a possibility which hollows it out' (Miller 1982, 9). Acknowledging this, and thereby conceding that which is also, already, admitted – and therefore doubled, divided – I will turn back to my title even as it returns to me, in order to move on, by taking responsibility for *responsibilities of J*.

What exactly is being articulated in this phrase, *responsibilities of J*? Who, or what, is *J*, supposing even that this single letter stands (in) for an identity, that it is the sign of an identity, however encrypted or however transparent? What are *J's responsibilities*? Does this mark, this *trait*, sign or assign responsibility, does it stand in for the promise to be responsible? Or does it in some manner dictate or demand responsibility? Certainly, this merest figure, at once both readable and enigmatic, invites as much as it resists reading, and '[t]he reader can never know any of these secrets' (Miller 2003, 30). As I have just rewritten the phrase, wherein there appears the *turn* of phrase (and which thereby turns the screw on translation's responsibilities), *responsibilities of J* is translated, not quite symmetrically, as *J's responsibilities*. So, another double genitive appears, one that is, of course, already in place in the former version through the articulating fulcrum of *of*. On the one hand, as you can no doubt read, this expression, which perhaps aspires if not to being an aphorism then at least to some axiomatic status, announces itself in different hands; to the ghost of one hand in the hand of the other we might say, in which there is that visible-invisible touch of discontinuous relation without relation, 'a complex tissue of repetitions and of repetitions within repetitions, or of repetitions linked in chain fashion to other repetitions' (Miller 1982, 2–3). The phrase with all its possible repetitions announces therefore the responsibilities that are *J's* – who, or whatever, *J* might be. On the other hand, it also gives us to understand those undeniably inscrutable responsibilities traced in the very letter *J*, which, in seeking to read them, I will have *be-trayed*. And this, it might be said, is the double bind of writing and reading, the double bind that finds itself re-marked, traced, and treated in *J*, from one *J* to another, between the *Js*. Or, in another language, recalling another *J's* remark,[2] in the *jeu* between that *J* (hear this in French) which is an other and the *Je*, which, touched by an other, that other *J* that, aphoristically calls on and in me/*Je*, inscribing me every time I write and read and every time *I* is written with that gift which is also the call to responsibility. (Just because you can no longer hear the other *J*, that *J* which is the multiply other in and of the Greco-Latinate-English *I*, as you can in a certain fashion in French, does not mean to say that *I* is not haunted by *J* for all that.) For, if the question of *J* is indeed one of the *trait d'esprit*, it is also one of the *jeu d'esprit*, wherein '[t]he act of trying to understand repeats the enigmatic, unknowable event that is the object of anxious interrogation'. An act such as this is 'a way of doing things with words rather than the constative expression of achieved knowledge' (Miller 2001b, 214). The critic's act of response in its responsibility seeks to personify, if only through the inscription of *I* and at least in part, as a means of economizing on the abyss (Derrida 1987b, 37)[3] of *J*, as it were, as a way of opening the encryption that is *J*. And, to re-cite in other words the assertion just cited in a gesture of haunting citation concerning performativity, such personifications or 'prosopopoeias . . . are potent speech acts. They have to do with doing rather than knowing' (Miller 1995, 8).

APHORISM 3: YET ANOTHER MODE OF CHARACTER READING IS DISPLAYED, WITH AN EXPLICIT REFERENCE TO HIEROGLYPHS

Yet where am *I*? Where is *I* to be found, on what ground, as you open this volume to this page? Or, to put this another way, what are the grounds for saying, writing I, except that call of *J*? Do *I* accept the call of *J*, and how do I know it is meant for me? *I am*, in Miller's own words, is 'suspended always on a vibrating tightrope over the abyss of its own impossibility' (1998, 157). Moreover, in having to acknowledge seriously, in the face of my subject's writing, the 'impossibility of criticism in the sense of [the impossibility of criticism's ability to effect] a demonstrable decoding of meaning' (1998, 157), I have to take responsibility and admit that I am faced with an impossible task. But the very fact that it is impossible in no way alleviates the responsibility I have. The task involves a series of obligations and responsibilities, all having to do in some manner, more or less directly, with the fraught question of reading, along with a number of related matters. And all of this is written – take it as read – in the letter *J*. *J* calls and thus names me, *J* taking place every time I respond, I is written. To call, as we know, is to name, and naming, as *J* has occasion to remind us, 'is an initiatory performative utterance, a "calling"'. I find myself called, but '[t]hat calling is based or *grounded* on nothing but the call from the other that impassions me' (emphasis added), hence the very nature of what you are reading, because '[t]his call I respond to in another calling, for example in writing an essay or a book'. This act of writing, which is also one of reading, in turn 'constitutes another demand for response. It is a demand for which I, as the one who has first responded, must, and hereby do, take responsibility' (2001b, 215). Yet this can always be missed. Even my attempted manoeuvre, my opening strategy if you will, of announcing my obligation, itself intended to be both a response to and a reading of what is at stake in the writings of J. Hillis Miller, runs a risk here: the chance of its being read (misread, not read at all), as being merely a formula, just a gambit and not the necessary admission of what takes place when one is seeking, without totalizing summary or synthesis, to respond to the other, to the wholly other and to every other.

Yet, despite – indeed, because of – this, in being faced; *no*, more accurately, in attempting (impossible scenario) to come face-to-face with every other and the wholly other that comes to appear in the text, in the guise of the text and signed in the name of *J. Hillis Miller*, what can be said in the face of every other and the wholly other, which is every text, every inscription of a critical singularity? It has to be admitted that the 'wholly other otherness of the other' arrives 'as a perturbation

... in language' (2001b, 269), and, moreover, 'individual works, even those by the same author, must be read as a unique testimony to otherness' (2001a, 3). Thus, I read as a short-hand encryption for this perturbation, this singularity and otherness, the figure or siglum *J*[4] that appears to say everything and all the rest; and all the while this being, I would like to imagine, a figure for a particular, singular *revenance*, an arrival that is a return, as well as a disclosure that nonetheless retains its secrets. What is it about *J* that authorizes me to say this? What takes place in the passage between *I* and the other, between *J* and *I*, between *J* and *J*? It is of course the case that 'argument cannot pass from here to there [or from there to here, even though, you will recall, we cannot say where *there* is or, for that matter, if it is possible to speak, ontologically as it were, of a *there is*, an *il y a*, which is not, first and foremost, the deconstruction of ontology, through the spectral passage of the other haunting the phrase *es gibt*] without the help of ... quotations. This happens according to the law of each text's dependence on other texts' (1998, 161). Every time I write – and all the more so, whenever I write *I* – *J* haunts and disables, even as it makes possible, authorizes, and demands my response. Thus *I* – as the column of a haunted house, an architecture in ruins. Reading, responding to, accepting the *responsibilities of J* discloses the necessary 'substitution of language for consciousness, figural for literal, interliterary for mimetic generation of meaning' (Miller 2000, xviii), so that consciousness – that false consciousness at least to which I ascribe through certain assumptions concerning *I* – 'may be a function of language, a fictive appearance generated by language, rather than something language describes or reflects' (2000, xv). So reading gets going by opening itself to that somewhat 'mazy' motion always already underway, and it is this motion that is caught for me in the singularity, and in the singular call, of the letter *J*. *J* gives; it gives (to) *I*; *J* lends *I* a hand, as it were, even though this hand has long since become invisible, a ghost writer causing *I* to appear, in part at least by disappearing under the sign of the phallic illusion of the Greco-Latinate-English column, and recognizable as that phantasm named by Miller 'the "consciousness of the author"' (2000, xv). Thus *I* is doubled and divided from within, the surety of its ground disrupted, 'haunted by itself', to recall and be disturbed by an earlier citation, 'as if it were its own uncanny *revenant*'. In responding to the aphoristic call of *J*, then, I am taking responsibility for this revenant that divides me from and within myself, that divides *I* and, in doing so, exceeds it.

Such an act of reading is only ever a 'hypothetical fiction' of course, an act that seeks to take possession of the other and so to 'build its structure of interpretation on that heterogeneous base, partly its own and partly' the other's (2000, xv). As images in fiction are understood to give the self material form, so might citations be said to function, at least analogously, in criticism, but in a manner that doubles: on the one hand, *I* cites for the purpose of taking partial possession of the work; on the other citation haunts the self as so many aphoristic resonances of the other, an identity in ruins. The responsibility of reading and writing chances everything in its attempt to map the unmappable 'domain where the reality *beyond* or *within* may be momentarily apprehended' (Miller 1958, 329). But how will I know whether my reading gets anything right? 'The consequences', Miller reminds us, 'of taking seriously the otherness and singularity of the other are by no means trivial' (Miller 2001a, 268). So, *once again*, what can one do except to write, to respond, in obligation to the singularity of *le tout autre*, a phrase which, though not Miller's, has taken possession of his writing on a number of occasions in recent years as the gift of the other, as he admits in 'A Profession of Faith'? What can one do, indeed, except write and read, hoping all the while to figure oneself as the merest approximation of the good reader that Miller desires, even though 'the consequences may be intolerable, the intolerable as such, something that no one can bear to see face to face'? (2001a, 268) Faced with *le tout autre*, one might answer the previous question in French by saying: *Bon qu'à ça*. It's all I can do, it's all I'm fit for, what else can I do?

APHORISM 4: THESE ARE UNGROUNDED DOUBLINGS WHICH ARISES FROM DIFFERENTIAL INTERRELATIONS AMONG ELEMENTS WHICH ARE ALL ON THE SAME PLANE

Perhaps at the most fundamental level, the problem of the task of seeking to begin to read Miller, and so respond to the aphorism of the other that marks the surface of his text through so many dangerous tropic motions and yet calling one to responsibility, must begin with unreasonable, and doubtless violent, acts of making choices. Given all that Miller has written concerning acts of good reading, of ethical commitment, and the responsibility of the good reader to bearing witness faithfully and with necessary patience, diligence, and rigour to the singularity of a given text or subject, how is it even thinkable that one could ignore such singularity at each and every turn of the page, and pretend to produce a reading that is in some manner representative, and which, by implication, elides all difference between each singular text in some double act of violence and betrayal in the name – or, indeed, semblance – of resemblance? Doubtless, it is patently clear by now that this is, according to my reading of Miller's ethical standards, just not possible, to stress the point once more. More than that, it is unthinkable, it is 'the intolerable as such', as you have just read. Yet, I have to try; it is necessary that I do, this is unavoidable. So, to reiterate, this is the irresolvable impossibility with which I find myself faced, with which I have repeatedly found myself faced, moving within and across – and as a result of – a series of doublings which it would be a mistake to regard as merely rhetorical – with which I have come face to face, again and again, in the process of arriving at the point at which you are now reading.

Inescapably, I am faced with the fact that I have committed already, in so many ways, the unthinkable. Yet despite such difficulties – and they are as real as they are insurmountable if we are faithful to Miller's own thought – another procedure might be to pull at one strand from amongst what Miller calls, with reference to Gerard Manley Hopkins's writing, this 'heterogeneous collection of documents'. In doing this, another question arises, one in which I find myself anticipated by Miller, yet again: might it be possible, or at least permissible, to proceed (quoting the essay on Hopkins, again) to take, as a limited objective the attempt to reveal '[a] pervasive imaginative structure', a structure that stands provisionally, as the approximation of the 'substance of thought', for the 'very substance' of Miller himself? This last question should not be misread. The very last thing I wish to imply here is that what the reader will find (and, doubtless, there will be some 'readers' who will find what they want despite all the precautions I take) is an image or representation of J. Hillis Miller. Rather, let us say that *J. Hillis Miller* becomes the signature for which I take responsibility. This involves and invokes not some essence or presence, not some essence within presence; instead a structure of what Miller has called 'related minds' comes to be embodied by the words, and this pattern 'exists as a temporal structure' (1968, 29), the temporality of which is that improper time of reading and citation, 'according to the law [let us remind ourselves of this] of each text's dependence on other texts' (1998, 161) – therefore, not *J. Hillis Miller*, but *J* as the mark of relation without relation.

One manner in which the structures and patterns come to appear is through the work of the question. The iteration of questions allows for a certain structure of responsibilities in the form of a theoretical matrix to be constructed, however precarious this might be. Clearly, asking myself such questions, I recognize that I am faced not simply with particular responsibilities, even though these are daunting, as I have already indicated. More significantly, I am forced to acknowledge, if not address, once again, those ethical responsibilities in response to the other, that in pursuing various acts of reading there is *always already* at work a certain force of translation, wherein one is always caught in the snares of both fidelity and betrayal.

Now, it may well be that the 'consciousness of the author' is an 'illusion or phantasm generated by the words on the page' and that 'this phantasm may have nothing necessarily to do with the actual mind of the person who put those words down on paper' (2000 xv); *I* may well be. Moreover, 'a linguistic function in a process that occurs of its own accord and is authorized by no independent witnessing "I"', but this does not let me off the hook from ethical responsibility, as Miller makes unequivocally clear. Of *I*, he remarks

> It is not an 'I' who speaks or writers . . . It is an impersonal possibility of thinking, speaking, and writing, there already within language, that takes possession of the 'I' to think itself, speak itself, or write itself, and thereby enter into history . . . The ethics of reading, 'I' have once more discovered, is this impersonal response to an implacable and impersonal demand . . . At the same time, however, by an equally inescapable necessity . . . that 'I' must in its own proper name take responsibility for the results of its acts of reading, writing, or speaking. (1991, 126–7)

So, this is where we might begin, in conclusion; it is the point to which we must return even as it returns insistently to us. The ethical moment 'in the act of reading . . . if there is one . . . is a response to something, responsible for it, responsive to it, respectful of it' (Miller 1987, 4). Of course, otherness and the ethical response is not simply a matter of literature, even if it is *always* a question of reading and even though the strangeness of literature gives place to the other's most enigmatic and aphoristic apparitions. Here is Miller in an essay titled 'Literary Study in the Transnational University': 'the radical otherness of another culture or its artifacts, ... the radical otherness of another person, possibly the result of a different gender or sexual orientation, but possibly also an otherness in other persons, of whatever gender or sexual orientation, [there is a] relay for an absolute otherness that speaks through them and makes demands on me for ethical commitment, decision, and action' (Miller 2005, 377). This demand is where Miller's good reader begins, with the commitment to raising the question of such ethical issues and acts, and acting upon them. Indeed, the very questions by which I find myself suspended are announced, as I have already shown in passing, where and wherever one encounters from the outset the inescapable awareness that reading is difficult, impossible, always fallible, *but necessary*. Even as both these (and every other one of the) essays announces in its own singular fashion the inescapable responsibilities of reading, of responding to the other, to each and every other, so too does this responsibility come to be received in, through, and from, each and every singular analysis by J. Hillis Miller, whether one refers immediately to the essays gathered here, or to any, and every, other essay, review, or book that is signed by him, that bears his name, and which arrives to call us to bear witness. These are the *responsibilities of J*. Beginning to recognize this, the good reader might desire the appropriate aphorism, as the call, the act of naming, the demand and gift of the other. To risk a location after all that has been said about the impossibility of locating the ground, I would like to suggest that such an aphorism is given here in another of Miller's essays, 'The Imperative to Teach', which opens appropriately with the question of the call: 'who or what (today) calls on us to teach?' The aphorism is not Miller's but arrives from Franz Kafka:

There is a goal but no way. What we call the way is only wandering.

Endnotes

Chapter 1: Toward a Phenomenology of Urban Gothic

1   'Realism' and 'realist fiction' are umbrella terms used throughout this book. While there is a
     danger that the terms are taken for granted, I am not implying that there is a single practice
     identified by that name. Although Dickens, Eliot, Thackeray, Trollope and other novelists of
     the first generation of Victorian fiction are loosely termed realists, they all write very differ-
     ently from each other. With some caution – and, doubtless, this will still be insupportable – I
     am using 'realist', 'realism' and so on, to refer to those modes of narrative where the 'average
     experience' of the middle orders of society are presented with the implicit understanding
     that this is how the world comports itself, and that what is represented is, if not all the
     world, then all the world that matters. Whilst the everyday is 'derailed' in small, local ways,
     all events creating detours and departures from the norm are understood as being within a
     more or less realistic paradigm. So, for example, someone may die of a disease, be run over by
     a train, lose a fortune, or prohibit a daughter to marry for love, but rarely do the characters
     in realist fictions stare intently at the minutiae of architectural detail until they lose sense of
     themselves. Characters in realist fictions rarely become involved in any narrative strand that
     is odd, disquieting or overly exciting beyond a certain range of convention (sensation novels
     from the mid-nineteenth-century onwards push such boundaries, as elements of Gothic
     begin to creep back into domestic fiction), unless narrative becomes generically mixed, as is
     frequently the case with Dickens. Additionally, their tales are told in a prose, which, whilst
     capable of delving into the minds of its characters, nevertheless maintains, on the one hand,
     an omniscient position over the world that is created, and, on the other hand, a narrative
     distance. Dickens may employ such devices, but he also frequently departs from them in
     different formal ways as well as in a manner that invites one to question what is going on. As
     Roger Fowler argues, 'all theories of realism, however sophisticated, rest on the assumption
     that the novel imitates reality, and that reality is more or less stable and commonly accessible'.
     However, he does go on to admit that all definitions 'prove unsatisfactory' (1973, 201). Of
     course, it can be said that Hardy – more or less – conforms to realist practices so understood.
     There are several problems with this, however, including the problematic 'interruptions'
     that are to be found everywhere in Dickens's writing. Ultimately though, the terms 'realist'
     and 'realism' are largely unhelpful, hindrances at worst, while, at best, prompts for critique
     and departure into a discussion of singularity and difference, and why the realist novel, if

such a thing exists, cannot, by example, be exemplified, seeing as every example differs from every other.

Chapter 4: *Contested Grounds*

1 'Oh, there's repristination! Just a spirt / O' the proper fiery acid o'er its face. / And forth the alloy unfastened flies in fume' (l.23–35). In these lines, as some readers will have observed undoubtedly, the alliteration of *f* signifies, perhaps, the sound of a momentary spurt of acid on the face of the metal, which is caught also in the *is* of 'repristination'. It is also perhaps worth noting that the shift between lines from 'Oh' to 'O', with the silent diacritical register in the latter ('O') of the vanished 'h' of the former ('Oh') is readable as a performative gesture on Browning's part, whereby graphically the reader is invited to observe a *repristination* of sorts. The letter O is returned to its purity in the movement, more purely itself than in that onomatopoeic phonic representation of itself given as an exclamatory vocalization at the beginning of the previous line. In this, the 'repristination' of the production of the ring is also enacted, the letter *O* becoming what it always was, the figure or symbol of the 'thing signified' in this case, the ring – but also *The Ring and the Book*. For Browning closes his book, and with that the circle, with a twelfth book entitled 'The Book and the Ring'.
2 The articles by Bagehot on which Armstrong draws are a review of *The Ring and the Book*, published in *Tinsley's Magazine*, III (January 1869, 665–74), and 'Wordsworth, Tennyson and Browning; or, "Pure, Ornate, and Grotesque Art" in English poetry', *National Review*, N.S., I (1864), 27–67. This article is also reprinted in full in Collins and Rundle, eds. (1999, 1308–19).
3 In *Modern Painters*, Ruskin sought to develop a theory of symbolic typology within realist representation, given exemplary expression for the critic by Tintoretto's *The Annunciation*. Ruskin's understanding of typological symbolism was a major influence on the Pre-Raphaelite Brotherhood.

Chapter 5: *(Sub) Urbi et Orbi*

1 The reference to Senate House and Russell Square acknowledges the initial presentation of this chapter as an invited lecture at the Institute of English Studies in February 2009, as part of the Literary London Seminar, organized by Lawrence Phillips and Brycchan Carey, both of whom I would like to thank for arranging the event.

Chapter 6: *Professions*

1 In the hypothesis presented here, and in those references to the notions of professing, professional, professor, and so forth, are the signs of this chapter's initial 'oral' transmission, given as an inaugural professorial lecture at Loughborough University, 28 May 2008. I have retained these markers throughout, given the chapter's emphasis on 'voice'.
2 See Derrida: 'I have only one language; it is not mine' (Derrida 1998a, 1).

3 *Destitution*, from the Latin *de* + *statuere*, means being removed or taken away from, place; it is not wholly illegitimate therefore to suggest *destitution* as a supplement or proxy for *diaspora* or, for that matter, in a chain of non-synonymous substitutions, *dissemination*.

4 Chris Wood, Liner Note to 'Bleary Winter'. *The Lark Descending*.

5 Verity Sharp, *Late Junction*, BBC Radio 3, Wednesday 23 April 2008.

6 Hugh Lupton, 'A Chain of Voices', Radio 4, February 2005.

7 Chris Wood, 'Not Icons but Jewels: Music and Loss in England', *Journal of Music in Ireland* (March–April, 2006). On-line version at: www.englishacousticcollective.org.uk/JMI/index.html

8 Coming to replace Anglo-Norman with the form many now refer to as Middle English, Chancery Standard, a legislative and bureaucratic London-English introduced in the reign of Henry V and based largely on London and East Midlands dialects, not only created the notion of a standard, against which other dialects were placed in marginal and hierarchical relation, it also became widespread as a standardized written form through the introduction of the printing press in the latter half of the fifteenth century. Printing and institutionalization; administrative, official form reliant for its power on technological reproducibility – Chancery Standard determines the English language as an homogeneous form. More than this it inaugurates historically and culturally, through an official voicing, a potentially infinite 'phantasm of indivisible sovereignty' given form in language (Derrida, 'Future of the Profession', 26). And with that it introduces consciousness of identity, either as standardizable, centralizable, or otherwise eccentric to the propagation of homogeneity and a concomitant war-economy. Any effort, as a result of what I am calling a war-economy of difference, which tends towards 'the construction of a homogeneous we' (Lyotard 1988, 98), an undifferentiated notion of English, of Englishness, of identity and literature as English, does so with the advent of secular written English and so conceals multiple, often fractured, exploited or violated, heterogeneities. The very profession of English both masks and announces this in every phrase, with each articulation.

9 Wood, 'Not Icons but Jewels'.

Chapter 7: *No, Not, None, Nothing, Nobody*

1 I am grateful to Emma Lister for raising the distinction between windows and doors as liminal forms, and as phenomenological indices. I would also like to thank those students at the Scottish Universities International Summer School, whose questions and comments were so invaluable in rethinking this essay.

Chapter 9: *'Theory' & the novel* (and *The Novel?*)

1 I say 'so-called' for two reasons: first, the name 'theory' assumes, however implicitly, an undifferentiated body of knowledge with an equally homogeneous ontology. That body of knowledge is not defined by what comprises it, but by the fact that, from the outside, it can be called 'theory', as opposed to other forms of writing, which supposedly are not 'theoretical' in any way. Such a supposition is a nonsense. The nineteenth-century novel, often concerned

with economics, engages with this 'theory'. Second, 'theory' is so-called, because, as I elaborate, the assumption in academic departments is that theory is entirely separable from other more obviously – i.e., given over to unthinking institutional consensus – literary forms. From this point forward, the phrase 'so-called' is implied wherever theory in the singular is referred to, and theory is placed in quotation marks in order to invite the reader to hold off from an unthinking and uncritical acceptance of the term, and more specifically its use in academic contexts.

2   If the metaphors and the images they invoke seem a little hyperbolic, excessive, exaggerated or alarmist, consider, through the medium of another anecdote, the following: upon it being suggested in passing that a course on 'critical thinking' intended for MA students studying post-1800 literature be made available also to those working on early modern studies, the response came, with not a small degree of forceful, if friendly, assertion, within which there was an equally forceful resistance to thinking the idea, that such 'critical thinking' had absolutely no relevance to the study of early modern literature. The 'intensity' of figural language in the passage of the chapter to which this note is appended, and to which it refers, is merely, if you will, a performative countersignature, which seeks to appropriate from the experience of the articulation of resistance the very energy that was made manifest in it.

3   For a comprehensive discussion of the scene in Gaskell, see Chapter Two, 'Our Society: *Cranford*', from my *Dickens to Hardy 1837–1884* (2007, 51–80).

Chapter 10: Ghosts

1   Spivak's translation includes 'tense' in parentheses, following the first reference to time, in order to distinguish between the two uses of *temps* in Derrida's text. Derrida's chiasmus relies in part on that which is legible, and so comprehensible, between the two uses as a 'writing effect' not available through voice. To have given the translation as 'the age [or epoch] . . . thus disturbs the tense of the line and the line of time' would have lost the disruptive graphic motion that Derrida inscribes in the iterable term *temps*, and thus render invisible that which haunts the French original. Another point to make here concerns Derrida's use of 'époque'. Generally, Spivak's translation favours 'age'. While both 'age' and 'epoch' can be used, commonly, to refer to periods of time, epoch also, and in contradistinction to the common use, signifies in its Greek roots the suspension or stoppage of time. Derrida's preference here has this double sense in mind arguably, especially as the notion of epoch in its other sense would serve, presumably, in the 'demand that reading should free itself, at least in its axis, from the classical categories of history' (1967, lxxxix).

2   There is a relation between the idea of dwelling, as that pause, or momentary cessation of activity and, on the one hand, perception, as a coming to consciousness of something, apprehension, or spiritual awareness, and, on the other hand, the idea of theory, its roots being in the Greek, meaning a looking at, a viewing, contemplation or speculation.

Chapter 11: The Reiterable Circularity Of Being

1   In thinking *obstinacy* and the *ostinato*, I am indebted to Jacques Derrida's discussions on

contre (next to/against) in a number of texts. *Contre* expresses both opposition and relation, defence or exchange, depending on the context in which it is found.

2 The first page number refers to the poem in German, the second to the facing English translation. Of the three 'versions' of the citation, the second is my translation, the third that of Pierre Joris.

3 The first page number refers to the poem in French, the second to the facing English translation.

4 On the vulgar concept of time, see Derrida's explication of the notion of 'spirit' in Heidegger contra Hegel (1989c, 23–30).

5 In Varèse's translation, 'Je est un autre' is given as 'I is someone else'.

Chapter 12: *Teaching Derrida*

1 This chapter was written in response to a request from Richard Bradford to contribute an essay to a book, the common theme of which is 'teaching theory'. As is the way of these things, whilst Richard was fully supportive of the article, which originally began after the italicized parenthesis, and which was titled 'Teaching Derrida' without the subtitle, he received readers' reports from the publisher, which effectively did not want the essay to say what it was saying. Responding to the misperceptions that one report in particular had, I argued, as I come to do in the parenthesis, which now begins the chapter, against the report and the repeated errors of non-reception in the face of Derrida that it perpetuated. Taking my comments back to the publisher and reader, the publisher suggested a 'compromise', effectively that I preface the essay as it appears here. The essay was, however, ultimately rejected because it did not give way to the reader's demands. I have left that commentary in place, rather than removing it, because I think it instructive regarding particular institutions of reception and reading. The subtitle, appended with the amended version, offers an almost oblique commentary, perhaps an aphorism or, possibly, a ventriloquial act, in which a recorded voice emerges, stepping forth to interrupt matters, and redirect the audience, on the process just described; as such, this 'voice', a mere subject, a 'tympanum' as Beckett would have it, resonates in the response to the reader and outwards towards any possible audience. The subtitle reiterates the first line of the parenthetical reference. Included after that line was written as a subtitle, there is a structural acknowledgement here of the disordered times of writing and response.

2 The phrase 'dark [or hard] sentence', is found in Bible translations, signifying a difficult problem. Gnome (from Gr. γνωμη): thought, judgement, opinion.

3 Given the phrase 'signifier of the signifier': if the first (first here designated through the assumption of an unbroken linear progression dictated by the semantic and grammatical protocols of reading and writing) 'signifier' is A^1 and the second 'signifier' (sequentially) is A^2, then, in a movement that folds back on itself, an wherein = is the signifier of equivalence, then:

$$A^1 = A^2$$
$$\| \qquad \|$$
$$A^2 = A^1$$

The figure is given as a square or phantom gnomon, rather than as a line or in imitation or representation of a sentence, in order to make clearer iterability and doubling, and the way in which, in the phrase, re*pli*cation is caught up in, and shadows ex*pli*cation. The first model appears closed. Thus, it is necessary to modify it in the following manner:

$$
\begin{array}{c}
+ \\
A^1 = A^2 \\
\| + \ + \| \\
A^2 = A^1 \\
+
\end{array}
$$

which modification serves to signify both finite structure, within which we remain, and an endless motion or iterability, intimating an excess beyond representation. (For an oblique commentary on this, or to take this as an oblique commentary on that chapter, see Chapter Eleven). For even as equivalence is seen to be staged, so one term or figure, being the double and supplement of the other, so addition is implied simultaneously to equivalence, for $A^1 + A^2$ equals both A^1 *and* A^2, and so on, and so forth . . .

However, because one mark is neither the representation nor logical equivalent of the other, there is no true or absolute equivalence, other than in (the undecidability that informs) the operation of either term in a differential relationship, therefore ($\|$ determining incomparability), leaving us with the possibility that:

$$
\begin{array}{c}
A^1 \| A^2 \\
= \ = \\
A^2 \| A^1
\end{array}
$$

Every figure, being both singular and iterable, it necessarily follows that no figure, whilst being a tropic double of every other figure, nonetheless is and remains in its singularity as incomparable with each and every other figure, no figure therefore being recuperable as an example, or exemplary of an economy of writing conventionally understood. Thus, a distance ($| \ldots |$) is implied and revealed, which distance *qua* spacing, is also, simultaneously, a determination of a displacement, displacement itself, absolute displacement, and, at the same time and additionally, a deferral, which maintains *both* singularity *and* iterability; différance, marking both the becoming-space of time and the becoming-time of space, institutes a 'norm', both finite and endless, which is also the determinant of a matrix ($| \ldots |$), thus:

$$
| \ | A^1 = A^2 \ | = | \ A^1 \pm A^2 \ | \ |
$$

(equivalence in the first pairing signifying not absolute repetition but, instead, two possible and different values, as figured in the second pairing).

The projection and working of the matrix is remarked on the understanding that what takes place between is irreducible to a determinable or fixable signification, other than the recognition of différance as an open interval, indicated thus (,) whereby $\{(A^1, A^2) =] A^1, A^2 [\}$ signifies an irreducible undecidability as the work of différance, even as meaning takes place, because the figure signifies, on the one hand, an ordered pair and, on the other hand, an open interval, within and as a result of which, representation and logic collapse into the abyssal taking-place, that we name, provisionally, deconstruction (as in the work, and supplement, of the copula 'of', in the phrase 'signifier of the signifier', which points in more than one direction).

Chapter 13: 'The strong dead return'

1   I have translated *Schatten* as 'shade' rather than 'shadow'. This is, on the one hand, to elicit the more poetic resonance in the German that is lost when one uses the latter translation, while, on the other hand, to hint at the connection, via a poetics of the spirit, to the dead, the ghostly, the spectre, which 'shade' announces. If 'I' is a shade, then I am always already haunted, and so transgressed by my daemonic other, that spectral alterity that countersigns my being, my identity, and all that I misread as being proper to myself, to the self.
2   I am drawing here, generally and specifically, from Derrida, *Force de Loi: Le 'Fondement mystique de l'autorité'* (1994b, 46). On the excessive and incalculable, see *Force* (44).

Chapter 14: *Face to Face with Agamben or, the Other* in *Love*

1   Heidegger first observes the intertwining of *phainomenon* and *logos* in the expression 'phenomenology' in Part II, § 7 of *Being and Time* (1996b, 24).

Chapter 15: *Responsibilities of J, or, Aphorism's Other*

1   I am paraphrasing, and partially citing, Diane Elam's essay, 'Waiting in the Wings' (2003, 46). Elam is addressing waiting and its relation to temporality in Henry James's *The Wings of the Dove* and Maurice Blanchot's *The Writing of the Disaster*. Waiting *qua* reading and the question of impossible temporality of reading is most acutely brought to consciousness through the problematic of aphorism.
2   The comments, and the play between *Je, Jeu*, and *J* are Derrida's, from his essay 'Justices' (2005c). The collection, drawn from a conference, 'J: Around the work of J. Hillis Miller' (April 18–19, 2003), celebrating the work of Miller, also has several articles which consider the letter *J*, and what is written in this letter, with regard to the text of J. Hillis Miller.
3   Jacques Derrida: 'economize on the abyss: not only to save oneself from falling into the bottomless depths by weaving and folding back the cloth to infinity, textual art of the reprise, multiplication of patches within patches, but also establish the laws of reappropriation, formalize the rules which constrain the logic of the abyss and which shuttle between the economic *and* the aneconomic ... the abyssal operation which can only work toward the *relève and* that in it which regularly reproduces collapse' (1987b, 37). See also, Derrida on that which gets reading underway: 'every thesis (bands erect) a prosthesis; what affords reading affords reading by citations (necessarily truncated, clippings, repetitions, suctions,

sections, suspensions, selections, stitchings, scarrings, grafts . . .). Thus does a text become infatuated. With another' (1986, 168).

4   Which among the histories or genealogies of *J* might be told? *J* might be said to be the singular manifestation of James Joyce's (*JJ's*) assertion that 'Jewgreek is greekjew' (1986, 411). First appearing or first returning in the middle ages as the excess of *I* and difference that had previously haunted *I*, *J's* parentage, so to speak, is Greek and Semitic, a vowel and consonant, *iota* and *yod*. *Yod*, itself having descended from the Phoenician symbol for hand, and which is taken to be a precursor to *J*, is, in Hebrew, the letter used in prefixes for future conjugations and tenses. There is thus no proper time for *J*; arriving from a past, which has never been present, as an encrypted, hieratic figure, it figures its own non-presence through its gesture towards an arrival to come that writing remarks. The work of the prefix in Hebrew thus uncannily prosthetizes in a performative manner the letter's *revenance* as the other within, and in excess of, the hegemonic Greco-Latinate-English *I*. *I* is therefore never simply *I*. Indeed, *I* is an other/*Je est un autre*. In French, *J* is already the graphic return of the other in *Je*, the play of *différance* by which *I*/*Je* comes to speak, but never as itself.

Bibliography

Abraham, Nicholas, and Maria Torok. *The Shell and the Kernel.* Ed., trans., and int. Nicholas T. Rand. Chicago, IL: University of Chicago Press, 1994.

Ackroyd, Peter. *Dickens.* New York: Harper Collins, 1990.

Agamben, Giorgio. *Language and Death: The Place of Death.* Trans. Karen E. Pinkus, with Michael Hardt. Minneapolis, MN: University of Minnesota Press, 1991.

Agamben, Giorgio. *Infancy and History: Essays on the Destruction of Experience.* Trans. Liz Heron. London: Verso, 1993a.

Agamben, Giorgio. *Stanzas: Word and Phantasm in Western Culture.* Trans. Ronald L. Martinez. Minneapolis, MN: University of Minnesota Press, 1993b.

Agamben, Giorgio. *The Coming Community.* Trans. Michael Hardt. Minneapolis, MN: University of Minnesota Press, 1993c.

Agamben, Giorgio. *Idea of Prose.* Trans. Michael Sullivan and Sam Whitsitt. Albany, NY: State University of New York Press, 1995.

Agamben, Giorgio. *Potentialities: Collected Essays in Philosophy.* Ed., trans. and int. Daniel Heller-Roazen. Palo Alto, CA: Stanford University Press, 1999.

Agamben, Giorgio. *Means without End: Notes on Politics.* Trans. Vincenzo Binetti and Cesare Casarino. Minneapolis, MN: University of Minnesota Press, 2000.

Agamben, Giorgio. *State of Exception.* Trans. Kevin Attell. Chicago, IL: University of Chicago Press, 2005.

Alderson, David. 'An Anatomy of the British Polity: *Alton Locke* and Christian Manliness'. In *Victorian Identities: Social and Cultural Formations in Nineteenth-Century Literature.* Eds Ruth Robbins and Julian Wolfreys. Basingstoke: Macmillan, 1996. 43–61.

Appelbaum, David. *Jacques Derrida's Ghosts: A Conjuration.* Albany, NY: State University of New York Press, 2009.

Armstrong, Isobel. *Victorian Poetry: Poetry, Poetics and Politics.* London: Routledge, 1993.

Attridge, Derek. *The Singularity of Literature.* London: Routledge, 2004.

Bachelard, Gaston. *The Poetics of Space.* Trans. Maria Jolas. Foreword John R. Stilgoe. Boston, MA: Beacon Press, 1994.

Bagehot, Walter. 'Wordsworth, Tennyson and Browning; or, "Pure, Ornate, and Grotesque Art" in English poetry', *National Review*, N.S., I (1864), 27–67. Rpt. Thomas J. Collins and Vivienne J. Rundle, eds. *The Broadview Anthology of Victorian Poetry and Poetic Theory*. Peterborough, ON: Broadview Press, 1999. 1308–19.

Barbaras, Renaud. *Desire and Distance: Introduction to a Phenomenology of Perception*. Trans. Paul B. Milan. Palo Alto, CA: Stanford University Press, 2006.

Barrell, John. *The Idea of Landscape and the Sense of Place 1730–1840: An Approach to the Poetry of John Clare*. Cambridge: Cambridge University Press, 1972.

Barzilai, Shuli. 'A Review of Paul de Man's "Review of Harold Bloom's *Anxiety of Influence*"', *Yale French Studies*, 69 (1985): 134–41.

Beach, Christoper. 'Ezra Pound and Harold Bloom: Influences, Canons, Traditions, and the Making of Modern Poetry', *ELH*, 56:2 (Summer 1989): 463–83.

Beckett, Samuel. *The Beckett Trilogy: Molloy, Malone Dies, The Unnamable*. London: Picador, 1979.

Benjamin, Walter. *Illuminations*. Ed. and int. Hannah Arendt. Trans. Harry Zohn. New York: Schocken Books, 1969.

Bennett, Arnold. *Riceyman Steps and Elsie and the Child*. Ed. and int. Edward Mendelson and Robert Squillace. London: Penguin, 1991a.

Bennett, Arnold. *Buried Alive*. Int., Nicholas Mander. Stroud: Alan Sutton Publishing, 1991b.

Bennett, Arnold. *The Man from the North*. Int. Nicholas Mander. Stroud: Alan Sutton Publishing, 1994.

Bivona, Daniel. 'Disraeli's Political Trilogy and the Antinomic Structure of Imperial Desire.' *Desire and Contradiction: Imperial Visions and Domestic Debates in Victorian Literature*. Manchester: Manchester University Press, 1990. 1–31.

Bivona, Daniel. *Desire and Contradiction: Imperial Visions and Domestic Debates in Victorian Literature*. Manchester: Manchester University Press, 1999.

Bloom, Harold. *The Anxiety of Influence: A Theory of Poetry*. Oxford: Oxford University Press, 1973.

Bloom, Harold. *A Map of Misreading*. Oxford: Oxford University Press, 1975.

Bloom, Harold. *The Breaking of the Vessels*. Chicago, IL: University of Chicago Press, 1982.

Blythe, Ronald. *Akenfield: Portrait of an English Village*. London: Penguin, 2005.

Boss, Medard. 'Preface to the American Translation of Martin Heidegger's *Zollikon Seminars*'. Martin Heidegger, *Zollikon Seminars: Protocols – Conversations – Letters*. Ed. Medard Boss. Trans. Franz Mayr and Richard Askay. Evanston, IL: Northwestern University Press, 2001.

Bowen, John. *Other Dickens: Pickwick to Chuzzlewit*. Oxford: Oxford University Press, 2000.

Bowen, John. 'Introduction'. Charles Dickens. *Barnaby Rudge*. London: Penguin, 2003. xiii–xxxiv.

Briggs, Asa. 'The Language of "Class" in Early Nineteenth-Century England'. In *Essays in Labour History*. Ed. Asa Briggs and J. Saville. London: Macmillan, 1967.

Brontë, Anne. *Agnes Grey*. Ed. Angeline Goreau. London: Penguin, 1988.

Brontë, Anne. *The Tenant of Wildfell Hall*. Ed. Herbert Rosengarten. Int. Margaret Smith. Oxford: Oxford University Press, 1993.

Browning, Robert. *The Ring and the Book*. Ed. Richard D. Altick and Thomas J. Collins. Peterborough, ON: Broadview Books, 2001.

Butt, John, and Kathleen Tillotson. *Dickens at Work*. London: Methuen, 1957.

Carroll, David. 'Representation or the End(s) of History: Dialectics and Fiction'. *Yale French Studies*, 59 (1980): 201–29.

Caruth, Cathy. 'Speculative Returns: Bloom's Recent Work', *MLN*, 98:5 (December 1983): 1286–96.

Celan, Paul. 'Als Wenn das Weisse Anfiel' / 'When Whiteness Assailed Us'. *Breathturn*. Trans. Pierre Joris. Los Angeles, CA: Sun & Moon Press, 1995. 111/112.

Celan, Paul. 'Reply to a Questionnaire from the Flinker Bookstore, Paris, 1958'. *Collected Prose*. Trans. and int. Rosemarie Waldrop. New York: Routledge, 2003, 15–16.

Chambers, Iain. *Migrancy, Culture, Diaspora*. London: Routledge, 1994.

Chaucer, Geoffrey. *The Riverside Chaucer*. 3rd edn. Ed. Larry D. Benson. Oxford: Oxford University Press, 2008.

Childers, Joseph W. *Novel Possibilities: Fiction and the Formation of Early Victorian Culture*. Philadelphia, PA: University of Pennsylvania Press, 1995.

Cixous, Hélène. *Stigmata: Escaping Texts*. London: Routledge, 1998.

Cixous, Hélène, and Jacques Derrida. 'From the Word to Life: A Dialogue between Jacques Derrida and Hélène Cixous'. *New Literary History*, 2005 (37): 1–13.

Clare, John. *Selected Poems*. Ed. Geoffrey Summerfield. London: Penguin, 2000.

Coleridge, Samuel Taylor. *The Statesman's Manual; or the Bible, the Best Guide to Political Skill and Foresight; A Lay Sermon*. London: n.p., 1816.

Collins, Wilkie. *The Moonstone*. Ed. Steve Farmer. Peterborough, ON: Broadview Books, 1999.

Connor, Steven. *Charles Dickens*. Oxford: Basil Blackwell, 1985.

Copper, John, and Sheila Chandra, "Ouses, 'Ouses, 'Ouses'. *Imagined Village*, EMI, 2007.

Cottom, Daniel. *Social Figures: George Eliot, Social History, and Literary Representation*. Foreword Terry Eagleton. Minneapolis, MN: University of Minnesota Press, 1987.

Crosby, Christina. *The Ends of History: Victorians and 'The Woman Question'*. London: Routledge, 1991.

Davie, Donald. *With the Grain: Essays on Thomas Hardy and Modern British Poetry*. Ed. and int. Clive Wilmer. Manchester: Carcanet, 1998.

Davies, Stevie. 'Introduction'. Anne Brontë. *The Tenant of Wildfell Hall*. Ed. Stevie Davies. London: Penguin, 1996.

de Bolla, Peter. *The Discourse of the Sublime: History, Aesthetics and the Subject.* Oxford: Blackwell, 1989.

de Man, Paul. *Aesthetic Ideology.* Ed. and int. Andrzej Warminski. Minneapolis, MN: University of Minnesota Press, 1996.

de Man, Paul. *Blindness and Insight: Essays in the Rhetoric of Contemporary Criticism*, 2nd edn. London: Methuen, 1983.

Defoe, Daniel. 'The True-Born Englishman'. *The Earlier Life and Chief Earlier Works of Daniel Defoe.* Ed. Henry Morley. London: George Routledge and Sons, 1889. 175–218.

Deguy, Michel. 'Recumbants'. *Recumbants: Poems.* Trans. Wilson Baldridge. Middletown, CT: Wesleyan University Press, 2005. 84/85.

Deleuze, Gilles. *Empiricism and Subjectivity: An Essay on Hume's Theory of Human Nature.* Trans. and int. Constantin V. Boundas. New York: Columbia University Press, 1991.

Deleuze, Gilles. *Negotiations, 1972–1990.* Trans. Martin Joughin. New York: Columbia University Press, 1995.

Derrida, Jacques. *Speech and Phenomena and Other Essays on Husserl's Theory of Signs.* Trans. and int. David B. Allison. Preface Newton Garver. Evanston, IL: Northwestern University Press, 1973.

Derrida, Jacques. *De la grammatologie.* Paris: Éditions de Minuit, 1967. Trans. Gayatri Chakravorty Spivak as *Of Grammatology.* Baltimore, MD: The Johns Hopkins University Press, 1976.

Derrida, Jacques. 'Living On • Borderlines'. *Deconstruction and Criticism.* Harold Bloom, *et al.* New York: Continuum, 1979, 75–176.

Derrida, Jacques. *Margins of Philosophy.* Trans. Alan Bass. Chicago, IL: University of Chicago Press, 1982.

Derrida, Jacques. 'Deconstruction and the Other'. Trans. Richard Kearney. *Dialogues with Contemporary Thinkers: The Phenomenological Heritage.* Ed. Richard Kearney. Manchester: Manchester University Press, 1984. 107–26.

Derrida, Jacques. 'Letter to a Japanese Friend'. Trans. David Wood and Andrew Benjamin. *Derrida and Différance.* Ed. David Wood and Robert Bernasconi. Coventry: Parousia Press, 1985. 1–6.

Derrida, Jacques. *Glas.* Trans. John P. Leavey, Jr., and Richard Rand. Lincoln: University of Nebraska Press, 1986.

Derrida, Jacques. *The Post Card From Socrates to Freud and Beyond.* Trans. Alan Bass. Chicago, IL: University of Chicago Press. 1987a.

Derrida, Jacques. *The Truth in Painting.* Trans. Geoff Bennington and Ian McLeod. Chicago, IL: University of Chicago Press, 1987b.

Derrida, Jacques. *Edmund Husserl's* Origin of Geometry: *An Introduction.* Trans., with Preface and Afterword, John P. Leavey, Jr. Lincoln, NB: University of Nebraska Press, 1989a.

Derrida, Jacques. *Memoires for Paul de Man.* Rev. edn. Trans. Cecile Lindsay, Jonathan Culler, Eduardo Cadava, and Peggy Kamuf. New York: Columbia University Press, 1989b.

Derrida, Jacques. *Of Spirit: Heidegger and the Question.* Trans. Geoffrey
   Bennington and Rachel Bowlby. Chicago, IL: University of Chicago Press,
   1989c.

Derrida, Jacques. '"This Strange Institution Called Literature": An Interview
   with Jacques Derrida'. Trans. Geoffrey Bennington and Rachel Bowlby. *Acts of
   Literature.* Ed. Derek Attridge. New York: Routledge, 1992a. 33–75.

Derrida, Jacques. 'Ulysses Gramophone: Hear Say Yes in Joyce'. *Acts of Literature.*
   Ed. Derek Attridge. New York: Routledge, 1992b. 253–309.

Derrida, Jacques. 'On a Newly Arisen Apocalyptic Tone in Philosophy'. Trans.
   John P. Leavey, Jr. *Raising the Tone of Philosophy: Late Essays by Immanuel
   Kant, Transformative Critique by Jacques Derrida.* Ed. Peter Fenves. Baltimore,
   MD: The Johns Hopkins University Press, 1993. 117–73.

Derrida, Jacques. *Specters of Marx: The State of the Debt, the Work of Mourning,
   & the New International.* Trans. Peggy Kamuf, int. Bernd Magnus and Stephen
   Cullenberg. New York: Routledge, 1994.

Derrida, Jacques. *Force de loi.* Paris: Galilée, 1994b.

Derrida, Jacques. *Archive Fever: A Freudian Impression.* Trans. Eric Prenowitz.
   Chicago, IL: University of Chicago Press, 1995a.

Derrida, Jacques. *Khora. On the Name.* Ed. Thomas Dutoit. Trans. David Wood,
   John P. Leavey, Jr. and Ian McLeod. Palo Alto, CA: Stanford University Press,
   1995b. 89–130.

Derrida, Jacques. *Monolingualism of the Other or, The Prosthesis of Origin.* Trans.
   Patrick Mensah. Palo Alto, CA: Stanford University Press, 1998a.

Derrida, Jacques. 'Economimesis'. *The Derrida Reader: Writing Performances.* Ed.
   Julian Wolfreys. Edinburgh: Edinburgh University Press, 1998b. 264–93.

Derrida, Jacques. *Resistances of Psychoanalysis.* Trans. Peggy Kamuf, Pascale-Anne
   Brault and Michael Naas. Palo Alto, CA: Stanford University Press, 1998c.

Derrida, Jacques. '"*As if* I were dead": an interview with Jacques Derrida'.
   Applying to Derrida Ed. John Brannigan, Ruth Robbins and Julian Wolfreys.
   Basingstoke: Macmillan, 1996. 212–27.

Derrida, Jacques. *Demeure: Fiction and Testimony.* Maurice Blanchot and Jacques
   Derrida, *The Instant of My Death / Demeure: Fiction and Testimony.* Trans.
   Elizabeth Rottenberg. Palo Alto, CA: Stanford University Press, 2000a.
   13–104.

Derrida, Jacques. 'Et Cetera'. Trans. Geoffrey Bennington. *Deconstructions: A
   User's Guide.* Ed. Nicholas Royle. Basingstoke: Palgrave, 2000b. 282–305.

Derrida, Jacques. 'The Future of the Profession or the University Without
   Condition (thanks to the "Humanities," what *could take place*, tomorrow').
   Jacques Derrida and the Humanities: A Critical Reader. Ed. Tom Cohen.
   Cambridge: Cambridge University Press, 2001a. 24–57.

Derrida, Jacques. *The Work of Mourning.* Ed. and int. Pascale-Anne Brault and
   Michael Naas. Chicago, IL: University of Chicago Press, 2001b.

Derrida, Jacques. *Who's Afraid of Philosophy? Right to Philosophy I.* Trans. Jan
   Plug. Palo Alto, CA: Stanford University Press, 2002a.

Derrida, Jacques. 'Typewriter Ribbon: Limited Ink (2)'. *Without Alibi.* Ed., trans. and int. Peggy Kamuf. Palo Alto, CA: Stanford University Press, 2002b. 71–160.

Derrida, Jacques. *On Touching – Jean-Luc Nancy.* Trans. Christine Irizarry. Palo Alto, CA: Stanford University Press, 2005a.

Derrida, Jacques. *Rogues: Two Essays on Reason.* Trans. Pascale-Anne Brault and Michael Naas. Palo Alto, CA: Stanford University Press, 2005b.

Derrida, Jacques. 'Justices'. *Justices: for J Hillis Miller.* Ed. Barbara L. Cohen and Dragan Kujundzic. New York: Fordham University Press, 2005c.

Derrida, Jacques. *Psyche: Inventions of the Other, Vol. I.* Ed. Peggy Kamuf and Elizabeth Rottenberg. Trans. Peggy Kamuf, *et al.* Palo Alto, CA: Stanford University Press, 2007.

Derrida, Jacques *The Gift of Death.* Trans. David Wills. Chicago, IL: University of Chicago Press, 1995. Second edn. published as *The Gift of Death 2nd Edition* and *Literature in Secret.* Trans. David Wills. Chicago, IL: University of Chicago Press, 2008.

Derrida, Jacques, and John Caputo. *Deconstruction in a Nutshell: A Conversation with Jacques Derrida.* New York: Fordham University Press, 1997.

Dickens, Charles. *Dombey and Son.* Ed. Peter Fairclough. Int. Raymond Williams. London: Penguin, 1985.

Dickens, Charles. *Nicholas Nickleby.* Ed. and int. Michael Slater. Harmondsworth: Penguin, 1986a.

Dickens, Charles. *Oliver Twist.* Ed. Peter Fairclough. Harmondsworth: Penguin, 1986b.

Dickens, Charles. *Letters.* Vol. 6 1850–1852. Ed. Madeline House, *et al.* Oxford: Clarendon, 1988.

Dickens, Charles. *Sketches By Boz and Other Early Papers 1833–39.* Ed. Michael Slater. London: J. M. Dent, 1994.

Dickens, Charles. *Selected Journalism 1850–1870.* Ed. and int. David Pascoe. London: Penguin, 1997a.

Dickens, Charles. *Our Mutual Friend.* Ed. and int. Adrian Poole. Harmondsworth: Penguin, 1997b.

Dickens, Charles. *Little Dorrit.* Ed. and int. Stephen Wall and Helen Small. Harmondsworth: Penguin, 1998.

Dickens, Charles. *Bleak House.* Ed. and int. Nicola Bradbury. Preface Terry Eagleton. London: Penguin, 2003.

Disraeli, Benjamin. *Sybil or The Two Nations.* Int. R. A. Butler. Ed. Thom Braun. Harmondsworth: Penguin, 1985.

Disraeli, Benjamin. *Coningsby or The New Generation.* Ed. Thom Braun. Harmondsworth: Penguin, 1989.

Donne, John. *The Complete English Poems.* Ed. A. J. Smith. Harmondsworth: Penguin, 1987.

Doyle, Brian. *English and Englishness.* London: Routledge, 1989.

Düttmann, Alexander Garcia. *The Gift of Language: Memory and Promise in Adorno, Benjamin, Heidegger and Rosenzweig.* Trans. Arline Lyons. Syracuse, NY: Syracuse University Press, 2000.

Eagleton, Terry. *Criticism and Ideology: A Study in Marxist Literary Theory.* London: Verso, 1978.

Ebbatson, Roger. 'Hardy and Class'. *Thomas Hardy Studies.* Ed. Phillip Mallett. Basingstoke: Palgrave Macmillan, 2004. 111–34.

Ebbatson, Roger. *Heidegger's Bicycle: Interfering with Victorian Texts.* Eastbourne: Sussex Academic Press, 2006.

Elam, Diane. '"Another day done and I'm deeper in debt": *Little Dorrit* and the Debt of the Everyday'. In *Dickens Refigured: Bodies, Desires and Other Histories.* Ed. John Schad. Manchester: Manchester University Press, 1996. 157–77.

Elam, Diane. 'Waiting in the Wings'. *Acts of Narrative.* Ed. Carol Jacobs and Henry Sussman. Palo Alto, CA: Stanford University Press, 2003.

Eliot, George. *Daniel Deronda.* Ed. and int. Barbara Hardy. Harmondsworth: Penguin, 1986.

Eliot, George. *Middlemarch: A Study of Provincial Life.* Ed. and int. David Carroll. Oxford: Oxford University Press, 1988.

Eliot, George. *Middlemarch: A Study of Provincial Life.* Ed. Rosemary Ashton. London: Penguin, 2003.

Eliot, T. S. *Four Quartets. Collected Poems 1909–1962.* London: Faber & Faber, 1963. 187–224.

Eliot, T. S. 'Eeldrop and Appleplex' pt I. *The Little Review.* [New York] vol. IV, no. 1 (May, 1917) 7–11; 'Eeldrop and Appleplex'. Pt. II *The Little Review.* [New York] vol. IV, no. 5 (September, 1917) 16–9.

Ermath, Elizabeth Deeds. *The English Novel in History 1840–1895.* London: Routledge, 1997.

Everett, Percival. *Glyph.* St Paul: Greywolf Press, 1999.

Fasick, Laura. 'Charles Kingsley's Scientific Treatment of Gender'. *Muscular Christianity: Embodying the Victorian Age.* Ed. Donald E. Hall. Cambridge: Cambridge University Press, 1994. 91–113.

Forster, E. M. *The Longest Journey.* Ed. and int. Elizabeth Heine. London: Penguin, 1989.

Forster, E. M. *Howards End.* Ed. and int. David Lodge. London: Penguin, 2000.

Forster, E. M. 'The Celestial Omnibus'. *Selected Stories.* Ed. and int. David Leavitt and Mark Mitchell. London: Penguin, 2001. 30–47.

Fowler, Roger. *A Dictionary of Modern Literary Terms.* London: Routledge, 1973.

Francis, Mark, and John Morrow. *A History of English Political Thought in the Nineteenth Century.* London: Duckworth, 1994.

Freeman, Nicholas. *Conceiving the City: London, Literature, and Art 1870–1914.* Oxford: Oxford University Press, 2007.

Freud, Sigmund. 'Screen Memories'. *The Uncanny.* Trans. David McLintock. Int. Hugh Haughton. London: Penguin, 2003. 1–23.

Fynsk, Christopher. *Language and Relation: . . . that there is language.* Palo Alto, CA: Stanford University Press, 1996.

Gallagher, Catherine. *The Industrial Reformation of English Fiction: Social*

Discourse and Narrative Form 1832–1867. Chicago, IL: University of Chicago Press, 1985.

Gasché, Rodolphe. 'The Witch Metapsychology'. Trans. Julian Patrick. *Returns of the "French Freud": Freud, Lacan, and Beyond*. Ed. Todd Dufresne. New York: Routledge, 1997. 169–208.

Gaskell, Elizabeth. *Cranford*. Ed. Elizabeth Porges Watson. Int. and notes Charlotte Mitchell. Oxford: Oxford University Press, 1998.

Gibson, Peter, and Julian Wolfreys. *Peter Ackroyd; The Ludic and Labyrinthine Text*. Basingstoke: Macmillan, 2000.

Goldsmith, Oliver. *Goldsmith's* The Traveller *and* The Deserted Village. Ed. Rose M. Barton. London: BiblioBazaar, 2008. 47–63.

Gosetti-Ferencei, Jennifer Anna. *Heidegger, Hölderlin, and the Subject of Poetic Language: Toward a New Poetics of Dasein*. New York: Fordham University Press, 2004.

Gramsci, Antonio. *Selections from Cultural Writings*. Ed. David Forgacs and Geoffrey Nowell-Smith. Trans. William Boelhower. Cambridge, MA: Harvard University Press, 1991.

Grossmith, George and Weedon. *The Diary of a Nobody*. Ed. and int. Ed Glinert. London: Penguin, 1999.

Guy, Josephine M. *The Victorian Social-Problem Novel: The Market, the Individual and Communal Life*. Basingstoke: Macmillan, 1996.

Hall, Donald E., ed. *Muscular Christianity: Embodying the Victorian Age*. Cambridge: Cambridge University Press, 1994.

Hamacher, Werner. 'To Leave the Word to Someone Else'. *Thinking Difference: Critics in Conversation*. Ed. Julian Wolfreys. New York: Fordham University Press, 2004.

Hardy, Thomas. *The Pursuit of the Well-Beloved and the Well Beloved*. Ed. and int. Patricia Ingham. London: Penguin, 1997a.

Hardy, Thomas. *The Trumpet-Major*. Ed. Linda M. Shires. London: Penguin, 1997b.

Hardy, Thomas. *Desperate Remedies*. Ed. and int. Mary Rimmer. London: Penguin, 1998a.

Hardy, Thomas. *Jude the Obscure*. Ed. and int. Dennis Taylor. London: Penguin, 1998b.

Hardy, Thomas. *Under the Greenwood Tree*. Ed. and int. Tim Dolin. London: Penguin, 1998c.

Hardy, Thomas. *A Pair of Blue Eyes*. Ed. Pamela Dalziel. London: Penguin, 1998d.

Hardy, Thomas. *The Return of the Native*. Ed. Penny Boumelha. London: Penguin, 1999.

Hardy, Thomas. *Far from the Madding Crowd*. Ed. and int. Rosemarie Morgan with Shannon Russell. London: Penguin, 2000.

Hardy, Thomas. *Thomas Hardy's 'Facts' Notebook: A Critical Edition*. Ed. William Greenslade. Aldershot: Ashgate, 2004.

Harpold, Terry. *Ex-Foliations: Reading Machines and the Upgrade Path*. Minneapolis, MN: University of Minnesota Press, 2009.

Hegel, G. W. F. *Phenomenology of Spirit*. Trans. A. V. Miller. Foreword J. N. Findlay. Oxford: Oxford University Press, 1977.

Heidegger, Martin. *Being and Time*. Trans. John Macquarrie and Edward Robinson. New York: Harper & Row, 1962.

Heidegger, Martin. *The Metaphysical Foundations of Logic*. Trans. Michael Heim. Bloomington, IN: Indiana University Press, 1984.

Heidegger, Martin. *History of the Concept of Time: Prolegomena*. Trans. Theodore Kisiel. Bloomington, IN: Indiana University Press, 1985.

Heidegger, Martin. *Hegel's Phenomenology of Spirit*. Trans. Parvis Emad and Kenneth Maly. Bloomington, IN: Indiana University Press, 1988.

Heidegger, Martin. *Parmenides*. Trans. André Schuwer and Richard Rojcewicz. Bloomington, IN: Indiana University Press, 1992.

Heidegger, Martin. *Hölderlin's Hymn 'The Ister'*. Trans. William McNeill and Julia Davis. Bloomington, IN: Indiana University Press, 1996a.

Heidegger, Martin. *Being and Time*. Trans. Joan Stambaugh. Albany, NY: State University of New York Press, 1996b.

Heidegger, Martin. *Pathmarks*. Ed. William McNeill. Cambridge: Cambridge University Press, 1998.

Heidegger, Martin. *Ontology – The Hermeneutics of Facticity*. Trans. John van Buren. Bloomington, IN: Indiana University Press, 1999.

Heidegger, Martin. *Poetry, Language, Thought*. Trans. Albert Hofstadter. New York, Harper Perennial, 2001a.

Heidegger, Martin. *Zollikon Seminars: Protocols – Conversations – Letters*. Ed. Medard Boss. Trans. Franz Mayr and Richard Askay. Evanston, IL: Northwestern University Press, 2001b.

Heidegger, Martin. 'The Problem of Reality in Modern Philosophy'. Trans. Phillip J. Bossert and John van Buren. *Supplements: From the Earliest Essays to* Being and Time *and Beyond*. Ed. John Van Buren. Albany, NY: State University of New York Press, 2002. 39–48

Heidegger, Martin. *Four Seminars*. Trans. Andrew Mitchell and François Raffoul. Bloomington, IN: Indiana University Press, 2003.

Heidegger, Martin. *Mindfulness*. Trans. Parvis Emad and Thomas Kalary. London: Athlone Press, 2006.

Henry, Michel. *Material Phenomenology*. Trans. Scott Davidson. New York: Fordham University Press, 2008.

Hobsbawm, Eric. *The Age of Revolution 1789–1848*. New York: Vintage, 1996.

Husserl, Edmund. *The Origin of Geometry*. Trans. David Carr. In Jacques Derrida. *Edmund Husserl's* Origin of Geometry: *An Introduction*. Trans., with a Preface and Afterword, John P. Leavey, Jr. Lincoln, NB: University of Nebraska Press, 1989. 155–80.

Husserl, Edmund. *On the Phenomenology of the Consciousness of Internal Time (1893–1917)*. Trans. John Barnett Brough. Dordrecht: Kluwer Academic, 1991.

Husserl, Edmund. *Cartesian Meditations: An Introduction to Phenomenology*. Trans. Dorion Cairns. Dordrecht: Kluwer Academic Publishers, 1995.

Hyppolite, Jean. *Genesis and Structure of Hegel's* Phenomenology of Spirit. Trans. Samuel Chernaik and John Heckman. Evanston, IL: Northwestern University Press, 1974.

Imagined Village, The. Audio CD. Real World B000T4F0J8, 2007.

Ingham, Patricia. *The Language of Gender and Class: Transformation in the Victorian Novel.* London: Routledge, 1996a.

Ingham, Patricia. 'Nobody's Fault: The Scope of the Negative in *Little Dorrit*'. In *Dickens Refigured: Bodies, Desires and Other Histories.* Ed. John Schad. Manchester: Manchester University Press, 1996b. 98–116.

Iser, Wolfgang. *The Implied Reader: Patterns of Communication in Prose Fiction from Bunyan to Beckett.* Trans. anon. Baltimore, MD: The Johns Hopkins University Press, 1974.

Jackson, Wallace. 'Review of *The Breaking of the Vessels* by Harold Bloom', *South Atlantic Review* 50:3 (September 1985): 90–3.

Joyce, James. *Ulysses.* (1922). Ed. Hans Walter Gabler, *et al.* London: Bodley Head, 1986.

Joyce, James. *Dubliners.* Ed. Terence Brown. London: Penguin, 1993.

Joyce, James. *Ulysses.* Ed. Jeri Johnson. Oxford: Oxford University Press, 2008.

Kamuf, Peggy. *Book of Addresses.* Palo Alto, CA: Stanford University Press, 2005.

Kant, Immanuel. *Critique of Pure Reason.* Trans. N. Smith. New York: St Martin's Press, 1963.

Kant, Immanuel. *Political Writings.* Ed. Hans Reiss. Trans. H. B. Nisbet. Cambridge: Cambridge University Press, 1970.

Kant, Immanuel. *Opus Postumum.* Ed. and int. Eckart Förster. Trans. Eckart Förster and Michael Rosen. Cambridge: Cambridge University Press, 1993.

Kant, Immanuel. 'What Does it Mean to Orient Oneself in Thinking?' *Kant, Religion and Rational Theology.* Trans. and ed. Allen W. Wood and George Di Giovanni. Cambridge: Cambridge University Press, 1996. 1–18.

Karatani, Kojin. *Architecture as Metaphor: Language, Number, Money.* Trans. Sabu Kohso. Ed. Michael Speaks. Cambridge, MA: MIT Press, 1995.

Karatani, Kojin. *Transcritique: On Kant and Marx.* Trans. Sabu Kohso. Cambridge, MA: MIT Press, 2005.

Kates, Joshua. *Fielding Derrida: Philosophy, Literary Criticism, History, and the Work of Deconstruction.* New York: Fordham University Press, 2008.

Kermode, Frank. *The Genesis of Secrecy: On the Interpretation of Narrative.* Cambridge, MA: Harvard University Press, 1979.

Kincaid, James R. *Child-Loving: The Erotic Child and Victorian Culture.* New York: Routledge, 1992.

Kingsley, Charles. *Alton Locke.* Ed. and int. Elizabeth A. Cripps. Oxford: Oxford University Press, 1987.

Kingsley, Charles. *Yeast.* Int. Julian Wolfreys. Stroud: Alan Sutton, 1994.

Kingsley, Charles. *The Water-Babies.* Ed. and int. Brian Alderson. Oxford: Oxford University Press, 1995.

Kofman, Sarah. *Lectures de Derrida.* Paris: Galilée, 1984.

Krell, David Farrell. 'General Introduction: The Thinking of Being'. In *Martin*

Heidegger: Basic Writings from Being and Time (*1927*) *to* The Task of Thinking (*1964*). Revised and expanded edn. Ed. David Farrell Krell. London: Routledge, 1993. 1–36.

Kristeva, Julia. *Powers of Horror: An Essay on Abjection.* Trans. Leon S. Roudiez. New York: Columbia University Press, 1982.

Lacan, Jacques. *Écrits: a Selection.* Trans. Alan Sheridan. New York: Norton, 1977.

Lacan, Jacques. *My Teaching.* Trans. David Macey. Preface Jacques-Alain Miller. London: Verso, 2008.

Laclau, Ernesto and Chantal Mouffe. *Hegemony and Socialist Strategy: Towards a Radical Democratic Politics.* London: Verso, 1985.

Lacoste, Jean-Yves. *Experience and the Absolute: Disputed Questions on the Humanity of Man.* Trans. Mark Raftery-Skehan. New York: Fordham University Press, 2004.

Lacoue-Labarthe, Philippe. *Poetry as Experience.* Trans. Andrea Tarnowski. Palo Alto, CA: Stanford University Press, 1999.

Langland, Elizabeth. *Nobody's Angels: Middle-Class Women and Domestic Ideology in Victorian Culture.* Ithaca, NY: Cornell University Press, 1995.

Leavis, F. R. *The Great Tradition.* London: Allen Lane, 1948.

Lee, Robert. *Unquiet Country: Voices of the Rural Poor 1820–1880.* Macclesfield: Windgather Press, 2005.

Levy, Amy. *Reuben Sachs.* Ed. Susan David Bernstein. Peterborough, ON: Broadview Press, 2006a.

Levy, Amy. *The Romance of a Shop.* Ed. Susan David Bernstein. Peterborough, ON: Broadview Press, 2006b.

Liu, Alan. *Wordsworth: The Sense of History.* Palo Alto, CA: Stanford University Press, 1989.

Luckhurst, Roger. 'Trance-Gothic, 1882–1897'. *Victorian Gothic: Literary and Cultural Manifestations in the Nineteenth Century.* Ed. Ruth Robbins and Julian Wolfreys. Basingstoke: Palgrave, 2000. 148–67.

Lupton, Hugh. 'A Chain of Voices'. BBC Radio 4, February 2005.

Lyotard, Jean-François. *The Differend: Phrases in Dispute.* Trans. Georges Van Den Abbeele. Minneapolis, MN: University of Minnesota Press 1988.

Marsh, Richard. *The Beetle.* Ed. Julian Wolfreys. Peterborough, ON: Broadview Press, 2004.

Marx, Karl. *Capital: A Critique of Political Economy Vol. I.* Trans. Ben Fowkes. Harmondsworth: Penguin, 1976.

McEachern, Claire. *The Politics of English Nationhood 1590–1612.* Cambridge: Cambridge University Press, 1996.

McLaughlin, Kevin. 'Losing One's Place: Displacement and Domesticity in Dickens's *Bleak House*', *MLN* 108:5 (December 1993): 875–90.

McSweeney, Kerry. 'Dream-Representation in *Wuthering Heights, Crime and Punishment,* and *War and Peace*'. *Symposium* (Fall 2005): 163–78.

Merleau-Ponty, Maurice. *The Prose of the World.* Ed. Claude Lefort. Trans. John O'Neil. Evanston, IL: Northwestern University Press, 1973.

Merleau-Ponty, Maurice. *Phenomenology of Perception*. Trans. Colin Smith. London: Routledge, 1995.

Merleau-Ponty, Maurice. *The World of Perception*. Trans. Oliver Davis. Foreword, Stéphanie Ménasé. Int. Thomas Baldwin. London: Routledge, 2008.

Mighall, Robert. *A Geography of Victorian Gothic Fiction: Mapping History's Nightmares*. Oxford: Oxford University Press, 1999.

Miles, Robert. *Gothic Writing 1750–1820: A Genealogy*. London: Routledge, 1993.

Mill, John Stuart. 'The Present State of Literature'. Vol. xxvi. *Collected Works*. Ed. F. L. L. Priestly and John M. Robson. 33 vols. London: Routledge, 1964–1991.

Miller, J. Hillis. *Charles Dickens: The World of His Fiction*. Cambridge, MA: Harvard University Press, 1958.

Miller, J. Hillis. *The Form of Victorian Fiction: Thackeray, Dickens, Trollope, George Eliot, Meredith and Hardy*. Notre Dame, IN: Indiana University Press, 1968.

Miller, J. Hillis. *Fiction and Repetition: Seven English Novels*. Cambridge, MA: Harvard University Press, 1982.

Miller, J. Hillis. *The Linguistic Moment from Wordsworth to Stevens*. Princeton, NJ: Princeton University Press, 1985.

Miller, J. Hillis. *The Ethics of Reading: Kant, de Man, Eliot, Trollope, James, and Benjamin*. New York: Columbia University Press, 1987.

Miller, J. Hillis. *Hawthorne and History: Defacing it*. Oxford: Blackwell, 1991.

Miller, J. Hillis. *Topographies*. Palo Alto, CA: Stanford University Press, 1995.

Miller, J. Hillis. *Reading Narrative*. Norman, OK: University of Oklahoma Press, 1998.

Miller, J. Hillis. *The Disappearance of God: Five Nineteenth-Century Writers*. Urbana, IL: University of Illinois Press, 2000.

Miller, J. Hillis. *Others*. Princeton, NJ: Princeton University Press, 2001a.

Miller, J. Hillis. *Speech Acts in Literature*. Palo Alto, CA: Stanford University Press, 2001b.

Miller, J. Hillis. *On Literature*. London: Routledge, 2002.

Miller, J. Hillis. 'Lying Against Death: Out of the Loop'. *Acts of Narrative*. Ed. Carol Jacobs and Henry Sussman. Palo Alto, CA: Stanford University Press, 2003. 195–235.

Miller, J. Hillis. 'A Profession of Faith'. *The J. Hillis Miller Reader*. Ed. Julian Wolfreys. Edinburgh: Edinburgh University Press, 2005. 282–8.

Miller, J. Hillis. 'Literary Study in the Transnational University'. *The J. Hillis Miller Reader*. Ed. Julian Wolfreys. Edinburgh: Edinburgh University Press, 2005. 339–90.

Miller, J. Hillis. *For Derrida*. New York: Fordham University Press, 2009.

Moretti, Franco. *An Atlas of the European Novel 1800–1900*. London: Verso, 1999.

Nancy, Jean-Luc. *Corpus*. Trans. Richard A. Rand. New York: Fordham University Press, 2008.

Natanson, Maurice. 'Phenomenology, Anonymity, and Alienation', *New Literary History* 10:3 (Spring, 1979): 533–46.

Niranjana, Tejaswini. *Siting Translation: History, Post-Structuralism, and the Colonial Context*. Berkeley, CA: University of California Press, 1992.

Nietzsche, Frederich. *Gesammelte Werke*. 23 vols. Munich: Muusarion Verlag, 1920–29.

Nolan, Emer. *James Joyce and Nationalism*. London: Routledge, 1995.

O'Toole, Tess. 'Siblings and Suitors in the Narrative Architecture of *The Tenant of Wildfell Hall*'. *Studies in English Literature, 1500–1900*, 39:4 (Autumn 1999): 715–31.

Parmenides. *Fragments*. http://philoctetes.free.fr/parmenides.htm

Polansky, Steve. 'A Family Romance: Northrop Frye and Harold Bloom: A Study of Critical Influence'. *Boundary 2*, 9:2 (Winter 1981): 227–46

Poovey, Mary. *Uneven Developments: The Ideological Work of Gender in Mid-Victorian England*. Chicago, IL: University of Chicago Press, 1988.

Porter, Roy. *London: A Social History*. London: Hamish Hamilton, 1994.

Punter, David. Review of *The Failure of Gothic: Problems of Disjunction in an Eighteenth-Century Literary Form*, by Elizabeth Napier. *The Times Higher Education Supplement*, 20 March 1987.

Rabaté, Jean-Michel. *James Joyce: Authorized Reader*. Baltimore, MD: The Johns Hopkins University Press, 1991.

Rancière, Jacques. *The Flesh of Words: The Politics of Writing*. Trans. Charlotte Mandell. Palo Alto, CA: Stanford University Press, 2004a.

Rancière, Jacques. *The Philosopher and His Poor*. Ed. and int. Andrew Parker. Trans. John Drury, Corinne Oster, and Andrew Parker. Durham, NC: Duke University Press, 2004b.

Rigney, Ann. *Imperfect Histories: The Elusive Past and the Legacy of Romantic Historicism*. Ithaca, NY: Cornell University Press, 2001.

Rimbaud, Arthur. *Illuminations and Other Prose Poems*. Trans. Louise Varèse. New York: New Directions, 1957.

Robertson, Fiona. *Scott, Gothic, and the Authorities of Fiction*. Oxford: Clarendon Press, 1994.

Rossetti, William Michael, ed. *Poems of Hood*. New York: Putnam and Sons, 1872.

Royle, Nicholas. *Telepathy and Literature: Essays on the Reading Mind*. Oxford: Basil Blackwell, 1990.

Royle, Nicholas. *The Uncanny*. London: Routledge, 2003.

Royle, Nicholas. 'Clipping'. *Forum: The University of Edinburgh Postgraduate Journal of Culture and the Arts* 7 (Autumn 2008): 1–8.

Russett, Margaret. 'Race Under Erasure'. *Callaloo* 28:2 (Spring 2005): 358–69.

Schlicke, Paul, ed. *Oxford Reader's Companion to Dickens*. Oxford: Oxford University Press, 1999.

Schwenger, Peter. *Fantasm and Fiction: On Textual Envisioning*. Palo Alto, CA: Stanford University Press, 1999.

Seel, Martin. *Aesthetics of Appearing*. Trans. John Farrell. Palo Alto, CA: Stanford University Press, 2005.

Sharp, Verity. *Late Junction*, BBC Radio 3, Wednesday, 23 April 2008.

Shklovsky, Viktor. *Theory of Prose*. Trans. Benjamin Sher. Int. Gerald L. Bruns. Elmwood Park, IL: Dalkey Archive Press, 1991.

Shuttleworth, Sally. *Charlotte Brontë and Victorian Psychology*. Cambridge: Cambridge University Press, 1994.

Simonsen, Peter. *Romantic Textualities: Literature and Print Culture, 1780–1840*, 16 (Summer 2006): 41–74.

Smith, Anne Marie. *New Right Discourse on Race and Sexuality: Britain 1968–1990*. Cambridge: Cambridge University Press, 1994.

Szafraniec, Asja. *Beckett, Derrida, and the Event of Literature*. Palo Alto, CA: Stanford University Press, 2007.

Tambling, Jeremy. *Dickens, Violence and the Modern State*. Basingstoke: Macmillan, 1995.

Todorov, Tzvetan. *The Fantastic: A Structural Approach to a Literary Genre*. Trans. Richard Howard. Int. Robert Scholes. Ithaca, NY: Cornell University Press, 1975.

Tricky. 'Brand New, You're Retro'. *Maxinquaye*. Island Records, 1995.

Vance, Norman. *The Sinews of the Spirit: The Ideal of Christian Manliness in Victorian Literature and Religious Thought*. Cambridge: Cambridge University Press, 1985.

Vidler, Anthony. *The Architectural Uncanny: Essays in the Modern Unhomely*. Cambridge, MA: MIT Press, 1992.

Vrettos, Athena. 'Displaced Memories in Victorian Fiction and Psychology'. *Victorian Studies: An Interdisciplinary Journal of Social, Political, and Cultural Studies*, 49:2 (Winter 2007): 199–207.

Weber, Samuel. *Mass Mediauras: Form, Technics, Media*. Palo Alto, CA: Stanford University Press, 1996.

Welsh, Alexander. *From Copyright to Copperfield: The Identity of Dickens*. Cambridge, MA: Harvard University Press, 1987.

Wheeler, Michael. *Heaven, Hell, & the Victorians*, abridged edn. Cambridge: Cambridge University Press, 1994.

Wigley, Mark. *The Architecture of Deconstruction: Derrida's Haunt*. Cambridge, MA: MIT Press, 1993

Williams, Raymond. *Writing in Society*. London: Verso, 1981.

Williams, Raymond. 'Introduction'. Charles Dickens. *Dombey and Son*. Ed. Peter Fairclough. London: Penguin, 1985.

Wolfreys, Julian. *Being English: Narratives, Idioms, and Performances of National Identity from Coleridge to Trollope*. Albany, NY: State University of New York Press, 1994.

Wolfreys, Julian. *Dickens to Hardy 1837–1884: The Novel, the Past, and Cultural Memory in the Nineteenth Century*. Basingstoke: Palgrave Macmillan, 2007.

Wolfson, Susan. 'Representing some Late Romantic Era, Non-Canonical Male Poets: Thomas Hood, Winthrop Mackworth Praed, Thomas Lovell Beddoes',

Romanticism on the Net, 19 (August 2000), Online: Internet [2 August 2006], http://www.erudit.org/revue/ron/2000/v/n19/005932ar.html

Wood, Chris. 'Not Icons but Jewels: Music and Loss in England', *Journal of Music in Ireland* (March-April 2006). www.englishacousticcollective.org.uk/JMI/index.html

Wood, Chris. 'Walk this World'. Lyrics Hugh Lupton, music Chris Wood. *The Lark Descending*. RUF CD10, 2005.

Wood, Chris. Liner Note, 'Bleary Winter'. *The Lark Descending*. RUF CD10, 2005.

Woolf, Virginia. 'Henry James's Ghost Stories'. *The Essays of Virginia Woolf: 1919–1924*. Ed. Andrew McNeillie. Vol. 3. New York: Harcourt Brace Jovanovich, 1988. 319–26.

Woolf, Virginia. *The Complete Shorter Fiction*. Ed. Susan Dick. London: Grafton, 1991. 90–6.

Wyclif, John. *Selected English Works* Vol. I. London: n.p., 1869–71.

Zemka, Sue. *Victorian Testaments: The Bible, Christology and Literary Authority in Early-Nineteenth-Century British Culture*. Palo Alto, CA: Stanford University Press, 1997.

Index of Proper Names